ONLY

SKIN

CHANGING VISIONS OF THE AMERICAN SELF

DEEP

EDITED BY COCO FUSCO AND BRIAN WALLIS

ONLY SKIN

CHANGING VISIONS OF THE AMERICAN SELF

DEEP

INTERNATIONAL CENTER OF PHOTOGRAPHY, NEW YORK / HARRY N. ABRAMS, INC., PUBLISHERS

This publication was produced in conjunction with the exhibition
Only Skin Deep: Changing Visions of the American Self organized
by the International Center of Photography.
Exhibition Dates: December 12, 2003 through February 29, 2004.
Visit the exhibition website at www.onlyskindeep.icp.org

Only Skin Deep: Changing Visions of the American Self is a Millennium
Project supported in part by the National Endowment for the Arts
with major funding provided by Corbis, Altria Group, Inc., The
Rockefeller Foundation, Ford Foundation, and additional support
from Samuel L. and Dominique Milbank.

For the International Center of Photography, Publications Staff:
Project Manager: Karen Hansgen
Text Editor: Marion Kocot
Designer: Bethany Johns
Rights and Reproductions: Erin Barnett and Nola Tully
Research: Michelle-Lee White

For Harry N. Abrams, Inc., Publishers:
Project Manager: Deborah Aaronson
Production Manager: Maria Pia Gramaglia

Library of Congress Cataloging-in-Publication Data

Only skin deep : changing visions of the American self / edited by
Coco Fusco and Brian Wallis.
    p. cm.
  ISBN 0-8109-4635-1 (hardcover)
  ISBN 0-8109-9165-9 (softcover)
1. Portrait photography—United States—Exhibitions. 2.
Race awareness—United States—Pictorial works—Exhibitions.
I. Fusco, Coco, 1960–
II. Wallis, Brian, 1953–

  TR680.O55 2003
  779'.2'0973074—dc21

                2003004120

Printed and bound in China

10 9 8 7 6 5 4 3 2 1

Front cover:
Gordon Parks
Emerging Man, Harlem, 1952
Gelatin silver print
16 1/8 x 19 7/8 in. (40.9 x 50.4 cm)
International Center of Photography, New York.
Purchased by the ICP Acquisitions Committee, 2003

Back cover:
Tseng Kwong Chi
Statue of Liberty, New York, from the
expeditionary series, "East Meets West," 1979
Gelatin silver print
36 x 36 in. (91.4 x 91.4 cm)
Estate of Tseng Kwong Chi /
Muna Tseng Dance Projects, Inc.

Page 2:
John Gutmann
The Artist Lives Dangerously (detail), 1938
Gelatin silver print
7 5/8 x 10 1/4 in. (19.4 x 26 cm)
Center for Creative Photography,
University of Arizona, Tuscon

Harry N. Abrams, Inc.
100 Fifth Avenue
New York, N.Y. 10011
www.abramsbooks.com

Abrams is a subsidiary of
LA MARTINIÈRE
GROUPE

International Center of Photography
1133 Avenue of the Americas
New York, N.Y. 10036
www.icp.org

CONTENTS

The long, slow turn into the new millennium has been an auspicious and revealing process for Americans, an opportunity to assess the past and a chance to imagine the future in a different way. When, in 1999, staff members from the International Center of Photography began discussions with representatives from the National Endowment for the Arts about how the agency's Millennium Initiative programs might best evaluate contemporary visual art, the issues were both challenging and self evident. One of the most striking features of American culture at this historical juncture, we all agreed, is the profound and unresolved issue of national identity. What does it mean to be an American? What are the boundaries of the nation? Who qualifies for citizenship? Who is excluded? Central to these questions is the troubling issue of race, the aspect of national identity that continues to defy explanation and to incite divisiveness. Despite the regular media claims that we have moved beyond race or that shifting demographics have made the concept irrelevant, ongoing political and social clashes attest to the contrary. If race is a myth, it remains an explosive one.

It was, therefore, with a mix of humility and ambition that we initially formulated the concept for *Only Skin Deep: Changing Visions of the American Self*. The goal of this ambitious project is to challenge some of the central myths or preconceptions governing American identity. In particular, this book—and the exhibition and website it accompanies—aims to show how fluctuating conceptions of race, nation, and self have been fixed or transformed through the unique attributes and strategic uses of photography. What the curators propose here is, in effect, a different reading of the archive of historical and contemporary photographs, not one that accuses or valorizes but one that studies the deep and lasting social impact of photographic representations. It is entirely appropriate that the International Center of Photography, with its long history of political engagement through "concerned photography," should attempt this task. For this project is above all a political one, one that asks each reader and each viewer to question her or his own identity and the ways it is shaped by and linked to wider social ideas through photography.

Clearly, such a complex intellectual investigation could not have been possible without the advice and leadership of many individuals. First and foremost, we must express our gratitude to the coorganizers of this project, Brian Wallis, Director of Exhibitions and Chief Curator at the International Center of Photography, and Coco Fusco, Associate Professor at Columbia University, as well as a leading artist and critic. As two key voices in the cultural debates of the last decade, Wallis and Fusco have worked together for three years to produce a thought-

DIRECTOR'S FOREWORD

Willis E. Hartshorn
Ehrenkranz Director

provoking book and exhibition that will surely serve as an important critical intervention for years to come.

An exhibition of this magnitude could have been realized without timely logistical and financial support. In this case, we are proud to acknowledge our partnership with the National Endowment for the Arts, which awarded this project a generous Millennium Grant at a crucial early stage. The Endowment's bold leadership commitment helped to generate a number of matching grants from private donors. We gratefully acknowledge these major sponsors: the Rockefeller Foundation, the Ford Foundation, Altria, and Corbis, with its enlightened commitment to expanding the public's awareness of the important role pictures play in our culture.

Given the national scope of this exhibition, it is significant that loans to this exhibition have come from over one hundred artists, collectors, galleries, and museums throughout the country. We offer our appreciation to those individuals and institutions that have so selflessly aided us in this undertaking; their cooperation and generosity have been invaluable. Finally, we at the International Center of Photography extend our deepest gratitude to the artists and photographers included in *Only Skin Deep*. Their ideas and images give form to this project and help us to better understand how photographs have shaped notions of national and individual identity. It is our hope that through *Only Skin Deep* their work will stimulate a widespread and lively conversation about what it means to be an American today.

Few issues are as controversial as race and nation. After years of debate we still understand very little about how these terms of self-definition and identity work. Their meaning seems to find its most powerful expression in photographs. America as a safe haven for immigrants and an Edenic paradise for pioneers and entrepreneurs, these are images formed in our consciousness through photography. Equally powerful photographs show us a society fraught by racial conflict and struggles to transform the social order. And even those photographs that might appear somewhat more disassociated from social issues—those more overtly concerned with style or with personal expression—can be indirectly or unintentionally inflected with racial tropes. In this book and exhibition, we argue that race and nation—and, indeed, photography itself—are fictions, cultural constructions that shape our social interactions. If photographs are not inherently truthful representations of identity, but must be read to find their meaning, can a different reading of these images break down their distorting stereotypes? This is the central question posed by *Only Skin Deep*.

As with any undertaking of this scale, *Only Skin Deep: Changing Visions of the American Self* would not have happened without the commitment and involvement of many people. My first thanks go to Coco Fusco, who graciously agreed to work with me as cocurator of this exhibition. Without her, the multifaceted project would not have happened. For three years, she has pursued this task with characteristic enthusiasm and intelligence. Her probing research and conceptual acumen have shaped this exhibition into one that demonstrates surprising historical and geographical breadth, and includes objects of remarkable aesthetic richness.

I would also like to thank the board of the International Center of Photography, led by Raymond J. McGuire, who has unwaveringly supported this challenging endeavor. On the staff, I particularly want to thank Ehrenkranz Director Willis E. Hartshorn and Deputy Director for Programs Philip S. Block, who had the audacity to conceptualize this project in the first place and the perseverance to see it through.

Assistant Curator Cynthia Fredette worked tirelessly and with great intellectual creativity on many aspects of project planning, and she served as curator of the *Only Skin Deep* National Survey, an online companion exhibition that includes work by over 150 contemporary artists and photographers. Such exhibitions invariably involve thousands of details to coordinate; in this case, our great curatorial assistants, Carmen Higginbotham and Michelle-Lee White, deftly handled them. Registrar Barbara Woytowicz skillfully managed the loan and care of works from other collections; curatorial assistant Cynthia Young

CURATORS' ACKNOWLEDGMENTS

Brian Wallis
Director of Exhibitions and Chief Curator,
International Center of Photography

Coco Fusco
Associate Professor, Columbia University
Curator, International Center of Photography

coordinated loans from the Permanent Collection of the International Center of Photography; and curatorial assistant Vanessa Rocco organized the exhibition tour and many other complicated aspects of the project.

Additional staff members at the International Center of Photography who were instrumental to the realization of *Only Skin Deep* include: Steve Rooney, Deputy Director for Finance; Annie LaRock, Deputy Director for External Affairs; Mackarness Goode, Deputy Director for External Affairs; Marie Spiller, Director of Development; Amy Poueymirou, Associate Director of Development; Phyllis Levine, Director of Communications; Suzanne Nicholas, Associate Director of Education; and Lacy Austin, Coordinator of Community Programs.

Publications Coordinator Karen Hansgen heroically engineered the complex production of this book, with the able assistance of Erin Barnett and Nola Tully. We are also grateful to ICP's editor Marion Kocot and to designer Bethany Johns for her extraordinary book design. Our deepest thanks go to editor Deborah Aaronson at Harry N. Abrams for the dedication she brought to this publication. And, of course, we thank all the authors whose writings in this book have strengthened the project as a scholarly intervention in the field of visual cultural studies by opening up new questions and areas of analysis.

Many of the authors in this book were part of the *Only Skin Deep* advisory team, who generously provided insights, contacts, and wonderful suggestions for photographic works to see. For their critical insights and support, we express our deep appreciation to the *Only Skin Deep* Advisory Committee, chaired by Merry Foresta: Maurice Berger, Susan Cahan, C. Ondine Chavoya, Thelma Golden, Karin Higa, Kellie Jones, Catherine Lord, Kobena Mercer, Nicholas Mirzoeff, James Moy, Aleta Ringlero, Caroline Vercoe, Ricardo Viera, Deborah Willis, and Fred Wilson.

Many colleagues—curators, librarians, archivists, scholars, arts administrators, artists, and photographers—have generously assisted with the many loans to this exhibition. They are thanked individually elsewhere in this volume, but I wish to express here my deep personal appreciation for their time and collaboration.

Finally, I wish to acknowledge with profound gratitude the invaluable exchanges with others that have helped me to understand how visual culture shapes our views of people in the world. In particular, I thank Kobena Mercer, Stuart Hall, Lucy Lippard, Thelma Golden, Okwui Enwezor, Robin Kelley, Carol Squiers, Tricia Rose, George Yudice, Maurice Berger, Jonathan Weinberg, Christopher Phillips, Andrew Ross, James Clifford, Miwon Kwon, Barbara Kirschenblatt-Gimblett, Maren Stange, Renee Green, Julie Ault, Michele Wallace,

Philomena Mariani, bell hooks, Allan Sekula, and Katherine Dieckmann. This project is meant as a continuation of those and many other dialogues, and hopefully it will contribute to a deeper understanding of our identities, our positions, our differences, and our shared goals.— **B.W.**

Only Skin Deep: Changing Visions of the American Self could not have come to fruition without the efforts of many people. I have benefited from support from other curators, museum staff, librarians, archivists, scholars, and artists throughout the United States. I would like to offer special thanks to the staff of the International Center of Photography, particularly to curatorial assistants Carmen Higginbotham and Michelle-Lee White. I would also like to thank my research assistants: Marcial Godoy-Anativia, Marisol Martinez, Claire Tancons, and Alexandra Whitney. The *Only Skin Deep* advisory team, C. Ondine Chavoya, Karin Higa, Nicholas Mirzoeff, Aleta Ringlero, and Deborah Willis, has generously provided insights, contacts, and made wonderful suggestions of photographic works. The essayists who have contributed original texts to the catalogue have strengthened the project as a scholarly intervention in the field of visual cultural studies. I am also greatly indebted to scholars James Faris, Lucy Lippard, Kellie Jones, Patricia Johnston, Jane Desmond, Lynn Davis, and Benito Vergara. And without the astute professional advice from Thelma Golden and Okwui Enwezor, I would not have been capable of envisioning a venture of this nature and scale.

The research for this exhibition took me on the road all over the United States and Puerto Rico to public and private collections. I was helped along the way by numerous people who took interest in *Only Skin Deep* and graciously led me to crucial materials and resources. I would like to thank Carol Johnson at the Library of Congress, Paula Richardson Fleming and Jeanie Sklar at the National Anthropological Archives, Chester Cowan at the Oklahoma Historical Society, Carolyn Davis at Syracuse University's Department of Special Collections, Becky Simmons, Joseph Struble, and Rachel Stuhlman at the George Eastman House, DeSoto Brown and Deanne DuPont at the Bishop Museum, Robert Spindler at the Arizona State University Library, Kathleen Hubehschmidt at the Arizona State Museum, Susan Sheehan at the Arizona Historical Society, Tricia Loscher at the Heard Museum, Beth Ann Guynn at the Getty Research Institute for the History of Art and the Humanities, Robert Sobieszek at the Los Angeles County Museum, Therese Babineau at the Phoebe A. Hearst Museum of Anthroplogy, Melissa Rountree at the Hallmark Collection,

Joseph Traugott at the Museum of New Mexico, Arthur Olivas at the Palace of the Governors in Santa Fe, Diane Bird at the Museum of Indian Arts and Culture, Steve Thomas at the California Museum of Photography, and Harry Persaud at The British Museum's Department of Ethnography. In Puerto Rico, I was assisted by Marimar Benitez, Haydee Venegas, Mercedes Trelles, and Michelle Marxuach, and in Hawaii, by Gaye Chan.

Many of the ideas in this project emerged from a course I taught at the Tyler School of Art for five years called "Art, Race and the American Experience." I am grateful to my students there, whose questions and comments helped me to clarify my own thoughts on a complicated subject. I began working on the exhibition while I was on a junior faculty research leave from Temple University. I offer my special thanks to Rochelle Toner and Stanley Whitney for their constant support during my tenure at Tyler, and to Bruce Ferguson, Janet Wolff, Gary Okihiro, Farah Jasmine Griffin, and Kendall Thomas at Columbia University, where I now teach, for their encouragement and assistance.

My own curiosity about America's colonial archive was sparked by studying with Mary Pratt at Stanford University and subsequently nourished through dialogues with many artists and writers. Nearly two decades of invaluable conversations and collaborations with Black British colleagues Isaac Julien, John Akomfrah, Lina Gopaul, Pervaiz Khan, Martina Attile, David Bailey, Kobena Mercer and Stuart Hall have contributed to the development of a critical framework for understanding the images in the exhibition. I have also benefited immeasurably from more recent conversations with Ricardo Dominguez, Jennifer González, Lisa Nakamura, and Maria Fernandez.

Thanks to the generous resources provided by this project's many funders, particularly the National Endowment for the Arts, I was able to engage in extensive primary research that would otherwise have been beyond my reach. More than any other venture I have been involved with, this exhibition has shown me how and why entire fields of inquiry go untouched, even though the need to broaden our understanding of American culture is widely recognized. My greatest hope for this project is that it can provide a resource for current and future students of American culture and photography. —**C.F.**

Coco Fusco

RACIAL TIME, RACIAL MARKS, RACIAL METAPHORS

Race has become metaphorical—a way of referring to and disguising forces, events, classes, and expressions of social decay and economic division far more threatening to the body politic than biological "race" ever was. Expensively kept, economically unsound, a spurious and useless political asset in election campaigns, racism is as healthy today as it was during the Enlightenment. It seems that it has a utility far beyond economy, beyond the sequestering of classes from one another, and has assumed a metaphorical life so completely embedded in daily discourse that it is perhaps more necessary and more on display than ever before.
—Toni Morrison, *Playing in the Dark*, 1992[1]

Race in the making of the American self

The photographic image plays a central role in American culture. Americans are avid producers and consumers of photographs and as our culture shifts from being predominantly print based to image based, we grow increasingly reliant on photographs for information about histories and realities that we do not experience directly. But we also create and use photography to see ourselves. By looking at pictures we imagine that we can know who we are and who we were. Though the fashioning of one's self-image may be most frequently associated with family snapshots or portraits, the endeavor to see, and thus to know oneself is also a public, communal activity. Photography offers the promise of apprehending who we are, not only as private individuals but also as members of social and cultural groups, as public citizens, as Americans. No other means of representing human likeness has been used more systematically to describe and formulate American identity than photography. Envisioning and exhibiting the American self has been a photographic venture since the inception of the medium. It is an ongoing social, cultural, and political project.

For most of our country's history, one of the most forceful means of circumscribing American identity has been race. From the establishment of the United States until the 1960s, access to American citizenship and to the full exercise of civil rights was restricted on the basis of race. As noted by historian Manning Marable, American national identity "was largely defined by 'whiteness': racial categories of privilege that rationalized and justified the domination and exploitation of 'others' who are nonEuropean, poor, and/or female."[2] He goes

1. Toni Morrison, *Playing in the Dark: Whiteness and the Literary Imagination* (New York: Vintage Books, 1992), p. 63.
2. Manning Marable, "The Problematics of Ethnic Studies," *Black Renaissance* 3, no. 19 (Fall 2000): 10.

Gordon Parks, *L.A. Courtroom, Malcolm X displaying picture of Muslim Ronald Stokes, killed by police a year earlier*, 1963. Gelatin silver print, 11 x 14 3/8 in. (27.9 x 36.4 cm). International Center of Photography, purchased by the ICP Acquisitions Committee, 2003.   13

on to explain "whiteness was literally codified as part of the Consti-
tution, particularly in Article I, Section 2, which defined enslaved
African Americans for the purposes of taxation and representation
as the equivalent of three-fifths of a human being."[3] Once slavery
was abolished, segregation, which was upheld by the Supreme Court
in 1896, remained in place until 1954; only after the passage of the
1965 Voting Rights Act were blacks guaranteed enfranchisement in
all fifty states.

Beginning in the 1830s, Native Americans were forcibly relocated
to reservations, thus facilitating the opening of the Western territories
to white settlement. They were subsequently enjoined by the 1887
Dawes Severalty Act to adopt an individualistic and capitalist concept
of property, and subjected to several decades of assimilationist re-
education projects that were designed to sever their connection to
their respective languages, religions, and other traditional customs.
A byproduct of this process of uprooting and deculturation was the
development of a pan-Indian racial consciousness, which led to the
formation of the American Indian Movement in the 1960s. Until the 1924
Indian Citizenship Act, the indigenous peoples of the United States
could only obtain citizenship through marriage to a white male or
military service, and until 1948 several states continued to bar them
from voting. To this day, federally recognized tribal affiliation is determined by equating identity with biological lineage.

Marable differentiates between blacks who were racialized through
slavery and legally enforced segregation and Asian and Latin American
immigrants who were racialized by means of laws and *de facto* segregation. After the U.S.–Mexican War of 1846–48, only Mexicans who
were defined as Spanish or white could claim U.S. citizenship. The
Chinese were subjected to restricted entry from 1870 until the 1940s,
and those who did reside in the United States could not become
citizens until 1943. Japanese immigration was restricted by Congress
in 1907 and 1924, Asian Indian immigration was halted in 1917, and
Filipino immigration was curtailed in 1934.[4] Only after the passage of
the McCarran–Walter Act of 1952 were racial barriers to immigration
removed, which finally made it possible for all Asians to become naturalized citizens. Still, it was not until 1965, when the quotas favoring
Europeans were terminated, that racial distinctions were completely
eliminated from U.S. immigration policy.

At one time, the limitations placed upon nonwhites and the
concomitant privileging of whites did not represent an untenable
contradiction of the idea of America as a democracy or even as a
melting pot. Race was not understood as something that American
law could reconstruct or abolish through the concept of political

3. Ibid., p. 11.
4. Ibid., p. 12.

equality—it was seen as a fact of nature. As the legendary *Plessy v. Ferguson* Supreme Court decision states regarding the right of states to enforce segregation in public spaces:

> *A statute which implies merely a legal distinction*
> *between the white and colored races—a distinction*
> *which is founded in the color of the two races and*
> *which must always exist so long as white men are*
> *distinguished from the other race by color—has*
> *no tendency to destroy the legal equality of the two*
> *races.... The object of the [Fourteenth Amendment] was*
> *undoubtedly to enforce the absolute equality of the two*
> *races before the law, but in the nature of things it could*
> *not have been intended to abolish distinctions based*
> *upon color, or to enforce social, as distinguished from*
> *political equality, or a commingling of the two races*
> *upon terms unsatisfactory to either.*[5]

During the first 150 years of U.S. history, race was considered a theoretically coherent system of human classification; from the

5. Justice Henry Billings Brown, "Majority Opinion in *Plessy v. Ferguson*," in *Desegregation and the Supreme Court*, ed. Benjamin Munn Ziegler (Boston: D.C. Heath and Company, 1958), pp. 50–51.

Garry Winogrand, *Central Park Zoo, New York City*, 1967. Gelatin silver print, 8 ¹/₂ x 13 ¹/₂ in. (21.6 x 32.5 cm). Courtesy of The Fraenkel Gallery, San Francisco; Center for Creative Photography, University of Arizona, Tuscon.

mid-nineteenth to mid-twentieth century, racial hierarchies were widely accepted as having a basis in science. Because of its purported technological objectivity as a recording device, photography during this period was marshaled to document the "fact" of racial difference. This was a particularly challenging task, considering that forced and consensual interracial unions in the segregated United States were generating a population with an ever-increasing variety of complexions and features even though the protection of white privileges demanded a clearly defined binary system of identification. The premise of this exhibition, however, is that rather than *recording* the existence of race, photography *produced* race as a visualizable fact.

I am making a point of referencing this history because it is not uncommon in the present to assume that in America, racial awareness is the result of self-segregation impulses among its ethnic minorities. This assumption notwithstanding, the historical record indicates that the organization of this country's population into racial categories has been a constituent element of American identity. The more difficult and controversial question is whether this is still the case, and if so, how are we to explain why. Politicians, media pundits, intellectuals, and activists debate these issues incessantly, and at times it seems as if their discussions are designed to defer rather than to engage in analysis. Over and over again, the same questions are posed. If equality has been achieved, then what does race mean? If race is still meaningful, does that mean that racism has not been eliminated?

The relationship between racism and racialized self perception is never a purely philosophical matter. Racism represents a social and political dilemma for the society that defines itself as democratic, so public acknowledgement and organization of the knowledge of race and racial imagery must be carefully managed. Ascribing racist character to any public cultural expression or image invokes the specter of deleterious economic effects—boycotts, protests, withdrawal of sponsorship, decline in value, and so forth. These effects are not qualitatively or quantitatively comparable to the long-term impact of racism indiscriminately directed at an entire group and sanctioned by law and custom. It is not uncommon for members of groups who are unaccustomed to being racialized in American terms—which includes both white Americans and newly arrived middle-class immigrants of all backgrounds—to equate freedom of expression with freedom from racial consciousness as a tactic of self-defense. The fear of the aforementioned potential economic effects informs the presumption that behind any discussion of race lurks an accusation of racism waiting to spring forth. Therefore one's interests are best protected by asserting

that culture no longer has anything to do with race unless it is obviously and univocally celebratory. And since art, or at least "good" art, should not be monological or instrumental, it should be thought of as being above such considerations. Contemporary public discussion of art abounds in variations on this theme, all of which fabricate an opposition between a concern with race and a concern with beauty. The arguments that develop out of this opposition are: art is about beauty, so art that is beautiful is not about race; photography defined as art is not about race; and artists who make beautiful images of themselves and others are not making pictures about race. Therefore, there is no need to discuss the relationships between race and representation in art photography. I hope to demonstrate in this exhibition why this opposition is spurious.

It is safe and easy to point to a past with a clearly demarcated racial hierarchy and grasp how it is connected with the propagandistic use of racial imagery. Much in the same way, it is no great feat to point to racist hate groups and understand how their rhetoric expresses their beliefs. In an age when racial discrimination against nonwhite legal residents of the United States has been made punishable by law and individual racist acts have been criminalized, it is more difficult to ascribe a single meaning or function to racial imagery, especially if it is not produced or used specifically for didactic purposes. Is the logical deduction that racial history can never drop out of the picture?

Unidentified photographer, *"Fun in black,"* ca. 1900. Albumen print stereograph, 4 1/8 x 7 1/8 in. (10.5 x 18.0 cm). UCR/California Museum of Photography, University of California, Riverside, Keystone-Mast Collection.

More than a few intellectuals in the past decade, recoiling in dismay at the entertainment industry's blatant commodification of ethnicity on the one hand, and the global rise of ethnic fundamentalism on the other, have gone on record as being "against race." But does it really make sense to claim that American culture has moved beyond race?

There is ample evidence that racial perception has not disappeared and racial imagery continues to proliferate, but there is no consensus as to the effect that historical legacy has on racial perception in the present. This is not only because racial obstacles to equality have been removed from our legal system—though that makes it much more difficult to measure the effect of race and the effect of racial imagery. As an individualistically oriented society with a market-driven economy and a thriving entertainment industry that reaches a global audience, the United States maintains a clear line in law and popular consciousness between public acts with measurable effects and the private world of image consumption and fantasy. Financial interests are served by keeping the politics of the consumption of racial imagery produced by the private sector away from public scrutiny, and finding recourse in the discourse of the individual rights of expression and privacy is the most unimpeachable rationale.

The efforts to dismiss racial analysis in the present, however, if viewed as part of a larger historical pattern, can be interpreted as a means of negotiating apprehensions about the decline of Western influence in the course of the twentieth century. According to sociologist Frank Füredi, these anxieties emerged during the transition from a dominant worldview prior to World War II that celebrated white superiority, to a formal acceptance of racial equality in the postwar period. In *The Silent War: Imperialism and the Changing Perception of Race*, Füredi describes how Western powers in the postwar era have been fearful of the potentially destabilizing consequences of racial conflict, and have thus developed defensive philosophies of race relations as preemptive strategies.[6] Those strategies have included: supporting knowledge production that pathologizes individuals and groups who espouse racial consciousness; promoting schools of thought that advance views of racism as universal and indistinguishable from one geopolitical context to another; circulating arguments that characterize racial conflict as irrational; and instituting cultural and educational policies that restrict redress of racial inequality to a celebratory expression of cultural difference. These approaches to race management inform most variants of multiculturalism *and* the conservative movements opposed to it.

America's relationship with its imaginary racial distinctions is not only a juridical and moral matter—in other words, it is not reducible to

6. Frank Füredi, *The Silent War: Imperialism and the Changing Perception of Race* (London: Pluto Press, 1998).

AS WE FOUND THEM.

These children were owned by Thomas White, of Mathews Co.,
Va., until Feb. 20th, when Capt. Riley, 6th U. S. C. I., took them
and gave them to the Society of Friends to educate at the Orphan's
Shelter. Philadelphia.

Profits from sale, for the benefit of the children.

AS THEY ARE NOW

The Mother of these children was beaten, branded and sold at
auction because she was kind to Union Soldiers. As she left for
Richmond. Va., Feb. 13th, 1864. bound down in a cart, she prayed
"O! God send the Yankees to take my children away."

Profits from sale, for the benefit of the children.

whether we treat people as equals or whether a given ascription is inherently racist. Regardless of whether we believe that race can tell us anything significant or "true" about people, we don't need to be forced to see it nor can we completely avoid it. Racial thinking is not experienced or enforced exclusively through repressive means. Photography has not only been deployed in the pursuit of scientific truths about race; it has played an absolutely fundamental role in the construction of racialized viewing as a positive, pleasurable, and desirable experience. Michel Foucault's notion of "the positive production of power" is crucial to this understanding: "What makes power accepted is that it traverses and produces things, induces pleasure, forms of knowledge."[7]

The knowledge of race operates, to use Foucault's terms, as a "productive network that runs through a social body." I am not alluding here to theories about the need to compensate for negative stereotyping with positive images of ethnic minorities, but to the ways that photography generates a distinct mise en scène and provides material that is visually reminiscent of but phenomenologically distinct from

7. Michel Foucault, "Truth and Power,"
in *Power/Knowledge: Selected Interviews
and Other Writings, 1972–1977*, ed. Colin
Gordon (New York: Pantheon, 1980),
p. 119.

Peregrine F. Cooper, *As We Found Them*, 1864. Carte-de-visite, 3 ³/₈ x 2 ¹/₄ in. (8.6 x 5.8 cm);
As They Are Now, 1864. Carte-de-visite, 3 ³/₁₆ x 2 ¹/₈ in. (8.1 x 5.4 cm). George Eastman House, Rochester, New York.

reality for voyeuristic engagement. The parameters of the pleasurable and the articulation of "beauty" in racial imagery were first established by and for a middle-class audience that was white. As Allan Sekula has said, "Perhaps more than any other single technical invention of the mid-nineteenth century, photography came to focus the confidence and fears of an ascendant industrial bourgeois…the contradictory role played by photography within the culture dominated by that class… combined a coldly rational scientism with a sentimental and often antirational pursuit of the beautiful."[8]

The representations of race in photography have never been restricted to denigration of racialized subjects; racial difference has also been seen as a spectacle and a commodity over the course of a century. Race has often been visualized in "high" and popular culture as a display of difference, as natural beauty and style, and as an eroticized encounter with alterity. Photography renders and delivers interracial encounters that might be dangerous, forbidden, or unattainable as safe and consumable experiences. Mass-marketed photography in the second half of the nineteenth century made racialized viewing into a form of entertainment. It created a domain for the imagination where fantasies did not have to remain within the boundaries of time, space, law, or decorum—but where pleasure was predicated on the awareness of limits and roles. In the scenes that have been staged in studios and exotic exteriors, cabarets and burlesque revues, theme parks and festivals, and now also in video games and cyberspace, racial difference has been dramatized as the interplay of irreconcilable extremes and ritualized as role play, yielding a fantasy world akin to what Jessica Benjamin described in her analysis of sadomasochistic eroticism as "the sensationalism of power and powerlessness."[9]

While social mores do affect what kind of racial imagery is considered marketable to mass audiences for public viewing, the possibilities of private production and consumption that were opened by photography enabled image makers to cater to a much wider range of racialized tastes and desires, and to foment and diversify demand by means of continuous exposure. The most obviously denigrating forms of racist caricature have long been targeted as evidence of visual culture as an agency of oppression, but the repertoire of racial imagery that Americans inherited from the nineteenth century is somewhat broader in style and scope and quite varied in emotional tone. A good deal of it erased the traces of racial or colonial domination altogether with picturesque tableaux that provided a site where the power to look and the pleasure derived from it appear to be detached from what Sarah Suleri calls "questions of colonial culpability."[10]

Fetishistic disavowal of race operates on more than one level in these photographic encounters. The scenes enable a psychic denial of

8. Allan Sekula, "The Traffic in Photographs," *Art Journal*, no. 41 (Spring, 1981): 21. In this volume, pp. 79–109.
9. Jessica Benjamin, "Master and Slave: The Fantasy of Erotic Domination," in *Powers of Desire: The Politics of Sexuality*, ed. Ann Snitow, Christine Stansell, and Sharon Thompson (New York: Monthly Review Press, 1983), p. 296.
10. Fatimah Tobing-Rony, *The Third Eye: Race, Cinema and Ethnographic Spectacle* (Durham: Duke University Press, 1996), p. 90.

the violent roots of racial difference, and counter the destabilizing effect of difference-as-unpredictable through the repetition of visual tropes. The apparent beauty of nature and of the "others" who are integral to it masks the cultural and political act of constructing the racial other. The aestheticizing of nature and of preindustrial societies, and the exaltation of the racial other's beauty has the incredible effect of reversing the power dynamic between the viewer and the viewed in the real world: in the fantasy of the photographic encounter, the viewer is "overcome" by the beauty of the other. I have outlined the mechanics of this process because it continues to be relevant in the present as these dynamics are repeated in contemporary art and advertising.

The abstraction of artifacts and human elements from their contexts, the mythologizing of "vanishing natives" as "noble savages," and the romanticizing of the rural South and its "happy Negroes" were the racialized versions of early photography's sentimental and antirational pursuit of the beautiful. Long before simulation entered our theoretical lexicon as a defining characteristic of postmodern imaging, photographers and filmmakers routinely entered already-colonized spaces and rearranged them to concoct images of a "pure" and "primitive" world that did not exist. Edenic pastoral scenes with exquisite others untouched by modernity have been and continue to be staged routinely for vicarious and genuine tourists who symbolically transcend time and space in the act of looking at others. On the global art circuit, contemporary art photography, with its imposing scale, its exuberant colors, and its never-ending parade of exotic bodies, is better understood as an extension of this racialized discourse on beauty than as a negation of race.

The ethnographic trope of staging evolutionary time, however, was not the only means of establishing the distance that frames and structures the scenarios of racial fantasy. The foregrounding of artifice with ironic editorial text and parodic theatricality was also common, if not the norm. Not surprisingly, the photographs produced to entertain white audiences were more openly humorous than those that served as political or scientific propaganda, and photographers often used exaggeration and transgression to entice viewers. Postcards and stereoscopic photographs titillated them with intimations of sexual attraction between white women and black or Native American men; images of costumed microcephalics, masquerading as examples of "backward" races, were grotesque parodies of positivist reasoning. Though the color line was clearly drawn in public life, photography studios were veritable laboratories for the fabrication of multiple selves. Photographed performances of racial transvestism in which whites could express their repressed "inner primitives" and nonwhites were dressed as wild savages, or demonstrated their abilities to "perform whiteness" were popular. These pictures from the past suggest that many peoples' views of race were not simplistic or literal-minded, in spite of the belief that only recently have Americans become more ironic and risqué in our attitudes toward race. These scenarios still inform photographic representation in art and entertainment in the present.

In American society today, race is *both* a volatile political agenda and a multimillion-dollar-culture industry. I offer just a few examples to highlight its prevalence in the immediate present. Even as the legitimacy of racial profiling has been restored by the threat of terrorism, affirmative action is in jeopardy and likely to be abolished when the University of Michigan case reaches the Supreme court this year. In the brief period that I have been working on this essay, Senate majority leader Trent Lott stepped down after the public outcry at his nostalgia for segregation, and nine hundred Middle Eastern men were arrested and detained when they voluntarily reported visa irregularities to immigration authorities in California. The reversal of the conviction of three black and two Latino youths in the 1989 Central Park rape case, as a result of the introduction of DNA evidence that linked another man to the crime, detonated yet another vituperative public debate about whether the American criminal justice system is prone to racial prejudice.

Meanwhile, Americans consume an astounding amount and variety of racial imagery and fantasy in music, literature, film, television, pornography, tourism, advertising, fashion, and beauty products. Sensationalized racial conflicts that accentuate racial polarities and enforce stereotypes are just as popular grist for the media mill as the prospect of eliminating, accentuating, or transforming racial characteristics through miracle treatments and morphing machines. The recently released Michael Moore documentary *Bowling for Columbine* features an interview with a producer of the television series *Cops*, who confesses that despite his liberal politics, he continuously features police officers chasing black men on his program because shows about white-collar crime are far less attractive to television audiences. Miscegenation as a means of neutralizing racial conflict through sexual domination still yields solid box office returns: Halle Berry won an Oscar in 2002 for playing a southern black woman who falls in love with the white prison guard who executed her black husband. Wayne Wang's new film *Maid in Manhattan* features a love affair between a Puerto Rican chambermaid, played by Jennifer Lopez, and a blueblood politician who discovers that a Bronx-bred Latina can be sexy and "Mediterranean-looking" when seen in a five-star hotel wearing pilfered Dolce & Gabbana. Todd Haynes's *Far From Heaven*, set in 1958,

leaves a love-starved white suburban housewife longing for her black gardener, but unable to have him.

The act of visualizing and looking at racial difference continues to seduce and enthrall American viewers, whether or not the racial discourse is objective, and whether or not all Americans even agree on the existence of racism. The sheer volume of racial imagery that has been and continues to be produced for private consumption, public education and entertainment, erotic stimulation, and aesthetic appreciation signals that America's attraction to race exceeds the boundaries of a discussion of institutional racism. In that sense, it is possible and indeed probable that we like to *see* race even if we don't consider ourselves racist. Some would hold that consuming racial imagery proves one's love for the other or is a substitute for engagement with the social and political realities of race relations. Others argue that the inclusion of images of nonwhite people in mainstream media and art indicates that racism is over and race is no longer salient. Serious discussion of the meaning of our desire to *see* race in visual representation is impeded by the difficulties we have in distinguishing between racialization as a visual process, and racism as an ethical and political dilemma.

Unidentified photographer, *Portrait of Young Kru Woman from Village Near Monrovia with Body Paint and in Costume*, 1893. Postcard, 6 x 4 in. (15.2 x 10.2 cm). National Anthropological Archives, Smithsonian Insititution, Washington D.C.
Walery Studio, *Josephine Baker*, 1926. Gelatin silver print, 10 x 8 in. (25.4 x 20.3 cm). Private collection.

The racial exhibition in context

Only Skin Deep: Changing Visions of the American Self began as a National Endowment for the Arts Millennium project, an initiative launched at the end of the Clinton Administration that was designed to showcase the quality and richness of American art and culture and thus, tacitly endorse the Endowment's role in its production. I was specifically asked to address the issue of race in America. I wanted to avoid several predictable responses to this request, and in particular I did not consider advocating the now-popular position that art and scholarship should move beyond race. If I embraced the argument that contemporary image-makers have moved on to a postracial and post-identitarian mode of representation, I would have been unable to assess the ways that race persists in American visual culture and social life. I did not want to visualize diversity as a taxonomic display of recognizably distinct and attractive ethnic faces, which is the convention that now dominates corporate advertising. Nor did I want to recast it as the geographic dispersal of universal art forms, which is the underlying premise of most global art shows and biennials.

I also did not wish to repeat the compensatory gesture of showcasing the self-imaging of minority groups as authentic, superior, or more self-reflective than what is generally identified as colonialist photography. The flip side of this method would be the modernist tactic of singling out works based on purely aesthetic criteria. The presumption that museums are able to effectively dismantle the history of institutional racism by attributing "master" status to a handful of nonwhite photographers based on the "discovery" of quality in their work implies that the economic and cultural power of art institutions to designate value should replace a critical analysis of Western forms of racial thought and how those forms are manifest in our culture.

Each one of these presentational strategies has yielded interesting and edifying exhibitions, broadened our understanding of photography, and helped many artists' careers. Because of the origin of this project in a government-sponsored initiative that was specifically aimed at conveying ideas about our *national* culture, I felt it necessary to pay close attention to the political implications of each method. I am not trying to suggest that exhibitions that manifest the abovementioned curatorial strategies should never be organized. However, they share an approach to multiculturalism that can be summed up as what Ann duCille calls "additive campaigns" that "augment but do not necessarily alter the Eurocentric status quo."[11] As such, they can all be understood as attempts at race management and containment that circumvent analysis of racial logic as a visual system that is distinguishable from the status of race as a indicator of some "truth" about identity.

11. Ann duCille, "Black Barbie and the Deep Play of Difference," in *The Feminism and Visual Culture Reader*, ed. Amelia Jones (London: Routledge, 2003), p. 336.

Because of the expectation that an exhibition about race is nothing more than a show about racism and how artists have endorsed or debunked it, I have tried to outline how that presumption is informed by our history and to explain why I have sought a different approach in developing this project. I hope this approach can move the discussion of photography's complicated relationship with identity, race, and nation around the critical impasse resulting from a focus on stereotyping of and discrimination against nonwhite people.

In an effort to work against the grain, I have tried to broaden the discussion of racial representation in American photography in many ways. The geographic area identified as America is here extended to include territories and protectorates to suggest that our political influence beyond national boundaries has also contributed to our changing views of race. The exhibition also includes many explorations of how whiteness is configured in photography and how it may even be expressed through nonfigurative means as the exercise of power over others through their very distinction. By this I mean, for example, that the representation of whiteness includes how it functions as a normative standard against which the physical and moral characteristics of nonwhite people are measured and how it operates as a force in the physical world separate from white bodies. To stress that race is a system of representation rather than an indicator of truths about any group of people, I have not divided the work in the exhibition according to the ethnicities of the subjects or their makers. The photographs are not displayed by genre or arranged in chronological order to emphasize how visual strategies resurface and are reformulated at different historical moments and how they cut across a range of photographic styles.

The images in the exhibition are grouped into five thematic categories that are organized in binary terms. "Looking Up/Looking Down" comprises images that endorse or subvert the objectivity of racial hierarchies. "All for One/One for All" examines the distinction between the embodiment of an ideal American, and specific ethnic types. "Humanized/Fetishized" contrasts images that emphasize a subject's individuality with those that objectify and dehumanize. "Assimilate/Impersonate" compares images of nonwhites attempting to "look or act white" with those of whites assuming the characteristics of nonwhites. And finally, "Progress/Regress" explores how racial imagery is tied to ideas about America's future and past.

The categories were devised to stress how photographic techniques communicate ideas about what race means through a recognizable set of visual symbols. In other words, *Only Skin Deep* explores the manifold strategies embedded in photographic discourses that make race visible, intelligible, and attractive. The exhibition is an inquiry into *racial imagery* rather than racism, and it features works that evoke popularly held ideas about race regardless of the intent of the photographers who took them. The logic and meaning of that imagery is too complicated to be explained by determining whether the photographer, his or her subject, or the viewer is consciously for or against racism. America's relationship with race, I would contend, is fraught with ambivalence; with *Only Skin Deep* I have tried to chart the traces of that irresoluteness.

Only Skin Deep is an investigation of how racial imagery in photography of many kinds has shaped understanding of what Americanness is and who Americans are. It is a historical survey and a multidisciplinary investigation. This exhibition also proposes ways of reading photographs and understanding the complicated relationships between images and the social realities they convey. The technological visualization of any identity involves—and often blurs—two key functions we regularly impute to photography: to record preexisting material realities and to visualize our fantasies of what reality could or should look like. Because race is an imaginary construct that is also a social fact with political ramifications, the act of making it visible entails generating believable fictions and demonstrating the effect of their credibility. This exhibition looks at the interplay of these functions.

Racial imagery as mythical speech

I began my research with the theoretical concept of Roland Barthes's notion of mythical speech, a kind of expression whose meaning relies on a preexistent set of signs, or images, and the concepts they convey. According to Barthes, mythical speech is defined by its intent more than its literal sense. When we recognize myth in a picture, we intuit that it is about more than the sum total of its elements. The intent thus appears naturalized. In "Myth Today," his landmark essay from 1957, Barthes relied on an image of a black male in order to explain how photographs function as mythical speech.[12] His principal example was a cover from the magazine *Paris Match* that featured a youthful black soldier in a French uniform saluting the French flag. Barthes's point was that the image made the political and historical effects of French imperialism seem harmless, even logically necessary.

Though he does not state it directly, Barthes relied on a Fanonian understanding of the soldier's blackness as a threat of difference: the image of a black man in a French uniform cast doubt on the general assumption that to be French meant to be white. Colonial subjects who were not white had to demonstrate their assimilation into Frenchness through the enactment of subservience and patriotism.

12. Roland Barthes, "Myth Today," in *Mythologies*, trans. and comp. Annette Lavers (New York, Hill and Wang, 1972), pp. 109–59.

The anticolonialist struggles of blacks, Arabs, and Asians in the 1950s struck at the legitimacy of French imperialism. But the representation of a black French soldier on the cover of a popular magazine in effect nullified their radical position. The black soldier's salute affirms both the justness of his colonial status and the validity of the French Empire. His blackness is visible, but its threat is neutralized.

We could apply this method of reading images to Laura Gilpin's photograph from 1932, *Hardbelly's Hogan*. In it, an elderly Navajo man lies on the earthen floor of a traditional Navajo abode. He is surrounded by three native women, one with a child in her lap, who sit with hands lowered and gaze somewhat blankly into space. A younger native male stands by the old man's head, looking down at a bespectacled white woman crouched by the side of the supine figure. She holds a small receptacle in her hand as she leans forward as if to offer it to him. Her gesture to the prostrate man before her, together with the three small chemical bottles and two tin bowls in the foreground, suggest that she is a nurse. A ray of light falls on her, accentuating the difference in her dress and further distinguishing her as the active agent in the scene. This intercultural configuration of figures can easily be read as a story about the power and superiority of Western science poised to sustain a race whose own life energy appears on the wane. The white nurse, perhaps at the behest of the presiding young adult male, arrives at the hogan to save the sickly Navajo patriarch with a dose of medicine that she has concocted on site, while the ineffectual family witnesses the act and learns a necessary lesson.

Significantly, illness is shown as the cause of the trouble in the hogan. The white presence in the Navajo home takes the form of a maternal savior, an "angel of mercy" responding to their call. The violent conquest and colonization of native land, culture, and people are not in the foreground, or even in the background here: Hardbelly's problem is biological. The relation between two cultures is epitomized by the benevolent administration of knowledge that the Navajo man must absorb to stave off his own death. The photograph was made during a transitional period in American history after the closing of the American frontier. Treaties between the federal government and native peoples required that the United States provide them with housing, education, and medical services, on the one hand, while prevailing notions of white superiority underlay the official policy of cultural termination via assimilation. The social context of U.S. Indian policy informs this intercultural scenario and proffers a set of assumptions about race and science, the photographed family, and by extension, the Navajo and other indigenous peoples of the Southwest: namely, that after the conquest of the American West traditional knowledge

would no longer be known or considered effective, and the indigenous would have to depend on white civilization and scientific knowledge for survival.

Anthropologist James Faris notes that the photograph, though usually classified and presented as "documentary," was to an extent composed by Gilpin, who was following her companion on a visit to the family, and is known to have removed European objects from hogans in order to reinforce their purely tribal aesthetic. The scene, he explains, either demanded that the subjects hold their poses for an extended period, or is likely to have required artificial light.[13] One way or another, the claims published in a 1986 museum catalogue on Gilpin, that it was lit by "sunlight filtering through the overhead smoke hole," and that the Navajo women accepted the photographer and were "sitting peacefully," are questionable, if not a direct attempt to downplay the violence of colonization and obfuscate any ethical questions about Gilpin's approach to photographing the Navajo.

13. James C. Faris, *Navajo and Photography* (Albuquerque: University of New Mexico Press, 1996), pp. 241 and 246.

Laura Gilpin, *Hardbelly's Hogan, Arizona*, 1932. Gelatin silver print, 9 $\frac{1}{2}$ x 13 $\frac{1}{2}$ in. (24 x 32.4 cm). Amon Carter Museum, Fort Worth, Texas, bequest of the artist.

When it works effectively, then, mythical speech makes a particular view of history seem like nature. If we analyze the intent of the myth, we discredit its content as a simple fact of life. If we argue that an image was created to make something arbitrary seem necessary, we undercut the possibility of seeing it as "just a picture." For example, what is it about the black man and white woman holding baby monkeys in Garry Winogrand's *Central Park Zoo* (1967) that makes them notable? Do they only draw attention because they appear to be an interracial couple or because the primates in their arms evoke common fantasies about the dangers of miscegenation? Or why would George Trager's photograph of Big Foot lying dead in the snow after the 1891 battle at Wounded Knee continue to be reproduced as a postcard decades later (as were images of the dead Pancho Villa) and circulated among people who had no direct relationship to the scene?

Some would say that this approach imposes a purpose on a photograph, making it an instrument. But even an ambiguous or polysemous photograph exists in a visual field and a collective imagination together with other images and real things. That nexus affected the choices that lead to the making of the image in the first place, and our understanding of it shapes our experience of the image and enables us to interpret it. Why, for example, did Richard Avedon title one of photographs in his American West series *Unidentified Migrant Worker* when his other subjects are named? Why is this man, who seems to be Mexican, bare-shirted and dripping wet when he was standing inside under hot lights? Are we to see him as a degraded version of an ethnic type, a "wetback?" Why has the imprimatur of the auteur foreclosed these questions when a similar image in another context would raise eyebrows? Some artists intentionally play with the potential for mythical resonance, while others may do so more inadvertently. Some approaches are overtly didactic, others more ludic, or oblique. The dialogue with the world outside the frame, what is at times described as a photograph's intertextuality, can be made manifest through the incorporation and quotation of documentary elements, historical allusions, and recycled icons, forms, and compositions. My point is that the dialogue exists, even if certain methods of generic classification, interpretation, and appraisal of photography sidestep or suppress it.

To expand upon this idea, let us look at one of Paul Pfeiffer's digital images from 1998, in which a closeup of a flattened doll's head covered with blonde hair fills the frame. The size of the follicles and the tone and texture of the skin constitute telltale signs of the scalp's artificiality. So does the monochromatic blondness of the hair whose waves appear here to parody painterly brushstrokes. Those synthetic locks caricature the formalist experiments with organic forms of such early twentieth-century photographers as Edward Weston, denaturing the universalistic pretense of such modernist gestures. In an oddly deadpan manner, Pfeiffer points to clichéd notions of abstraction as the prime example of Americanness in art.

Pfeiffer's blond doll head simultaneously recalls Kenneth Clark's landmark study in the 1950s that demonstrated racism's impact on black children by their preference for white dolls. That study, poignantly documented by Gordon Parks, and referenced with melodramatic flair by Douglas Sirk in *Imitation of Life*, his classic tale of a mulatta's self-hatred, has sparked innumerable debates about how cultural artifacts affect children's self-images. In the decades since then, the toy industry has diversified the complexions of its most popular dolls to mollify its critics, but as Ann duCille points out in her essay "Black Barbie and the Deep Play of Difference," the effort to represent the heterogeneity of the world population stops at skin. "Mattel and other toymakers have got around the problem by making the other at once different and the same. In this sense, Mattel's play with mass-produced difference resembles the nation's uneasy play with a melting pot pluralism that both produces and denies difference."[14]

Artists from different backgrounds who explore the representation of whiteness have repeatedly touched on the ideological power of blond dolls. Todd Haynes used and defaced Barbie dolls to convey

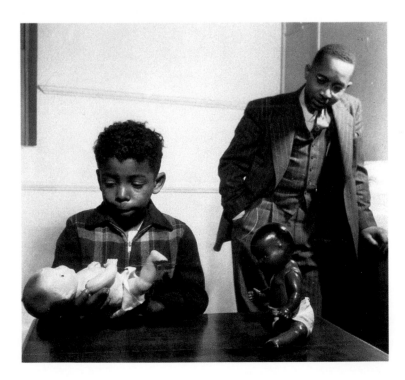

14. duCille, "Black Barbie," p. 337.

Gordon Parks, *Dr. Kenneth B. Clark conducting the "Doll Test" with male child*, 1947. Modern gelatin silver print from original negative, 11 x 14 in. (27.9 x 35.5 cm). Library of Congress, Washington D.C.

"LA YODO," OR IODINE, WAS THE NAME I GAVE MY IMAGINARY FRIEND. SHE WAS FAIR AND LIGHT COMPLECTED.

SHE HAD A BROTHER WHO WE WATCHED PLAY IN THE SNOW WHEN WE HAD TO STAY INDOORS. HE WAS OLDER.

"LA YODO" WAS ALWAYS GETTING INTO TROUBLE, SO I WOULD TAKE HER BY THE EAR AS PUNISHMENT FOR HER ACTIONS.

THE OTHER DAY I CALLED MY MOTHER TO ASK IF "LA YODO" WAS EVER REAL.

"YES," SHE ANSWERED, "SHE LIVED A BLOCK AWAY FROM OUR HOUSE. HER NAME WAS HONEY.

AND SHE WAS A VERY SWEET LITTLE GIRL."

Karen Carpenter's status as a cultural icon and her obsession with attaining impossible body shape in his short film *Superstar: The Karen Carpenter Story*. The East Los Angeles multimedia art collective ASCO, whose members had participated in the 1968 Chicano student protests against racist public education, set white dolls on fire as performance in the 1970s. In Celia Alvarez Muñoz's "La Honey," the text contrasts her mother's and her own memories of a fair-haired figure from the artist's childhood; the photo series culminates with the image of the back of a white doll's head where the hair has been pulled out. Pfeiffer's rendering may not be figurative, but his selection of the blond doll head is not exclusively formal. Pfeiffer makes other key choices here that invite a reading of the work as racially inflected myth. The artist's use of scale—the work is seven feet by three feet— spatializes the symbolism of the work's title, *Leviathan*. Pfeiffer projects Jonas's biblical encounter with the great white whale onto the viewer by engulfing us with the image of blond hair. The title connects the artist's work to a plethora of other literary and philosophical references, among the most notable being Thomas Hobbes's treatment of the whale as a metaphor for the manmade state that circumscribes the individual.

Celia Alvarez Muñoz, *La Honey Nos. 1–6*, 1983. Mixed media (rock maple, gelatin silver print, letterpress text, seven boxes, each 12 x 17 x 14 in. (30.5 x 43.2 x 35.5 cm), images 11 x 14 in. (27.9 x 35.5 cm). Courtesy of the artist.

Whereas Barthes's black soldier saluted the flag while we watched, Pfeiffer places us in front of a mythical reference to the state in order to point to both its capacity to dwarf us, and its visible artifice. He offers us a commentary on whiteness as an all-encompassing construct. That flaxen-haired scalp, rendered abject by its being so obviously plastic, is nonetheless presented to us as the flayed hide of leviathan. And if leviathan is the whale, then we as American viewers are latter-day versions of Herman Melville's Ahab, so immersed in our pursuit of whiteness that we cannot see beyond the detail in front of our eyes. Pfeiffer twists that infamous seafarer into a child whose nemesis is a dismembered towheaded toy.

The evolution of "race"

Thus far, I have asserted that racial imagery is central to American culture and have given examples of how it can operate as mythic speech about the nation and its people. Nonetheless, I have not yet provided a genealogy of the term "race" and how its development affected its use as organizing concept in American society. After many years of teaching about race and visual culture and encountering students who have all experienced some form of racial awareness and fear, but regularly conflate race, ethnicity, and nationality when they write and speak, I have learned not to confuse unconscious racial behavior with the awareness of race as signification. To make sense of how and why race resonates in contemporary America, one must examine how its significance has evolved.

The existence of the term "race" actually precedes the formation of the United States. The word first entered the English language in 1508, and was then used to signify lineage. In the seventeenth century, the word was used by European natural historians to refer to all living species. Throughout the history of its usage, the idea of race has posed a philosophical dilemma for a Judeo-Christian world that posited all human beings as descendants of one source, Adam and Eve. If there was only one human race, several philosophers argued, how could the physical diversity of the world's peoples be explained?

At the very beginning of colonization of the Americas, the legitimacy of hierarchical racial relations was cast in religious terms, as is evidenced by theological debates of that period about whether native peoples had souls. The Bible contains passages about the punishment of Ham that were used to justify enslavement of blacks. Those hierarchies were reinforced visually by representations in which non-Europeans resembled animals and the mythical beings of medieval folklore other than humans. Even though indigenous American peoples would soon be determined to be human, the vestiges of earlier attempts to represent them as another species of animal altogether would remain in Western visual culture, eventually resurfacing in the nineteenth-century imagery that likened blacks and the Irish, for example, to primates.

The political and economic pressures that propelled European colonialism and American expansionism also called for more arguments that would sustain the notion that people in fact were not all the same. By the early nineteenth century, the meaning of race had changed as scientists turned to zoology as a defining paradigm and began to rely on the concept of biological type. From this came the notion that the human species was actually divisible into a number of subspecies that had developed into distinct groups. Some theorists explained those distinctions as the result of geographic dispersal, while others saw them as the product of miscegenation. Still others adhered to the notion of polygenesis, which stipulated that each race was a distinct species. The latter school of thought became widely accepted in the United States in the decade before the Civil War.

Shortly thereafter, Charles Darwin's theories of evolution were added to the cauldron of pseudoscientific theories about human diversity, and they were construed to serve racist ends. The races were placed on a scale of evolutionary development that ranked whites at the top, blacks and Australian aboriginals at the bottom, and Asians, Arabs, and Amerindians in between. According to this interpretation, Caucasians had evolved more than other races. The allegedly less-developed races needed to be disciplined by the more developed ones in order to survive and be useful, and the most "primitive" groups would die out as a result of natural selection. Those whose job it was to capture the vanishing strains of humanity were racing, in theory, against the clock. The belief system that mapped the historical evolution of the human species onto a static topography of phrenological types, known as Social Darwinism, also equated racial superiority with technological accomplishment. This logic, however, generated a self-fulfilling prophecy, since controlling the nonwhite population's access to technology could be legitimized by using body type to determine intellectual or technological ability.[15]

Throughout the second half of the nineteenth century, proponents of the new social sciences of anthropology and sociology undertook the task of organizing a vast encyclopedia of humanity. The diversity of visual characteristics of human beings could be used as evidence of the reality of racial differentiation. Photography, with its apparent objectivity, seemed to be the perfect means of documenting the purportedly objective reality of the existence of distinct human types. Scientists, photographers, and the viewers of the photographs operated

15. Michael Adas, *Machines and the Measure of Men: Science, Technology, and Ideologies of Western Dominance* (Ithaca: Cornell University Press, 1989).

in a world in which phrenology and physiognomy were considered legitimate, and those disciplines demanded that material evidence could be extracted from the human body to explain invisible traits and human potential.

Scientific racism relied on linking physical traits with invisible group characteristics and remained a widely accepted view until the mid-twentieth century, when its use by the Nazis compelled the international scientific community to formally repudiate it. There were significant prior attempts to contest it, but the empirical evidence of its devastating effects in Europe sealed its demise and catalyzed subsequent political moves by European and American governments to undo legalized systems of racial domination. This epistemological shift did not take place by fiat nor did it lead to the negation of race as an operative category; instead race generates a sphere of public contestation, a terrain in which defensive management strategies are organized for and against every theory of what the term means. Visual culture, and photographic imagery in particular, is the key locus for the articulation of these battles.

The historical legacy of nineteenth-century ideas about race lives on in common language: we still speak of race as synonymous with differences based on pigmentation or human typologies, even though there is no scientific basis to support such usages. In the present there are still many efforts to resurrect this myth through supposed new evidence in social science and genetics. Digital-media artists entertain their audiences with spectacular displays of racial alteration and recombination. The speed of this technological operation reinforces the notion of race as pure visual phenomenon located on the surface of the human body, and appears to dislocate this epidermal logic from its origins in social relations of power. *Only Skin Deep* on the other hand, posits race as a historically rooted myth through which we read physical appearance, a conceptual crutch that we use to organize humanity into culturally meaningful groupings. By referring to race as a myth, however, I do not mean to suggest that the concept does not have ramifications in the real world. On the contrary, racialization of human beings, though not grounded in science, is a historical process with real effects, what leading racial theorist Howard Winant calls a social fact.

Winant notes that because race is now widely understood as socially constructed, many conservatives argue that it is an illusion and therefore without valence.[16] He argues forcefully for the need to challenge "the widely reported death of the category of race."[17] Indeed, it has become commonplace in the so-called postidentity era to suggest that any mention of race necessarily entraps one in an antiquated

16. Howard Winant, "The Theoretical Status of the Concept of Race," in *Theories of Race and Racism*, ed. Lee Back and John Solomos (London: Routledge, 2002), p. 181. In this volume, pp. 51–61.
17. Ibid., p. 182.

logic. The position that race is meaningless because it is illusory over-looks the fact that imaginary constructs can and do wield political and cultural power. As Winant writes, "the salience of a social construct can develop over half a millennium of diffusion… as a fundamental principle of social organization and identity formation."[18] Winant also warns against assuming that race and racial identity have always meant the same thing to everyone. That view does not account for their mutability, which is to say how ideas about race change, how group affinities shift, how roles are performed, and so on. He defines race as a concept that is adapted by its users; at the same time, because it is rooted in a logic that emerges from binary relationships of domination, its meaning is constrained by poles of difference.[19]

Framing whiteness

It is fairly clear that race as a measurement of inferiority could be deployed to legitimize colonization and slavery, and to defend segregation, xenophobia, and imperialist adventurism. Sociologist Michael Banton notes that theories of white superiority were most prevalent between 1890 and 1920, a period when European colonialism was at its zenith;[20] Jim Crow reigned in the American South, the U.S. government's genocidal campaign against Native Americans had been completed, and the Spanish-American War brought Cuba, Puerto Rico, and the Philippines under U.S. control. What is less obvious is how whiteness makes itself visible photographically, even when racial difference is

18. Ibid., p. 185.
19. Marable, "Problematics of Ethnic Studies," p. 10.
20. Michael Banton, Racial Theories (Cambridge: Cambridge University Press, 1987) p. 76.

Don Normark, *Lladro Madrid, home from WWII*, from the "Chavez Ravine, 1949" series, 1949/1997. Gelatin silver print, 14 3/8 x 11 in. (36.5 x 27.9 cm). International Center of Photography, purchased by the ICP Acquisitions Committee, 2003.
Jack Iwata, *Queen of Manzanar*, ca. 1943. Gelatin silver print, 9 1/2 x 7 3/4 in. (24.1 x 19.7 cm). Japanese American National Museum, Los Angeles, gift of Jack and Peggy Iwata.

clearly delineated and legally enforced, as it was during that period. Many historical exhibitions have limited the issue of whiteness in photography to images of white ethnics—Irish, Italian, and Eastern European immigrants who emigrated to the United States in the late nineteenth and early twentieth century, and who underwent a process of Americanization that broadened the category of whiteness beyond its original Anglo-Saxon Protestant base. However, in his book *White*, British cultural theorist Richard Dyer explains that the centrality of whiteness in Western visual culture depends on Christian ideas about incarnation and embodiment, specifically the notion that white people are *more than* bodies.[21]

21. Richard Dyer, *White* (London: Routledge, 1997), chap. 2, pp. 1–41. See also in this volume, pp. 301–311.

John Baldessari, *California Map Project*, 1969. Type R prints and typewritten sheet mounted on board; eleven prints, each 8 x 10 in. (20.3 x 25.4 cm); text 8 1/2 x 11 in. (21.6 x 27.9 cm). Private collection.

Whereas systems of racial classification from the eighteenth century onward reduced people of color to the corporeal, whiteness was understood as a spirit that manifests itself in a dynamic relation to the physical world. Whiteness, then, does not need to be made visible to be present in an image; it can be expressed as the spirit of enterprise, as the power to organize the material world, and as an expansive relation to the environment. We might consider some of the photographs in the exhibition that mythologize the construction of the transcontinental railroad and the opening of the Panama Canal in relation to these concepts of whiteness. Michael Heizer's earthwork *Double Negative* and its aestheticized "opening" of southwestern lands as heroic gesture, and John Baldessari's *California Map Project* could also be reconsidered in light of Dyer's formulations. Similarly, Richard Misrach's photographs of the U.S. Navy bombing exercises in the Nevada Desert—territory considered sacred by the Northern Paiute—provides a chilling coda to the triumphal version of the history of American expansionism.

Dyer underscores the centrality of images of the conquest of the West and of the metaphor of borders to the formation of white American identity. Postcards such as William S. Prettyman's *The Race* (1907) helped to draw whites to areas being opened for settlement. The image shows scores of white men on horseback dashing across a field in Oklahoma, presumably carrying the markers they would use to stake out their own plot of land. Eugene Omar Goldbeck's 1926 panoramic view of a row of armed U.S. Immigration officers at the Texas–Mexico border merges notions of white authority with the right to territorial control of the United States. Don Bartletti's photo of the 1991 "Light Up The Border" campaign in Southern California with its motto "Control Immigration or Lose America," an expression of white backlash against the perceived threat of illegal immigration, shows how the expansive urge to take over land is now recast as a frantic plea to hold onto it.

Dyer also points out how crucial cowboys were to the construction of white masculinity. It bears emphasizing here that the dominant cultural representation of cowboys as white men supported by Indian scouts—the stuff of Hollywood Westerns—obscures the historical evidence of the widespread existence of black, Native American, and Mexican cowboys, and the Mexican origins of cowboy culture. Richard Prince's postmodern reframing of the cowboy icon in his "Marlboro Man" series leaves this aspect of history untouched. On the other hand, Isaac Julien's video *The Long Road to Mazatlan* underscores the intercultural dimensions of what is often conceived of as a quintessentially American cultural identity. Nonetheless, because whiteness is

distinguishable from embodiment, it is a somewhat mercurial category. Whiteness often requires otherness to become visible. In other words, white people look whiter when there are nonwhite people around them. Whiteness can also be articulated as the capacity to masquerade as a racial other without actually being one. Whiteness emerges most clearly when it can mold others into imitations of itself.

By the early twentieth century, it had become more expedient and socially productive for official propaganda to stress the legitimacy of reasoned rule, and to present white Americanness as a civilizing force. The notion of whiteness as an implicit normative code of appearance pervades the before-and-after photographs of black and Native American children "saved" by assimilationist boarding schools education. Photographs taken during the Puerto Rican Reconstruction campaign illustrated the view that the "backward" Puerto Rican peasantry lived in overcrowded, unsanitary conditions that could be remedied by proper instruction in modern American ways, including methods of personal hygiene that would enable them to work as servants in the United States. These performances of civilized, industrious, and patriotic behavior would become the basis for many contemporary artists' ironic commentaries on the psychosocial dynamics of inclusion. Tseng Kwong Chi's well known self-portraits in a Mao suit posing with American icons that range from the Twin Towers to Mickey Mouse, and Pedro Meyer's image of a man clinging to the face of the Statue of Liberty are but two of many examples of the playful and at times sardonic repositioning of national icons characteristic of a great deal of photography about cultural identity from the 1980s and 1990s.

Threats to national security have frequently led to the resurrection of racial profiling techniques. After the bombing of Pearl Harbor in 1941, *Life* magazine published "How to Tell Japs from the Chinese"

Eugene Omar Goldbeck, *Immigration Border Patrol, Laredo, Texas, February 1926, M. M. Hanson, Inspector in Charge*, 1926.
Gelatin silver print, 9 3/4 x 40 3/8 in. (24.7 x 102.5 cm). Harry Ransom Humanities Research Center, The University of Texas at Austin.

with a comparative phrenological study to instruct the general public in how to distinguish the new enemy from other Asians. Although that particular magazine spread makes the Japanese man in it look deviant, the photographs of Japanese internees taken for the U.S. government make them look quite docile, industrious, and unencumbered by their detention—indeed, internment camp life was made to seem like a cross between a technical school and a military academy. During the 1950s and early 1960s, when the moral authority of the United States was impugned by the circulation of images of the segregated South and of white supremacist brutality, the United States retaliated in international magazines such as *Life en Español*, with displays of "exceptional" black talent from politicians and athletes to artists and musicians. Lee Friedlander's photographs of that period of jazz luminaries were published in *Art in America*. More recently, "new and improved" biometric imaging technologies that digitally recognize racial "types" are touted as a necessary means of protection from terrorism. At the same time, government-funded publicity campaigns featuring Muslims who enjoy freedom and prosperity in the United States circulate at home and abroad.

During the period when dominant political forces endorsed racial hierarchies by means of photographic illustration of "objective" principles, and a burgeoning entertainment industry capitalized on the spectacle of racial difference as a panorama of archetypal polarities and human oddities, antiracist efforts, quite logically, sought to visualize the immorality of racism with documentary "evidence" of its deleterious effects. Most of what is identified by American audiences in the post-Civil Rights era as "photography about race" is more precisely defined as documentary photography about racism. Scores of socially engaged documentarians throughout the twentieth century have

Don Bartletti, *Border Opinions, San Ysidro, California. Protestors gather within sight of the US/Mexico border to demonstrate their opinions about immigration*, 1991. Digital chromogenic print, 16 x 20 in. (40.6 x 50.8 cm). Courtesy of the artist and the *Los Angeles Times*.

produced a vast archive of photographs that link inequality with injustice, and that foreground the merits of the racially oppressed with images that elegize their dignity and will to resist in the face of adversity.

The finest examples of this counter-hegemonic humanism are distinguishable from what Allan Sekula describes as the liberal humanism of the Cold War period epitomized by the photographs chosen by Edward Steichen for *The Family of Man*. The works I am interested in suggest an antiuniversalist politics of race and foreground the impact of racism on the raced individual. The most visually striking images render race relations as a poetic drama about political idealism in the subaltern population. I am thinking here of the poignancy of Roy DeCarava's teenaged black girl in a party gown who stands alone in a garbage strewn lot looking at a billboard advertisement for a Chevrolet sedan; the quiet defiance of Horace Poolaw's relative as she stands before a sign in a field that says "Stop State Law"; and the remarkable intimacy of Don Normark's view of a Mexican-American migrant worker who, four years after World War II, still wears his soldier cap as he prepares his breakfast. In works such as these, the visual contrasts are not about ritualized role play—they detail how subaltern people negotiate their subjection, not just in public confrontations but also in orchestrated private moments.

Postmodern critique of documentary realism has focused on the fallacy of the logic that asserts that positive images can refute negative ones. The premise of the critique is that photographs are representations, not unmediated documents of preexisting realities, and therefore positive images are no truer than negative ones—no picture can "tell it like it is." While I do not dispute that assertion, I would suggest that it has at times led to the problematic assumption that documentary realism is inherently nonreflexive. This hypothesis does not give sufficient consideration to how the subjects of a photograph, not just its maker, may self-consciously construct the "real." This is not so much a matter of whether, in the early days of photography, nonwhite people reinvented themselves in commissioned studio portraits, just as whites did. I am more concerned here with pointing out that counterhegemonic humanism entailed a self-conscious politics of realism. In the early twentieth century, Leigh Raiford notes, the NAACP appropriated the postcards taken for whites of lynchings and used them in their antilynching campaigns. They also sponsored "Beautiful Baby" contests and commissioned portraits of the winners for black magazines. Gordon Parks's 1963 photograph of Malcolm X holding up a photograph of a murdered black man suggests an awareness of the power of a carefully chosen iconic image to shape a discourse on reality, rather than an unquestioning faith in photographic indexicality.

Racial politics and racial fantasies

In outlining some of the ways that photography has been used both to endorse and to denounce racism, I would not want to suggest that all racialized images can be understood as falling into this paradigm. The project of classifying humanity into a hierarchy was facilitated by the professionalization of the social sciences, which engendered a network for the production and circulation of knowledge about racial difference, and by the technological development of photography. But these material conditions, even when coupled with the demand for ideological justification of colonialism, enslavement, and segregation, are insufficient as explanations for why racial imagery was popular and desirable for the largely white public that has consumed it voraciously for more than a century. The attraction to racial fantasies should be distinguished from racism as a punitive politics of power, not because fantasy has nothing to do with reality but because it is not a mimetic reflection of it. Photography is a field where the psychic power of fantasy meets the power of the marketplace. The economic incentive to stimulate viewers who enjoyed visualization of racial difference has affected the ways that numerous photographers in America have represented all the peoples of this country, as well as their very choice to do so.

Not every photographer who produced racial imagery has done so exclusively—on the contrary, many well-known nineteenth and early-twentieth-century photographers did so only occasionally. Eadweard Muybridge's stereoscope photograph *Heathen Chinee*, for example, is the sole example of racial stereotyping in his work that I could find, and it is not clear that the title is his. Edward Steichen's photographs of Hawaiian hula dancer Tootsie Steer, taken on assignment for the Matson Cruise Line in 1941, are also quite different from the fashion photography for which he is known. Nonetheless, it appears that Steichen had a clear sense of how to stage his version of an untarnished "native," because Steer recalls that in addition to seeking out dramatic natural sites as backdrop, he instructed her to stop cutting her hair, to cut off her nails, and to stop using nail polish.[22] It seems safe to estimate that in these and many other cases, financial gain was a much stronger motive than fanatical Social Darwinism, or belief in the existence of the primitive. In the first decades of mass-marketed photography, consumers were largely European immigrants in urban areas who were learning to see themselves as white Americans and simultaneously to enjoy how technology brought the rest of the world into view. Photographing racial difference was a lucrative business, whether it involved ethnic types, frontier myths, or exotic paradises. The images blurred official "scientific" discourse with a parallel world

22. Jan C. Desmond, *Staging Tourism: Bodies on Display from Waikiki to Sea World* (Chicago: The University of Chicago Press, 1999), p. 192.

Jack Delano, *In the convict camp in Greene County, Georgia*, 1941. Gelatin silver print, 11 x 14 in. (27.9 x 35.5 cm). Library of Congress, Washington D.C.

of exaggerated artifice as a sales strategy.

Numerous scholars have pointed out how crucial the photograph was to the nineteenth-century concept of the European and American self. Those studies often focus on how photography transformed portraiture, a painting genre that had originally served to legitimate the bourgeois self, into a mass-cultural venture that enabled the more humble members of Western societies to participate in the performance of individuation. The Euro-American middle classes not only used pictures of themselves to explain who they were, but also to know who they were different from. Mass-produced images of ethnographic types circulated far beyond the domain of science. The world beyond their immediate surroundings was coming into view through the act of looking at representations that objectified and miniaturized their referents; personal collections of these images of racial others as types symbolically linked the acquisition of racial knowledge with the possession of other people as things. Photographs of racial others put white viewers at the center of that world regardless of whether they appeared in the pictures or not.

When I have asked scholars and curators in the course of my research on this project to explain the popularity of early racial imagery, particularly ethnographic photographs, they have often commented on how these images offer a vicarious experience of power. In other words, while some people might have been drawn westward by the prospect of picturesque natives or may have accepted the validity of U.S. military adventures in the Caribbean and the Pacific, it is also likely that more viewers were enjoying the "views" as a conduit for the fantasy of omnipotence. Psychoanalytic theory posits that the voyeur's fantasies of omnipotence arise from the anxiety about being overwhelmed in an encounter with difference, and racial differentiation functions as a master narrative for dramatizing the making of the American self. Malek Alloula, in his study of the artificial construction of the harem in French colonial postcards of Algeria, argues that the political act of colonization was transferred to the visual register and transfigured as an erotic unveiling of the female colonial subject.[23] A similar argument could be made about the plethora of images of awkwardly posed, bare-breasted Southwestern indigenous women and Hawaiian hula dancers taken by studio photographers in America at the turn of the twentieth century. These are usually classified as ethnography by fastidious archivists who are completely cognizant of the irony in the captions. Mass participation in the blatant fetishizing of the Polynesian native was institutionalized by the Kodak Hula Show, which has been providing tourists with dancers to photograph

23. Malek Alloula, *The Colonial Harem*, trans. Myrna Godzich and Wlad Godzich, introduction Barbara Harlow (Minneapolis: University of Minnesota Press, 1986).

since 1937. That today the "natives" are paid serves as evidence of the consent that is supposed to balance the power between tourists and the others.

The legal apparatus of American racism has been dismantled, but the photographic apparatus that produced race has not. In stating this I am not advocating the elimination of photography, but I do endorse its deconstruction, if for no other reason than that images are much too pervasive and powerful in American culture to be taken for granted, *especially* when they are pleasurable. That the management of racial representation is important to contemporary power structures is evident by how carefully the symphony of diversity is orchestrated. Global corporate advertising, regardless of what it is designed to sell, conveys the message that racial difference is attractive, comprehensible, and essentially nonantagonistic through endless displays of "rainbow coalitions" of happy workers, students, patients, athletes, and clients. Technological innovation is made to seem interchangeable with subaltern empowerment when photographs of Cesar Chavez and Gandhi appear in Apple's "Think Different" ad campaign, for example. In her analysis of Internet advertising, cultural theorist Lisa Nakamura notes that the spectacle of race acts as an antidote to the insecurities provoked by the real possibility of a technological world where differences break down. In this "globalizing Coca-Colonization of cyberspace," beautiful racialized others are used to sell a product by seducing viewers and simultaneously reminding them of who they are not.[24] Referring to a 1997 advertisement for MCI, she writes:

> The ad gestures toward a democracy founded upon
> disembodiment and uncontaminated by physical
> difference, but it must also show a dizzying parade
> of difference in order to make its point. Diversity is
> displayed as the sign of that which the product will
> eradicate. Its erasure and elision can only be understood in terms of its presence; like the word race on
> the chalkboard, it can only be crossed out if it is
> written or displayed. This ad writes race and poses it
> as both a beautiful spectacle and a vexing question.[25]

The visual landscape of today's mainstream media resembles a "multiplication table of living breathing faces," as Carl Sandburg referred to *The Family of Man* exhibition. Whereas that table evoked the idea that all the different peoples of the world were the members of the same kinds of families, the message these days is that all those different peoples serve the global economy. In his brilliant analysis of that exhibition, Allan Sekula explains how its "aestheticized job of

24. Lisa Nakamura, *Cybertypes: Race, Ethnicity and Identity on the Internet* (London: Routledge, 2002), p. 99.
25. Ibid., p. 22.

global accounting" was strategically designed to forge an ideological alignment between the United States and the third world at the height of the Cold War.[26] At present, the staggering economic polarization of the world population, the rising tide of xenophobia in wealthier nations, the emergence of ethnic fundamentalism in poor ones, and the pervasiveness of immigration and border "crises" suggest that the visual celebration of racial diversity just might be diverting our attention from other far less attractive racial scenes.

The question that still disrupts the photographic pleasure machine is: what does racial imagery, even when it is perceived as beautiful, communicate to us about the meaning of race in the present? If many visual tropes from earlier periods have retained their allure, is it because our society has not changed? Or is the recycling of racial paradigms a perverse form of nostalgia, the fixation of a few hardcore fetishists, something akin to fascist chic? Similar debates have taken place since the 1970s about sadomasochistic eroticism, or more precisely, about the relationship of staged scenarios of domination between partners to the actuality of sexual violence in real life. Most feminist arguments in favor of the idea that ritualized domination and submission are entirely distinct from real violence have been predicated on the informed consent of the participants and the fluidity of the roles. However, in her legendary essay "Fascinating Fascism," Susan Sontag argues for the need to scrutinize those rituals carefully when they adopt the trappings of a heinous political moment from the past. She exhorts those who defend the photographs and films that endorse fascist ideals on the basis of their "beauty," using the example of the rehabilitation in the 1970s of the work of Nazi filmmaker Leni Riefenstahl. Instead of neutralizing the politics of fascism by treating it as purely aesthetic, Sontag advocates that we should ponder the motives underlying the renewed attraction to it on the part of those who are too young to have experienced it firsthand during the 1930s and 1940s. At the same time she recognizes that separate from the ideology, many would find some fascist ideals generally acceptable.[27]

In an increasingly individualistic and hyperrational society where religion and politics no longer offer possibilities of enjoying emotional fusion with collectives, rituals of domination offer respite from numbness. For Sontag, certain forms of eroticized fascism are controlled expressions of longing for temporary dissolution of the self. Those forms of sexual theater, she explains, are different from the self-consciously ironic "playing with cultural horror" of certain artists. Sontag's arguments here are apropos not only because fascism was a horrific example of how state-sanctioned racism could lead to mass genocide but also because she offers a cogent example of how one might reflect on the

26. Sekula, "Traffic in Photographs," p. 20. In this volume, pp. 79–109.
27. Susan Sontag, "Fascinating Fascism" in *Under the Sign of Saturn* (New York: Farrar, Straus & Giroux, 1975).

delicate relationships of erotic drives, political violence, theatricalized domination, and beauty to arrive at informed consent. Understanding the representation of race in photography and our sublimated erotic attraction to its various manifestations entails this very same process. Analysis of racial rhetoric in visual culture then does not lead to the complete erasure of the generic distinctions between art and propaganda, between functionalism and beauty; but it does involve critical reflection about the implications of how those lines are drawn.

The postcolonial investigation of the photographic archive by many artists of color that began in the 1970s and then flourished in the 1980s and 1990s ushered in a watershed period for the development of that informed consent and for the changing of roles regarding

Larry McNeil, *The Raven Series*, 1999. Digital chromogenic prints. Courtesy of the artist.

"Americans show
greater differences
gesturally"

"Do crossed arms
mean that 'I am
frustrated?'"

"A hand to the
face may serve
as a barrier"

"Crossed legs point
to each other."

"Crossed arms do
the same thing"

"Crossing arms
defines posture"

"Does she try to
avert attention
avoiding your eyes?"

"Is she sitting
stiffly and not
relaxed?"

"Covering legs
reveals frigidity,
fear of sex."

ROBERTA'S BODY LANGUAGE CHART

(photographed during a psychiatric session)

January 24, 1978

the construction and reception of racial imagery. The artists not only underscored the relevance of historical records and of marginalized nonwhite photographers of earlier generations, but also placed a new emphasis on the ways that bodies had been racialized by photographic discourses; on how ethnic imagery had been classified within cultural institutions; on how cultural institutions and the media perpetuated fictions about ethnic identities; and on how audience desires had been defined in racial terms. The 1970s Chicano experimental collective ASCO, for example, created film stills for a cinema they never produced. Called "No-Movies," these images about the absence of a "real" Chicano cinema were a conceptual statement about two factors that made Chicano cinema impossible to realize: the artists' poverty, and the exclusionary practices of the mainstream media. In *Accused/Blowtorch/Padlock*, Pat Ward Williams's furiously scribbled questions around the edges of an enlarged magazine photo of a lynched black man literally

Lynn Hershman, *Roberta's Body Language Chart*, from the "Roberta Breitmore in Therapy Session" series, 1978. Eight gelatin silver prints with text, overall 60 x 40 in. (152.4 x 101.6 cm). Courtesy of Gallery Paule Anglim and Robert Koch Gallery, San Francisco.

thrust the ethical dilemma of witnessing and reviewing racial violence into the process of reception. Glenn Ligon's *Notes on the Margins of the Black Book* masterfully foregrounds of the question of consent. This compendium of comments of the models who posed for Robert Mapplethorpe's photographs, and of other viewers of those images is a multilayered act of reframing, not just of those portraits but also of the history of modernist photography's objectification of blackness. The conservative backlash against multiculturalism in the 1990s may have resulted in the tempering of more strident forms of questioning, but some resourceful artists have elaborated other less verbally driven means of addressing these issues. Daniel Martinez, for example, has turned his skin, neck, and tongue into unsettling sites of violent inscription that somaticize the social construct of race as an act of wounding. In *Self Portrait #4 (Second attempt to clone mental disorder or How one philosophizes with a hammer)*, he tilts his head toward the camera to draw attention to the stitched wound that runs across his forehead.

Extrapolating from the work of the Annales School historians who have tried to explain historical logic in terms of how material life was produced, sociologist Howard Winant suggests that we can understand Western time as a racial *longue durée*, "in which a slow inscription of phenotypical signification took place upon the human body, in and through conquest and enslavement, to be sure, but also as an enormous act of expression, of narration."[28] *Only Skin Deep* is about how photography acts as a site and agent for the enunciation of racial history. Race has a special relationship with photography, more than with other art forms. As the most pervasive technology of visualization, photography has served as the primary guarantor of race as a visual indicator of invisible differences. All forms of photography have been created and used to prove and disprove the validity of racial theories while shaping an image of the American nation and its citizenry. No one effort ever completely succeeds in fulfilling either task—instead, photography continuously repeats and reformulates this project. This is due in part to the fact that all the factors involved—America, its population, ideas about race and photography—have changed over the past one hundred and fifty years. But it is also indicative of how photography communicates the ambivalence of Americans toward race in its various formulations—our dependence on it as a frame of reference, our attraction to its logic, and our fears of its implications.

The notion that the current state of affairs signals a transcendence of valence of race becomes difficult to maintain if one takes the history of race relations into account. Where and when Americans have expected or wanted to see race, as well as where and when we don't want to see it, tells us a great deal about how we negotiate our

28. Winant, "Theoretical Status of the Concept of Race," pp. 187–88. In this volume, pp. 51–61.

ambivalent relation to the historical legacy of racialization. That ambivalence has informed the ways that photographs are classified and interpreted. That some photographs are identified as being about race within the larger field of photography—and those are usually limited to images of nonwhite people or demonstratively racist whites—does not simply enable racial imagery to become visible, but permits us to maintain the belief that other photographic images are not about race.

The perceived effect that race has on the status and coherence of America's image as a nation makes any discussion of race and representation appear politically charged, and this supposed threat has motivated most attempts to camouflage or otherwise suppress public analysis of racial discourse. Numerous social theorists have pointed out that since the middle of the twentieth century, American race relations have been the most influential factor in undermining national and international perceptions of America as a democracy, and thus have greatly affected our country's ability to exercise influence in the rest of the world. That American story is not unique; on the contrary, it is part of a global history.

The story of how the construction of race intersects with the emergence of nations is central to the history of the modern world, and has wide ranging implications for the interpretation of culture. Postcolonial theorists consistently argue that modernity, capitalism, and the very idea of Western society cannot be fully understood without taking slavery and colonization into account—race is a signifying system that emerges from that history. Since its inception America has been a territory inhabited by many peoples who saw themselves as different from each other in one way or another—the racialization of its populations is an integral component of the formation of the nation, and the evolution of power relations among those groups is a key element its development as a democracy.

Barbara Kruger, *Untitled* [Your Fictions Become History], 1983. Gelatin silver print, 76 1/4 x 39 1/2 in. (193.7 x 100.3 cm).
Milwaukee Art Museum, gift of Contemporary Art Society.

Howard Winant

Race used to be a relatively intelligible concept; only recently, we have seriously challenged its theoretical coherence. Today there are deep questions about what we actually mean by the term. But before (roughly) World War II, before the rise of Nazisim, before the end of the great European empires, and particularly before the decolonization of Africa, before the urbanization of the U.S. black population and the rise of the modern civil rights movement, race was still largely seen in Europe and North America (and elsewhere as well) as an essence, a natural phenomenon, whose meaning was fixed, as constant as a southern star.

THE THEORETICAL STATUS
OF THE CONCEPT OF RACE

In the earlier years of this century, only a handful of pioneers, people like W. E. B. DuBois and Franz Boas, conceived of race in a more social and historical way. Other doubters included avant-garde racial theorists emerging from the intellectual ferment of the Harlem Renaissance; black nationalists and pan-Africanists who sought to apply the rhetoric of national self-determination expressed at Versailles to the mother continent, and who returned from the battlefields of France to the wave of antiblack race riots that swept the United States in 1919; a few Marxists (whose perspectives had their own limitations); and to some extent the Chicago school of sociology led by Robert Ezra Park. But even these intellectuals and activists made incomplete breaks with essentialist notions of race, whether biologistic or otherwise deterministic.

That was then; this is now. Today the theory of race has been utterly transformed. The socially constructed status of the concept of race, which I have labeled the *racial formation* process, is widely recognized,[1] so much so that it is now often *conservatives* who argue that race is an illusion. The main task facing racial theory today, in fact, is no longer to critique the seemingly "natural" or "common-sense" concept of race—although that effort has not by any means been entirely completed. Rather, the central task is to focus attention on the *continuing significance and changing meaning of race*. It is to argue against the recent discovery of the illusory nature of race; against the supposed contemporary transcendence of race; against the widely reported death of the concept of race; and against the replacement of the category of race by other, supposedly more objective, categories like ethnicity, nationality, or class. All these initiatives are mistaken at best, and intellectually dishonest at worst.

In order to substantiate these assertions, we must first ask, what is race? Is it merely an illusion? An ideological construct utilized to manipulate, divide, and deceive? This position has been taken by many theorists, and activists as well, including many who have heroically served the cause of racial and social justice in the United States.

1. Michael Omi and Howard Winant, *Racial Formation in the United States: From the 1960s to the 1980s* (New York: Routledge, 1986).

Or is race something real, material, objective? This view too has its adherents, including both racial reactionaries and racial radicals.

In my view both of these approaches miss the boat. The concept of race is not an ideological construct, nor does it reflect an objective condition. Here I first reflect critically on these two opposed viewpoints on the contemporary theory of race. Then I offer an alternative perspective based on the approach of racial formation.

Race as an ideological construct

The assertion that race is an ideological construct—understood in the sense of a "false consciousness" that explains other "material" relationships in distorted fashion—seems highly problematic. This is the position taken by the prominent historian Barbara Fields in a well-known article, "Slavery, Race and Ideology in the United States of America." Although Fields inveighs against various uses of the race concept, she directs her critical barbs most forcefully against historians who "invoke race as a historical explanation."[2]

According to Fields, the concept of race arose to meet an ideological need: its original effectiveness lay in its ability to reconcile freedom and slavery. The idea of race provided "the means of explaining slavery to people whose terrain was a republic founded on radical doctrines of liberty and natural rights." But, Fields says, to argue that race—once framed as a category in thought, an ideological explanation for certain distinct types of social inequality—"takes on a life of its own" in social relationship is to transform (or "reify") an illusion into a reality. Such a position could be sustained "only if *race* is defined as innate and natural prejudice of color:"

2. Barbara Jeanne Fields, "Slavery, Race and Ideology in the United States of America," *New Left Review*, no. 181 (May/June 1990): 101.

Edie Winograde, *Indians on Horseback*, from "The Legend of the Rawhide" series, 1999/2003. Chromogenic print, 8 x 10 in. (20.3 x 25.4 cm). Courtesy of the artist.

*Since race is not genetically programmed, racial preju-
dice cannot be genetically programmed either, but must
arise historically.... The preferred solution is to suppose
that, having arisen historically, race then ceases to be a
historical phenomenon and becomes instead an external
motor of history; according to the fatuous but widely
repeated formula, it "takes on a life of its own." In other
words, once historically acquired, race becomes heredi-
tary. The shopworn metaphor thus offers camouflage for
a latter-day version of Lamarckism.*[3]

Thus, race is either an illusion that does ideological work or an
objective biological fact. Since it is certainly not the latter, it must be
the former. No intermediate possibility—consider, for example, the
Durkheimian notion of a "social fact"—is considered.

Some of this account—for example, the extended discussion of
the origins of North American race thinking—can be accepted without
major objection.[4] Furthermore, Fields effectively demonstrates the
absurdity of many commonly held ideas about race. But her position
is so extreme that at best it can only account for the *origins* of race
thinking, and then only in one social context. To examine how race
thinking evolved from these origins, how it responded to changing
sociocultural differences, is ruled out. Why and how did race thinking
survive after emancipation? Fields cannot answer, because the very
perpetuation of the concept of race is ruled out by her theoretical

3. Ibid., pp. 101, 114.
4. Minor objections would have to do with
Fields's functionalist view of ideology,
and her claim that race concept only
"came into existence" when it was
needed by whites in North American
colonies beginning in the late seventeenth century. The concept of race, of
course, has a longer history than that.

Max Becher and Andrea Robbins, *German Indians: Campfire*, 1996. Chromogenic print, 20 x 24 in. (50.8 x 60.9 cm). Courtesy of
Sonnabend Gallery, New York.

approach. As a relatively orthodox Marxist, Fields could argue that changing "material conditions" continued to give rise to changes in racial "ideology," except that even the limited autonomy this would attach to the concept of race would exceed her standards. Race cannot take on a life of its own; it is pure ideology, an illusion.

Fields simply skips from emancipation to the present, where she disparages opponents of "racism" for unwittingly perpetuating an illusory concept of race. In denunciatory terms, Fields concludes by arguing for abolition of the concept:

> Nothing handed down from the past could keep race alive if we did not constantly reinvent and reritualize it to fit our own terrain. If race lives on today, it can do so only because we continue to create and recreate it in our social life, continue to verify it, and thus continue to need a social vocabulary that will allow us to make sense, not of what our ancestors did then, but of what we choose to do now.[5]

Fields is unclear about how "we" should jettison the ideological construct of race, and one can well understand why. By her own logic, racial ideologies cannot be abolished by acts of will. One can only marvel at the ease with which she distinguishes the bad old slavery days of the past from the present, when "we" anachronistically cling, as if for no reason, to the illusion that race retains any meaning. We foolishly throw up our hands and acquiesce in race thinking, rather than … doing what? Denying the racially demarcated divisions in society? Training ourselves to be "color blind?"[6]

I venture to say that only a historian (however eminent) could have written such an article. Why? Because at the least a sociologist would know W. I. Thomas's famous dictum that if people "define situations as real, they are real in their own consequences."[7] Nor is Fields alone in claiming that racial ideology persists because people insist on thinking racially. Her position is espoused by many, on both the left and the right of racial debates.[8]

In any case, the view that race is a kind of false consciousness is held not only by intellectuals, based on both well-intentioned and ulterior motivations; it also has a commonsense character. One hears in casual discussion, for example, or in introductory social science classes, variations on the following statement: "I don't care if a person is black, white, or purple, I treat them exactly the same; a person's just a person to me.…" Furthermore, some of the integrationist aspirations of racial minority movements, especially civil rights movement, invoke this sort of idea. Consider the famous line from the "I Have a Dream" speech, the line that made Shelby Steele's career: "that someday my

5. Fields, "Slavery, Race and Ideology," p. 118.
6. Fields's admirer David Roediger also criticizes her on this point: "At times she nicely balances the ideological creation of racial attitudes with their manifest and ongoing important and their (albeit ideological) *reality*.… But elsewhere, race disappears into the 'reality' of class." David R. Roediger, *The Wages of Whiteness: Race and the Making of the American Working Class* (New York: Verso, 1991), pp. 7–8.
7. W. I. Thomas and Dorothy Swaine Thomas, *The Child in America* (New York: Knopf, 1928), p. 572.
8. Another important thinker who has at least flirted with the idea of race as illusion is Kwame Anthony Appiah. See Kwame Anthony Appiah, "The Uncompleted Argument: DuBois and the Illusion of Race," in *"Race," Writing, and Difference*, ed. Henry Louis Gates (Chicago: University of Chicago Press, 1986).

four little children will be judged, not by the color of their skin, but by the content of their character."

The core criticisms of this "race as ideology" approach are two: First, it fails to recognize the salience a social construct can develop over a half a millennium or more of diffusion, or should I say enforcement, as a fundamental principle of social organization and identity formation. The longevity of the race concept and the enormous number of effects race thinking (and race acting) has produced a guarantee that race will remain a feature of social reality across the globe, and *a fortiori*, in the United States, despite its lack of intrinsic or scientific merit (in the biological sense). Second, and related, this approach fails to recognize that at the level of experience, of everyday life, race is a relatively impermeable part of our identities. U.S. society is so thoroughly racialized that to be without racial identity is to be in danger of having no identity. To be raceless is akin to being genderless. Indeed, when one cannot identify another's race, a microsociological crisis of interpretation results, something perhaps best interpreted in ethnomethodological or Goffmanian terms. To complain about such a situation may be understandable, but it does not advance understanding.

Race as an objective condition

On the other side of the coin, it is clearly problematic to assign objectivity to the race concept. Such theoretical practice puts us in quite heterogeneous, and sometimes unsavory company. Of course, the biologistic racial theories of the past do this: here I am thinking of such precursors of fascism as Gabineau and Chamberlain,[9] of the eugenicists such as Lothrop Stoddard and Madison Grant, of the "founding fathers" of scientific racism such as Agassiz, Broca, Terman, and Yerkes.[10] Indeed, an extensive legacy of this sort of thinking extends right up to the present. Stephen Jay Gould[11] makes devastating critiques of such views.

But much liberal and even radical social science, though firmly committed to a social as opposed to a biological interpretation of race, nevertheless also slips into a kind of objectivism about racial identity and racial meaning. This is true because race is afforded an easy and unproblematic coherence all too frequently. Thus, to select only prominent examples, Daniel Moynihan, William Julius Wilson, Milton Gordon, and many other mainstream thinkers theorize race in terms that downplay its flexibility and historically contingent character. Even these major thinkers, whose explicit rejection of biological forms of racial theory would be unquestioned, fall prey to a kind of creeping objectivism of race. For in their analyses a modal explanatory approach emerges as follows: sociopolitical circumstances change over historical

9. George Mosse, *Toward the Final Solution: A History of European Racism* (New York: Howard Fertig, 1978).
10. Daniel J. Kevles, *In the Name of Eugenics: Genetics and the Uses of Human Heredity* (New York; Knopf, 1985); and Allan Chase, *Legacy of Malthus: The Social Costs of the New Scientific Racism* (New York: Knopf, 1977).
11. Stephen Jay Gould, *The Mismeasure of Man* (New York: Norton, 1981).

time, racially defined groups adapt or fail to adapt to these changes, achieving mobility or remaining mired in poverty, and so on. In this logic there is no reconceptualization of group identities, or the constantly shifting parameters through which race is thought about, group interests are assigned, statuses are ascribed, agency is attained, and roles are performed.

Contemporary racial theory, then, is often "objectivistic" about its fundamental category. Although abstractly acknowledged to be a sociohistorical construct, race in *practice* is often treated as an object fact: one simply *is* one's race; in the contemporary United States, if we discard euphemisms, we have five color-based racial categories: black, white, brown, yellow, and red.

This is problematic, indeed ridiculous, in numerous ways. Nobody really belongs in these boxes; they are patently absurd reductions of human variation. But even accepting the nebulous "rules" of racial classification—"hypodescent," [12] and so forth—many people do not fit anywhere: into what categories should we place Turks, for example? People of mixed race? South Asians? Objectivist treatments, lacking a critique of the *constructed* character of racial meanings, also clash with experimental dimensions of the issue. If one does not "act" black, or white, or whatever, that is just deviance from the norm. There is in these approaches an insufficient appreciation of the *performative* aspect of race, as postmodernists might call it.[13]

To summarize the critique of this "race as objective condition" approach, then, it fails on three counts: First, it cannot grasp the processual and relational character of racial identity and racial meaning. Second, it denies the historicity and social comprehensiveness of the race concept. And third, it cannot account for the way actors, both individual and collective, have to manage incoherent and conflictual racial meanings and identities in everyday life. It has no concept, in short, of what Omi and I have labeled *racial formation*.

Toward a critical theory of the concept of race

The foregoing clearly sets forth the agenda that any adequate theorization of the race concept must fulfill. Such an approach must be theoretically constructed so as to steer between Scylla of "race as illusion" and the Charybdis of "racial objectivism." Such a critical theory can be consistently developed, I suggest, drawing upon the racial formation approach. Such a theoretical formulation, too, must be explicitly historicist: it must recognize the importance of historical context and contingency in the framing of racial categories and the social construction of racially defined experiences.

What would be the minimum conditions for the development of a

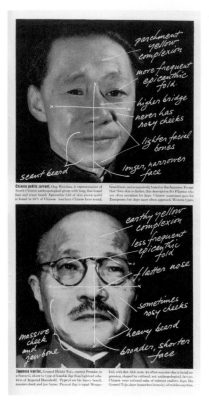

12. The concept is developed in Marvin Harris, *Patterns of Race in the Americas* (New York: Walker, 1964).
13. "The question of identification is never the affirmation of a pregiven identity, never a self-fulfilling prophecy—it is always the production of an image of identity and the transformation of the subject in assuming that image." Homi K. Bhabha, "Interrogating Identity; The Postcolonial Prerogative," in *Anatomy of Racism*, ed. David Theo Goldberg (Minneapolis: University of Minnesota Press, 1990). p. 188.

Life, *How to Tell Japs from the Chinese*, December 22, 1941. Magazine interior (detail). Private collection.

critical, processual theory of race? I suggest three conditions for such a theory:

> —*It must apply to contemporary political relationships.*
> —*It must apply in an increasingly global context.*
> —*It must apply across historical time.*

Let us address each of these points very briefly.

Contemporary political relationships

The meaning and salience of race is forever being reconstituted in the present. Today such new relationships emerge chiefly at the point where some *counterhegemonic* or *postcolonial* power is attained. At that point the meanings and the political articulations of race proliferate.

Examples include the appearance of competing racial *projects*, by which I mean efforts to institutionalize racial meanings and identities in particular social structures: notably those of individual, family, community, and state. As egalitarian movements contend with racial "backlash" over sustained periods of time, as binary logics of racial antagonism (white/black, *ladino*/*indio*, settler/native, etc.) become more complex and decentered, political deployment of the concept of face comes to signal qualitatively new types of political domination, as well as new types of opposition.

Consider the U.S. example. In terms of domination, it is now possible to perpetuate racial domination without making any explicit reference to race at all. Subtextual or "coded" racial signifiers, or the mere denial of the continuing significance of race, may suffice. Similarly, in terms of opposition, it is now possible to resist racial domination in entirely new ways, particularly by limiting the reach and penetration of the political system into everyday life, by generating new identities, new collectivities, new (imagined) communities that are relatively less permeable to the hegemonic system.[14] Much of the rationale for Islamic currents among blacks in the United States, for the upsurge in black anti-Semitism, and to some extent for the Afrocentric phenomenon, can be found here. Thus the old choices—integration versus separatism, assimilation versus nationalism—are no longer the only options.

In the "underdeveloped" world, proliferation of so-called postcolonial phenomena also have significant racial dimensions, as the entire Fanonian tradition (merely to select one important theoretical current) makes clear. Crucial debates have now been occurring for a decade or more on the question of postcolonial subjectivity and identity, the insufficiency of the simple dualism of "Europe and its others," the subversive and parodic dimensions of political culture at and beyond the edges of the old imperial boundaries, and so forth.[15]

14. The work of Paul Gilroy on the significance of black music in Afro-diasporic communities is particularly revealing on this point. Paul Gilroy, *"There Ain't No Black in the Union Jack": The Cultural Politics of Race and Nation* (Chicago: University of Chicago Press, 1991).

15. There is vast literature by now on these matters. The founding statement is undoubtedly Edward Said's *Orientalism* (New York: Pantheon, 1978); also useful is Homi K. Bhabha, "DissemiNation: Time, Narrative and the Margins of the Modern Nation," in *Nation and Narration*, ed. Bhabha (London: Routledge, 1990).

Patrick Nagatani and Andree Tracey, *Radioactive Reds*, 1986. Polacolor ER print, 24 x 20 in. (60.9 x 50.8 cm). Center for Creative Photography, University of Arizona, Tuscon.

The global context of race

The geography of race is becoming more complex. Once more easily seen in terms of imperial reach, in terms of colonization, conquest and migration, racial space is becoming *globalized* and thus accessible to a new kind of comparative analysis. This only becomes possible now, at a historical moment when the distinction "developed/underdeveloped" has been definitely overcome. Obviously, by this I do not mean that now there are no disparities between North and South, rich and poor. Rather, I mean that the movement of capital and labor has internalized all nations, all regions. Today we have reached the point where the empire strikes back,[16] as former (neo)colonial subjects, now redefined as "immigrants," challenge the majoritarian status of the formerly

16. I borrow this phrase not from George Lucas but from the book of that title by the Centre for Contemporary Cultural Studies. See *The Empire Strikes Back: Race and Racism in 70's Britain*, ed. Centre for Contemporary Cultural Studies, Birmingham (London: Hutchinson, 1982).

Tseng Kwong Chi, *Statue of Liberty, New York,* from the expeditional series "East Meets West," 1979. Gelatin silver print, 36 x 36 in. (91.4 cm x 91.4 cm). Estate of Tseng Kwong Chi/Muna Tseng Dance Projects, Inc.

17. David Lopez and Yen Espiritu define panethnicity as "development of bridging organizations and solidarities among subgroups of ethnic collectivities that are often seen as homogeneous by outsiders." Such a development, they claim, is a crucial feature of ethnic change—"supplanting both assimilation and ethnic particularism as the direction of change for racial/ethnic minorities." While panethnic formation is facilitated by an ensemble of cultural factors (e.g., common language and religion) and structural factors (e.g., class, generation, and geographical concentration), Lopez and Espiritu conclude that a specific concept of race is fundamental to the construction of panethnicity. David Lopez and Yen Espiritu, "Panethnicity in the United States: A Theoretical Framework," *Ethnic and Racial Studies*, no. 13 (1990): 198.

18. Similar points are made in V. Y. Mudimbe, *The Invention of Africa: Gnosis, Philosophy, and The Order of Knowledge* (Bloomington: Indiana University Press, 1988); Paul Rabinow, "Representations are Social Facts: Modernity and Post-Modernity in Anthropology," in *Writing Culture: The Poetics and Politics of Ethnography*, ed. James Clifford and George E. Marcus (Berkeley: University of California Press, 1986); and Sandra Harding, *The Science Question in Feminism* (Ithaca, N.Y.: Cornell University Press, 1987).

metropolitan group (the whites, the Europeans, the "Americans," or "French," etc.). Meanwhile, phenomena such as the rise of "diasporic" models of blackness, the creation of "panethnic"[17] communities of Latinos and Asians (in such countries as the United Kingdom and the United States), and the breakdown of borders in both Europe and North America all seem to be internationalizing and racializing previously national polities, cultures, and identities. To take just one example, popular culture now internationalizes racial awareness almost instantaneously, as reggae, rap, samba, and various African pop styles leap from continent to continent.

Because of these transformations, a global comparison of hegemonic social/political orders based on race becomes possible. I think that in a highly specified form—that is, not as mere reactions or simple negations of "Western" cultural/theoretical dominance—such notions as diasporic consciousness or racially informed standpoint epistemologies deserve more serious attention as efforts to express the contemporary globalization of racial space.[18] Furthermore, to understand such phenomena as the construction of new racial identities or in terms of the panethnicity dynamic is to recognize that the territorial reach of racial hegemony is now global.

The dissolution of the transparent racial identity of the formerly dominant group, that is to say, the advancing racialization of whites in Europe and the United States, must also be recognized as proceeding from the increasingly globalized dimensions of race. As previous assumptions erode, white identity loses its transparency, the easy elision with "racelessness" that accompanies racial domination. "Whiteness" becomes a matter of anxiety and concern.

The emergence of racial time

Some final notes are in order to respect to the question of the epochal nature of racial time. Classical social theory has an Enlightenment-based view of time, a perspective that understood the emergence of modernity in terms of the rise of capitalism and the bourgeoisie. This view was by no means limited to Marxism. Weberian disenchantment and the rise of the Durkheimian division of labor also partake of this temporal substrate. Only rarely does the racial dimension of historical temporality appear in this body of thought, as, for example, in Marx's excoriation of the brutalities of "primitive accumulation":

> *The discovery of gold and silver in America, the extirpa-*
> *tion, enslavement, and entombment in mines of the*
> *aboriginal population, the beginning of the conquest*
> *and looting of the East Indies, the turning of Africa into*
> *a warren for the commercial hunting of black skins,*
> *signalized the rosy dawn of the era of capitalist produc-*
> *tion. These idyllic proceedings are the chief momenta*
> *of primitive accumulation. On their heels treads the*
> *commercial war of the European nations with the globe*
> *for a theater. It begins with the revolt of the Netherlands*
> *from Spain, assumes giant dimensions in England's*
> *Anti-Jacobin War, and is still going on in the opium wars*
> *with China, etc.*[19]

Yet even Marx frequently legitimated such processes as the inevitable and ultimately beneficial birth pangs of classlessness—by the way of the ceaselessly revolutionary bourgeoisie.

Today such teleological accounts seem hopelessly outmoded. Historical time could well be interpreted in terms of something like a racial *longue durée*: for has there not been an immense historical rupture represented by the rise of Europe, the onset of African enslavement, the *conquista*, and the subjugation of much of Asia? I take the point of much poststructural scholarship on these matters to be quite precisely an effort to explain "Western" or colonial time as a huge project demarcating human "difference," or more globally as Todorov, say, would argue, of framing partial collective identities in terms of externalized "others."[20] Just as, for example, the writers of the *Annales* school sought to locate the deep logic of historical time in the means by which material life was produced—diet, shoes, and so on[21]—so we might usefully think of a racial *longue durée* in which the inscription of phenotypical signification took place upon the human body, in and through conquest and enslavement, to be sure, but also as an enormous act of expression, of narration.

19. Karl Marx, *Capital*, vol. 1 (New York: International Publishers, 1967), p. 751.
20. Tsvetan Todorov, *The Conquest of America: The Question of the Other*, trans. Richard Howard (New York: Harper & Row, 1985).
21. For example, the magisterial work of Fernand Braudel, *The Structures of Everyday life: The Limits of the Possible*, vol. 1 of Braudel, *Civilization and Capitalism, 15th–18th Century*, trans. Sian Reynolds (New York: Harper & Row, 1981).

In short, just as the noise of the big bang still resonates through the universe, so the overdetermined construction of the world "civilization" as a product of the rise of Europe and the subjugation of the rest of us still defines the race concept. Such speculative notes, of course, can be no more than provocations. Nor can I conclude this effort to reframe the agenda of racial theory with a neat summation. There was a long period—centuries—in which race was seen as a natural condition, an essence. This was succeeded although not entirely superseded by a shorter but potent way of thinking about race as subordinate to supposedly more concrete, "material" relationships; during that period, down to now, race was understood as an illusion, an excrescence. Perhaps now we are approaching the end of that racial epoch, too.

To our dismay, we may have to give up our familiar ways of thinking about race once more. If so, there also may be some occasion for delight. For it may be possible to glimpse yet another view of race, in which the concept operates neither as a signifier of comprehensive identity nor of fundamental difference, both of which are patently absurd, but rather as a marker of the infinity of variations we humans hold as a common heritage and hope for the future.

Romare Bearden, *Untitled*, 1964. Gelatin silver print photomontage, 35 x 48 in. (88.9 x 121.9 cm). Private collection.

I.
LOOKING UP/
LOOKING DOWN

James W. Queen, *The Darkey's Vanity*, ca. 1860. Hand-tinted albumen print stereograph (one side shown), 3 ¹/₂ x 7 in. (8.9 x 17.8 cm). Wm. B. Becker Collection/American Museum of Photography.

Vanessa Beecroft, *VB39, US Navy SEALS, Museum of Contemporary Art, San Diego*, 1999. Digital chromogenic print, one of three panels, overall 96 x 120 in. (230 x 288 cm). Private collection. Courtesy of Deitch Projects, New York.

Miguel Calderon, *Evolucion del Hombre (Evolution of Man)*, 1995. Chromogenic prints, overall 36 $^{1}/_{2}$ x 151 in. (92.7 x 383.5 cm).
Private collection. Courtesy of Andrea Rosen Gallery, New York.

Will Connell, Film still from *Roman Scandals*, 1933. Gelatin silver print, 14 x 11 in. (35.5 x 27.9 cm). UCR/California Museum of Photography, University of California, Riverside, Will Connell Collection.

F. Holland Day with **Clarence H. White**, *F. Holland Day with Model*, ca. 1897. Platinum print, 9 $\frac{1}{2}$ x 7 $\frac{3}{8}$ in. (24.2 x 18.8 cm).
Gilman Paper Company Collection, New York.

Hulleah Tsinhnahjinnie, *This is Not a Commercial, This is My Homeland*, 1998. Digital chromogenic print, 16 x 20 in. (40.6 x 50.8 cm). Courtesy of the artist.

John Vachon, *Billboard*, 1948. Modern print from original negative, 8 x 10 in. (20.3 x 25.4 cm). International Center of Photography, Museum purchase, 2003.

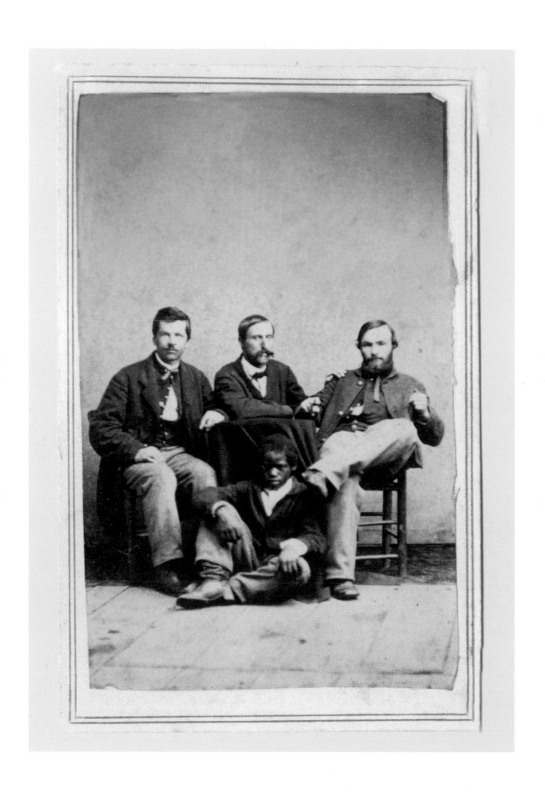

Unidentified photographer, *Civil War Soldiers with a "Contraband,"* ca. 1863. Carte-de-visite, 4 x 2 ¹/₂ in. (11.6 x 6.3 cm).
Wm. B. Becker Collection/American Museum of Photography.

Underwood & Underwood, *Border Guard inspecting suspicious Mexican*, ca. 1916. Gelatin silver print, 9 ³/₁₆ x 7 ¹/₈ in.
(23.3 x 18 cm). National Archives, Washington D.C.

Barbara Norfleet, *Private Home, New Providence Is., Lyford Cay Club*, 1982. Gelatin silver print, 11 x 14 ³/₈ in. (27.9 x 36.5 cm).
International Center of Photography, purchased by the ICP Acquisitions Committee, 2003

Ken Light, *Strip Search, Shakedown Room of Visiting Area*, from the "Texas Death Row" series, 1994. Gelatin silver print, 16 x 20 in. (40.6 x 50.8 cm). Courtesy of the artist.

An-My Lê, *Small Wars (Sniper I)*, 1999–2002. Gelatin silver print, 26 x 37 $^1/_2$ in. (66 x 95.2 cm). Courtesy of the artist.

Dinh Q. Lê, *Persistence of Memory #10*, 2000–01. Chromogenic print and linen tape, 45 x 63 in. (114.3 x 160 cm). Courtesy of P.P.O.W., New York.

Patty Chang, *Contortion*, 1999–2000. Digital chromogenic prints, 40 x 60 in. each (101.6 x 152.4 cm). Courtesy of Jack Tilton/ Anna Kustera Gallery, New York.

William Pope.L, *Susan Smith Goes to Haiti*, 2001. Digital chromogenic print, 67 $\frac{1}{2}$ x 37 in. (171.4 x 93.9 cm). Courtesy of The Project, New York.

I SELL THE SHADOW TO SUPPORT THE SUBSTANCE.

SOJOURNER TRUTH.

Allan Sekula

THE TRAFFIC IN PHOTOGRAPHS

Introduction: Between aestheticism and scientism

How can we work toward an active, critical understanding of the prevailing conventions of representation, particularly those surrounding photography?[1] The discourse that surrounds photography speaks paradoxically of discipline and freedom, of rigorous truths and unleashed pleasures. Here then, at least by virtue of a need to contain the tensions inherent in this paradox, is the site of a certain shell game, a certain dance, even a certain politics. In effect, we are invited to dance between photographic truths and photographic pleasures with very little awareness of the floorboards and muscles that make this seemingly effortless movement possible.

By discourse, then, I mean the forceful play of tacit beliefs and formal conventions that situates us, as social beings, in various responsive and responsible attitudes to the semiotic workings of photography. In itself constrained, determined by, and contributing to "larger" cultural, political, and economic forces, this discourse both legitimates and directs the multiple flows of the traffic in photographs. It quietly manages and constrains our abilities to produce and consume photographic imagery, while often encouraging, especially in its most publicized and glamorous contemporary variants, an apparently limitless semiotic freedom, a timeless dimension of aesthetic appreciation. Encoded in academic and "popular" texts, in books, newspapers, magazines, in institutional and commercial displays, in the design of photographic equipment, in schooling, in everyday social rituals, and—through the workings of these contexts—within photographs themselves, this discourse exerts a force that is simultaneously material and symbolic, inextricably linking language and power. Above all, in momentarily isolating this historically specific ideology and practice of representation, we shouldn't forget that it gives concrete form to—thus lending both truth and pleasure to—other discursively borne ideologies: of "the family," of "sexuality," of "consumption" and "production," of "government," of "technology," of "nature," of "communications," of "history," and so on. Herein lies a major aspect of the affiliation of photography with power. And as in all culture that grows from a system of oppressions, the discourses that carry the greater force in everyday life are those that emanate from power, that give voice to an institutional authority. For us, today, these affirmative and supervisory voices speak primarily for capital, and subordinately for the state. This essay is a practical search for internal inconsistencies, and thus for some of the weaknesses in this linkage of language and power.

Photography is haunted by two chattering ghosts: that of bourgeois science and that of bourgeois art. The first goes on about the truth of

1. An earlier, shorter version of this essay was published in the *Australian Photography Conference Papers,* Melbourne, 1980. I am grateful to the editors of *Working Papers on Photography,* Euan McGillvray and Matthew Nickson, for the opportunity to present the preliminary version there.

Unidentified photographer, *Sojourner Truth: I Sell the Shadow to Support the Substance,* 1864. Carte-de-visite, 4 x 2 ³/₈ in. (20.3 x 6 cm). International Center of Photography, Museum purchase, 2003.

appearances, about the world reduced to a positive ensemble of facts, to a constellation of knowable and possessable *objects*. The second specter has the historical mission of apologizing for and redeeming the atrocities committed by the subservient—and more than spectral—hand of science. This second specter offers us a reconstructed *subject* in the luminous person of the artist. Thus, from 1839 onward, affirmative commentaries on photography have engaged in a comic, shuffling dance between technological determinism and auteurism, between faith in the objective powers of the machine and a belief in the subjective, imaginative capabilities of the artist. In persistently arguing for the harmonious coexistence of optical truths and visual pleasures, in yoking a positivist scientism with a romantic metaphysics, photographic discourse has attempted to bridge the philosophical and institutional separation of scientific and artistic practices that has characterized bourgeois society from the late eighteenth century onward. The defenders of photography have both confirmed and rebelled against the Kantian cleavage of epistemology and aesthetics; some argue for truth, some for pleasure, and most for both, usually out of opposite sides of the mouth. (And a third voice, usually affiliated with liberalism, sporadically argues for an ethical dimension to photographic meaning. This argument attempts to fuse the separated spheres of fact and value, to graft a usually reformist morality onto empiricism.) This philosophical shell game is evidence of a sustained crisis at the very center of bourgeois culture, a crisis rooted in the emergence of science and technology as seemingly autonomous productive forces. Bourgeois culture has had to contend with the threat and the promise of the machine, which it continues to both resist and embrace.[2] The fragmentary and mechanically derived photographic image is central to this attitude of crisis and ambivalence; the embracing issue is the nature of work and creativity under capitalism. Above all else, the ideological force of photographic art in modern society may lie in the apparent reconciliation of human creative energies with a scientifically guided process of mechanization, suggesting that despite the modern industrial division of labor, and specifically despite the industrialization of cultural work, despite the historical obsolescence, marginalization and degradation of artisanal and manual modes of representation, the category of the artist lives on in the exercise of a *purely mental, imaginative* command over the camera.[3]

But during the second half of the nineteenth century, a fundamental tension developed between uses of photography that fulfill a bourgeois conception of the *self* and uses that seek to establish and delimit the terrain of the *other*. Thus every work of photographic art has its lurking, objectifying inverse in the archives of the police. To the

2. In 1790, Kant separates knowledge and pleasure in a way that fully anticipates the bastard status of photography: "'If art which is adequate to the *cognition* of a possible object performs the actions requisite therefore merely in order to make it actual, it is mechanical art; but if it has as its immediate design the feeling of pleasure, it is called *aesthetical* art." Immanuel Kant, *Critique of Judgment*, trans. J. H. Bernard (New York: Hafner Press, 1951), p. 148.

A number of texts seem relevant to the question of the photographer as mere "appendage to the machine." Of specific importance is Bernard Edelman's *Ownership of the Image. Elements for a Marxist Theory of Law* (London: Routledge and Kegan Paul, 1979). Less directly related, but valuable are Harry Braverman's *Labor and Monopoly Capital* (New York: Monthly Review Press, 1974); Alfred Sohn-Rethel's *Intellectual and Manual Labor* (London: Macmillan, 1978); and an essay by Raymond Williams, "The Romantic Artist," in *Culture and Society* (New York: Columbia University Press, 1958), pp. 30–48.

3. I am grateful to Sally Stein for discussions about the relationship between scientific management and the development of a mechanized visual culture in the early twentieth century, and especially for showing me an unpublished essay written in 1980 on this issue, "The Graphic Ordering of Desire: Modernization of *The Ladies' Home Journal*, 1914–1939." Her criticisms and support were very important. Also, Bruce Kaiper deserves thanks for a lucid essay, "The Human Object and its Capitalist Image," *Left Curve*, No. 5, 1976, pp. 40–60, and for a number of conversations on this subject.

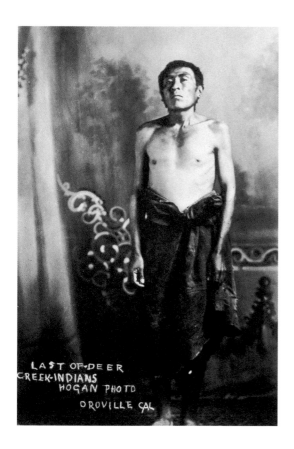

extent that bourgeois society depends on the systematic defense of property relations, to the extent that the legal basis of the self lies in property rights, every proper portrait of a "man of genius" made by a "man of genius" has its counterpart in a mug shot. Both attempts are motivated by an uneasy belief in the category of the individual. Thus also, every romantic landscape finds its deadly echo in the aerial view of a targeted terrain. And to the extent that modern sexuality has been invented and channeled by organized medicine, every eroticized view of the body bears a covert relation to the clinical depiction of anatomy.

With the rise of the modern social sciences, a regularized flow of symbolic and material power is engineered between fully-human subject and less-than-fully-human object along vectors of race, sex, and class. The social-scientistic appropriation of photography led to a genre I would call *instrumental realism,* representational projects devoted to new techniques of social diagnosis and control, to the systematic naming, categorization, and isolation of an otherness thought to be determined by biology and manifested through the "language" of the body itself. Early anthropological, criminological, and psychiatric

John H. Hogan, *Ishi, Last of the Deer Creek Indians*, ca. 1911. Real photo postcard, 5 ¹/₂ x 3 ¹/₂ in. (14 x 9 cm). Phoebe Apperson Hearst Museum of Anthropology and the Regents of the University of California.
Unidentified photographer, *Portrait of Ishi*, ca. 1911. Modern print from original glass plate negative, 5 x 7 in. (12.7 x 17.8 cm). Phoebe Apperson Hearst Museum of Anthropology and the Regents of the University of California.

photography, as well as motion-study photography used somewhat later in the scientific analysis and management of the labor process, constitute ambitious attempts to link optical empiricism with abstract, statistical truth, to move from the specificity of the body to abstract, mathematical laws of human nature. Thus photography was hitched to the locomotive of positivism.

But consider for a moment the symbolist cult of metaphor, so central to the rhetoric of emergent avant-garde art photography in the United States in the first quarter of this century. In its attempt to establish the free-floating metaphorical play, or equivalence, of signifiers, this symbolist-influenced photography was fundamentally reactive, the outcome of a desire to seize a small area of creative autonomy from a tainted, instrumentalized medium, a medium that had demonstrated repeatedly its complicity with the forces of industrialism. Thus the free play of metaphorical associations was implicitly contrasted to the slavish metonymy of both instrumental realism and the sentimental realism of late nineteenth-century family photography. With symbolism the ultimate goal of abstraction also looms, but in metaphysical and spiritualist rather than positivist guise. But both modern science and modernist art end up worshipping in floating cathedrals of formal, abstract, mathematical relations and "laws." Perhaps the fundamental question to be asked is whether or not traditional photographic representation, whether symbolist or realist in its dominant formal rhetoric, can transcend the pervasive logic of the commodity form, the exchange abstraction that haunts the culture of capitalism. Despite its origins in a radical refusal of instrumental meaning, symbolism appears to have been absorbed by mass culture, enlisted in the spectacle that gives imaginary flesh to the abstract regime of commodity exchange.[4]

No theory of photography can fail to deal with the hidden unity of these extremes of photographic practice without lapsing into mere cultural promotion, into the intellectual background-music that welcomes photography into the shopping mall of a bureaucratically administered high culture that has, in the late-capitalist period, become increasingly indistinguishable from mass culture in its structural dependence on forms of publicity and stardom. The goals of a critical theory of photography ought, ultimately, to involve the practical, to help point the way to a radical, reinvented cultural practice. Other more powerful challenges to the order of monopoly capitalism need to be discovered and invented; resistances that unite culture and politics. Symbolic revolts are not enough, nor is a purely instrumental conception of politics. This essay is an attempt to pose questions that I take to be only preliminary, but necessary, steps in that direction.

4. For an earlier discussion of the relation between symbolist and realist photography see my "On the Invention of Photographic Meaning" in *Photography Against the Grain: Essays and Photo Works 1973–1983* (Halifax: Nova Scotia College of Art and Design, 1984).

It goes almost without saying that photography emerged and proliferated as a mode of communication within the larger context of a developing capitalist *world order.* No previous economy constituted a world order in the same sense. As an inherently expansionist economic system, capitalism seeks ultimately to unify the globe in a single system of commodity production and exchange. Even tribal and feudal economies at the periphery of the capitalist system are drastically transformed by the pressures exerted from the aggressive centers of finance and trade. These forces cause local economies and cultures to lose much of their self-sufficiency, their manner of being tied by necessity and tradition to a specific local ecology. This process of global colonization, initially demanding the outright conquest, extermination, and pacification of native peoples, began in earnest in the sixteenth century, a period of expanding mercantile capitalism. In the late twentieth century this process continues in a fashion more intensive than extensive, as modern capitalism encounters national political insurrections throughout the colonized world and attempts to fortify its position against a crisis that is simultaneously political, economic, and ecological, a crisis that is internal as well as external. Despite these changes, a common logic of capital accumulation links, for example, the European slave trade in West Africa in the seventeenth and eighteenth centuries to the late twentieth-century electronics sweatshops operated by American multinationals in Singapore and Malaysia. And today, even established as well as recently insurgent socialist economies are increasingly forced to adjust to the pressures of a global system of currency dominated by the large multinational enterprises of the West.[5]

What are we to make then, of the oft-repeated claim that photography constitutes a "universal language"? Almost from 1839 to the present, this honorific has been expansively and repetitively voiced by photographers, intellectuals, journalists, cultural impresarios, and advertising copy writers. Need I even cite examples? But the very ubiquity of this cliché has lent it a commonsensical armor that deflects serious critical questions. The "universal language" myth seems so central, so full of social implications that I'd like to trace the argument as it surfaced and resurfaced at three different historical conjunctures.

An initial qualification seems important here. The claim for semantic universality depends on a more fundamental conceit: the belief that photography constitutes a language in its own right. But photography is *not* an independent or autonomous language system, but depends on larger discursive conditions, invariably including those

5. A useful introduction to some of the cultural implications of an international capitalist economy can be found in Samir Amin's "In Praise of Socialism," in *Imperialism and Unequal Development* (New York: Monthly Review Press, 1977), pp. 73–85. In this connection, a recent, and perhaps sardonic remark by Harold Rosenberg comes to mind: "Today, all modes of visual excitation, from Benin idols to East Indian chintz, are both contemporaneous and American." Harold Rosenberg, "The Problem of Reality," in *American Civilization: A Portrait from the 20th Century*, ed. Daniel J. Boorstin, (London: Thames and Hudson, 1972), p. 305.

Lee Friedlander, *Manuel "Fess" Manetta*, 1957. Gelatin silver print, 14 x 11 in. (35.5 x 27.9 cm). Courtesy of Janet Borden, Inc., New York.

established by the system of verbal-written language. Photographic meaning is always a hybrid construction, the outcome of an interplay of iconic, graphic, and narrative conventions. Despite a certain fugitive moment of semantic and formal autonomy—the Holy Grail of most modernist analytic criticism—the photograph is invariably accompanied by, and situated within, an overt or covert text. Even at the level of the artificially "isolated" image, photographic signification is exercised in terms of pictorial conventions that are never "purely" photographic. After all, the dominant spatial code in the Western pictorial tradition is still that of linear perspective, institutionalized in the fifteenth and sixteenth centuries. Having made this point, only in passing and only too briefly, suppose we examine what is necessarily the dependent claim, a claim grounded in the dubious conception of a "photographic language."

My first example consists of two texts that constituted part of the initial euphoric chorus that welcomed and promoted the invention of photography in 1839. In reading these, we'll move "backwards," as it were, from the frontiers of photography's early proliferation to the ceremonial site of invention, tracing a kind of reverse geographical movement within the same period of emergence.

Early in 1840, a glowing newspaper account of the daguerreotype (mistranslated understandably enough as the "daguerreolite") was published in Cincinnati, Ohio. Cincinnati was a busy center for river-borne shipping in what was then the western United States, a city that would soon support one of the more ornate and culturally pretentious of American photographic portrait establishments, Ball's Daguerrian Gallery of the West.[6] Here then is a fragment of what was undoubtedly the first local announcement of the novel invention which was soon to blossom into the very embodiment of Culture:

> Its perfection is unapproachable by human hand and its
> truth raises it above all language, painting or poetry. It is
> the first universal language addressing itself to all who
> possess vision, and in characters alike understood in
> the courts of civilization and the hut of the savage. The
> pictorial language of Mexico, the hieroglyphics of Egypt
> are now superseded by reality.[7]

I find it striking that this account glides from the initial trumpeting of a triumph over "all language," presumably including all previous European cultural achievements, to the celebration of a victorious encounter with "primitive" and archeologically remote pictographic conventions, rendering these already extinct languages rather redundantly "obsolete." This optimistic hymn to progress conceals a fear of the past. For the unconscious that resides within this text, dead

6. See Richard Rudisill, *Mirror Image: The Influence of the Daguerreotype on American Society* (Albuquerque: University of New Mexico Press, 1971), p. 201.
7. "The Daguerreolite," *The Daily Chronicle* (Cincinnati), vol. 1, no. 38, January 17, 1840, p. 2, quoted in Rudisill, *Mirror Image*, p. 54.

Was a Yuma chief in days of prosperity.

languages and cultures may well be pregnant with the threat of rebirth. Like zombies, they must be killed again and embalmed by a "more perfect union" of sign and referent, a union that delivers "reality" itself without the mediation of hand or tongue. This new mechanical language, by its very closeness to nature, will speak in civilizing tones to previously unteachable "savages." Behind the rhetoric of technologically derived egalitarianism lurks a vision of the relentless imposition of a new pedagogical power.

Consider also a related passage from one of the central ideological documents of the early history of photography, the report on the daguerreotype by the physicist and left-republican representative François Arago addressed to his colleagues in the French Chamber of

Andrew Miller, *Was a Yuma Chief in Days of Prosperity*, ca. 1885. Albumen print, 6 $^1/_2$ x 4 $^1/_4$ in. (16.5 x 10.8 cm). Museum of New Mexico, Palace of the Governors, Santa Fe.

Deputies. This report was published along with the texts of related speeches by the chemist Gay-Lussac and the Interior Minister Dûchatel in the numerous editions in many languages of Daguerre's instruction manual. As is well known, Arago argued for the award of a state pension to Daguerre for his "work of genius"; this purchase would then be offered "generously to the entire world." Not without a certain amount of maneuvering (involving the covert shunting aside of photographic research by Hippolyte Bayard and the more overt down-playing of Nicéphore Nièpce's contribution to the Nièpce-Daguerre collaboration), Arago established the originality of Daguerre's invention.[8] Arago also emphasized the extraordinary efficiency of the invention—its capacity to accelerate the process of representation—and the demonstrable utility of the new medium for both art and science. Thus the report's principal ideological service was to fuse the authority of the state with that of the individual author—the individuated *subject* of invention. But while genius and the parliamentary monarchic state bureaucracy of Louis-Phillipe are brought together within the larger ideological context of a unified technical and cultural progressivism, the report also touches on France's colonial enterprises and specifically upon the archival chores of the "zealous and famous scholars and artists attached to the army of the Orient."[9] Here is the earliest written fantasy of a collision between photography and hieroglyphics, a fantasy that resurfaced six months later in Ohio:

> While these pictures are exhibited to you, everyone will imagine the extraordinary advantages which could have been derived from so exact and rapid a means of reproduction during the expedition to Egypt; everybody will realize that had we had photography in 1798 we would possess today faithful pictorial records of that which the learned world is forever deprived by the greed of the Arabs and the vandalism of certain travelers.
>
> To copy the millions of hieroglyphics which cover even the exterior of the great monuments of Thebes, Memphis, Karnak, and others would require decades of time and legions of draughtsmen. By daguerreotype one person would suffice to accomplish this immense work successfully.... These designs will excel the works of the most accomplished painters, in fidelity of detail and true reproduction of atmosphere. Since the invention follows the laws of geometry, it will be possible to re-establish with the aid of a small number of given factors the exact size of the highest points of the most inaccessible structures.[10]

8. See Helmut and Alison Gernsheim, *L. J. M. Daguerre: The History of the Diorama and the Daguerreotype* (New York: Dover, 1968), pp. 88, 99.
9. François Arago, "Report," in Josef Maria Eder, *History of Photography*, trans. Edward Epstean (New York: Columbia University Press, 1945), p. 235. The earliest English translation of this address appears in L. J. M. Daguerre, *An Historical and Descriptive Account of the Daguerreotype and the Diorama* (London: McLean, 1839).
10. Arago, "Report," pp. 234–35.

In this rather marked example of what Edward Said has termed "Orientalist" discourse, a "learned" Occident colonizes an East that either always has lacked or has lost all memory of learning.[11] A seemingly neutral, mathematical objectivism retrieves, measures, and preserves the artifacts of an Orient that has "greedily" squandered its own heritage. In a sense, Arago's argument here is overdetermined: France, a most civilized nation, a nation aware of its historical mission, must not fail to preserve and nurture its own inventions. In effect, Arago's speech conflates photography-as-an-end and photography-as-a-means. This should not be at all surprising, given the powerful tendency of bourgeois thought to collapse all teleology into the sheer, ponderous immanence of technological development. Rational progress becomes a matter of the increasingly quantitative refinement of technical means; the only positive transformations are those that stem from orderly technical innovations. Hence Arago's emphasis on the conquest of vandalism, greed, and ignorance through speed and the laws of geometry.

In a very different historical context—that of the last crisis-ridden years of Weimar Germany—a text appeared that is reminiscent of both Arago's refined promotion and the hyperbolic newspaper prophecy from Ohio. August Sander, that rigorously and comprehensively sociologistic portraitist of the German people, delivered a radio talk in 1931 entitled "Photography as a Universal Language." The talk, which ran fifth in a series by Sander, stresses that a liberal, enlightened, and even socially critical pedagogy might be achieved by the proper use of photographic means. Thus Sander's emphasis is less on the pictorial archive anticipated by Arago in 1839 than on a global mode of communication that would hurdle barriers of illiteracy and language difference. But at the same time, Sander echoes the scientistic notions of photographic truth that made their initial authoritative appearance in Arago's report:

> Today with photography we can communicate our
> thoughts, conceptions, and realities, to all the people on
> the earth; if we add the date of the year we have the power
> to fix the history of the world....
>
> Even the most isolated Bushman could understand a
> photograph of the heavens—whether it showed the sun or
> the moon or the constellations. In biology, in the animal
> and plant world, the photograph as picture language can
> communicate without the help of sound. But the field in
> which photography has so great a power of expression
> that language can never approach it, is physiognomy....[12]

11. Edward Said, *Orientalism* (New York: Pantheon Books, 1978).
12. August Sander, "Photography as a Universal Language," trans. Anne Halley, *Massachusetts Review*, 19, no. 4, (Winter 1978): 474–75.

Perhaps it is understandable that in his enthusiasm for photographic enlightenment Sander led his unseen radio audience to believe that a Copernican cosmology and a mechanically rendered Albertian perspective might constitute transhistorical and transcultural discourses: photography could deliver the heliocentric and perspectival truths of the Renaissance to any human viewer.

Further, Sander describes photography as the truth vehicle for an eclectic array of disciplines: not only astronomy, but history, biology, zoology, botany, physiognomy (and clearly the list is not meant to be exhaustive). Two paragraphs later, his text seeks to name the source of the encyclopedic power to convey virtually all the world's knowledges:

> *No language on earth speaks as comprehensively*
> *as photography, always providing that we follow the*
> *chemical and optic and physical path to demonstrable*
> *truth, and understand physiognomy. Of course you have*
> *to have decided whether you will serve culture or the*
> *marketplace.*[13]

In opposing photographic truth to commercial values, and in regarding photography as "a special discipline with special laws and its own special language,"[14] Sander is assuming an uncompromisingly modernist stance. This position is not without its contradictions. Thus, on the one hand, Sander claims that photography constitutes a "language" that is both autonomous and universal; on the other, photography is subsumed within the logical order of the natural sciences. The "laws" that are "special" to photography turn out to be those of chemistry and optics. From this subordinate position photography functions as the vehicle for a scientific pedagogy. For Arago, photography is a means of aggressively acquiring the world's truth; for Sander, photography benignly disseminates these truths to a global audience. Although the emphasis in the first instance is on acquisition, and in the second on distribution, both projects are fundamentally rooted in a shared epistemology. This epistemology combines a faith in the universality of the natural sciences and a belief in the transparency of representation.

For Sander, physiognomy was perhaps the highest of the human sciences, which are in turn merely extensions of natural-scientific method. Physiognomic empiricism serves as the basis for what the novelist and physician Alfred Döblin, in his preface to Sander's *Antlitz der Zeit* described as a project methodologically analogous to medical science, thereby collapsing history and sociology into social anatomy:

> *You have in front of you a kind of cultural history, better,*
> *sociology of the last 30 years. How to write sociology*
> *without writing, but presenting photographs instead,*

13. Ibid., p. 675.
14. Ibid., p. 679.

Walker Evans, *Mask, profile view; Africa, Cameroon, Bandjoun, Bamendjo Kingdom, #272, from African Negro Art portfolio*, 1935. Gelatin silver print, 8 7/8 x 6 in. (22.5 x 15.2 cm); *Mask; Africa, Cameroon, Bandjoun, Bamendjo Kingdom, #271, from African Negro Art portfolio*, 1935. Gelatin silver print, 8 7/8 x 7 in. (22.5 x 18.8 cm). New York University, Institute of Fine Arts, Visual Resource Collection Photography.

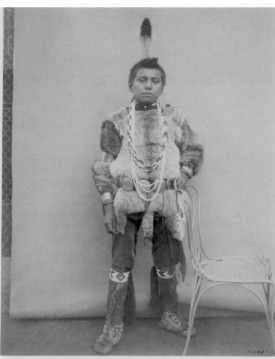

Collection anthropologique du Prince Roland Bonaparte.   *Collection anthropologique du Prince Roland Bonaparte*

photographs of faces and not national costumes, this is what the photographer accomplished with his eyes, his mind, his observations, his knowledge and last but not least his considerable photographic ability. Only through studying comparative anatomy can we come to an understanding of nature and the history of the internal organs. In the same way this photographer has practiced comparative anatomy and therefore found a scientific point of view beyond the conventional photographer.[15]

The echoes of nineteenth-century positivism and its Enlightenment antecedents are deafening here, as they are in Sander's own implicit hierarchy of knowledge. The grim master-voice is that of Auguste Comte's systematic and profoundly influential effort to invent sociology (or "social physics," as he initially labeled the new discipline) on the model of the physical sciences, in his *Cours de Philosophie Positive* of 1830–42.[16]

Physiognomy predates and partially anticipates positivism. A number of social scientific disciplines absorbed physiognomic method as a means of implementing positivist theory during the nineteenth

15. Alfred Döblin, "About Faces, Portraits, and Their Reality: Introduction to August Sander," *Antlitz der Zen* (1929), in *Germany: The New Photography 1927–1933*, ed. David Mellor (London: Arts Council of Great Britain, 1978), p. 58.
16. Auguste Comte, *Cours de Philosophie Positive* (1830–42) in *Auguste Comte and Positivism: The Essential Writings*, ed. Gertrud Lenzer (New York: Harper & Row, 1975). Lenzer's introduction is especially valuable.

Roland N. Bonaparte, *Iga-she (Traveler), 13 years old, in costume with ornaments beside wrought iron chair, Omaha Bay, Ca.,* 1883.
Albumen prints, 15 x 12 in. (38.1 x 30.5 cm). National Anthropological Archives, Smithsonian Institution, Washington D.C.

century. This practice continued into the twentieth century and, despite a certain decline in scientific legitimacy, took on an especially charged aspect in the social environment of Weimar Germany. Sander shared the then still common belief—which dated back at least as far as Johann Caspar Lavater's *Physiognomische Fragmente* of 1775–78 — that the body, and especially the face and head, bore the outward *signs* of inner character. Lavater himself had first suggested that this "original language of Nature, written on the face of Man" could be deciphered by a rigorous physiognomic *science*.[17] This "science" proceeded by means of an analytic isolation of the anatomic features of the head and face—forehead, eyes, ears, nose, chin, and so on—and the assignment of a significance to each. "Character" was judged through a concatenation of these readings. Of course, Sander never proffered so rigorous a mode of physiognomical interpretation for his photographs. He never suggested that each fragment of facial anatomy be isolated through the kind of pictorial dissection sketched by Lavater and practiced by his myriad disciples. I suspect Sander wanted to envelop his project in the legitimating aura of science without violating the aesthetic coherence and semantic ambiguity of the traditional portrait form. Despite his scientistic rhetoric, his portraits never achieve the "precision" and "exactitude" so desired by physiognomists of all stripes. Sander's commitment was, in effect, to a sociologically extended variant of formal portraiture. His scientism is revealed in the ensemble, in the attempt to delineate a social anatomy. More than anything else, physiognomy served as a telling *metaphor* for this project.

The historical trajectories of physiognomy, and of the related practices of phrenology and anthropometrics, are extremely complicated and are consistently interwoven with the history of photographic portraiture. And as was the case with photography, these disciplines gave rise to the same contradictory but connected rationales. These techniques for reading the body's signs seemed to promise both

17. Johann Caspar Lavater, *Essays on Physiognomy*, trans. Henry Hunter (London: Printed for W. Locke, 1792), Vol. I, preface, n.p. This is the first English translation of *Physiognomische Fragmente, Zur Beförderung der Menschenkenntnis und Menschenliebe* (Leipzig: Weidman Erben und Reich, 1775–78).

18. I am preparing an essay which deals with the relation between physiognomy and instrumental realism in much greater detail. A great deal of this work revolves around a study of the two principal schools of late nineteenth-century European criminology, the Positivist School of the Italian forensic psychiatrist Cesare Lombroso and the Statistical School of the French police official Alphonse Bertillon. Lombroso advanced the profoundly racist and long-lived notion of an atavistic criminal *type,* while Bertillon, applying the social statistics developed by the Belgian statistician Adolphe Quetelet in the 1820s and 1830s, sought to absolutely identify the criminal "individuality" Bertillon's method of police identification, which linked a series of anthropometric measurements to a photographic *portrait-parlé* or "speaking likeness," was the first "scientific" system of police intelligence. Perhaps the most striking example of the mathematicism inherent in these searches for the absolute, objective truth of the incarcerated body is found, not in the criminological literature of the nineteenth century, but in the related field of psychiatric medicine.

McCrary & Branson, *Alligator Bait*, ca. 1897. Gelatin silver print, 8 3/8 x 23 in. (21.2 x 58.4 cm). International Center of Photography, Daniel Cowin Collection, 1990.

I would like to cite one example to emphasize the nature of this thinking. Hugh Welch Diamond, a minor English psychiatrist and founding member of the genteel Photographic Society, attempted to use photographic portraits of patients in the Surrey County Women's Asylum for empirical research, therapy, and surveillance of the inmate population. Diamond read a paper on his work to the Royal Society in 1856: "The photographer, on the other hand, needs in many cases no aid from any language of his own, but prefers rather to listen, with the pictures before him, to the silent but telling language of nature... the picture speaks for itself with the most marked pression and indicates the *exact* point which has been reached in the *scale of* unhappiness between the first sensation and its utmost height". (Italics mine). Hugh W. Diamond, "On the Application of Photography to the Physiognomic and Mental Phenomena of Insanity," in *The Face of Madness: Hugh W. Diamond and the Origin of Psychiatric Photography*, ed. Sander L. Gilman (New York: Brunner/Mazel, 1977), p. 19.

I have found the work of Michel Foucault particularly valuable in considering these issues, especially his *Discipline* and *Punish: The Birth of the Prison*, (New York: Pantheon Books, 1977). My interest in this area began in conversations with Martha Rosler; her video "opera" *Vital Statistics of a Citizen: Simply Obtained* (1976) is an exemplary study of the power of measurement science over the body, with a feminist inflection that is absent in the work of Foucault.

19. Lavater, *Essays on Physiognomy*, p. 13.

20. Anne Halley, "August Sander," *Massachusetts Review*, Vol. 19, no. 4 (Winter 1978): 663–73. See also Robert Kramer, "Historical Commentary," in *August Sander: Photographs of an Epoch* (Millerton, NY: Aperture, 1980), pp. 11–38, for a discussion of Sander's relation to physiognomic traditions.

egalitarian and authoritarian results. At the one extreme, the more liberal apologetic promoted the cultivation of a common human understanding of the language of the body: all of humanity was to be both subject and object of this new egalitarian discourse. At the other extreme—and this was certainly the dominant tendency in actual social practice—a specialized way of knowledge was opening harnessed to the new strategies of social channeling and control that characterized the mental asylum, the penitentiary, and eventually, the factory employment office. Unlike the egalitarian mode, these latter projects drew an unmistakable line between the professional reader of the body's signs—the psychiatrist, physiologist, criminologist, or industrial psychologist—and the "diseased," "deviant," or "biologically inferior" object of cure, reform, or discipline.

August Sander stood to the liberal side of positivism in his faith in a universal pedagogy. Yet, like positivists in general, he was insensitive to the *epistemological* differences between peoples and cultures. Difference would seem to exist only on the surface; all peoples share the same modes of perception and cognition, as well as the same natural bodily codes of expression. For nineteenth-century positivism, anthropological difference became quantitative rather than qualitative. This reduction opened the door to one of the principle justifications of social Darwinism. Inferiority could presumably be measured and located on a continuous calibrated scale. Armed with calipers, scalpel, and camera, scientists sought to prove the absence of a governing intellect in criminals, the insane, women, workers, and nonwhite people.[18] Here again, one lineage stretches back beyond positivism and social Darwinism to the benign figure of Lavater who proclaimed both the "universality of physiognomic discernments" and defined a "human nature" fundamentally constituted by a variable mixture of "animal, moral, and intellectual life."[19]

But Sander, in contrast to his nineteenth-century predecessors, refused to link his belief in physiognomic science to biological determinism. He organized his portraiture in terms of a social, rather than a racial, typology. As Anne Halley has noted in a perceptive essay on the photographer, herein lay the most immediate difference between Sander's physiognomic project and that of Nazi race "theorists" like Hans F. K. Günther who deployed physiognomic readings of photographic portraits to establish both the biological superiority of the Nordic "race" and the categorical otherness of the Jews.[20] The very universalism of Sander's argument for photographic and physiognomic truth may well have been an indirect and somewhat naive attempt to respond to the racial particularism of the Nazis, which "scientifically" legitimated genocide and imperialism.

The conflict between Sander and National Socialist *Rassentheorie,* which culminated in the Nazi's destruction of the plates for *Antlitz der Zeit* in 1934, is well remembered and celebrated by liberal historians of photography. One is tempted to emphasize a contrast between Sander's "good" physiognomic science and the "bad" physiognomic science of Günther and his ilk, without challenging the positivist underpinnings of both projects. That is, what is less apparent is that Sander, in his "scientific" liberalism, shared aspects of the same general positivist outlook that was incorporated into the fascist project of domination. But in this, Sander was little different from other social democrats of his time. The larger questions which loom here concern the continuities between fascist, liberal capitalist, social democratic, and bureaucratic socialist governments as modes of administration which subject social life to the authority of an institutionalized scientific expertise.[21]

The politics of social democracy, to which Sander subscribed, demand that government be legitimated on the basis of formal representation. Despite the sense of impending collapse, of crisis-level unemployment and imminent world war conveyed by Sander in his radio speech of 1931, he sustains a curiously inflected faith in the *representativeness* of bourgeois parliamentary government:

> *The historical image will become even clearer if we join together pictures typical of the many different groups that make up human society. For instance, we might consider a nation's parliament. If we began with the Right Wing and moved across the individual types to the farthest Left, we would already have a partial physiognomic image of the nation.*[22]

Just as a picture stands for its referent, so parliament stands for a nation. In effect, Sander regards parliament as a picture in itself, a synecdochic sample of the national whole. This conflation of the mythologies of pictorial and political representation may well be fundamental to the public discourse of liberalism. Sander, unlike Bertolt Brecht or the left-wing photomontagist John Heartfield, believed that political relations were evident on the surface of things.[23] Political revelation was a matter of careful sampling for Sander; his project shares the logic of the opinion poll. In this, Sander stands in the mainstream of liberal thinking on the nature of journalism and social documentation; he shares both the epistemology and the politics that accompany bourgeois realism. The deceptively clear waters of this mainstream flow from the confluence of two deep ideological currents. One current defends science as the privileged *representation* of the real, as the ultimate source of social truth. The other current defends parliamentary

21. Fascist ideology is overtly metaphysical in character, depending in large measure on cults of racial and national superiority and on the ostentatious display of charismatic authority. Nevertheless, the actual functioning of the fascist corporate state demands the sub rosa exercise of a bureaucratic rationalism that is profoundly rooted in positivist notions of the commanding role of science and of technical elites. Nazi ideologues felt the need, in fact, to scientifically legitimate the *Führer* cult. One text in particular is relevant to our discussion of Sander and physiognomy. Alfred Richter's *Unser Fuhrer im Lichte der Rassenfrage und Charakterologie* (Leipzig,1933), sought to demonstrate the racial ideality and innate political genius of Adolf Hitler and the host of top party officials by means of handsomely-lit formal portraits that were accompanied by flattering physiognomical analyses. This research project-cum-souvenir album provides unintended evidence that the seemingly charismatic authority of the fascist leader has the quality of an apparition, an Oz-like aspect that requires amplification through the media and legitimation through an appeal to the larger, abstract authority of Science. In this light, Hitler shines as the embodiment of a racial principle. In its assault on parliamentary pluralism, fascist government portrays itself not only as a means of national salvation, but as the organic *expression* of a nonrational, biologically driven will to domination.

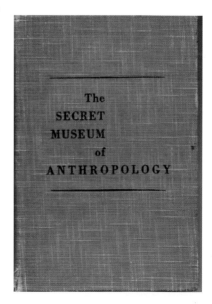

Author unknown, *The Secret Museum of Anthropology*, 1935. Book. Private Collection.

Author unknown, *The Secret Museum of Anthropology*, 1935. Book. Private Collection.

93

politics as the *representation* of a pluralistic popular desire, as the ultimate source of social good.

Despite Sander's tendency to collapse politics into a physiognomic typology, he never loses sight of the political arena as one of conflict and struggle. And yet, viewed as a whole, Sander's compendium of portraits from the Weimar period and before possess a haunting—and ideologically limiting—synchronicity for the contemporary viewer. One witnesses a kind of false stasis, the appearance of a tense structural equilibrium of social forces. Today, Sander's project suggests a neatly arranged chessboard that was about to be dashed to the floor by brown-shirted thugs. But despite Sander's and Döblin's claims to the contrary, this project was not then and is not now an adequate reading of German social history.

But what of an even more ambitious photographic project, one which managed not only to freeze social life, but also to render it invisible? I am thinking here of that celebrated event in American postwar culture, the exhibition *The Family of Man*. Almost thirty years after Sander's radio talk, the photographer Edward Steichen, who was director of the photography department at the Museum of Modern Art, voiced similarly catholic sentiments in an article published in *Daedalus,* the journal of the American Academy of Arts and Sciences. Despite the erudite forum, the argument is simplistic, much more so than anything Sander ever claimed:

> Long before the birth of a word language the caveman communicated by visual images. The invention of photography gave visual communication its most simple, direct, universal language.[24]

Steichen went on to tout the success of his Museum of Modern Art exhibition, *The Family of Man*, which by 1960 had been seen by "some seven million people in the twenty-eight countries." He continued, introducing a crude tautological psychologism into his view of photographic discourse:

> The audiences not only understand this visual presentation, they also participate in it, and identify themselves with the images, as if in corroboration of the words of a Japanese poet, "when you look into a mirror you do not see your reflection, your reflection sees you."[25]

Steichen, in this moment of fondness for Zen wisdom, understandably neglected to mention that the Japanese recipients of the exhibition insisted on the inclusion of a large photographic mural depicting the victims of the atomic bombings of Hiroshima and Nagasaki, thus resisting the ahistoricity of the photo essay's argument.

22. Sander, "Photography as a Universal Language," p. 678.

23. Walter Benjamin (in "A Short History of Photography" [1931], trans. Stanley Mitchell, *Screen* 13 [Spring 1972]: 24) quotes a very explicit and often cited statement by Brecht in this regard: "For, says Brecht, the situation is complicated by the fact that less than at any time does a simple *reproduction* of *reality* tell us anything about reality. A photograph of the Krupp works or GEC yields almost nothing about these institutions. Reality proper has slipped into the functional. The reification of human relationships, the factory, let's say, no longer reveals these relationships. Therefore something has actually to be *constructed,* something artificial, something set up."

One could argue that even the *assemblage* of portraits pursued by Sander merely reproduces the logic of assigned individual places, and thus of reification.

24. Edward Steichen, "On Photography," in *Photographers on Photography*, ed. Nathan Lyons (Englewood Cliffs, NJ: Prentice-Hall, 1966), p. 107.

25. Ibid., p. 107.

The Family of Man, first exhibited in 1955, may well be the epitome of American Cold War liberalism, with Steichen playing cultural attaché to Adlai Stevenson, the would-be good cop of U.S. foreign policy, promoting a benign view of an American world order stabilized by the rule of international law. The Family of Man universalizes the bourgeois nuclear family, suggesting a globalized, utopian family album, a family romance imposed on every corner of the earth. The family serves as a metaphor also for a system of international discipline and harmony. In the foreign showings of the exhibition, arranged by the United States Information Agency and cosponsoring corporations like Coca-Cola, the discourse was explicitly that of American multinational capital and government—the new global management team—cloaked in the familiar and musty garb of patriarchy. Nelson Rockefeller, who had served as president of the MoMA Board of Trustees between 1946 and 1953, delivered a preview address that is revealing in terms of its own father-fixation.

Rockefeller began his remarks in an appropriately internationalist vein, suggesting that the exhibition created "a sense of kinship with all mankind." He went on:

> There is a second message to be read from this profession of Edward Steichen's faith. It demonstrates that the essential unity of human experience, attitude and emotion are perfectly communicable through the medium of pictures. The solicitous eye of the Bantu father, resting upon the son who is learning to throw his primitive spear in search of food, is the eye of every father, whether in Montreal, Paris, or in Tokyo.[26]

For Rockefeller, social life begins with fathers teaching sons to survive in a Hobbesian world; all authority can be metaphorically equated with this primary relationship.

A close textual reading of The Family of Man would indicate that the exhibition moves from the celebration of patriarchal authority—which finds its highest embodiment in the United Nations—to the final construction of an imaginary utopia that resembles nothing so much as a protracted state of infantile, pre-Oedipal bliss. The best-selling book version of the exhibition ends with the following sequence. First, there appears an array of portraits of elderly couples, mostly peasants or farmers from Sicily, Canada, China, Holland, and the United States. The glaring exception in regard to class is a Sander portrait of a wealthy German landowner and his wife. Each picture is captioned with the repeated line from Ovid, "We two form a multitude." From these presumably archetypal parent-figures we turn the page to

26. Nelson Rockefeller, "Preview Address: 'The Family of Man,'" *U. S. Camera 1956*, ed. Tom Maloney (New York, 1955): p. 18. I am grateful to Alex Sweetman for calling my attention to this article.

find a large photograph of the United Nations General Assembly, accompanied by the opening phrases of the U. N. Charter. The next page offers a woman's lower body, bedecked in flowers and standing in water. The following five pages contain smaller photographs of children at play throughout the world, ending with W. Eugene Smith's famous photograph of his son and daughter walking from darkness into light in a garden. The final photograph in the book is quite literally a depiction of the oceanic state, a picture by Cedric Wright of churning surf.

A case could also be made for viewing *The Family of Man* as a more or less unintentional popularization of the then-dominant school of American sociology, Talcott Parsons's structural functionalism. Parsons's writings on the family celebrate the modern nuclear family as the most advanced and efficient of familial forms, principally because the nuclear family establishes a clearcut division of male and female roles. The male function, in this view, is primarily "instrumental" and oriented toward achievement in the public sphere. The female

W. Eugene Smith, *The Walk to Paradise Garden*, 1946. Gelatin silver print, 16 x 14 in. (40.6 x 35.5 cm). International Center of Photography, International Fund for Concerned Photography purchase, 1975.

27. See Talcott Parsons et al., *Family, Socialization and Interaction Process,* (Glencoe, Ill.: Free Press, 1955), and the critique provided in Mark Poster, *Critical Theory of the Family* (New York: Seabury Press, 1978), pp.78–84. Barbara Ehrenreich and Deirdre English, *For Her Own Good: 150 Years of Experts' Advice to Women* (Garden City, NY: Anchor Press, 1978), are excellent on the issue of familial ideology in the postwar period.

28. Russell Lynes presents evidence that Steichen's appointment to the position of Director of the MoMA Department of Photography in 1947 involved an unsuccessful plan to bring direct funding from photographic corporations into the museum. Although unsurprising today, in an era of direct corporate funding, this was a novel move in the late 1940s. (Russell Lynes, *Good Old Modern* [New York: Atheneum, 1973], pp. 259–60.

function is primarily "expressive" and restricted to the domestic sphere. Although *The Family of Man* exhibits a great deal of nostalgia for the extended family engaged in self-sufficient agrarian production, the overall flow of the exhibition's loosely knit narrative traces a generalized family biography that adheres to the nuclear model.[27]

The familialism of *The Family of Man* functions both metaphorically and in a quite specific, literal fashion as well. For audiences in the advanced capitalist countries, and particularly in the United States, the celebration of the familial sphere as the exclusive arena of all desire and pleasure served to legitimate a family-based consumerism. If nothing else, *The Family of Man* was a massive promotion for family photography, as well as a celebration of the power of the mass media to represent the whole world in familiar and intimate forms.[28]

The Family of Man, originating at the Museum of Modern Art but utilizing a mode of architecturally monumentalized photo-essayistic showmanship, occupies a problematic but ideologically convenient middle position between the conventions of high modernism and those of mass culture. The modernist category of the solitary author was preserved, but at the level of editorship. The exhibition simultaneously

Wayne Miller, *Edward Steichen working on* The Family of Man *exhibition*, 1954. Gelatin silver print, 5 x 7 in. (12.7 x 17.8 cm). International Center of Photography, gift of Jim and Evelyn Hughes, 1998.

suggested a family album, a juried show for photo hobbyists, an apotheosis of *Life* magazine, and the *magnum opus* in Steichen's illustrious career.

A lot more could be said about *The Family of Man*, particularly about its relation to the domestic sexual politics of the Cold War and about its exemplary relation to the changing conventions of advertising and mass-circulation picture magazines in the same period. This will have to wait. My main point here is that *The Family of Man*, more than any other single photographic project, was a massive and ostentatious bureaucratic attempt to *universalize* photographic discourse.

Five hundred and three pictures taken by 273 photographers in sixty-eight countries were chosen from two million solicited submissions and organized by a single, illustrious editorial authority into a show that was seen by nine million citizens in sixty-nine countries in eighty-five separate exhibitions, and into a book that sold at least four million copies by 1978—or so go the statistics that pervade all accounts of the exhibition. The exhibition claims to fuse universal subject and universal object in a single moment of visual truth and visual pleasure, a single moment of blissful identity. But this dream rings hollow, especially when we come across the following oxymoronic construction in Carl Sandburg's prologue to the book version of the exhibition: Sandburg describes *The Family of Man* as a "multiplication table of living breathing human faces."[29] Suddenly, arithmetic and humanism collide, forced by poetic license into an absurd harmony. Here, yet again, are the twin ghosts that haunt the practice of photography: the voice of a reifying technocratic objectivism and the redemptive voice of a liberal subjectivism. The statistics that seek to legitimate the exhibition, to demonstrate its value, begin to carry a deeper sense: the truth being promoted here is one of enumeration. This is an aestheticized job of global accounting, a careful Cold War effort to bring about the ideological alignment of the neocolonial peripheries with the imperial center. American culture of both elite and mass varieties was being promoted as more universal than that of the Soviet Union.

A brief note on the cultural politics of the Cold War might be valuable here. Nelson Rockefeller, who welcomed *The Family of Man* with the characteristic exuberance noted above, was the principal architect of MoMA's International Circulating Exhibitions Program, which received a five year grant from the Rockefeller Brothers' Fund beginning in 1952. Under the directorship of Porter MacCray, this program exhibited American vanguard art abroad, and, in the words of Russell Lynes, "let it be known especially in Europe that America was not the cultural backwater that the Russians during that tense period called 'the cold war' were trying to demonstrate that it was."[30] Eva Cockcroft

29. Carl Sandburg, "Prologue," *The Family of Man* (New York: Published for the MoMA by Simon and Schuster, 1955).
30. Lynes, *Good Old Modern*, p. 233.

The Family of Man

Created by Edward Steichen

Prologue by Carl Sandburg

The Museum of Modern Art, New York

31. Eva Cockcroft, "Abstract Expressionism as a Weapon of the Cold War," *Artforum* 12, no. 10 (June 1974): 39–41. See also Max Kozloff, "American Painting During the Cold War," *Artforum* 11, no. 9 (May 1973): 43–54; William Hauptman, "The Suppression of Art in the McCarthy Decade," *Artforum* 12, no. 2 (October 1973): 48–52. Of general interest is Christopher Lasch's "The Cultural Cold War: A Short History of the Congress for Cultural Freedom," in *Towards a New Past: Dissenting Essays in American History*, ed. Barton Bernstein (New York: Pantheon Books, 1969), pp. 322–59. It is interesting, if not terribly relevant to my present argument, to note that Harry Lunn, currently regarded as the biggest photographic dealer in the U.S., was a principal agent in the CIA's infiltration of the National Student Association in the 1950s and 1960s, according to Sol Stern, "NSA and the CIA, A Short Account of International Student Politics and the Cold War," *Ramparts* 5, no. 9 (March 1967): 33.

has shown convincingly that this nongovernmental sponsorship was closely allied with CIA efforts to promote American high culture abroad while circumventing the McCarthyist probings of right-wing congressmen who, for example, saw abstract expressionism as a manifestation of the international communist conspiracy.[31] But since the formal rhetoric of *The Family of Man* was that of photo-journalistic realism, no antagonisms of this sort developed; and although a number of the photographers who contributed pictures to the exhibition were or had been affiliated with left parties or causes, Steichen himself, the grand author of this massive photo essay, was above suspicion. Thus, *The Family of Man* was directly sponsored by the USIA, and openly embraced by the cosponsoring corporations as a valuable marketing and public relations tool. The exhibition was intended to have an immense *popular* appeal, and was more extensively circulated than any other MoMA production. Even medium-sized cities in the United States, Canada, Europe, Australia, Japan, and the Third World received the show. For example, in India alone the exhibition turned up in Bombay, Agra, New Delhi, Ahmedabad, Calcutta, Madras, and Trivandrum. In South Africa *The Family of Man* was shown in Johannesburg, Capetown, Durban, Pretoria, Windhoek (Southwest Africa), Port Elizabeth, and Uitenboge. In domestic showings in New York state alone, the original MoMA exhibit was followed by appearances in Utica, Corning, Rochester, and Binghamton. Shades of American television, but with higher pretensions.

From my reading of the records of foreign showings of *The Family of Man*, it seems clear that the exhibition tended to appear in political "hot spots" throughout the Third World. I quote from a United States Information Agency memo concerning the Djakarta showing in 1962:

> *The exhibition proved to have wide appeal … in spite of the fact that … the period coincided with a circus sponsored by the Soviet Union, complete with a performing bear.*
>
> *The exhibit was opened with a reception to which members of the most important target groups in Djakarta were invited.* [32]

In a more lyrical vein, Steichen recalled the Guatemala City showing in his autobiography, *A Life in Photography*:

> *A notable experience was reported in Guatemala. On the final day of the exhibition, a Sunday, several thousand Indians from the hills of Guatemala came on foot or muleback to see it. An American visitor said it was like a religious experience to see these barefoot country people who could not read or write walk silently through the exhibition gravely studying each picture with rapt attention.*
>
> *Regardless of the place, the response was always the same … the people in the audience looked at the pictures and the people in the pictures looked back at them. They recognized each other.* [33]

At the risk of boring some readers with more statistics, allow me to recall that in 1954, only fourteen months earlier, the United States directly supported a coup in Guatemala, overthrowing the democratically elected government of Jacobo Arbenz, who had received 72 percent of the popular vote in the 1950 elections. American pilots flew bombing missions during the coup. When Arbenz took office, 98 percent of the land in Guatemala was owned by 142 people, with corporations counted as individuals. Arbenz nationalized 200,000 acres of unused United Fruit Company land, agreeing to pay for the land with 25-year bonds, rather than engaging in outright expropriation. In establishing

32. United States Information Agency memo, subject "Djakarta showing of 'Family of Man,'" Feb. 5, 1962. A copy of this memo is in the files of the International Council Office of MoMA.
33. Edward Steichen, *A Life in Photography* (Garden City, NY: Doubleday, 1962).

the terms of payment, the Guatemalan government accepted the United Fruit valuation of the land at $600,000, which had been claimed for tax purposes. Suddenly, United Fruit claimed that the disputed land was worth $16 million, and approached the U.S. State Department for assistance. Secretary of State John Foster Dulles, who was both a United Fruit stockholder and a former legal counsel to the firm, touted the successful invasion and coup as a "new and glorious chapter in the already great tradition of the American States."[34] Following the coup, the U.S.-sponsored dictatorship of Colonel Castillo Armas dismantled agrarian reform and disenfranchised the 70 percent of the population that could, in Steichen's words, "neither read nor write." In this context, "visual literacy" takes on a grim meaning.

Finally, my last exhibit concerning this Cold War extravaganza: a corporate commentary on the showing of *The Family of Man* in Johannesburg, South Africa, in 1958 attempted to link the universalism of the exhibition to the global authority of the commodity.

> *At the entrance of the hall the large globe of the world encircled by bottles of Coca-Cola created a most attractive eye catching display and identified our product with Family of Man sponsorship.*[35]

And thus an orbiting soft drink answered the technological challenge of Sputnik. *The Family of Man* worked to make a bottled mixture of sugar, water, caramel color, and caffeine "humanly interesting" to recall Steichen's expressed ambition for his advertising work of the late 1920s and 1930s. In the political landscape of apartheid, characterized by a brutal racial hierarchy of caloric intakes and forced separation of black African families, sugar and familial sentiment were made to commingle in the imagination.

Clearly, both the sexual and international politics of *The Family of Man* are especially interesting today, in light of the headlong return of American politics to the familialism and interventionism of a new cold war, both domestic and international in scope. *The Family of Man is* a virtual guidebook to the collapse of the political into the familial that so characterizes the dominant ideological discourse of the contemporary United States. In a sense, *The Family of Man* provides a blueprint of sorts for more recent political theater; I am thinking here of the orchestrations of the Vietnam P.O.W. "homecoming" and the return of the American hostages from Iran. However, it would be a mistake not to realize that *The Family of Man* eschewed the bellicosity and racism that accompanies these latter dramas; in this, it represented the limit of an official *liberal* discourse in the Cold War era.[36] The peaceful world envisioned by *The Family of Man* is merely a smoothly functioning international market economy, in which economic bonds have been

34. Department of State White Paper, *Intervention of International Communism In Guatemala*, 1954, p. 33, quoted in David Horowitz, *Free World Colossus* (New York: Hill and Wang, 1965), p. 160. The summary of events in Guatemala here is taken largely from Felix Greene, *The Enemy: Notes on Imperialism and Revolution* (London: Cape, 1970), pp. 196–98, with some references to Horowitz, pp. 160–81.

35. *Coca-Cola Overseas*, December 1958, p. 15.

36. In 1955, the conservative critic Hilton Kramer attacked *The Family of Man* for displaying liberal naiveté in an era of harsh political realities, claiming that the exhibition was "a reassertion in visual terms of all that has been discredited in progressive ideology." Hilton Kramer, "Exhibiting the Family of Man," *Commentary* 20, no. 4 (October 1955).

translated into spurious sentimental ties, and in which the overt racism appropriate to earlier forms of colonial enterprise has been supplanted by the "humanization of the other" so central to the discourse of neocolonialism.[37]

Again, what are we to make of the argument that photography constitutes a universal language? Implicit in this claim is the suggestion that photography acts as a miraculous universal solvent upon the linguistic barriers between peoples. Visual culture, having been pushed to an unprecedented level of technical refinement, loses specificity, cultural difference is cancelled and a "common language" prevails on a global scale. Paradoxically, a medium that is seen as subtly responsive to the most minute details of time and place delivers these details through an unacknowledged, naturalized epistemological grid. As the myth of a universal photographic language would have it, photography is more natural than natural language, touching on a common, underlying system of desire and understanding closely tied to the senses. Photography would seem to be a way of *knowing* the world directly— this is the scientist aspect of our faith in the powers of the photographic image. But photography would also seem to be a way *of feeling* the world directly, with a kind of prelinguistic, affective openness of the visual sense—this is the aestheticist aspect of our faith in the medium. As a symbolic practice, then, photography constitutes not a universal language but a paradoxical yoking of a primitivist, Rousseauian dream, the dream of romantic naturalism, with an unbounded faith in a technological imperative. The worldliness of photography is the outcome, not of any immanent universality of meaning, but of a project of global domination. The language of the imperial centers is imposed, both forcefully and seductively, upon the peripheries.

Universal equivalent

Photography was dreamt of and slowly invented under the shadow of a fading European aristocracy; it became practical and profitable in the period of the continental European revolutions of 1848, the period in which class struggle first took the clear form of an explosive political confrontation between bourgeoisie and urban proletariat waged against the conflict-ridden backdrop of everyday industrial production. Photography proliferated, becoming reproducible and accessible in the modern sense, during the late nineteenth-century period of transition from competitive capitalism to the financially and industrially consolidated monopoly form of capitalist organization. By the turn of the century, then, photography stands ready to play a central role in the development of a culture centered on the mass marketing of mass-produced commodities.

37. For further criticism of *Family of Man* from the political left see Roland Barthes, "The Great Family of Man," in *Mythologies*, trans. Annette Lavers (New York: Hill and Wang, 1972), pp. 100–2. I also found an unpublished English translation of an essay by Edmundo Desnoes, "The Photographic Image of Underdevelopment" (translator unknown) extremely valuable. This essay appeared in Spanish in *Punto de Vista*, Havana, 1967.

Perhaps more than any other single technical invention of the mid-nineteenth century, photography came to focus the confidence and fears of an ascendant industrial bourgeoisie. This essay is an attempt to understand the contradictory role played by photography within the culture dominated by that class. As we have seen briefly and will see again, this role combined a coldly rational scientism with a sentimental and often antirational pursuit of the beautiful.

But my argument here seeks to avoid simple deterministic conclusions: to suggest that the practice of photography is entirely and inseparably bound by capitalist social relations would be reductive and undialectical in the extreme. As a social practice, photography is no more a "reflection" of capitalist society than a particular photograph is a "reflection" of its referential object. Conversely, photography is not a neutral semiotic technique, transparently open to both "reactionary" and "progressive" uses. The issue is much more complicated than either extreme would have us believe. Although I want to argue here that photography is fundamentally related in its normative way of depicting the world to an epistemology and an aesthetics that are intrinsic to a system of commodity exchange, as I have suggested before, photography also needs to be understood as a simultaneous *threat and promise* in its relation to the prevailing cultural ambitions of a triumphant but wary Western bourgeoisie of the mid-nineteenth century. The historical context was one of crisis and paradox; to forget this is to risk achieving an overly harmonized understanding of the contradictory material and symbolic forces at work in the development of bourgeois culture.

John L. Lovell, *Composite of Class of '87, Harvard*, 1887. Gelatin silver print, 3 1/8 in. (7.9 cm) diameter; *Composite Class of Harvard Annex*, 1887. 3 1/8 in. (7.9 cm) diameter. The Hallmark Photographic Collection, Kansas City, Missouri.

With this warning in mind, I would like to turn to an extraordinary text written by the American physician, essayist, and poet, Oliver Wendell Holmes, published in 1859 in the *Atlantic Monthly*. Holmes is in many senses an exemplary, even if unique, figure in nineteenth-century New England culture. Furthermore, he embodies the oscillating movement between scientism and aestheticism that so pervades the discourse of photography. Holmes was both a practical man of science—an advocate of positivism—and a genteel man of letters—the archetypal Boston Brahmin, autocrat, poet, and professor of the breakfast table. He was a founding member of the American Medical Association and, in company with Emerson, Lowell, and Longfellow, a founder of the *Atlantic Monthly*. Characteristically, Holmes's writing veers between surgical metaphors and allusions to the classics. Perhaps there was no American writer who was better prepared, both rhetorically and ideologically, to envelop photography in the web of Culture.

Holmes's essay on "The Stereoscope and the Stereograph" was one of many optimistic early attempts to both philosophize and prognosticate about photography. Significantly, English and American physicians seem to have been prominent in voicing unqualified enthusiasm for the powers of the camera. Holmes, however, goes to hyperbolic extremes. Citing Democritus, he suggests that photography establishes a means of capturing the visual effluvia that are continuously "shed from the surfaces of solids."[38] Arguing, as was common at the time, that photographs are products of the sun's artistry, he coins the phrase "mirror with a memory,"[39] thereby implying that the camera is a wholly passive, reflective, technical apparatus. In this view, nature reproduces itself. Thus, while Holmes casually prefaces his discussion of photography with a mention of the railroad, the telegraph, and chloroform, it would seem that photography constitutes a uniquely privileged technical invention in its refusal or inability to dominate or transform the realm of nature. Photography would seem to offer an inherently preservationist approach to nature. So far, there is nothing in Holmes's argument that is not relatively common to what is by now the thoroughly institutionalized discourse of photographic naturalism.

But the essay takes a rather bizarre turn as Holmes ventures to speculate about the future of photography in a conclusion that seems somewhat prototypical of science fiction, even if entirely deadpan in its apocalyptic humor:

> Form is henceforth divorced from matter. *In fact, matter as a visible object is of no great use any longer, except as the mould on which form is shaped. Give us a few negatives of a thing worth seeing, taken from different*

38. Oliver Wendell Holmes, "The Stereoscope and the Stereograph," *Atlantic Monthly* III, no. 20 (June 1859): 738. My attention was directed to this essay by an insightful article by Harvey Green, "'Pasteboard Masks,' the Stereograph in American Culture, 1865–1910," in *Points of View: The Stereograph in America—A Cultural History*, ed. Edward Earle (Rochester, NY: Visual Studies Workshop, 1979), p.109.
39. Holmes, "Stereoscope," p. 739.

*points of view, and that is all we want of it. Pull it down
or burn it up, if you please.* (emphasis in original).[40]
    Perhaps it is important to interject that Holmes is discussing
the stereograph apparatus, the most effective of nineteenth-century
illusionistic machineries in its ability to reconstruct binocular vision
and thus offer a potent sensation of three-dimensional depth. (Holmes
invented a hand-held stereo viewer, and was an avid collector of
stereo views.)
    Also, like the diorama and the lantern-slide show, the stereo-
scope delivered a total visual experience: immersed within the field of
the illusion, eyes virtually riveted to the sockets of the machine, the
viewer lost all sense of the pasteboard or glass material substrate of

40. Ibid., p. 747.

Lewis W. Hine, *Composite Photograph of Child Laborers Made from Cotton Mill Children*, 1913. Gelatin silver print, 6 5/8 x 4 5/8 in.
(16.8 x 11.7 cm). National Gallery of Canada, purchased 1978.

the image. Despite the slight discomfort of the body that bore the weight of the machine, the experience was one of disembodied vision, vision lacking the illusion-shattering boundary of a frame. Thus, the stereo process was particularly liable to give rise to a belief in dematerialized form.

But would it be absurd for me to suggest that Holmes is describing something analogous to the capitalist exchange process, whereby exchange values are detached from, and exist independently of, the use values of commodities? The dominant metaphor in Holmes's discussion is that of bourgeois political economy; just as use value is eclipsed by exchange value, so the photographic sign comes to eclipse its referent. For Holmes, quite explicitly, the photograph is akin to money. The parallel with political economy becomes even more apparent as Holmes continues:

> Matter in large masses must always be fixed and dear;
> form is cheap and transportable. We have got hold of
> the fruit of creation now, and need not trouble ourselves
> with the core. Every conceivable object of Nature and
> Art will soon scale off its surface for us.[41]

But we are not talking simply about a global political economy of signs, we are also invited to imagine an epistemological treasure trove, an encyclopedia organized according to a global hierarchy of knowledge and power. Diderot's ghost animates Holmes's Yankee enthusiasm:

> The time will come when a man who wishes to see
> any object, natural or artificial, will go to the Imperial,

41. Ibid., p. 748.

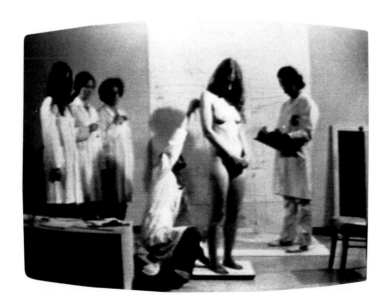

Martha Rosler, Still from *Vital Statistics of a Citizen, Simply Obtained*, 1977. Video, 40 minutes. Courtesy of the artist and Video Data Bank, Chicago.

*National, or City Stereographic Library and call for its skin
or form, as he would for a book at any common library.*[42]

How prophetic and typical that an American, writing in an aggressively expanding republic, should invoke the fictitious authority of empire in his vision of the future. Finally, Holmes gets down to brass tacks:

*Already a workman has been traveling about the country
with stereographic views of furniture, showing his employer's patterns in this way, and taking orders for them. This
is a mere hint of what is coming before long.*[43]

(In fact, by 1850, traveling clock salesmen are known to have carried boxes of daguerreotypes illustrating their line of products.) Holmes's vision of an expanded system of photographic advertising leads to a direct appeal for an expanded economy of images:

*And as a means of facilitating the formation of public
and private stereographic collections, there must be
arranged a comprehensive system of exchanges, so
that there might grow up something like a universal
currency of these banknotes, on promises to pay in
solid substance, which the sun has engraved for the
great Bank of Nature.*[44]

Note that Holmes, true to the logic of commodity fetishism, finds the origin of this money-like aspect of the photograph, not in human labor, but in a direct "miraculous" agency of Nature. Recall Marx's crucial definition of the commodity fetish, first published in 1867, in the first volume of *Capital:*

*… the definite social relation between men themselves
… assumes here, for them, the fantastic form of a relation
between things. In order, therefore, to find an analogy we
must take flight into the misty realm of religion. There
the products of the human brain appear as autonomous
figures endowed with a life of their own, which enter into
relations both with each other and with the human race.
So it is in the world of commodities with the products
of men's hands. I call this the fetishism which attaches
itself to the products of labour as soon as they are
produced as commodities, and is therefore inseparable
from the production of commodities.*[45]

For Holmes, photographs stand as the "universal equivalent," capable of denoting the quantitative exchangeability of all sights. Just as money is the universal gauge of exchange value, uniting all the world goods in a single system of transactions, so photographs are imagined to reduce all sights to relations of formal equivalence. Here, I think, lies one major aspect of the origins of the pervasive formalism

42. Ibid., p. 748.
43. Ibid., p. 748.
44. Ibid., p. 748.
45. Karl Marx, *Capital*, Vol. I, trans. Ben Fowkes (New York: Vintage Books, 1977), p. 165.

Bharat Sikka, *Anurag*, 2002. Chromogenic print, 32 1/2 x 42 1/2 in. (82.5 x 108 cm). Courtesy of Riva Gallery, New York.

that haunts the visual arts of the bourgeois epoch. Formalism collects all the world's images in a single aesthetic emporium, torn from all contingencies of origin, meaning, and use. Holmes is dreaming of this transcendental aesthetic closure, while also entertaining a pragmatic faith in the photograph as a transparent gauge of the real. Like money, the photograph is both a fetishized end in itself and a calibrated signifier of a value that resides elsewhere, both autonomous and bound to its referential function:

> To render comparison of similar objects, or of any that we may wish to see side by side, easy, there should be a stereographic metre or fixed standard of focal length for the camera lens…. In this way the eye can make the most rapid and exact comparisons. If the "great elm" and Cowthorpe Oak, the State-House and Saint Peter's were taken on the same scale, and looked at with the same magnifying power, we should compare them without the possibility of being misled by those partialities which might make us tend to overrate the indigenous vegetable and the dome of our native Michel Angelo.[46]

In what may be a typically American fashion, Holmes seems to be confusing quantity with quality, even in modestly suggesting the inferiorities of the American natural and architectural landscape. More generally, Holmes shares the pervasive faith in the mathematical truth of the camera.

Oliver Wendell Holmes, like most other promoters of photography, manages to establish a false discursive unity; shifting schizophrenically from instrumentalism to aestheticism, from Yankee pragmatism and empiricism to a rather loose romanticism, thus recalling that other related incongruity, Ralph Waldo Emerson's linkage of the "natural fact" and the "spiritual fact."[47] The ideological custodians of photography are forced to periodically switch hats, to move from positivist to metaphysician with the turn of a phrase. It is the metaphysician who respiritualizes the rationalized project of photographic representation. Thus, Holmes in a later essay on photography, speaks of carte-de-visite portraits as "the sentimental 'greenbacks' of civilization."[48] All of this is evidence of a society in which economic relations appear, as Marx put it, "as material relations between persons and social relations between things."[49] Holmes ends his first essay with an appropriately idealist inversion of the Promethean myth:

> … a new epoch in the history of human progress dates from the time when He … took a pencil of fire from the hand of the "angel standing in the sun" and placed it in the hands of a mortal.[50]

46. Holmes, "Stereoscope," p. 748.
47. Ralph Waldo Emerson, "Nature" (1844), *The Collected Works of Ralph Waldo Emerson, Vol. 1* (Cambridge, Mass.: Belknap Press, 1971), p. 18.
48. Oliver Wendell Holmes, "Doings of the Sunbeam," *Atlantic Monthly* 13, no. 49 (July 1863): 8.
49. Marx, *Capital*, p. 166.
50. Holmes, "Stereoscope," p. 748.

So much for bourgeois humanism: Prometheus is no longer an arrogant rebel but a grateful recipient of divine favors. And so technical progress is reconciled with theology. Photography, as it was thus conceived in mid-nineteenth-century America, was the vocation of pious accountants.

Conclusion

A final concluding anecdote to end this essay, much too long already. Crossing the cavernous main floor of New York's Grand Central Station recently, I looked up to see the latest installment in a thirty-odd-year exhibition of monumental, back-illuminated dye-transfer transparencies; a picture, taken low to the wet earth of rural Ireland, a lush vegetable apparition of landscape and cottage, suspended above this gloomy urban terminal for human traffic. With this image—seemingly bigger and more illusionistic, even in its stillness, than Cinerama—everything that is absent is made present. Above—stillness, home, hearth, the soil, the remote old country for many travelers, an affordable or unaffordable vacation spot for others, a seductive sight for eyes that must strain hurriedly in the gloom to read timetables. Below—the city, a site for the purposeful flow of bodies. Accompanying this giant photograph, a caption reads, as nearly as I can remember:

PHOTOGRAPHY: THE UNIVERSAL LANGUAGE
EASTMAN KODAK 1880–1980

And what of the universality of this name, Kodak, unknown to any language until coined in 1888 by George Eastman, inventor of roll film, pioneer in horizontal and vertical corporate integration, in the global mass-marketing of consumer goods? Eastman offered this etymological explanation in 1924, in *American Photography:*

> *Philologically, therefore, the word "Kodak" is as meaningless as a child's first "goo." Terse, abrupt to the point of rudeness, literally bitten off by firm unyielding consonants at both ends, it snaps like a camera shutter in your face. What more could one ask?*[51]

And so we are introduced to a "language" that is primitive, infantile, aggressive—the imaginary discourse of the machine. The crucial question remains to be asked: can photography be anything else?

51. Eastman, quoted in Eder, *History of Photography*, p. 489.

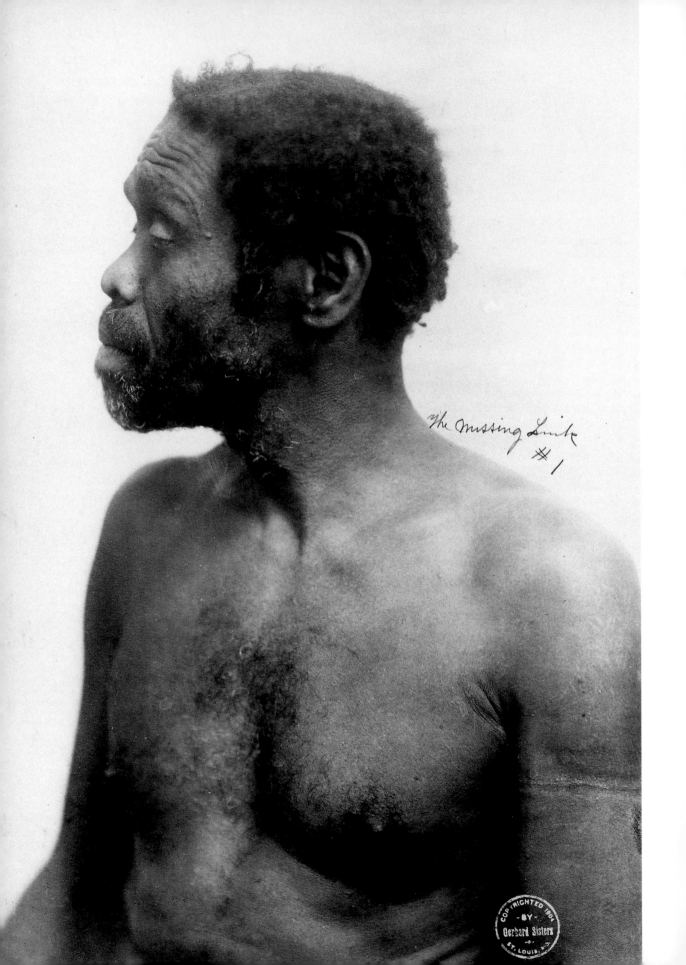

The missing Link
#1

Nicholas Mirzoeff

THE SHADOW AND THE SUBSTANCE

Race, Photography, and the Index

My thanks to Coco Fusco and Brian Wallis for inviting me to be involved with *Only Skin Deep*; to the Sterling and Francine Clark Art Institute whose Visiting Scholarship award facilitated the writing of this essay; and to Geoffrey Batchen, Darby English, and Kathleen Wilson for their generous help in improving it.

1. According to Peirce, "An *index* is a sign which would, at once, lose the character which makes it a sign if its object were removed, but would not lose that character if there were no interpretant. Such, for example, is a piece of mould with a bullet-hole in it as a sign of a shot; for without the shot there would have been no hole; but there is a hole there, whether anybody has the sense to attribute it to a shot or not," Charles Sanders Peirce, quoted by Mieke Bal and Norman Bryson, "Semiotics and Art History," *Art Bulletin* 73, no. 2 (June 1991): 189.
2. John Tagg, *The Burden of Representation* (London: Macmillan, 1988), p. 63. This notion was endorsed recently by Elizabeth Edwards, *Raw Histories: Photographs, Anthropology and Museums* (Oxford and New York: Berg, 2001), p. 11.

Writing about "race" and photography is a paradoxical endeavor. A clear scientific consensus exists that there are no biological grounds to distinguish human beings into separate "races" (hence the quotation marks which I will assume for the remainder of this discussion). Nonetheless, the social practices of slavery, segregation, and racism have made race a social fact in the United States. The photograph, marked as it is by that which actually was in front of the lens at the time of exposure, is held to be a directly indexical medium. As derived from the work of Charles Sanders Peirce, the index is a sign that designates a truly existing thing (in commonsense terms) in the way that a bullet-hole indicates the passing of a bullet.[1] At the same time, in the influential opinion of John Tagg, "photography has no identity. Its status as technology varies in the power relations that invest it."[2] In this dialectical view, the photograph is a screen upon which wider social forces become visible. Racism thus exists and photography makes it visible. But it is a process in which a "nothing" is made visible by something that does not exist.

Racism itself has been intensely ambivalent about the place of skin or other physical features in determining race. Numerous accounts argue that while these signs may be important, what matters is the internal quality of difference that may be as effectively concealed as revealed by external appearance. Even in overtly racist discourse, race flickers in and out of sight, frustrating efforts to refute it by refusing a stable definition. Caught between the desire to assert the obvious— that race is what is visibly different—and the impossibility of sustaining such a position in the face of the always-mixed population of the United States, discourses on race came to rely heavily on photographic representation.

The photograph became a prime locus of the performance of the racialized index. By performance, I mean to suggest something that is constituted each time it is enacted and that may vary according to circumstance. As race is not an indisputable fact, the index here is posed as a question of the racial difference in which all citizens of the United States are skilled readers. Each time a photograph is looked at, a viewer consciously or unconsciously decides whether and how it indexes the race of its object. When the editors of *Time* magazine darkened the skin tone on a cover photograph of O. J. Simpson in June 1994, readers everywhere recognized both the nature of the alteration and the intended racialized connotation that a person of darker skin is more likely to be a criminal. As Allan Sekula has argued, there is a certain "shadow archive" against which such judgments are made,

Gerhard Sisters, *The Missing Link No. 1 (Photograph of Indigenous Filipino from St. Louis Fair)*, 1904. Gelatin silver print, 20 1/2 x 11 3/4 in. (52 x 29.8 cm). Library of Congress, Washington D.C.

consciously or unconsciously.[3] In this essay, I want to argue that this indexicality of race in the United States was created in the paradoxically modern and segregated society that emerged after the abolition of slavery in 1863. Photography had already existed for a quarter-century (a sixth of its lifetime to date) by this time and in the United States had generated its own peculiar racialization to which the archived, indexical photograph of the 1880s and 1890s was a powerful and dangerous supplement. This new indexicality was part of a wider move to exhibit difference of all kinds at fairs, sideshows, cinemas, and so on that created and sustained a desire to see racially. As that culture of amusement has been replaced by mass media, photography has an opportunity to reinvent itself that paradoxically has been enabled by the rise of digital media. It may be that contemporary artists are now in the best position to make the indexicality of race incoherent.

Photography in the Atlantic World

Neither race nor photography can be conceived solely in a national context. Both arose from the world created by Atlantic slavery, the violent interplay of cultures and peoples from Africa, Europe, and the Americas. In the early nineteenth century, the Atlantic world was the scene of abolition, enslavement, and emancipation in different localities. As this historic drama unfolded, repeated efforts were being made by at least twenty-five people around the world to create a light-sensitive image-generating process, until William Henry Fox Talbot (1800–1877) and Louis Daguerre (1787–1851) announced their success in 1839.[4] The tensions at stake become clear when we consider the very different pioneers of photography on either side of the Atlantic. In Britain, Thomas Wedgwood (1771–1805) was the son of the famous potter Josiah Wedgwood, and shared his father's abolitionist sentiments. These were expressed in the famous Wedgwood medallion "Am I Not a Man and a Brother?" that became one of the leading images of the abolition movement. His experiments with light-sensitive copying in 1802 were all a part of a life that included associations with political radicals like William Godwin. In a similar vein, Talbot, the legendary pioneer of British photography, was a Reform member of Parliament in 1832 and voted for the emancipation of slaves in the British Empire. In the Americas, matters were necessarily different. The French artist Hercules Florence (1801–1878) was the first man to use the term "photography," in 1833. Florence settled in Campinas, now part of São Paolo, Brazil, a district of slave-run coffee plantations. According to his own account, in "1832, on August 15, while strolling on my verandah, an idea came to me that perhaps it is possible to capture images in a *camera obscura* by means of a substance which changes color through

3. Allan Sekula, "The Body and the Archive," *October*, no. 39 (Winter 1986).
4. See Geoffrey Batchen, *Burning With Desire: The Conception of Photography* (Cambridge, Mass. and London: MIT Press, 1997).

the action of light....I captured a negative view of the jailhouse."[5] His verandah would have given a view of a world created and sustained by slavery and the jail would have housed runaways and otherwise disobedient slaves. In the United States, the best-known experimenter with photographic processes was Samuel F. B. Morse, the painter and later inventor of the famous telegraph code that bears his name. Morse experimented with silver nitrate in New Haven, probably in 1821, but once he succeeded in generating what we would now call a negative image, he abandoned his researches.[6] Sadly, Morse was also a convinced advocate of slavery, based on his constantly reasserted opinion that it was no sin but rather "a social condition ordained from the beginning of the world for the wisest purposes, benevolent and disciplinary by Divine Wisdom."[7]

In these circumstances, it is no surprise that the slave-owning United States received photography very differently than its European counterparts. The identity of photography was unclear at first.

5. Quoted in Boris Kossoy, "Hercules Florence, Pioneer of Photography in Brazil," *Image*, 20, no. 1 (1977): 12–21.
6. Batchen, *Burning With Desire*, p. 41.
7. Quoted in *Samuel F. B. Morse: Letters and Journals*, ed. Edward Lind Morse (New York: Da Capo Press, [1914] 1973), vol. 2, p. 331.

Charles Eisenmann, *Microcephalics: Maximo and Bartola—Aztecs of Ancient Mexico*, ca. 1880. Cabinet card, 6 1/2 x 4 1/2 in. (15.9 x 10.8 cm). Syracuse University Library, Syracuse, New York, Becker Collection.

Whereas Talbot was prone to refer to his process as "natural magic," his colleague David Brewster called it the "black art" as early as February 1839.[8] By March, *The Spectator* was calling it "necromancy,"[9] giving a racialized affect to the question that was no idle matter in the slave economy, where magic and poison were the constant fears of the planter. In the United States, the question was prominent in the very first reports of photography's existence, such as *The New Yorker*'s account of April 13, 1839:

> *Wonderful wonder of wonders!! Steel engravers, copper engravers, and etchers, drink up your aquafortis and die! There is an end of your black art—"Othello's occupation is no more." The real black art of true magic arises and cries avaunt. All nature shall paint herself.*[10]

The black arts of engraving and etching (in part a pun on black-and-white images) no longer had enough power to resist the "true black art" of photography. This magical transformation is explicitly racialized with the quotation taken from Shakespeare's drama of the African soldier Othello[11] at the very moment when he discovers Desdemona's apparent infidelity in the form of the infamous handkerchief, proffered to him by Iago, and declares "Othello's occupation's gone"—*The New Yorker* writer misquoted. In the play, Othello follows his lament with a demand that Iago provide "the ocular proof" that so many private investigators would later offer suspicious spouses in the form of photographs. This quotation from Shakespeare suggested far more than a simple transposition of reproductive technologies from engraving to photography. It set in play an ambiguous range of dangerous ideas from the foundational Western drama of cross-ethnic relationships—the specter of miscegenation that haunted and haunts the United States—to emancipation, performance, betrayal, and deception.

Slavery and after

American photography was characterized in its first thirty years by the peculiar longevity and prominence of daguerreotypy. One then-obscure example of daguerreotypy has now taken a prominent role in the history of African Americans and enslavement. In 1850, the Swiss scientist Louis Agassiz (1807–1873) employed a daguerreotyper named Joseph T. Zealy to take a series of plates of enslaved Africans in South Carolina. Stored in the Peabody Museum at Harvard for over a century, their accidental rediscovery in 1975 led to their becoming some of the best-known images of slavery.[12] As Brian Wallis has shown, Agassiz was engaged in attempting to find evidence for his controversial thesis of polygenesis, that is to say, the idea of entirely separate human

8. David Brewster to Talbot, 12 February 1839, in *Selected Correspondence of William Henry Fox Talbot 1823–1874*, ed. Larry J. Schaaf (London: Science Museum and National Museum of Photography, Film and Television, 1994), p. 18.

9. Batchen, *Burning With Desire*, p. 92.

10. "New Discovery in the Fine Arts," *The New Yorker*, April 13, 1839, reprinted in *Secrets of the Dark Chamber: The Art of the American Daguerreotype*, ed. Merry A. Foresta and John Wood (Washington, DC: National Museum of American Art, Smithsonian Institution Press, 1995), p. 223.

11. Enslaved Africans were often given such names as Shakespeare in the United States; see Susie King Taylor, *Reminiscences of My Life in Camp* (Boston, 1902), reprinted in *Collected Black Women's Narratives* (New York and Oxford, 1988), p. 2.

12. For an account of their rediscovery and the detective work required to identify them, see Melissa Banta, *A Curious & Ingenious Art: Reflections on Daguerreotypes at Harvard* (Iowa City: University of Iowa Press, 2000), pp. 43–52.

races. He had photographs taken of what he took to be the dominant African racial groups, such as a man called Renty who was photographed to depict the Congo. By Congo, slavers meant a vast area incorporating modern Congo, Angola, and the Congo Republic, all of which in fact contained a wide array of languages and cultural groups. In many of the plates, such as those of Drana, Delia, Fassena, and Renty, Agassiz's desire to see the half-naked body was fulfilled but the clothes worn by the enslaved men and women are still visible. In the cases of Drana and Delia, we can see that the women were wearing quite elaborate print dresses. The half-on, half-off dresses highlight the absurdity of the project and, taken together with the apparent "refusal to engage with the camera or its operator" noted by Wallis, contribute to the failure of the daguerreotypes to signify what Agassiz had hoped to show.[13] That is to say, these images fail to perform race in a satisfactory manner, which perhaps contributed to their being forgotten even by subsequent race science. As a series, they constitute an attempt to call a mode of identification into being that was

13. Brian Wallis, "Black Bodies, White Science: Louis Agassiz's Slave Daguerreotypes," *American Art* 9, no. 2 (Summer 1995). In this volume, p. 165.

Mathew B. Brady, *William Henry Johnson (Zip the Pinhead)*, ca. 1872. Modern gelatin silver print from original wet-plate collodion negative, 3 9/16 x 2 3/8 in. (9 x 6.1 cm). National Portrait Gallery, Smithsonian Insititution, Washington D.C., Courtesy of Art Resource.
Unidentified photographer, *Ku Klux Klansman*, 1869. Tintype, 3 1/4 x 1 7/8 in. (8.1 x 4.9 cm). Gilman Paper Company Collection, New York.

EMANCIPATED SLAVES BROUGHT FROM LOUISIANA BY COL. GEORGE H. HANKS.

The Children are from the Schools established by order of Maj. Gen. Banks.

WILSON CHINN.   MARY JOHNSON.   ROBERT WHITEHEAD.

CHAS. TAYLOR. AUGUSTA BROUJEY.   ISAAC WHITE. REBECCA HUGER.   ROSINA DOWNS.

Entered according to Act of Congress, in the year 1863, by GEO. H. HANKS, in the Clerk's Office of the United States for the Southern District of New-York.

Photographed by M. H. Kimball, 477 Broadway.

unsuccessful, precisely because their very insistence on one single idea could not be visually or intellectually sustained.

Agassiz insisted on the inferiority of Africans while opposing slavery, a position that strains credulity in modern eyes. Yet in that period, such apparent inconsistency was the means by which the system of social and ethnic distinction that supported first slavery and then segregation became possible. Abolitionists circulated a photograph known as *The Scourged Back* (1863) that depicted a half-naked African man, whose horribly scarred back is turned to the camera. It was intended to highlight the evils of enforced labor and human bondage, made visible as the scars of whipping(s) inflicted by a cruel slave-owner. In the plantation world-view, *The Scourged Back* was simply evidence of a crime committed and properly punished. The wider point to be drawn, in this view, was the irrepressible malfeasance of Africans, who, therefore, could only be controlled by force.[14] In two key sets of photographs from the moment of abolition these tensions became fully visible. After Union forces took New Orleans in 1863, schools were established for African American children, often for the

14. See Kenneth S. Greenberg's remarkable book, *Honor and Slavery: Lies, Duels, Noses, Masks, Dressing as a Woman, Gifts, Strangers, Humanitarianism, Death, Slave Rebellions, The Pro-Slavery Argument, Baseball, Hunting and Gambling in the Old South* (Princeton: Princeton University Press, 1996), p. 15.

Myron H. Kimball, *Emancipated Slaves*, 1863. Albumen print, 5 1/4 x 7 1/4 in. (13.2 x 18.3 cm). Gilman Paper Company Collection, New York.

Learning is Wealth.

first time. As funds to support the project were low, a series of photographs, such as M.H. Kimball's *Emancipated Slaves* (1863), were created for sale. In an oval frame, two rows of people face the camera directly. In front are five children, four seeming to be "white" (namely Charles Taylor, Augusta Broujey, Rebecca Huger, and Rosina Downs) standing on either side of a "black" child, Isaac White.[15] The children are smartly dressed, carefully disposing their hands so as not to create a blur for the camera. Behind them stand three adults, whose dark skin and servants' clothing leaves no apparent doubt as to their African American origins. Wilson Chinn, standing on the left, had several letters branded into his forehead as a mark of being chattel. As he was branded in a place that could not be concealed, he may very well have been an apprehended runaway. No such visible marks appear on the four white children in the front row. The selling point and scandal of the photograph was precisely the fact that all the children, by virtue of their status as former slaves, were African American. The very whiteness of the children's skin was the sign that they had no place in slavery. Slavery was to be abolished, then, not only because it was violent and inherently immoral, but because the "wrong" kind of people were being enslaved. The older enslaved people shown in these photographs were all dark-skinned, whereas dark-skinned children only appeared as a minority, and many photographs showed just the light-skinned children. These compositions were designed to tell a story of rampant miscegenation by the Southern planters, creating an emergent generation of slaves that was more white than not. Reinforced by abolitionist newspapers and slave narratives, these photographs present slavery as a scandal of miscegenation, rape, and violence, without needing to address the fundamental issues of owning people as property or distinguishing people into distinct races.

These pictures can be contrasted with the cartes de visite sold by the abolitionist Sojourner Truth to fund her activities.[16] In these carefully posed images, Truth sought to counter the ambivalence of earlier abolitionist photography with a series of well-chosen signs. Dressed in respectable middle-class attire, Truth posed as if caught in the middle of knitting. Her gender-appropriate (in view of the period) activity and dress allowed her to signify her engagement with ideas and learning, shown by her glasses and the open book. The caption that she provided for the cards showed her awareness of the ambivalences of photography: "I sell the shadow to support the substance." Here the emancipated woman makes her image the object of financial exchange in place of the substance, her whole person, which had once been for sale. It indexes freedom rather than question whether we see race. Her recommodification of her "shadow" was justified by its substantive use

15. See Kathleen Collins, "Portraits of Slave Children," *History of Photography* 9, no. 3 (July–Sept. 1985): 187–207.
16. See Nell Painter, *Sojourner Truth: A Life, A Symbol* (New York: W. W. Norton, 1996).

Charles Paxton, *Learning is Wealth, Wilson, Charley, Rebecca and Rosa, Slaves from New Orleans*, 1864. Carte-de-visite, 4 x 2 ⁷/₁₆ in. (10.1 x 16.2 cm). International Center of Photography, Daniel Cowin Collection, 1990.

in campaigning for the abolition of the ownership of people. Following the antebellum use of daguerreotypy as a means of documenting African American freedom, Truth's use of photography shows that another "shadow archive" was possible. By insisting on her control over the financial process, Truth further asserted a freedom to dispose of her own image that the "emancipated slaves" did not possess. As Kenneth S. Greenberg argues, "an emancipation that assumed the form of a gift from the master could only be partial,"[17] leading W. E. B. DuBois to later insist that the enslaved had freed themselves. Truth made her shadow claim the substance of freedom, even beyond her person.

Exhibiting the index

At the end of the Civil War, the white Army colonel C. T. Trowbridge told his African American troops of the South Carolina Volunteers: "The prejudices which formerly existed against you are well-nigh rooted out."[18] But the 1875 Civil Rights Act that had offered some legal protections to back up such assurances was overturned by the Supreme Court in 1883, beginning a process known in the South as Redemption.[19] By 1896 with the prosegregation verdict in *Plessy v. Ferguson*, a profound separation of African Americans and whites had been enshrined in law and custom, creating what W. E. B. DuBois later famously called the "color line" in American life. Newly invested with an aura of scientific respectability, racism came to be a modern spectacle, enabled by visual technologies such as the camera. From the 1870s onward, anthropology renewed its engagement with photography as a key means of classifying human difference into distinct races. These visual classifications of race "science," unseen by most people, were enacted in public at fairs, sideshows, cinemas, World's Fairs, museums, zoos, and theaters. Timothy Mitchell has called this moment the "exhibitionary order," in which reality itself came to be "organized and grasped as though it were an exhibition."[20] The idea of indexicality was itself the subject of display, especially in "freak" shows. P. T. Barnum, the king of the fairs, offered Americans his "What Is It?" exhibitions on either side of the Civil War, featuring William Johnson, an African American, as an exhibit under the category "nondescript."[21] While such "intercultural performances," to use Coco Fusco's term, have a long history, the late nineteenth century enshrined them as part of a classificatory and visualized system of knowledge. These exhibits and the resulting photographs created and sustained a desire to understand people in terms of a racialized hierarchy. For the spectator, being in a place to make these abstract determinations was a mark of citizenship and reason that the object of display inevitably lacked.[22]

17. Greenberg, *Honor and Slavery*, p. 66.
18. Lt. Col. C. T. Trowbridge, 9 February 1866, quoted by Susie King Taylor, *Reminiscences*, p. 48.
19. Philip Dray, *At the Hands of Persons Unknown: The Lynching of Black America* (New York: Random House, 2002), pp. 56–57, 109–14.
20. Timothy Mitchell, "Orientalism and the Exhibitionary Order," in *Colonialism and Culture*, ed. Nicholas Dirks (Ann Arbor: University of Michigan Press, 1992), p. 296.
21. James W. Cook Jr., "Of Men, Missing Links, and Nondescripts: The Strange Career of P. T. Barnum's 'What Is It?' Exhibition," in *Freakery: Cultural Spectacles of the Extraordinary Body*, ed. Rosemarie Garland Thomson (New York: NYU Press, 1996).
22. See Dipesh Chakrabarty, "Museums in Late Democracies," *Humanities Research*, no. 1 (2002): 5–12.

The World's Fairs and other such international arenas of display were central locations of this new means of indexing the real. At events across Europe and the United States, new inventions, trade goods, and art displays mingled with recreations of colonized nations and their way of life, often with inhabitants of those countries displayed as living exhibits. These fairs were at once the place in which the Western classifications of cultural and racial hierarchies of difference were made visible—hence the object of extensive photography in themselves—and the model for Western visual constructions of their others. The sense of difference and distinction was heightened for white spectators because, in the North as well as the South, African Americans were excluded from these new amusements.[23] Photography became a key medium for this refashioning of the world. I want to trace one of these complex threads to show that the effects of

23. David Nasaw, *Going Out: The Rise and Fall of Public Amusements* (New York: Basic Books, 1993), pp. 72–79, 92–94; Grace Elizabeth Hale, *Making Whiteness: The Culture of Segregation in the South, 1890–1940* (New York: Pantheon Books, 1998), pp. 203–9.

Marlon Fuentes, Film still from *Bontoc Eulogy*, 1995. Gelatin silver print. Courtesy of the artist and the Cinema Guild, Inc., New York.

American constructions of racial difference were not limited to national boundaries. Following Henry Morton Stanley's exploration of the Congo River in the 1870s, Camille Coquilhat, one of his junior officers, became governor of an up-river province after the Belgian annexation of the Congo in 1885. In his travel narrative, Coquilhat provided an extensive description of what he called a human sacrifice by "Pygmies" (perhaps Mbuti people) in the region, illustrated with a dramatic print made by a Belgian artist. As there are no other sources to support this belief, it is most likely that Coquilhat had witnessed an execution ordered by the notoriously cruel Belgian mercenary forces. Nonetheless, this incident passed into anthropological lore as a feature of forest-dwellers' lives and was staged on a daily basis for visitors to the St. Louis World's Fair of 1904. There it was photographed and dis-tributed around the world as evidence of African primitivism. Another feature of the St. Louis fair was the Philippine exhibit, resulting from the 1898 annexation of the islands by the United States. Among the various displays performed by the indigenous Filipinos was one of war-riors lined up in a threatening pose, with bows and arrows ready to fire. This unlikely military posture was taken as scientific fact by many who witnessed the displays and the resulting photographs, leading the American anthropologist Herbert Lang to stage identical photographs during his 1909–14 field trip to the Belgian Congo. These photographs were then published in the *Journal of the American Museum of Natural History*, where together with ten thousand unpublished photographs that Lang deposited with the museum, they remained unseen by the vast majority of people. These images and many others like them came to constitute the "shadow archive" of photography as it pertained to indexing race in the United States. Its origins as a copy of a copy were quickly lost amid the welter of academic papers, statistics, and material gathered in the field. Its effectiveness was marked by the routine performance of the indexicality of race in everyday life.

The hooded archive

This shadow archive was itself sustained and guaranteed by the existence of what I call the "hooded archive" of lynching photographs. Slavery had been an economic institution dependent on biological reproduction; one of the peculiarities of slavery in the United States was that its population was self-sustaining, unlike the plantation economies of the Caribbean and Brazil. Lynching as biological extinc-tion was dependent on the mechanical reproduction of the photograph to achieve its fullest effect. While lynching existed under slavery and came to prominence during Reconstruction (1865–77), photography enabled the spectacular modern lynching (1878–1951). The extended

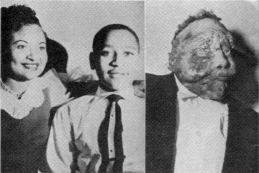

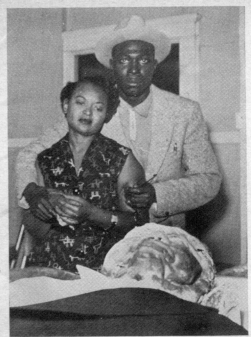

Negroes Often Lynched For Crimes Of Guilty Whites

intentionally ignored. So much so that the nearly 300 Negroes murdered in the romantic Magnolia State (documented by Ginzburg, between 1893 and the 1959 lynching of Mack Charles Parker) must represent no more of the real total number of victims than the visible portion of an iceberg represents the lurking danger of the bigger part under water.

There are true and thoroughly documented stories of Negroes lynched for white men's crimes, with the guilty whites, desperately seeking to dispel guilt feelings, often leading the blood-thirsty mobs. Negroes were lynched for marrying white women, or just on the word of the lowest white prostitute that she had been "insulted." Negro mothers and wives were raped and lynched when mobs were unable to locate their sons and husbands, and Ne-

Fished from river Emmett Till (l), 15, was blood-curdling sight. His alleged crime: whistling at Delta white woman.

8

Just like many mothers before her, choked, hurt Mrs. Mamie Bradley viewed gory features of son, Emmett, for last time.

9

torture and murder by fire or hanging that became a ritualized practice of the lynch mob manifested a desire to make the deviance of the racially segregated other visible. The victim's flesh would be plied with corkscrews, irons, and tongs in search of this impossible discovery that would be replaced by the coerced confession of the victim. At the same time, lynching created what Michael Hatt has called a "unified constituency of whiteness" that set aside the fragmenting consequences of modernity in the face of what seemed to be a single, identifiable enemy.[24] Even as lynching created such a terror for African Americans that, in the words of Richard Wright, "I was compelled to give my entire imagination over to it," it was perversely pleasurable for its white audience. The recent and remarkable exhibition of lynching photographs distributed as postcards, *Without Sanctuary*, highlighted DuBois's insight that "Negro baiting and even lynching became a form of amusement,"[25] that existed, like other amusements, to be photographed. Indeed, the culture of spectacular lynching took hold immediately following the invention of easy-to-use Kodak cameras in 1888. The resulting photographs ensured that race would remain indexical in modern American consumer culture.

24. Michael Hatt, "Race, Ritual and Responsibility: Performativity and the Southern Lynching," in *Performing The Body/Performing the Text*, ed. Amelia Jones and Andrew Stephenson (London: Routledge, 1999), p. 80.
25. DuBois, 1925, quoted by Hale, *Making Whiteness*, p. 199.

Ernest C. Withers, *Special Issue: Mississippi*, 1955. *Jet* magazine interior. International Center of Photography, Museum Purchase Fund, 2002

One of the first spectacular lynchings to incorporate the widespread public distribution of photographs was that of Ami "Whit" Ketchum and Luther H. Mitchell on December 10, 1878, in Custer County, Nebraska, where they had sought to become homesteaders, a crime in the eyes of the lynch mob. A photographic "artist" named H. M. Hatch made stereograph slides of their immolated bodies available for thirty-five cents or three dollars a dozen.[26] By the time a crowd of 15,000—conveyed to the site by special trains—saw Jesse Washington lynched in the self-declared modern city of Waco, Texas, in 1916, a photographer named Fred A. Gildersleeve had set his camera up before the fire was even lit.[27] His pictures of the burning of Washington's body and the dragging of the corpse through the city were sold at ten cents each; Washington's body parts changed hands for five dollars or more. Gildersleeve's photographs were also obtained by Elizabeth Freeman of the NAACP and were published as a cover picture and eight-page supplement in their magazine *The Crisis*.[28] Even as these photographs and many others like them ensured that lynching was a national and international scandal, their distribution perversely fulfilled the desire of the mob that their violence be seen. When Thomas Brookes was lynched in Tennessee in 1915, *The Crisis* reported: "Hundreds of Kodaks clicked all morning at the scene of the lynching."[29] This apparent free-dom to photograph was itself exercised under the threat of lynching. In 1956, the "head lady" of Choctaw County, Alabama, responded to Gordon Parks's *Life* magazine series "Background of Segregation" by saying to reporters, "If we'da got that nigger who took them pictures we'da tarred and feathered him and set him to fire."[30] Only a certain view of race could be photographed under lynch law.

At the core of the lynch mob's practice was an unbound desire in all its polymorphously perverse forms, a desire that wanted to perform its racialized vision without restraint. Lynching was very often justified as a reprisal for an alleged rape that rarely had any basis in fact. Or more exactly, sexual contact across the racialized divide, when it existed, was usually consensual. The phantasmatic intransigence of the color line, upheld in *Plessy*, was enacted as a gendered divide between black men and white women that was never to be questioned. Other unacknowledged desires were in play as well. The ritual of lynching almost always included the severing of the victim's penis that was often displayed to the crowd. The standardized account would often include a mention of the victim's "wild, superhuman energy" to quote a newspaper account of the lynching of Sam Hose in 1899.[31] This fasci-nation with the supposed hypermasculinity of African American men, itself evidence of their deviance, speaks to a repressed homosocial and even homoerotic desire that found its outlet through spectacular violence. No doubt this violence was in part a defense against

26. James Allen, Hilton Als, Congress-man John Lewis, and Leon F. Litwack, *Without Sanctuary: Lynching Photography in America* (Santa Fe, NM: Twin Palms Publishers, 2000), figs. 69 and 70.
27. Hale, *Making Whiteness*, p. 218.
28. Dray, *At the Hands of Persons Unknown*, pp. 214–19.
29. Leon F. Litwack, "Hellhounds," in *Without Sanctuary*, p. 11.
30. Quoted by Elizabeth Abel, "Bathroom Doors and Drinking Fountains: Jim Crow's Racial Symbolic," *Critical Inquiry* 25 (Spring 1999): p. 443.
31. Hale, *Making Whiteness*, p. 213.

recognizing certain truths about the circulation of desire across and adjacent to the color line that could not be entertained. Instead the "amusement" of lynching inescapably arose in all thinking about race and its representation in the United States. The lynching photograph became, as it was intended to be, that which made the index of race adhere to its object. It created another still more shadowy, even hooded, archive of race, housed on mantelpieces and in desk drawers across the United States from Minnesota and Illinois to the deep South. In 1951, the Civil Rights Congress presented a report to the United Nations on the condition of African Americans; it affirmed the power of this hooded archive to affect everyday life: "They are lynched in the thousands of glances from white supremacists all over the land every day."[32]

After the index?

This archive was not ended in a moment and still has a certain power even today. However, as the spectacular culture of amusement that had sustained it was replaced by the global village of mass media, it became possible first to counter and then to ironize the index. This formation may seem paradoxical, given that the 1950s and 1960s are often seen as the beginnings of what the Situationist Guy Debord called the "society of the spectacle." This global spectacle was of a different quality and created a different archive from its national predecessors. Debord claimed in 1967 that the hierarchical spectacle of difference had been replaced by a unitary domain in which "all that was once directly lived has become mere representation."[33] Thinking about the organization of knowledge, Michel Foucault similarly argued that the archive was now "the general system of the formation and transformation of statements,"[34] rather than a specific repository for documentation of a certain kind. If these ideas are taken to be indicative of the political climate of the 1960s, certain consequences become apparent. The elimination of traditional hierarchies opened the way for a new kind of citizenship from which no one was to be excluded. At the same time, the question of the fate of specific individuals and identities in the generalized archive and spectacle became acute.

The Civil Rights Movement in the United States generated a plethora of images that showed both the damage done by the general system of segregation and its individual consequences. The terrible 1951 photograph of the corpse of the fourteen-year-old Emmet Till in his coffin, lynched while on holiday from Chicago for supposedly disrespecting a white woman in Mississippi, inaugurated a counter-archive to the lynching photograph. As Mamie Till Bradley, Emmet's mother, said of the image: "It just looked as though all the hatred and all the scorn [the world] ever had for a Negro was taken out on that child."[35]

32. "We Charge Genocide: The Historic Petition to the United Nations for Relief from a Crime of the United States Government Against the Negro People," 1951, quoted by Dray, *At the Hands of Persons Unknown*, p. 411.
33. Guy Debord, *The Society of the Spectacle* (Detroit: Red and Black, 1977), p. 1.
34. Michel Foucault, *The Archaeology of Knowledge*, trans. A. M. Sheridan Smith (New York: Pantheon, 1972), p. 130.
35. Quoted by Dray, *At the Hands of Persons Unknown*, p. 425.

By making visible the effects of a system on one person's body, the picture brought the shadow archive into the open and countered it. The evidence presented in the landmark 1954 case *Brown v. Board of Education* showed that this hatred was generated by the system of segregation rather than by the evil of individuals. Gordon Parks's classic photograph depicted the experiment in which African American children chose white dolls as representing desirable human qualities, even as they acknowledged that these dolls did not look like them. Even though these photographs were not legal evidence, they sustained and energized the activism that would finally compel the United States to offer all its citizens equal rights.

It now became possible to use irony to counter the archive. Diane Arbus's satirical photograph *A Jewish giant at home with his parents in the Bronx* (1970) represented her sense that "something is ironic in the world and it has to do with the fact that what you intend never comes out like you intend it."[36] Her title suggests that the intended subject is the ironic contrast between the physically small Jewish parents, in their typically assimilated New York apartment, and their physically giant son. The plastic wrapping still in place on the lampshades, the ever-cautious economy of the immigrant and refugee is the sign of Jewishness in the image. The second irony is the very idea of a Jewish giant, a racialized contradiction in terms, embodied in his need for orthopedic shoes and a cane to stand upright. Here, Jewishness is inadequate to define what is seen in the intense glare of Arbus's flash, recalling a police crime scene photograph. At the same time, Arbus's own unacknowledged position as the secular daughter of Jewish parents is reinforced as the proper, because invisible, assimilation.

The next generation of photographers put such questions into the frame as part of their ironical reflection on the shadow archive. In Carrie Mae Weems's *Mirror, Mirror* (1986) an African American woman looks into the mirror only to be told that Snow White is the most beautiful "you black bitch and don't forget it." Here the punch line is almost literally a blow, causing a sharp exhalation of air even as it amuses. Weems makes the invisible racialized hierarchy of beauty the subject of her keen irony and visual imagination. This anger even challenged the lynching photograph itself in works like Pat Ward Williams's *Accused/Padlock/Blowtorch* (1986). Williams surrounded a reproduction of a spectacle lynching with a blackboard covered in handwritten text that expressed the full range of emotion evoked by these terrible images. In psychoanalytic terms, Williams's piece allows the viewer to work through the trauma of lynching rather than repeatedly act it out in each encounter with the hooded archive.

36. The Museum of Modern Art, New York, *Diane Arbus* (Millerton NY: Aperture, 1972), p. 2.

LOOKING INTO THE MIRROR, THE BLACK WOMAN ASKED,
"MIRROR, MIRROR ON THE WALL, WHO'S THE FINEST OF THEM ALL?"
THE MIRROR SAYS, "SNOW WHITE, YOU BLACK BITCH,
AND DON'T YOU FORGET IT!!!"

Just as these works appeared, it seemed to many people that
the digital era was about to end the indexical claims of photography
altogether. Treated by some as a liberation and by others as a moral
outrage, digital photography seemed poised to eradicate photography
as an index of the real. Ten years later, with the creation of intensely
detailed digital images that can now carry more information than
analog film, the digital image has simply been naturalized. In 2002,
New York State announced that digital photographs would be accepted
as evidence in cases of domestic violence. Given that questions of
intent and actual harm are key to such cases, it is remarkable that
the potentially manipulable digital photographs are now effective legal
evidence. Photography did not die. Rather it has become clear that
photography has always been and remains a medium susceptible to
a range of external interventions.

    Artists have jumped into this space as a means of making the
indexicality of race incoherent to the point of failure, even as the formerly

Carrie Mae Weems, *Mirror, Mirror*, from the "Joke" series, 1986. Gelatin silver print, 20 x 16 in. (50.8 x 40.6 cm).
International Center of Photography, gift of Julie Ault, 2001.

invisible quality of whiteness is now subject to the critical examination with which it formerly treated its others. Glenn Ligon created two over-life-size portraits *Self-Portrait Exaggerating My Black Features* and *Self-Portrait Exaggerating My White Features* (1997) that stand side-by-side. Our eyes scan them looking for difference and stop short when there is none to be found. Unlike Adrian Piper's famous 1981 drawing *Self-Portrait Exaggerating My Negroid Features* that made ironical use of the supposedly indexical signs of race, Ligon forces viewers to consider their own complicity in racializing the image. Somewhere between these two photographs there should be a color line, but it is elsewhere. The *Self-Portraits* followed a fascinating project in which Ligon had used the format of the slave narrative and advertisements for runaway slaves as a means of self-identification.[37] The *Self-Portrait* diptych can be seen as an attempt to represent the "twoness" that DuBois identified as the hallmark of being African American in such a way that the cut between the two qualities is not made by the color line. To know why there are two Glenn Ligons we have to think elsewhere. By the same token, in Albert J. Winn's *Jewish Summer Camp* (1997), there is no overt sign of Jewishness. The photograph shows one of the holiday camps that were popular with Jewish families in the mid-twentieth century as an escape from the city. The empty bunk beds offer a haunting parallel to those of the concentration camps but, for the artist, the ghosts belong to victims of the AIDS epidemic that has caused such havoc in California where the camp is situated. A camp on the West coast also cannot help but evoke memories of the internment camps created for Japanese Americans during World War II. But none of these responses is indexed in the photograph itself.

That is not to say that the photograph does not have indexical qualities: the objects in a photograph were really there. But history, identity, ethnicity, and sexuality never were indexical. In a sense, it seems that photography is ready to begin all over again, symptomatically attested to by the number of photographers using early photographic techniques like the pinhole camera, daguerreotypes, or cyanotypes. Into the fascinating emptiness left behind by the retreat of the racialized index emerge all the ghosts of photography represented in this exhibition. As a new archive that will create its own spectacle of difference and dissent, it marks what, following Glenn Ligon, we might call the "unbecoming" of identity. The photograph, in ceasing to become indexical, might become the document of the complexity of lived, embodied experience. In certain works there are also warnings against the possible return of the racialized index under the guise of genetics or as part of the total information system of the new Department of Homeland Security. It is, for the moment, open to question.

37. See *Glenn Ligon: Unbecoming* (Philadelphia: Institute of Contemporary Art, 1997).

Albert J. Winn, *Jewish Summer Camp, Southern California*, 1997. Gelatin silver print, 14 x 11 in. (35.5 x 27.9 cm).
Courtesy of the artist.

Javier Morillo-Alicea

*I must emphasize that it is easier to secure informa-
tion with reference to the insular possessions than
it is with reference to any other part of the country
under the American flag, due almost entirely to the
fact that the information has been concentrated
in one place in the United States.*
—General Frank McIntyre, Chief, Bureau of
Insular Affairs, U.S. War Department[1]

LOOKING FOR EMPIRE IN THE
U.S. COLONIAL ARCHIVE

*Perhaps we have an invincible resistance to believing
in the past, in History, except in the form of myth.
The Photograph, for the first time, puts an end to
this resistance: henceforth the past is as certain
as the present, what we see on paper is as certain
as what we touch.*
—Roland Barthes[2]

*Cuando se proclamó que la Biblioteca abarcaba
todos los libros, la primera impresión fue de
extravagante felicidad. Todos los hombres se
sintieron señores de un tesoro intacto y secreto.*
—Jorge Luis Borges[3]

The archival research in Washington,
D.C., would not have been possible
without the financial support of the
Smithsonian Institution, where I was a
member of the Latino Graduate Student
Training Seminar in June 1997.
1. Major General Frank McIntyre to
Rufus S. Tucker, March 24, 1926, Record
1322–61A, Records of the Bureau of
Insular Affairs, Record Group 350,
United States National Archives II,
College Park, Maryland (hereafter RG
350, USNA II).
2. Roland Barthes, *Camera Lucida:
Reflections on Photography*, trans.
Richard Howard (New York: Hill and
Wang, 1981), p. 88.
3. Jorge Luis Borges, "La Biblioteca de
Babel," *Ficciones* (Madrid: Alianza, 1971),
p. 94.
4. It is clear from the captions of many
of the photographs in RG 126 that,
despite their archival placement, they
were taken in the period of the BIA's
jurisdiction over the island. The records
of the Bureau were transferred to the
Department of Interiors Division of
Territories and Island Possessions in
1934, which might explain why, for
example, the children in Photo 8 shown
here appear in both Record Groups.

Trained as a historian, I went, of course, looking to find documents,
texts written and collected by those who had been bureaucrats and
officials of the post-1898 U.S. empire. Attempting to understand the
bureaucratic organization of the U.S. colonial apparatus and how it
adapted to the previously existing Spanish imperial circuit, I went to
the United States National Archive (USNA) to peruse the papers of
the Bureau of Insular Affairs (BIA), the office within the War Department in charge of the administration of Puerto Rico and the Philippines
during the first decades of this century. Made aware that the USNA
also holds photographic materials from the period, out of curiosity I
requested some of the images once collected by the Bureau. Somewhat to my surprise, my research trip became largely defined by
these photos and less by the texts for which I had gone in search.

It is these images that I would like to use in this essay as a spring-
board for a reflection not just on the photographs themselves but on
what their existence, collection, and preservation tell us about the
aftermath of 1898 in Puerto Rican history. Most of the photos here
are from Record Group 350, Records of the Bureau of Insular Affairs,
but two are taken from Record Group 126, the Records of the Office
of Territories, the agency with jurisdiction over the island after 1939.[4]

Jack Delano, *Guayanilla, Puerto Rico. Family of a sugar worker living behind the mill. All these people live in the same house*, 1942.
Gelatin silver print, 11 x 14 in. (27.9 x 35.5 cm). Library of Congress, Washington D.C. 129

I am interested not so much in using them to discover and present new "truths" about the United States and Puerto Rico's colonial past but rather to explore the island's role in the U.S. archival imagination. In this, I am following a line of thinking about the "colonial archive" forged recently by historians of colonialism.

Anthropologist and historian Ann Stoler has recently called for students of colonialism to analyze carefully the functionings of the colonial archive, the manners and institutions through which colonial powers collected and created information about their possessions.[5] Asking historians to read the archive "with the grain," Stoler suggests that interrogating the logic of the archive will enable us better to understand not only colonial situations but also how it is that our very epistemologies for interpreting them are deeply embedded in the forms of knowledge colonialism itself produces. Rather than seek to find a hidden, subaltern truth within the documents of the archive (reading "against the grain"), Stoler calls on us to try to decipher what the modes of producing information and collecting it tell us about the colonial state.[6] This would be, then, an exploration into what officials thought was worth knowing about colonies, what they thought they knew with certainty, and how all of this information was classified and stored. This does not mean that the historian accepts this classificatory logic but rather understands it as being as much a historical artifact as the documents themselves. We can then ask what the state attempted to control through the production and collection of information and, indeed, explore the limits of that control and the illusions of colonial knowledge.[7]

By calling this a reflection on the U.S. colonial archive, there are several things I mean to do with this concept. First, I want to present some preliminary readings of how the United States bureaucracy organized knowledge about what travel books of the period commonly called "Our New Possessions."[8] Secondly, by taking as a point of departure and comparison theoretical and historical work of scholars of colonial studies, I am making a conscious decision not simply to borrow from another field of study; rather, I am interested in thinking of the history of U.S. empire as integrated into the global history of modern empire and therefore as having a rightful place within the field of colonial and postcolonial studies. Puerto Rico and the United States should be thought of up against European colonies and metropoles not because they are merely "comparable" situations but rather because they are an integral part of the same kinds of global processes that created the modern Age of Empire.[9] Although much has changed in the historiography of U.S. imperialism since James Field declared in 1978 that the study of it constituted "The Worst Chapter in Almost Any Book," we still have much to learn about how to place the study of the United States as a colonial power in a global context.[10]

5. Ann Laura Stoler, "Unpacking Colonial Archives: New Movements on the Historic Turn," University of Rochester Lewis Henry Morgan lecture, April 22, 1996, cited with the author's permission. Along a different vein, Nicholas Dirks looks at the role that native informants play in the creation of a colonial archive, especially in the early years of British colonial-rule India. See, "Colonial Histories and Native Informants: Biography of an Archive" in *Orientalism and the Postcolonial Predicament*, ed. Carol A. Breckenridge and Peter van der Veer (Philadelphia: University of Pennsylvania Press, 1993), pp. 279–313. For the perspective of a literary critic who posits the question of the imperial archive interestingly, if too anglo-centrically, see Thomas Richards, *The Imperial Archive: Knowledge and the Fantasy of Empire* (London: Verso, 1993). For the case of Latin America, Roberto González-Echevarria has analyzed the origins of Latin American narrative as being intimately linked to the archive as metaphor and practice in the early colonial period. See his *Myth and Archive: A Theory of Latin American Narrative* (Cambridge: Cambridge University Press, 1991).

6. Hers is a different take than that of, for example, Ranajit Guha of the Subaltern Studies Collective, who Stoler cites as an example of someone attempting to read "against the grain." See Ranajit Guha, "The Prose of Counterinsurgency" in *Culture/Power/History*, ed. Nicholas Dirks, Geoff Eley, and Sherry Ortner (Princeton: Princeton University Press, 1994), pp. 336–71. The difference in modes of reading can be seen as Guha's concern with reading the document against the grain as opposed to Stoler's attempt to read the wider context of the archive.

7. See also Stoler's "In Cold Blood: Hierarchies of Credibility and the Politics of Colonial Narratives," *Representations*, no. 37 (Winter 1992): 151–89. In this earlier work, Stoler traces a criminal case in the Dutch East Indies through its paper trail, examining not just the "facts" of the case itself but also how bureaucratic networks created the very paper trail.

8. See Lanny Thompson-Womacks, "'Estudiarlos, juzgarlos, y gobernarlos': Conocimiento y poder en el archipiélago imperial estadounidense," in *Consuelo Naranjo, Miguel A. Puig-Samper, and Luis Migue Garcia Mora, eds, La Nacion Sonada: Cuba, Puerto Rico y Filipinas ante el 98*, (Madrid: Doce Calles, 1996), pp. 685–93.

Using these photographs, as well as some of the textual material produced and filed by the Bureau, I hope to point to some of the fruitful ways that an approach to colonial knowledge—one that is both global in its reach and local in its concerns—might provide new avenues for inquiry into the history of Puerto Rico, the United States, and the place of both in the history of modern empire. I do so with the intention of presenting glimpses of what kind of information was collected and reflecting on how the logic (and, indeed, seeming randomness) of its collection might tell us about this past. My comments will be neither extended interpretations of the photographs nor detailed information about who took them or how they were used. The purpose here is different: I aim to use them as starting points, as tools for reflection on Puerto Rico's history and on our ways of knowing it.

As we look back on 1898 in its aftermath, one hundred years later, we should seek to ask not just what happened but also *how* do we know what happened? How is our will to know this past, to write the history of colonialism, allowed by and also constrained by the forms of knowledge that colonialism itself has produced? What might looking into the history of these forms of knowledge production tell us about colonialism itself?

Counters and counted

The inhabitants are mostly of Spanish origin—emigrants from Spain during the last 400 years and their descendants. There is a large representation from the Canary Islands and the Balearic group in the Mediterranean, a large number of Corsicans and their descendants… Included in that one million are about 300,000 negroes and mulattoes, approximately a little more than that number. About one third of the entire population is of the negro or mixed race, what would be called in the United States "colored" people. Of pureblood negroes there are about 70,000, the remainder mulattoes, and all speaking Spanish, and largely slaves liberated in 1874.

—Brigadier General George W. Davis, Military Governor of Puerto Rico, 1900[11]

Allow me to begin with one item within one record group of the vast archive: a photograph, a portrait shot of a group of enumerators for the 1899 Puerto Rican census, the first survey of the population undertaken by the government of the new metropole.[12] What first drew me to request the photographic materials on Puerto Rico was the promise of seeing these portrait images of those who did the counting in the island's first U.S. census.[13] Interested in the idea of the census as a

9. Eric Hobsbawn, *The Age of Empire: 1875–1914* (London: Weidenfeld and Nicolson, 1987). In thinking of this history from a perspective different from the comparative history model, I am following the work of historians such as Frederick Cooper, who, in a recent review essay, calls for work that goes beyond the model of comparative history, which assumes that there are two distinct entities to be compared. Cooper suggests instead that emphasis be placed on uncovering the manners in which different areas of the world are already connected in concrete, material terms. See Frederick Cooper "Race, Ideology, and the Perils of Comparative History," *American Historical Review* 101, no. 4 (1996): 1122–38.
10. James Field, "American Imperialism: The Worst Chapter in Almost Any Book," *American Historical Review* 83 (1978): 644–83.
11. Brigadier General George W. Davis, Statement of January 13 and 17, 1900, *Hearings Before the Committee on Pacific Islands and Puerto Rico of the United States on Senate Bill 2264, To Provide a Government for the Island of Puerto Rico, and for other Purposes* (Washington DC: Government Printing Office, 1900), p. 4. Pamphlet filed as Record 834–12, RG 350, USNA II.
12. "Census Enumerators, Utuado PR," Photograph No. 350-PR-44C-21, Box 5, RG 350 Prints, USNA II.
13. United States War Department, Puerto Rico Census Office, *Report on the census of Porto Rico, 1899* (Washington D.C.: Government Printing Office, 1900).

tool of empire and in, as Arjun Appadurai has put it, the role of "number in the colonial imagination," I was eager to see the faces of those who did the counting in that survey.[14] What categories were they asked to count (families? income? race?) and who were these people? Although the photographs could not answer these questions for me, I requested them in the hope of getting some kind of concrete grasp on this past, to place faces with the process.

Of the many census enumerator group photographs, this one drew my attention for several reasons. It is the only one of the portraits where the enumerators are pictured with those satchels, which one can assume carried the survey forms for the census. The promise of the photograph—the detailed information probably held in those satchels, as opposed to the more general information provided by the published form of the census—is what makes the image for me. The very fact that all of these portraits were taken is of interest. The mat framing the picture and its handwritten title, "Census Enumerators Utuado P.R.," suggest perhaps that the image might have hung on a wall somewhere (in Washington? San Juan?). The stern faces of Puerto Rico's enumerators posing in front of that large American flag speaks to both the local practice of state counting (the local counters, their status, etc.) and its global importance (the U.S. empire, the American flag).

Contemporaneously in the Philippines, U.S. census officials were charting out vast territories, some of which were barely under the

14. See Arjun Appadurai's essay of that title in his *Modernity at Large: Cultural Dimensions of Globalization* (Minneapolis: University of Minnesota Press. 1996), pp. 114–38.

Unidentified photographer, *Census Enumerators, Utuado, P.R.*, ca. 1900, Silver printing out paper, 3 11/16 x 4 5/8 in. (9.7 x 11.7 cm). National Archives, Washington D.C.

15. See Vicente Rafael, "White Love: Surveillance: Surveillance and Nationalist Resistance in the U.S. Colonization of the Philippines" in *Cultures of United States Imperialism*, ed. Amy Kaplan and Donald E. Pease (Durham: Duke University Press, 1993), pp. 186–218, where the historian looks specifically at racial categorization in the census of the islands. See also "Mimetic Subjects: Engendering Race at the Edge of Empire," *differences 7*, no. 2 (1995): 127–49, where Rafael analyzes White North American women's images of Filipino race and also looks at the 1903 U.S. census of the archipelago. My thanks to John T. Stiles for bringing this article to my attention.

16. The only information about the record group that the archive holds is its accession date, the moment when it came to be a part of the USNA collection. This means that within the archive itself, I was not able to gather much more information about the nature of these photographs. I do not mean to suggest that the answers to all of the interrogatives suggested by these and other photos I discuss are somehow unanswerable. By asking the questions that the archiving process itself does not answer I merely wish to point to the limits of the archive and not to the absolute impossibility of knowledge.

17. "Type of Mestizo in Porto Rico," Photograph No. 350-PR-44C-14, Box 5, RG 350 Prints, USNA II.

18. "Type of 'Niger' not so black, Puerto Rico. Type of 'Negro' not so black, Puerto Rico," Photograph No. 350-PR-44C-15, Box 5, RG 350 Prints, USNA II.

19. "'Type of 'Negro' very black, Puerto Rico," Photograph No. 350-PR-44C-16, Box 5, RG 350 Prints, USNA II.

20. See Ann Laura Stoler, "Racial Histories and their Regimes of Truth." *Political Power and Social Theory, no. 11* (1997): 183–205.

political control of their Spanish predecessors. Vicente Rafael has analyzed the construction of race in the Philippines under U.S. rule, looking particularly at how census enumerators determined racial categorization and created grids for understanding the population of the new territory.[15] This process of information-gathering, in an area previously unknown to U.S. government officials, was an essential practice of rule. Viewed as a tool of empire-wide application, the census of Puerto Rico and its enumerators can be seen as participating in both the local process of counting and the global practice of Imperial control. We should view this group of enumerators of Utuado not simply in relation to insular history but also to the circuits of power and knowledge of which they were necessarily a part. In terms of their local importance, it is relevant for us to understand the categories that institutions like the census used because it is through them that Puerto Rico and Puerto Ricans were made intelligible to an American bureaucratic audience.

When I received box five of this collection, however, the photographs that initially drew my attention were not those of the census enumerators. I first and immediately came under the spell of a three-photograph series that gave no indication as to their origin, explained very little about the images themselves, and was generally baffling. Each of the images consists of two men posed in front of two oxcarts. Each man is holding a farm tool and all are looking straight at the camera. The repetition of the three photographs, the careful manner in which the subjects were posed almost identically, is what first made them stand out for me. They were all three very carefully mounted as if for framing.[16]

Turning the photographs over for clues as to their nature, I found handwritten captions on each. The first of the three had written on the back of it: "Type of Mestizo in Puerto Rico." Another colored pen later crossed out the word "Puerto," replacing it with "Porto," suggesting the labeling was done contemporaneously. Under this sentence, written in pencil and in capital letters was the word "MULATO."[17] The second photo in the series had written, in pencil, the following description: "Type of 'Niger' not so black in P.R." Under that pencil marking was a more official description, written in black ink: "Type of 'Negro' not so black, Puerto Rico."[18] The third photograph was described as "Type of 'Negro' very black, Puerto Rico."[19]

What is the criteria by which the distinction is created between a "'Negro' not so black" and a "'Negro' very black"? Race, after all, does not simply point to biological or observable difference—it is the cultural understandings of physical variance.[20] What cultural understandings went into the definition of "not so black," "very black," and "mestizo"

or "mulatto"? And what of the original categorization of the "not so black" men as "Nigers"? Is this a misspelled version of the North American epithet "nigger"? This begs us to inquire into how preexisting notions of race, as well as Spanish and Creole racism, gel with the conceptions of race in the new metropole. Puerto Rican nationalist mythology has made much of the "mix of three races" and of the mixed-blood *jibaro* who comes to symbolize the nation. In the example here, the mixed-blood category serves to set the men apart from the other two decidedly "Negro" categories. We can see a parallel here to what José Luis González describes as Creole nationalist efforts at distancing the nation from blackness through the use of the language of mestizaje.[21]

The fact that here, in the same box of the archive, were examples of both counters and counted, adds more than just poetry to the inquiry. Beyond the facts of these particular photographs, we still have much to learn about race in Puerto Rico, in this period and beyond. How are twentieth-century understandings of race on the island affected by the imperial transition of 1898? This must go beyond determining which colonial power was more or less "racist." What we need are clearer understandings of the conceptual tools that contemporaries used to determine and know race, as well as how these tools evolved during a period of imperial transition. Beyond the matter of who wrote these particular photo captions, at a more general level, who was making official racial determinations? To what extent were they informed by previous, local understandings of race and to what degree did North American conceptions of race figure? When General George Davis is able to detail, as in the quotation that opens this section, exact figures for race and racial mixture, how are these numbers produced?

21. José Luis Gonzalez, *El pais de cuatro pisos y otros ensayos* (Rio Piedras: Hurácan, 1980).

On reading the archive: texts

Upon the acquisition of the territory ceded to the United States by Spain as a result of the Spanish-American war, the necessity arose for the creation of an agency of the Federal Government especially equipped to administer the civil affairs of the new possessions. For this purpose there was established in the Office of the Secretary of War, on December 13, 1898, a Division of Customs and Insular Affairs, which was charged with "all matters pertaining to the customs of the Islands of Porto Rico, Cuba, and the Philippines, and all civil affairs relating to those islands as distinguished from matters of a military character connected with the government of the islands."
—USNA research guide for materials on Puerto Rico[22]

European and, subsequently, U.S. archival arrangement of textual material has developed historically according to two guiding principles: provenance and original order. The principle of provenance "provides that records should be grouped according to the nature of the institution that has accumulated them" while the standard of original order requires "that archives should be kept in the order originally imposed on them."[23] Unlike library methods of classification, where new materials are grouped according to a preexisting code of subject-indexing, archives, in principle, file materials according to the logic, random as it might have been, given to them by those who produced and originally preserved the information. This should mean, in theory, that the form of the archive can allow us to glean some information about what historical actors thought were meaningful, or perhaps just logistically useful, forms of classification.

If the officials of the Bureau of Insular Affairs, for example, thought it best to file materials chronologically, geographically, by subject matter, or by some other principle of arrangement, this should be reflected in how archives today hold these materials, according to the principal of original order. Looking through the textual records of the BIA for information about Puerto Rico, one of the striking things about these documents relating to the island is that—unlike the photographic holdings—there is no specific subgroup or series of file boxes that contains all materials on the island. Documents relating to Puerto Rico are scattered among texts about and from all other areas of the world that came under BIA jurisdiction.

Past archivists at the USNA have prepared a guide to textual materials held in the BIA papers regarding Puerto Rico, consisting of a list of subjects with the corresponding record numbers to be called

22. Kenneth Munden and Milton Greenbaum, comps, *Records of the Bureau of Insular Affairs Relating to Puerto Rico 1898–1934,* A List of Selected Files (Washington D.C.: USNA, 1943), p. vii.
23. See T. R. Schellenberg, "Archival Principles of Arrangement," in *A Modern Archives Reader: Basic Readings on Archival Theory and Practice,* ed. Maygene F. Daniels and Timothy Walch (Washington D.C.: USNA, 1984), pp. 151 and 150. For a historical overview of the history of European archival administration, see, in the same volume, Ernst Posner, "Some Aspects of Archival Development Since the French Revolution," pp. 3–14.

for when requesting files.[24] As a historian of Puerto Rico, one might well look at this list for categories of interest, request pertinent documents for an area of interest, and do no more. When one receives the box of the documents, however, all still numbered in the manner in which they were received from the BIA, one finds that information on the island was catalogued next to information of about, for example, the Panama Canal, Hawaii, and the U.S. Dominican Customs Receivership. While this might seem obvious—the BIA's responsibilities were wide-ranging in its history—it also speaks to the nearly worldwide reach of U.S. bureaucratic colonial knowledge and the manner in which Puerto Rico figured in projects of global scope.

Puerto Rico is also found among discussions of what the Bureau called the "Government of the World's Colonies."[25] When policy changes in Puerto Rico and other areas were considered, the Bureau often collected information regarding how other colonial powers dealt with similar problems in the government of their empire. Newspaper clippings from around the globe are filed among the Bureau's papers, with topics including, for example, France's methods of colonial rule and the proceedings of a British Imperial Conference in London.[26] When General Leonard Wood, Governor of the Philippines, was contemplating changes in the administration of the archipelago, he first wrote to the Bureau requesting that persons there collect information on the British and French imperial experience:

> I have been informed that during the last four years, the British empire has granted semi-responsible governments to India and Malta and has promulgated new constitutions in Ceylon, Burma and Nigeria. I am told that the same development has taken place in French Tunis and Senegal, which was given a parliament in 1920, and that in 1919 Italy established parliaments in Tripoli and Cyrenica.
>
> Will you please obtain for me and mail as soon as possible as many as you can of these new instruments of government?[27]

This is relevant in terms of understanding how the new colonial power saw its role vis-à-vis other empires. This is a complicated question because, on the one hand, the United States justified its takeover of the Spanish territories rhetorically by distancing itself from colonialism as defined by a brutal Spanish past.[28] When proexpansionist people spoke and wrote about the United States's "new possessions," the model often cited was the British one. For example, in a 1907 meeting of the American Academy of Political and Social Science dedicated to studying the administration of the new "dependencies,"

24. Munden and Greenbaum, comp., *Records of the Bureau of Insular Affairs.*
25. "Government of the World's Colonies." Record 1322, RG 350, USNA II.
26. See "Transmitting Specimen Copies of Newspaper Articles on the French Colonies," Record 1322-54, RG 350, USNA II; and "Imperial Relations Committee of the Imperial Conference issued at London on November 20, 1926," Record 1322-64, RG 350, USNA II.
27. Governor General Leonard Wood to Major General Frank McIntyre, Chief, Bureau of Insular Affairs, July 10, 1925, Record 1322-38, RG 350, USNA II.
28. I have addressed this stereotyped view of Spanish colonialism and provided an alternative reading in, "Demystifying Spanish Empire in Contemporary Colonial Studies," paper presented at the Annual Meeting of the Society for Spanish and Portuguese Historical Studies, Minneapolis, Minnesota, April 26, 1997.

the Ambassador of Great Britain to the United States was asked to deliver a talk on "some difficulties in colonial government."[29] One of the first things the first military governor of Puerto Rico did upon arriving on the island was to write to the colonial governor of Barbados, asking the latter for information that would aid him in administering the new U.S. territory. The governor of Barbados, in turn, sent along a copy of colonial laws there and attached a note saying, "I shall be glad to be furnished with any legislation which in Your Excellency's opinion may have reference to this Colony."[30] We still have much to learn about how to view local situations of Puerto Rico horizontally, across the U.S. empire and across the global stage of modern Empire. Looking at the place of Puerto Rico within the colonial archive is just one approach to achieving this kind of a reading.

In the archive, photographs are often catalogued following different principles than those that guide the preservation of textual sources.[31] Accession records of the USNA tell us that the photographic images discussed here were not originally all held together. They were found among the textual records of the Bureau and later extracted for research use as a separate photo collection. What we gain in having a photographic collection labeled "Puerto Rico"—direct access to images of the island—we lose in terms of being able to read the images horizontally, the way we can with textual records. These pictures, however, can and should lend themselves to broader readings that extend beyond the island. Keeping in mind the wider context provided by the textual records, let us turn now back to the photo records of the archive and some of the other images collected by the Bureau.

Educating for citizenship, or "Be good and be good for something"

Mr. Loomis said the principal fault with the United States in its attitude toward its colonials is the tendency to hand out textbooks and plenty of money and to let it rest there. Education, he stated, is essential, but sometimes too much of it works badly and produces agitators and reformers, who in time will work to the detriment of the mother government and who have no difficulty in spreading a feeling of unrest and discontent.
—"Tells of Colonies," newspaper clipping in BIA records[32]

A large portion of the photographs in the archive regarding the first decades of U.S. rule in Puerto Rico are of schools and schoolchildren. There are many images of physical-education exercises and agricultural

29. See the *Annals of the American Academy of Political and Social Science* 30, no. 1 (1907), special annual meeting number, "American Colonial Policy and Administration."
30. Letter from Government House of Barbados, June 28, 1899 (Fondo Fortaleza: Archivo General de Puerto Rico).
31. See Nancy E. Malan, "Organizing Photo Collections: An Introspective Approach" in *A Modern Archives Reader*, ed. Daniels and Walch, pp. 181–86.
32. "Tells of Colonies," newspaper clipping in BIA files with handwritten reference, *Washington Star*, June 11 [no year], Record 1322-37, RG 350, USNA II.

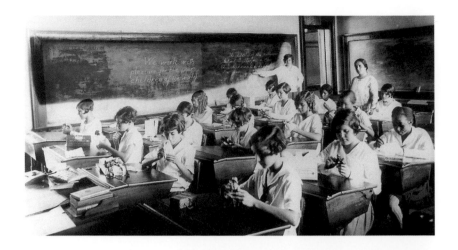

clubs, and numerous prints showing barefoot children posed with their teachers in front of dilapidated rural school buildings. The photos of children tell the story of Puerto Rico's modernization, of the U.S. narrative that assured islanders and the world that they were being moved out of barbarism and into modernity.

Reproduced here are two images of classrooms, one a girls' sewing class[33] and the other of a boys' star hat and basketry-making class.[34] In the first photo the girls are shown at work, none of them looking into the camera. The two women in the picture, however, are posing for the photographer, and one—presumably the teacher, Herminia

33. "Mayaguez, Porto Rico. Central Grammatical School. Class in sewing in charge of the teacher, Herminia Lebrón de Urrutéa." Photograph No. 350-PR-44B-5-4, Box 4, RG 350 Prints. USNA II. **34.** "Riera Palmer School, Mayagüez, Porto Rico. Pupils preparing hats and baskets under the direction of the teacher, Iva M. Woodruff" [no date], Photograph No. I26-PG-3A-1, Box 3, Record Group 126. Records of the Office of Territories. Prints: General Photographs of Puerto Rico 1935–1948, USNA II (hereafter RG 126 Prints). Although

Unidentified photographer, *Mayaguez, Porto Rico. Central Grammatical School. Class in sewing in charge of the teacher, Herminia Lebrón de Urrutéa*, ca. 1935. Gelatin silver print, 7 ¹⁵/₁₆ x 9 ³/₈ in. (20.0 x 23.8 cm). National Archives, Washington D.C.
Unidentified photographer, *Riera Palmer School, Mayagüez, Porto Rico. Pupils preparing hats and baskets under the direction of the teacher, Iva M. Woodruff*, ca. 1935. Gelatin silver print, 7 x 9 in. (17.8 x 22.9). National Archives, Washington D.C.

Lebrón de Urruteá—is pointing at a message on the blackboard. It reads: "The children of the Grammar School wish you a Merry Christmas and a Happy New Year." To the left of the holiday greeting is another message, placing the girls' labor literally in a global context: "We work with pleasure for the poor children of the world."

Photograph six shows a boys' classroom with a similar Christmas greeting on the blackboard. To the right of the holiday message is written a motto: "Be good and be good for something." But, for me, the point of interest in this photograph, what Roland Barthes calls the photograph's *punctum*, is not the text on the board but rather the face of the boy to the far right in the first row.[35] That boy's (to my eyes) sad face prefigures Jack Delano's famous Operation Bootstrap photographs and so many other images of Puerto Rico's twentieth century. The story of Puerto Rico's modernity and modernization has been written on the faces of children such as these.

It is not surprising that education and children should figure prominently in the photographs collected by colonial bureaucrats—it was through schooling that the story of progress was told and exhibited to the world. And education was one way of avoiding, in the language of fear demonstrated by the news clipping quoted above, that "agitators and reformers" might be growing up on the island. Education was cultural and material, consisting of the ideas taught (e.g., that they are examples of for the world's poor) as well as the structures and infrastructures built. Interspersed with the images of children are many photos of new school buildings, such as the one above.[36] Unlike the many photographs of the rural schools, shown with barefoot children posing in front of them, these new school structures are often pictured alone, the edifice speaking for itself. The story of education is told through persons, institutions, and physical structures.

the photograph is with RG 126, the caption does not date the photograph. Other similar photographs, some of the same school, are found in RG 350 and dated earlier as taken during the period of the BIA's jurisdiction in Puerto Rico. See, for example, "Mayaguez, Porto Rico Riera Palmer School. Class in sewing in charge of the teacher, Isabel Rodríguez." Photograph No. 350-PR-44B-4-18, Box 4, RG 350 Prints, USNA II.
35. He writes of the *punctum:* "whether or not it is triggered, it is an addition: it is what I add to the photograph and *what is nonetheless already there.*" Barthes, *Camera Lucida,* p. 55.
36. "A new type of school building constructed by the Department of Education—Graded school at Adjuntas." Photograph No. 350-PR-44B-4-10, Box 4, RG 350 Prints, USNA II.

Unidentified photographer, *A new type of school building constructed by the Department of Education—Graded school at Adjuntas,* ca. 1903. Silver printing out paper, 4 3/8 x 6 13/16 in. (11.0 x 17.3 cm). National Archives, Washington D.C.

Petite Yankees, performing colonialism

The focus on children, seen in the above section, is not surprising when one compares Puerto Rico to other colonial situations. A new and expanding body of scholarship on colonialism has brought increased attention to the importance of children to notions of colonial and imperial order. Anna Davin's now-classic essay "Imperialism and Motherhood" looked at how, in England, metropolitan discourses of motherhood, gender roles, and state family policy were intimately linked to the reality of British empire.[37] In policy concerns in both colonies and metropoles, ranging from debates about intermarriage and *mètissage* in Indonesia to the colonial state's interest in regulating breastfeeding in the Belgian Congo, discourses of race and gender intersected in ways that often put children at the center of colonial discourses.[38]

In the particular situation of Puerto Rico, where colonialism did not require or produce a large settlement of North Americans, what role did children play in notions of colonial order? Let us turn to two more images of children in the archive, beginning with *Minuet-Carolina*.[39] I first saw these children in the picture reproduced here, from Record Group 126. The photograph provided no information about its taking or who the children were; all it offered was the somewhat ornately script-ed title someone had written on the matting: "A Minuet—Carolina." I later found the same children posed in a different manner among the photographs of Record Group 350, where a caption provided some more information: "Carolina, P.R. Minuet danced by children of 1st grade under the direction of Miss Esperanza Cuin (Sept. 1927)."[40]

The boys are costumed in powdered wigs and other George Washington-era regalia, the girls in white gowns, string pearls, and feathered fans. The power of the image for me rests in the carriage of the girls, whose coquettish poses resist the straight-back formality of what historically might have been a minuet danced in colonial New England. Dressed in costumes of this bygone era, the children are petite yankees, in the most literal sense this phrase can take.

There are many costumed children among the archived photo-graphs of school activities throughout the island. American Education Week seems to have often been celebrated with "Folk Dances," which included a girl posing as Betsy Ross, girls dressed as leprechauns doing a version of an Irish folk dance, and several photographs of sim-ulated Native American rituals. It is one of these latter photographs that I will turn to now. The bottom photograph on the opposite page presents a group of children from Cabo Rojo on a parade float.[41]

If we juxtapose the minuet with this image, what we have are two different instances of children reenacting a colonial past, at least one—the "Indians"—in celebration of American Education Week.

37. Anna Davin, "Imperialism and Motherhood" (1978) in *Tensions of Empire: Colonial Cultures in a Bourgeois World*, ed. Fred Cooper and Ann Laura Stoler (Berkeley: University of California Press, 1996), pp. 87–151.
38. See Ann Laura Stoler, "Sexual Affronts and Racial Frontiers: European Identities and the Cultural Politics of Exclusion in Colonial Southeast Asia," *Comparative Studies in Society and History* 34, no. 2, pp. 514–51; on the Belgian Congo see Nancy Rose Hunt, "*Le bébé en brousse*; European Women, African Birth Spacing and Colonial Intervention in Breastfeeding in the Belgian Congo," *International Journal of African Historical Studies*, 21:3, pp. 401–32. See also Stoler's chapter, "Domestic Subversions and Children's Sexuality," in *Race and the Education of Desire* (Durham, N.C.: Duke University Press, 1995), pp. 137–64.
39. "A Minuet—Carolina." Photograph No. 136-PG-3A-2, Box 3, RG 126 Prints, USNA II.
40. The photograph of the minuet not reproduced here can be found as "Carolina. P.R. Minuet danced by children of 1st grade under the direction of Miss Esperanza Cuin, September 1927." Photograph No. 350-PR-44B-4-20, Box 4, RG 350 Prints, USNA II.
41. "Education Week. Float representing an Indian Teepee prepared by the teach-ers of the school Eugenio M. de Hato of Cabo Rojo, Porto Rico, (1928)" Photograph No. 350-PR-44B-5-1, Box 4, RG 350 Prints, USNA II.

The past being reenacted is a decidedly North American colonial one, where children are being encouraged to take on the roles of both petite colonizers and petite colonized. These are not Caribbean Tainos, after all, who the children are dressed to supposedly resemble. The teepees, and the bows and arrows, together with the powdered wigs of the minuet, display an imaginary and idyllic view of the U.S. main-land's period of colonial conquest. The word "colonial" here could only mean a romantic view of the eighteenth century, not the reality of the contemporary U.S. presence.

Unidentified photographer, *Minuet—Carolina*, ca. 1927. Gelatin silver print, 5 x 7 in. (12.7 x 17.8 cm). National Archives, Washington D.C.
Unidentified photographer, *Education Week. Float representing an Indian Teepee prepared by the teachers of the school Eugenio M. de Hato of Cabo Rojo, Porto Rico*, 1928. Gelatin silver print, 5 x 7 in. (12.7 x 17.8 cm). National Archives, Washington D.C.

There is no reason to interpret this purely as a colonizing imposition on the part of education officials. That would erase the agency of the colonized, of the children who dressed up for the minuet and of the Puerto Rican teachers involved in these events. Colonial culture is more dynamic than that view would allow. The challenge is not to view these images and simply label them colonialist or racist, as appropriate as those labels might be, but rather to sense the manners in which these images function in the island's colonial culture. We are also challenged to sift through the manners in which Puerto Ricans sometimes rejected, sometimes accepted, but always altered the meanings of these very powerful colonial signifiers. Our little Martha Washingtons may have been dressed up to dance a minuet, but the beauty of the image consists in the disjunction between the implications and limitations of its given title, "Carolina—A Minuet," and the redefinition of the minuet provided by the children.

Bureaucratic intimacies and imperial circuits

[T]he exercise of bureaucratic power itself involved
the colonial imagination...
—Arjun Appadurai [42]

Up to now, the photographs I have chosen to reproduce here—and, indeed, most of those I had to choose from—were images of islanders, of the colonized in the colonizer/colonized binary. This binary, as scholars in colonial studies have amply argued, is not absolute. The culture of colonialism worked to define and ensure the binary, but it was always destabilized by resistance.[43] If we are to speak of colonial culture we must pay attention to both sides of that binary and problematize the often unmarked category of the colonizer.

Along with the photos of schools, children, road construction, and other public works, the records also file the portrait photos of some of the early North American governors of the island. They are all similarly posed portraits, sitting, looking straight into the camera. Above is E. Mont Reily, governor of Puerto Rico from 1921 to 1923.[44] What is interesting to me about the photograph is not simply the chance to look at the local symbol of U.S. authority, the person who sat above everyone else pictured in the archive. What I find most engaging about the photo is its dedication, written by Reily himself: "To my friend, Gen. McIntyre, E. Mont Reily, Gov. Porto Rico 1921." Several of the governor portraits were dedicated in a similar manner, suggesting the photos were taken directly for the use and display of the BIA in Washington. The friend to whom Reily dedicated the portrait was, of course, head of the BIA. The dedication speaks to me of the circuits of power and

42. Appadurai, *Modernity at Large*, p. 115
43. Homi Bhabha, "Of Mimicry and Man: The Ambivalence of Colonial Discourse" in *Tensions of Empire*, ed. Cooper and Stoler (Berkeley: University of California Press, 1997) pp. 152–60. For theoretical and historical perspectives on colonial culture, see Nicholas B. Dirks, "Introduction: Colonialism and Culture." in *Colonialism and Culture*, ed. Dirks (Ann Arbor: University of Michigan Press, 1991).
44. "To my friend, Gen. McIntyre, E. Mont Reily, Gov. Porto Rico 1921," Photograph No. 350-PR-44B-6-6, Box 4.

Unidentified photographer, *To my friend, Gen. McIntyre, E. Mont Reily, Gov. Porto Rico*, 1921. Gelatin silver print, 9 x 6 in. (22.8 x 15.5 cm). National Archives, Washington D.C.

knowledge that the U.S. empire forged among its bureaucrats and officials. There are stories there yet to be told. What were the material, intellectual, and cultural circuits that tied officials in Puerto Rico to those in D.C., the Philippines, Guam, and elsewhere?

And then, of course, we should relate these imperial circuits to the local contexts in which these officials functioned. And how has history remembered the tenure of Reily as governor of the island? In the words of historian Francisco Scarano:

> Habria, además, ejecutivos como el gobernador E. Mont Reily—denominado "Moncho Reyes" por el genio popular puertorriqueño—, quienes, además de carecer de experiencia y preparación, se comportarian con insensibilidad hacia la cultura y la manera de ser de los puertorriqueños.[45]

45. Francisco Scarano, *Puerto Rico: Five Eras of History* (Mexico: McGraw-Hill, 1994), p. 647.

The two sides of this coin, the bureaucrat intimate with his superiors and insensitive to local culture are both crucial to comprehending Puerto Rico's colonial culture in the first decades of this century.

54—The Philippines, Porto Rico and Cuba—Uncle Sam's Burden. (With apologies to Mr. Kipling.)

Benjamin L. Singley, *The Philippines, Porto Rico and Cuba—Uncle Sam's Burden (with apologies to Mr. Kipling)*, 1899. Albumen print stereograph (one side shown), 3 1/2 x 7 in. (8.9 x 17.8 cm). Private collection.

II.
ASSIMILATE/
IMPERSONATE

George Bacon, *Dodie Bacon holding the March 12, 1959 edition of the Honolulu Star-Bulletin, announcing statehood of Hawaii, Honolulu, Hawaii*, 1959. Gelatin silver print, 8 ¹/₂ x 7 ¹/₄ in. (21.6 x 18.4 cm). Bishop Museum, Honolulu, Hawaii.

Ed Clark, *Going Home*, 1945. Gelatin silver print, 10 ⅝ x 12 ⅜ in. (26.9 x 31.4 cm). Hallmark Fine Art Collection, Kansas City, Missouri. Courtesy of Ed Clark/Getty Images.

Gordon Parks, *American Gothic*, 1942. Gelatin silver print, 20 x 16 in. (50.8 x 40.6 cm). Courtesy of the artist.

Jacob A. Riis, *The First Patriotic Election in the Beach Street Industrial School*, ca. 1890. Gelatin silver print, 7 3/4 x 9 5/8 in.
(19.7 x 24.4 cm). International Center of Photography, purchased by the David Schwartz Foundation, 1982.

Frances Benjamin Johnston, *Saluting the Flag at the Whittier Primary School*, 1899. Gelatin silver print, 7 ⁷/₁₆ x 9 ¹/₂ in. (18.8 x 24.1 cm). Library of Congress, Washington D.C.

Horace Poolaw, *Cletus Poolaw's Honor Dance, Carnegie, Oklahoma*, ca. 1952. Gelatin silver print, 9 $^{15}/_{16}$ x 12 $^{15}/_{16}$ in. (25.2 x 32.8 cm).

Courtesy of Charles Junkerman.

U.S.SENATOR LEWIS V.BOGY, WHILE INDIAN COMMISSIONER AT WASHINGTON 1867-8.
TAKEN IN INDIAN COSTUME WITH SAUK AND FOX CHIEFS.
(From Left to Right). Seated:MA-NA-TO-WAH.   KEOKUK. Standing: SEN.L.V.BOGY.

Alexander Gardner, *U.S. Senator Lewis V. Bogy while Indian Commissioner at Washington*, 1867–68. Albumen print, 12 x 19 in.
(30.5 x 48.2 cm). Harney Collection, Missouri Historical Society, St. Louis, Missouri.

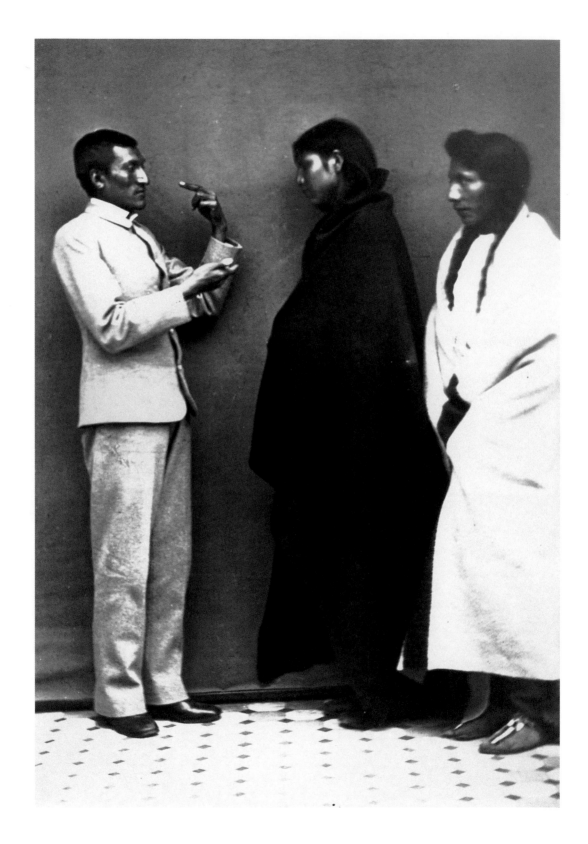

William Larrabee, *Little Chief (Con-way-how-nif, Cheyenne) Welcoming Two Newcomers from Dakota Territory*, 1878.
Albumen print, 9 x 7 ½ in. (22.8 x 19 cm). Hampton University Archives, Hampton, Virginia.

Collins Studio, *Geronimo, Apache Chief and Medicine Man*, 1903. Gelatin silver print on board, 7 ¹/₈ x 5 in. (18 x 12.7 cm).
International Center of Photography, Museum purchase, 2003.

Robertson Studio, *Principal Chief Pleasant Ponter*, 1904. Modern print from original glass plate negative, 7 x 5 in. (17.8 x 12.7 cm).
Oklahoma Historical Society, Oklahoma City, Archives and Manuscripts Division, Alice Robertson Glass Plate Collection.

Robertson Studio, *Principal Chief Pleasant Ponter as a Knight's Templar*, 1904. Modern print from original glass plate negative, 7 x 5 in. (17.8 x 12.7 cm). Oklahoma Historical Society, Oklahoma City, Archives and Manuscripts Division, Alice Robertson Glass Plate Collection.

Raoul Gradvohl, *Woman with feathered headdress, sitting within light circle*, ca. 1940. Gelatin silver print, 10 x 8 in. (25.4 x 20.3 cm).

UCR/California Museum of Photography, University of California, Riverside, Raoul Gradvohl Collection.

Eleanor Antin, *Eleanora Antinova in Pocahontas*, from the "Recollections of My Life with Diaghilev" series, 1980. Toned gelatin silver print, 14 x 11 in. (35.5 x 27.9 cm). Courtesy of Ronald Feldman Fine Arts, New York.

Cindy Sherman, *Untitled*, 1976/2000. Gelatin silver print, 10 x 8 in. (25.4 x 20.3 cm). Courtesy of the artist and Metro Pictures, New York.

Edward Weston, *Tehuana Costume [worn by Rose Roland, wife of Covarrubias]*, ca. 1920. Gelatin silver contact print, 9 5/8 in x 6 in. (24.9 x 15.2 cm). Courtesy of Throckmorton Fine Art; Center for Creative Photography, University of Arizona, Tuscon.

Louis Carlos Bernal, *Rosie Siqueiros, Barrio Anita*, 1978. Chromogenic print, 9 x 9 in. (22.8 x 22.8 cm). Center for Creative Photography, The University of Arizona, Tuscon.

Cindy Sherman, *Untitled Film Still #50*, 1979. Gelatin silver print, 8 x 10 in. (20.3 x 25.4 cm). Courtesy of the artist and Metro Pictures, New York.

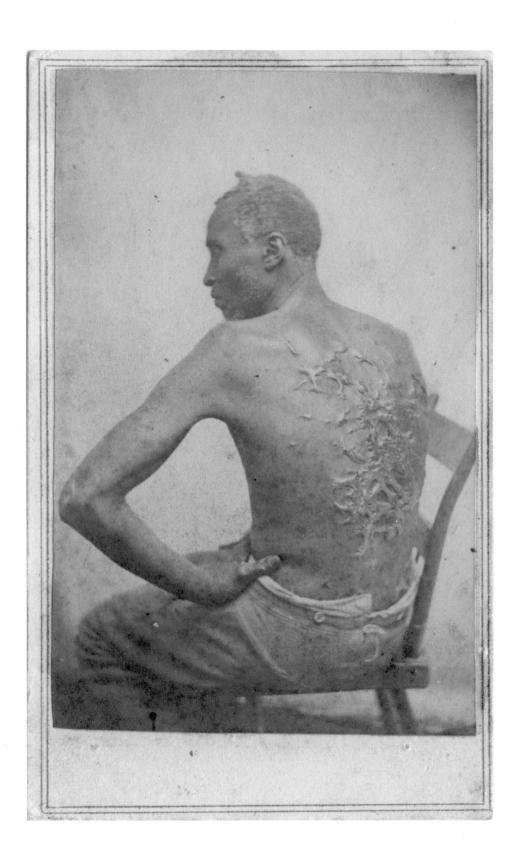

Brian Wallis

Recent discussions of multiculturalism, ethnicity, identity, and race have raised many new questions about the nature of cultural difference. Some critics have derided "political correctness" and challenges to Western canons of culture, while others have struggled to trace the genealogies of cultural oppression and to challenge normative structures of identity formation. In its methodology, this second group of critics has shifted the analysis away from essentialist or biological versions of race by trying to determine how fluctuant ethnic roles are constructed and articulated through a variety of positions, languages, institutions, and apparatuses. When race has been subjected to the critical gaze of these practices, it has inevitably been reinscribed as a complex and discursive category that cannot be separated from other formative components of identity.

BLACK BODIES, WHITE SCIENCE
Louis Agassiz's Slave Daguerreotypes

In other words, these debates have made clear that "race" is a political issue, a product of subjective choices made around issues of power, a function less of physical repression than of constructions of knowledge. Who determines what counts as knowledge? Who represents and who is represented? Whose voice will be heard? Whose stories will be remembered? Such questions go to the heart of how history is written and validated by society—through negotiations fraught with silent conflicts and profound implications. For this reason, it is important to historicize not only the concept of race but also the institutions and power-knowledge conjunctions that have fostered it.

Museums are central to the ways our culture is constructed. Despite the attention they now pay to spectacle and display, museums—like libraries, historical societies, and archives—are principally concerned with sorting and classifying knowledge. It is significant, then, that over the past few decades a great sea change has swept over all these institutions. In the wake of the photography boom of the 1970s, information once stored in the form of photographs and photographically illustrated books has been wrenched from its previous organizational and institutional contexts and reclassified according to its medium. As critic Rosalind Krauss has noted, the effect of this change has been "to dismantle the photographic archive—the set of practices, institutions, and relationships to which nineteenth-century photography belonged—and to reassemble it within the categories previously constituted by art and its history."[1]

Thus, in recent museum exhibitions of daguerreotypes, images once intended for personal, scientific, topographic, medical, or legal reasons have been reclassified, reunited under the ruling category of the "daguerrean aesthetic." Once-anonymous camera operators have

1. Rosalind Krauss, "Photography's Discursive Spaces," *Art Journal* 42 (Winter 1982) 311–19. See also Douglas Crimp, "The Museum's Old/The Library's New Subject," *Parachute*, no. 22, (Spring 1981): 32–37; and Allan Sekula, "Dismantling Modernism, Reinventing Documentary (Notes on the Policies of Representation)," *Massachusetts Review* 19 (Winter 1978): 859–83.

McPherson & Oliver, attr., *The Scourged Back*, 1863. Carte-de-visite, 3 $^{15}/_{16}$ x 2 $^{3}/_{8}$ in. (10 x 6 cm). International Center of Photography, Museum purchase, 2003.

been given names and accorded the status of artists. And works that formerly circulated in file cabinets, desk drawers, family albums, and local archives have now been displaced to the autonomous, unifying context of the art museum. If nothing else, this process proves that these putatively objective records are anything but, and that the notion of an autonomous image is a fiction. Moreover, this process also suggests that the classificatory systems of nineteenth-century objectivity may have a great deal to do with the formation of modernist versions of knowledge. This dual shift in seeing suggests that all knowledge is relative, historically situated, subjectively formed and catalogued, and bound to interests that color its meanings. But what is signaled by this

A. R. Henwood, *General Williams and Servant*, ca. 1863. Carte-de-visite, 4 1/4 x 3 in. (10.8 x 7.6 cm). International Center of Photography, Museum purchase, 2003.

shift in meaning? How has this reorientation of photographic knowledge actually produced new meanings and new insights? What is the relationship between changing attitudes toward race and simultaneous transformations in museum collection practices?

Louis Agassiz and racial typologies

A particularly revelatory case is that of the so-called slave daguerreotypes of Louis Agassiz, discovered at Harvard's Peabody Museum in 1975 and justifiably celebrated in the exhibition *Nineteenth-Century Photography* organized by the Amon Carter Museum in 1992. This extraordinary series consists of fifteen highly detailed images on silver daguerreotype plates, which show front and side views of seven Southern slaves, men and women, largely naked.[2] The individuals sit or stand facing the camera with a directness and forthrightness that is at once familiar and utterly strange. If it is a shock to see full frontal nudity in early American photography, it is even more surprising to see it without the trappings of shame or sexual fantasy. Here, the seated women calmly reveal their breasts, and the standing men are stark naked. But their attitudes are detached, unemotional, and workmanlike. In what seems to be a deliberate refusal to engage with the camera or its operator, they stare into the lens, their faces like masks, eyes glazed, jaws clenched. Fascinating and disturbing, these pictures raise compelling questions about the construction of—and the social investments in—the categories of "race," "science," "photography," and "the museum."

The daguerreotypes, which were taken for Agassiz in Columbia, South Carolina, in 1850, had two purposes, one nominally scientific, the other frankly political. They were designed to analyze the physical differences between European whites and African blacks, but at the same time they were meant to prove the superiority of the white race. Agassiz hoped to use the photographs as evidence to prove his theory of "separate creation," the idea that the various races of mankind were in fact separate species. Though strictly scientific in purpose, the daguerreotypes took on a very particular meaning in the context of prevailing political, economic, and aesthetic theories about race. Thus, they help to discredit the very notion of objectivity and call into question the supposed transparency of the photographic record.

The classificatory project that led to the production of the slave daguerreotypes was something of a departure for Agassiz, who, in 1850, was the most famous scientist in America.[3] Before coming to the United States, he had shown no interest in the growing American debates over slavery or the division of mankind into separate species. Born in Switzerland, Agassiz (1807–1873) had achieved his first success

2. See Martha A. Sandweiss, ed., *Photography in Nineteenth-Century America* (Fort Worth: Amon Carter Museum, 1991). One of the slave daguerreotypes was also featured on the cover of the catalogue for the exhibition *From Site to Sight*, organized by the Peabody Museum, Harvard University, and circulated by the Smithsonian Institution in 1986.
3. On Louis Agassiz, see Edward Lurie, *Louis Agassiz: A Life in Science* (Chicago: University of Chicago, 1960).

in Paris as the star student of the legendary Baron Georges Cuvier, the leading zoologist of his day and the founder of the modern science of comparative anatomy. Cuvier was so impressed with Agassiz that he turned over to him his own research on fossil fish. In 1829, when he was just twenty-two, Agassiz published his first scientific treatise, a mammoth, groundbreaking study of the fish of Brazil. This volume consisted of the meticulous drawing, classification, and ordering of more than five hundred species of fish found principally along the Amazon River.

Continuing his studies of fish, in 1830 Agassiz published the comprehensive catalogue *Fresh Water Fishes of Central Europe* and, from 1833 to 1844, the multipart publication *Research on Fossil Fish*. Previous to this project, only eight generic types of fossil fish had been identified; Agassiz's five-volume work catalogued more than 340 new genera. The methodology Agassiz used was comparative and relational: individual images or specimens held far less meaning for him than the cumulative consequence of a series properly ordered. Sorting and classifying were the bases of Agassiz's method. As a result, he was one of the principal collectors and archivists of natural history specimens in the nineteenth century. In the United States, he founded prominent natural history museums in Charleston, South Carolina, and Cambridge, Massachusetts, and established the fundamental rules for cataloguing and classifying. Indeed, the modern museum combines two nineteenth-century traditions—the organization schemes of Agassiz and the showmanship of P. T. Barnum.

When he emigrated to the United States in December 1846 to take a post at Harvard University, Agassiz's first stop was in Philadelphia to see "the American Golgotha," the famous skull collection of Dr. Samuel Morton. An eminent physician and anatomist, Morton had recently published two skull compendia, *Crania Americana* (1839) and *Crania Aegyptiaca* (1844), works that had profound influence on the understanding of race in America. Morton's first book collected data on the shape and capacity of the skulls of various North American types, classified as white, Indian, Eskimo, and Negro. Judging that the ancient skulls he had collected from Indian burials and other sites did not differ markedly from modern skulls of the same race, Morton concluded that the races always had the same physical and mental characteristics. In other words, he believed that racial factors were static rather than evolutionary. Moreover, from a comparison among skulls, Morton deduced that the races of mankind had been separately created as distinct and unequal species.[4]

Prior scientific theory about evolution was almost universally creationist; that is, it conformed to the Bible in its belief in the unity of

4. For the discussion of Morton and the American School of Ethnology, see William Stanton, *The Leopard's Spots: Scientific Attitudes Toward Race in America, 1815–59* (Chicago: University of Chicago, 1960). See also Stephen Jay Gould's classic *The Mismeasure of Man* (New York: W. W. Norton & Co., 1981). Gould restaged many of Morton's cranial measurements and discovered important discrepancies that demonstrated that there is little difference in the size of the cranial cavity of different individuals, regardless of race. The culminating document of the anti-Darwinist American School of Ethnology was J. C. Nott and George R. Gliddon, *Types of Mankind* (Philadelphia, 1854), which featured an introduction by Agassiz. Nott and Gliddon, though distinguished scientists, were both rabid segregationists who distorted art historical and archeological evidence (mainly from Egyptian tombs) to promote their view that blacks were historically inferior to other races.

all peoples as descendants of Adam and Eve. This theory, called mono-genism, asserted origin from a single source. Racial discrepancies were explained by subscribing to one of two views: one, the environmentalist, which said that separate races evolved into different body types and skin pigmentation because of climate, locale, and other physical effects; and two, miscegenist, which held that separate races were the result of intermarriage. But it was polygenesis, the theory of multiple, separate creations for each race as distinct species, that became the hallmark of the American School of Ethnology. For a brief time around 1850, the American theory of polygenesis, with Morton as its leader, enjoyed wide credence in international scientific circles.

Whether or not Morton and Agassiz discussed racial theory at their first meeting is unclear. Until that point, Agassiz had shown little interest in racial typologies and had not yet embraced the theory of separate creation. He was impressed by the skulls, though. For a collector like Agassiz, the effect was dramatic, and he wrote to his mother at once: "Imagine a series of 600 skulls, most of Indians from all tribes who inhabit or once inhabited North America. Nothing like it exists anywhere else. This collection, by itself, is worth a trip to America." However, in the same letter to his mother, Agassiz recorded another event that may have either reflected his conversations with Morton or simply jolted him into a confrontation with the issue of race. He wrote of his encounter, for the first time in his life, with a black man:

> All the domestics in my hotel were men of color. I
> can scarcely express to you the painful impression
> that I received, especially since the feeling that they
> inspired in me is contrary to all our ideas about the
> confraternity of the human type and the unique origin
> of our species.... Nonetheless, it is impossible for
> me to repress the feeling that they are not of the same
> blood as us. In seeing their black faces with their thick
> lips and grimacing teeth, the wool on their head, their
> bent knees, their large curved nails, and especially
> the livid color of their palms, I could not take my eyes
> off their face in order to stay far away.[5]

Despite his personal repugnance for the blacks he encountered, Agassiz later claimed that his beliefs on racial typologies were without political motivation, and he remained a staunch abolitionist, a position that seems contradictory given the later proslavery embrace of his views. Morton, a Quaker, also argued for disinterested science, although his assertion, in *Crania Aegyptiaca,* that ancient Egyptians were not black and in fact had employed blacks as their slaves seemed

5. Agassiz to his mother, December 1846 (Houghton Library, Harvard University), quoted in Gould, pp. 50, 44–45.

to support American slavery. But clearly, highly subjective political and aesthetic decisions governed the development of polygenesis, particularly among Southern scientists determined to prove the inferiority of African American slaves in the decades before the Civil War.

This "scientific" issue came to a head at the third meeting of the American Association for the Advancement of Science held in Charleston in March 1850. The central theme of the conference was the question of the unity or diversity of species, and the featured speaker was Agassiz. His comments to the Charleston audience, his first public statement regarding separate creation, were circumspect. But he made it clear that he sided with the Southern view of polygenesis and accepted the inferior status of blacks. The various races of mankind, he stated, were "well marked and distinct" and did not originate "from a common center ... nor a common pair."[6]

This statement elicited a firestorm of controversy with the conservative clergy in his hometown of Boston, and Agassiz was obliged to make his positions on Christianity and abolitionism clear in three long articles published in the *Christian Examiner.* In these, Agassiz stressed that his views regarding separate creation did not contradict the biblical notion of a unified human origin. Rather, he argued, the Bible referred only to the Caucasian inhabitants of one portion of the globe; Negroes, Indians, Hindus, and the other "species" he identified inhabited different and discrete geographical regions, having originated and evolved in unique ways. Regarding slavery, Agassiz tried specifically to divorce himself from any political implications (or intentions) of his project:

> We disclaim, however, all connection with any question involving political matters. It is simply with reference to the possibility of appreciating the differences existing between different men, and of eventually determining whether they have originated all over the world and under what circumstances, that we have tried to trace some facts representing the human races.[7]

Yet, immediately following his visit to Charleston in March 1850, Agassiz had been motivated to gather specific evidence for his theory in relation to Africans. That Agassiz would employ science in a project that implicitly supported the Southern view of slavery is significant because it demonstrates how the pose of disinterested empiricism actually fortified preexisting, though unstated, political views. Even the mode of statistical analysis had an ideological basis characteristic

6. Agassiz, quoted in Elinor Reichlin, "Faces of Slavery: A Historical Find," *American Heritage* 29 (June 1977): 4.
7. Agassiz, "The Diversity of Origin of the Human Races," *Christian Examiner* 49 (1850): 113.
8. See Jonathan Crary, *Techniques of the Observer: On Vision and Modernity in the Nineteenth Century* (Cambridge, Mass.: MIT Press, 1990).

Facing page:
Joseph T. Zealy, *Renty, Congo. Plantation of B.F. Taylor, Esq., Columbia, S.C.*, 1850. Two quarter-plate daguerreotypes, each 4 ¹/₄ x 3 ¹/₄ in. (10.8 x 8.3 cm). Peabody Museum, Harvard University, Cambridge.
Joseph T. Zealy, *Drana, country born, daughter of Jack, Guinea. Plantation of B.F. Taylor, Esq., Columbia, S.C.*, 1850. Two quarter-plate daguerreotypes, each 4 ¹/₄ x 3 ¹/₄ in. (10.8 x 8.3 cm). Peabody Museum, Harvard University, Cambridge.
Joseph T. Zealy, *Jack (driver), Guinea. Plantation of B.F. Taylor, Esq., Columbia, S.C.*, 1850. Two quarter-plate daguerreotypes, each 4 ¹/₄ x 3 ¹/₄ in. (10.8 x 8.3 cm). Peabody Museum, Harvard University, Cambridge.

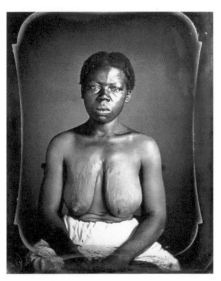

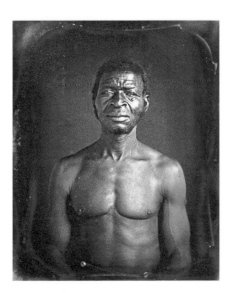

of increasing modernization. The mania for the collection and quantification of natural specimens coincided with other statistical projects, such as the beginning of the annual census, statistics for crime and health, and the mapping and surveying of new lands, exemplifying a new way of seeing the world.[8] Certainly, such scientific enumerations reduced individuals to statistics and involved depersonalization, but, its proponents argued, modern quantification would improve social organization by helping to catalogue the needs of citizens.

In attempting to organize his data regarding Africans, Agassiz sought firsthand evidence. Since the importation of Africans had been outlawed in 1808, Agassiz was doubtful about finding "pure" examples of the race in America. But Dr. Robert W. Gibbes, who had given two papers in Charleston, encouraged Agassiz to visit the plantations around Columbia. Gibbes, the son of a prominent South Carolina family, was a close friend of many of the leading plantation owners, including such families as the Hamptons, the Hammonds, and the Taylors. He was also Columbia's foremost authority on science and culture. He was a nationally recognized expert on American paleontology and, like Agassiz, an obsessive collector of scientific specimens.[9]

Whatever Agassiz may have thought about the racial status of Africans as he wrote out his lectures in Boston, his attitude was radically transformed once he witnessed the real-life situation of African American slaves in Columbia, South Carolina. There, he encountered a tiny caste of aristocratic white slaveowners who commanded vast plantations (Wade Hampton's alone was more than eighteen thousand acres) and owned as many as three thousand slaves. In 1850, the white population of Columbia was just over six thousand, whereas the slave population was in excess of a hundred thousand. Given this huge disparity, upcountry plantation owners were justifiably fearful of slave uprisings and used a variety of fear-inducing tactics to insure docility. Thus, if attitudes toward slaves were more tolerant, even paternalistic, in Massachusetts or even Virginia, in South Carolina discipline was deemed necessary, and the need for discipline seemed to encourage an attitude of contempt toward slaves.[10]

How Agassiz hit upon the idea of photographing the slaves is not fully known. The idea may have come from Morton, who had given Agassiz a daguerreotype of a young African boy he had exhibited before the Academy of Natural Sciences in Philadelphia.[11] Or Agassiz may have been familiar with various calls in contemporary European scientific journals for the creation of a photographic archive of human specimens, or types. For instance, Agassiz's colleague Étienne-Reynaud-Augustin Serres, a professor of comparative anatomy at the Jardin des Plantes and the president of the Academy of Sciences in

9. For more on Gibbs and the plantation owners around Columbia, see Carol Bleser, ed., *Secret and Sacred: The Diaries of James Henry Hammond, a Southern Slaveholder* (New York: Oxford University Press, 1988).

10. See George M. Frederickson, "Masters and Mudsills: The Role of Race in the Planter Ideology of South Carolina," in *The Arrogance of Race: Historical Perspectives on Slavery, Racism, and Social Inequality* (Middletown, Conn.: Wesleyan University Press, 1988), pp. 15–27.

11. This daguerreotype, taken by W. & J. Langenheim, is reproduced in Melissa Banta and George Hinsely, *From Site to Sight: Anthropology, Photography, and the Power of Imagery* (Cambridge, Mass.: Harvard University Press, 1986), p. 34.

Blake Brothers, *Portrait of a Man*, ca. 1860. Carte-de-visite, 4 x 2 7/16 in. (10.1 x 6.2 cm). International Center of Photography, Daniel Cowin Collection, 1990.

Unidentified photographer, *Stirrup Branch Plantation. Bishopville, S.C., on the 75th birthday of Capt. James Rembert, June 8, 1857 (Front view of house shows Capt. Rembert and family; rear view of house shows slave families)*, 1857. Tintypes, 2 ¼ x 5 ½ in. (5.8 x 8.9 cm). Library of Congress, Washington D.C.

Paris, had proposed the establishment of a museum of photographs of the races of mankind. And, in 1845, a French daguerreotypist named E. Thiesson had taken studies of Brazilians and Portuguese Africans in Lisbon.[12] But there was no precedent in America for the type of photographic collection that Agassiz sought to build.

In a letter to Morton, Gibbes explained that during a tour of plantations around Columbia, Agassiz had selected various slaves to be photographed: "Agassiz was delighted with his examination of Ebo, Foulah, Gullah, Guinea, Coromantee, Mandrigo and Congo Negroes. He found enough to satisfy him that they have differences from the other races." After Agassiz departed, Gibbes had the slaves brought to the local daguerreotypist, Joseph T. Zealy, and photographed. Gibbes carefully recorded the names, African origins, and current ownership of the slaves. In June 1850, Gibbes wrote to Morton, saying, "I have just finished the daguerreotypes for Agassiz of native Africans of various tribes. I wish you could see them."[13]

The fifteen daguerreotypes are divided into two series. The first consists of standing, fully nude images showing front, side, and rear views. This practice reflected a physiognomic approach, an attempt to record body shape, proportions, and posture. Four slaves were photographed in this manner—Alfred Jack's American-born daughter who lived on the Taylor estate; Renty, from the Congo tribe, who also worked at Taylor's estate; Delia, Renty's American-born daughter, who also lived on the Taylor estate; and Fassena, from the Mandingo tribe, a carpenter at the plantation of Wade Hampton II.

Typological systems

The efforts by Gibbes and Agassiz to systematize the slave daguerreotypes represent an early attempt not only to apply photography to anthropology, but also to form a coherent photographic archive. As critic Allan Sekula has pointed out in his landmark article "The Body and the Archive," almost from its inception the photograph was perceived as a form of currency within a closed system. As currency, the photograph ascribed value by both quantifying things and placing them in a circulating system that emphasized their similarity to or difference from other things. This system, generally perceived as an archive, attempts to give coherence and meaning to seemingly random components. Every photograph, Sekula says, takes its place in a "shadow archive," that ultimate, imaginary ranking and organizing of information implied by the very selective and classificatory nature of photography.[14]

In fact, primitive archival systems were immediately characteristic of the daguerrean era. The "shadow archive" of early photographs can be divided along two general organizational principles—the later-

12. For more on French attempts to use daguerreotypes for anthropological study, see Étienne-Reynaud-Augustin Serres, "Observations sur l'application de la photographie à l'étude des race humaines," *Comptes Rendus des Séances de l'Académie des Sciences* 21 (1845): 242–26; Harrmur Krech, "Lichtbilder vom Menschen: Vom Typenbild zur anthropologischen Fotographie," *Fotogeschichte* 4 (1984): 3–15; and "Anwendung der Photographie zum Studium der Menschenracen," *Dingler's Polytechnisches Journal* (Stuttgart) 97 (1845): 400. On Thiessen, in particular, see Janet E. Buerger, *French Daguerreotypes* (Chicago: University of Chicago Press, 1990), pp. 90–91, 229.
13. Robert W. Gibbes to Samuel G. Morton, 31 March and June 1850, Library Company of Philadelphia. Although little is known about Joseph T. Zealy, we can imagine the slaves' shock upon entering his gallery. The local newspaper editor wrote that Zealy's gallery was "fitted up with great taste...The room where he takes his pictures is handsomely furnished, and we notice therein an elegant piano, for the accommodation of his lady visitors. Immediately off this is an ante-room, for the proper adjustment of toilette, etc., by his visitors. It is magnificently lighted, having, besides numerous windows, a large skylight adjusted and constructed for the purposes of his art, and will undoubtedly insure a more perfect finish to his pictures." *Photographic Art-Journal* 2 (December 1851): 376–77.
14. Allan Sekula, "The Body and the Archive," *October*, no. 39 (Winter 1986): 3–64.

ally organized catalogue or the vertically organized genealogy. The catalogue attempted to establish similarity or difference across a spatial dimension. This concept thus included group portraits, panoramic views, and collections of portraits of famous people. The genealogy, on the other hand, assembled likeness or diversity across time. This category embraced family photographs (often assembled in frames or, later, in albums), postmortem or memorial photographs, records of changing scenes, or changes in an individual over time.

Within the "shadow archive," both of these systems for organizing photographs—and they often overlapped—implied a hierarchical ordering.[15] Individual images were linked comparatively and organized dichotomously, thus creating and enforcing divisions between self and other, healthy and diseased, normal and pathological. Strengthened by the seeming transparency of photographic realism, these categories and the divisions between them soon took on the authority of natural "facts." Supplying either too much or too little information, photographs soon muddied the easy distinctions between subjective knowledge and what was called "objective." Owing to its indexical properties— that is, that a photograph retains a "trace" of an actual existence, as does, say, a footprint—photography seemed to be entirely objective. But the very literalness of photographs produces an uncontrollable multiplication of meanings in even the most banal images. And the equally complex acts of taking, reading, or organizing photographs animate all the trajectories of power and desire, mastery and projection, self and other that triangulate the visual field and govern reception.

By supplying an overabundance of information, photography confuses and problematizes its message; it creates what author Roland Barthes calls a "reality effect," a semblance of realism bound to detail. In nineteenth-century parlance, two technical words gained a certain currency to describe how "reality" was construed: the word *daguerreotype* was distinguished from the word *stereotype*.[16] Stereotypes were originally molds for creating multiple copies of printing type; the word, therefore, came to connote generalized replication. The daguerreotype, on the other hand, was characterized by miniaturization, infinitesimal precision, and detail. These contrasting characteristics—the general category and the specific case—are precisely those poles that govern the logic of the archive.

The early ethnographic research conducted by Morton, Agassiz, and other members of the American School of Ethnology depended on the collapse of the specific and the generic into "types." The type represented an average example of a racial group, an abstraction, though not necessarily the ideal, that defined the general form or character of individuals within the group; it subsumed individuality. As Herbert H. Odom explains, "The term *type* roughly implies that the

15. Ibid., p. 10.
16. See Roland Barthes, "The Reality Effect," in *The Rustle of Language*, trans. Richard Howard (New York: Hill and Wang, 1986), pp. 141–48. For the etymology of the word *stereotype*, see Sander L. Gilman, *Difference and Pathology: Stereotype of Sexuality, Race, and Madness* (Ithaca, NY: Cornell University Press, 1989) pp. 15–35; on the uses of the word *daguerreotype*, see Alan Trachtenberg, "Photography: Emergence of a Keyword," in *Photography in Nineteenth-Century America*, ed. Sandweiss, pp. 13–47.

observed, apparently disordered phenomena are best explained as
deviations from certain determinate norms.... The function of classification is then to decide which observed creature may be considered
as deviations from each set norm, and, of course, how many norms
exist."[17] Photography strengthened the seeming reality of the type
by objectifying the individual and by using props and other details
to accentuate the "truth" of the depiction. Typological photographs—
particularly those that became popular in the 1860s and 1870s—
were assumed to be self-evident, to speak for themselves, and, at
the same time, to be generic. Typically, natives were identified only
by their country, tribe, or some other generic label (for example,
"A Burmese Beauty").

Another feature of type classification and the typological photograph was the emphasis on external appearance, on the measurement
and observation of the human form (that is, the skeletons and skulls),
rather than on cultural forms. This practice conformed to Agassiz's
method as well. He had worked principally with fossils and other
"hard" evidence to determine his classification of fish types. This
objectifying method was allied with physiognomy and phrenology, the
early nineteenth-century sciences that analyzed the exterior form of
the human body in an attempt to understand connections between
different human groups as well as the inner workings of the mind and
spirit. As Agassiz said, "The material form is the cover of the spirit";
this he regarded as "fundamental and self-evident." The discourse on
slavery and abolitionism was typified by such external views of the
body. Two images keyed to outward markings received wide circulation
in mid-nineteenth-century popular culture—the *Branded Hand* (1844)
and the *Scourged Back* (1863), showing, respectively, a punished slave
liberator and a slave's lash-scarred back.[18]

Typological systems depended on the widespread contemporary
interest in the body, especially the head. Silhouettes, portrait daguerreotypes, and phrenology all directed special attention to the shape,
size, or character of the head as a record of individuality. The polygen-
esists, by contrast, were interested in defining separate racial types.
Their charts, derived from phrenological models, often showed crude
rankings from the primate head to the African to the classical Greek.
This thinly disguised racism was also reflected in their field research,
which involved not only the physical measurement of the body, but an
assessment of the moral character, manner, and social habits of each
racial type. For instance, Morton wrote that the African Hottentots
were the "nearest approximation to the lower animals.... Their com-
plexion is yellowish brown, compared by travelers to the peculiar hue of
Europeans in the last stages of jaundice.... The women are represented

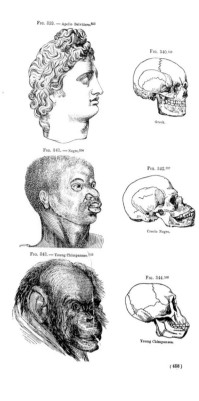

17. Herbert H. Odom, "Generalizations
on Race in Nineteenth-Century
America," *Isis* 58 (Spring 1967): 5–18.
See also Elizabeth Edwards, "Photo-
graphic 'Types': The Pursuit of Method,"
Visual Anthropology 3 (1990): 235–58.
Edwards notes that the Société
d'Ethnographie in Paris had initiated
a master archival project recording
"human types" as early as 1866.
18. Agassiz, quoted in *Dictionary of
American Biography*, vol. 1 (New York:
Charles Scribner's Sons, 1928), p. 120.
For information on the *Branded Hand*
and the *Scourged Back*, see, respectively,
Robert Sobieszek and Odette M. Appel,
*The Spirit of Fact: The Daguerreotypes
of Southworth & Hawes, 1843–1862*
(Boston: David R. Godine, 1980), p. 23;
and Kathleen Collins, "The Scourged
Back," *History of Photography* 9, no. 1
(January–March 1985): 43–45.
19. Morton, *Crania Americana* (Phila-
delphia: John Pennington, 1839), p. 90.

as even more repulsive in appearance than the men."[19] Needless to say, such observations were often casual and rarely dependent on what would today be called fieldwork. But as scientific description, such views were legitimized.

The construction of racial types, their ranking in a hierarchy of intellect, and the analysis of the meaning of their physiognomy in the general scheme of things all required the presence of a standard. Although these scientists argued that their studies were made without prejudice or without models, there is ample evidence that a standard was in place to characterize the Caucasian ideal. As historian George Mosse has argued, this view emerged from the appropriation by pre-revolutionary Enlightenment anthropology of the classicist idealism of Johann Joachim Winckelmann, best remembered as the founder of art history. Winckelmann argued that the "physical beauty of the ancient Greeks accounted for the excellence of their art." The ancient Egyptians and Africans, by comparison, had been handicapped by their own physical appearance, "which lacked the features that could stimulate the artist through an ideal of higher beauty."[20]

This aesthetic standard underlay every classificatory system in the polygenetic program, guaranteeing that the races would be considered not only separate but unequal. The embodiment of the classical ideal in America, the standard against which all the derogatory images of African Americans were judged, was the neoclassical statue in white marble, typified by Hiram Powers's *Greek Slave*. Various versions of this life-size standing nude sculpture, ostensibly representing a modern Greek woman captured by Turks, were wildly popular among American audiences from the time of its creation in 1844 until its triumph at the London Crystal Palace Exhibition in 1851. Critics praised its chaste purity and its classical proportions; male and female viewers swooned. Rather than suggesting violence, the slight chains on the *Greek Slave's* wrists only accentuated the work's mildly erotic and highly sentimentalized view of slavery and the body. But the irony that the model of purity and ideal beauty is depicted as a slave was not lost on the sculpture's earliest audiences, and the statue was embraced by the abolitionist cause. More pointed, however, was the cartoon in *Punch* that depicted the anti-ideal—an image of a black slave on a pedestal.[21]

In nineteenth-century anthropology, blacks were often situated along the evolutionary ladder midway between a classical ideal and the orangutan. From these pseudoscientific studies a Negro type emerged that was highly distorted and almost unique to ethnographic illustration. In comparing various skulls, taxonomists often relied on the device of the facial angle. This technique, invented by the

20. Winckelmann, paraphrased in Hugh Honour, *The Image of the Black in Western Art*, vol. 4., pt. 2 (Cambridge, Mass.: Harvard University Press), p. 14.
21. See Joy S. Kasson, *Marble Queens & Captives: Women in Nineteenth-Century American Sculpture* (New Haven: Yale University Press, 1990).

eighteenth-century Dutch taxonomist Peter Camper, involved the systematic evaluation of the profile measurement from the tip of the forehead to the greatest protrusion of the lips. For Camper and others, the mathematical capability of scientifically classifying such information offered a new tool for the investigation of evolution, or linear development. Camper described his project: "I observed that a line drawn along the forehead and upper lip indicated a difference in national physiognomy.... When I made these lines incline forwards, I obtained the face of an antique; backwards of a negroe; still more backwards, the lines which mark an ape, a dog, a snipe, etc."[22] Representations of the facial angle of the Negro skull almost always showed an abnormally pronounced brow, protruding lips and teeth, and a back-sloping forehead. Curiously, these "scientific" representations preceded most of the more familiar stereotypes and derogatory images of African Americans in popular culture. The popular images built on the scientific ones and enhanced or exaggerated distortions of the black body. The subject's clothes were often shown torn, partially removed, or missing altogether; the body itself was often shown being whipped, beaten, hung, pierced, bitten, branded, or otherwise subjugated to a white oppressor. Moreover, many of the exposed and attacked bodies were shown in explicitly erotic poses, raising the question of how these largely proslavery images functioned as a type of pornography.

It is perhaps not coincidental that by their unprecedented nudity, the slave daguerreotypes intersect with that other illicit regime of photography so central to the 1850s (at least in Europe) and so exclusively concerned with the representation of the tactile surface of the human body. While there is no absolute connection between photographs of the nude body and pornography, the vaguely eroticized nature of the slave daguerreotypes derives from the unwavering, voyeuristic manner with which they indiscriminately survey the bodies of the Africans, irrespective of the subjects' lives.

Agassiz was undoubtedly influenced in this regard by his great mentor, Baron Cuvier, who took a particular—if not perverse—interest in the Hottentot Venus, an African woman who was exhibited naked as a curiosity in Europe because of her unusually prominent posterior. After her death, Cuvier conducted an autopsy of her body and published a text about its distinguishing features.[23] The case of the Hottentot Venus marked the collapse of scientific investigation of the racial other into the realm of the pornographic. This sort of elision of the exotic and the erotic explains in part the mid-nineteenth-century fascination with distorting the features of blacks in popular representations. In many texts (including Agassiz's letter to his mother), blacks were made not only animal-like or simian, but also vulgar and overtly seductive.

22. Peter Camper, quoted in Honour, *Image of the Black*, p. 14.
23. See Sander L. Gilman's important but controversial treatment of this history in "Black Bodies, White Bodies: Toward an Iconography of Female Sexuality in Late Nineteenth-Century Art, Medicine and Literature," in *"Race," Writing, and Difference*, ed. Henry Louis Gates Jr. (Chicago: University of Chicago Press, 1986); and Stephen Jay Gould, "The Hottentot Venus," *Natural History* 19 (1982): 20–27.

Unidentified photographer, *Abolitionist Button*, ca. 1849. Daguerreotype, ⅝ in. (1.5 cm) diameter. Gilman Paper Company Collection, New York.

The type and the portrait

Given this history of the distortions wrought by typologies, it is particularly ironic that historian Alan Trachtenberg, in writing of the Agassiz
slave daguerreotypes, refers to them as portraits and even likens them
to classical Roman busts.[24] Here, it is necessary to draw the fundamental distinctions between the type and the portrait. Formally, the
type discourages style and composition, seeking to present the information as plainly and straightforwardly as possible. Thus, the images
are frequently organized around a clear central axis with a minimum
of external information that could distract from the principal focus.
Since objectivity is the goal, the typological image appears to have no
author. (In the case of the slave daguerreotypes, however, authorship
is multiple, applying equally to Agassiz and to the photographer Zealy.)
And, finally, the type is clearly situated within a system that denies its
subject even as it establishes overt relations between its mute subjects.
The emphasis on the body occurs at the expense of speech; the subject
as already positioned, known, owned, represented, spoken for, or constructed as silent; in short, it is ignored. In other words, the typological
photograph is a form of representational colonialism. Fundamentally
nonreciprocal, it masks its subjective distortions in the guise of logic
and organization. Its formations are deformations.

The portrait, on the other hand, is of value principally because
of the viewer's relationship to the sitter, the ability to recognize the

24. See Alan Trachtenberg, *Reading
American Photographs: Images as
History; Mathew Brady to Walker Evans*
(New York: Hill and Wang, 1989),
pp. 54–56.

Albert Sands Southworth and Josiah Johnson Hawes, *The Branded Hand of Captain Jonathan Walker, Boston, Mass.*, 1845.
Sixth plate daguerreotype, 2 3/4 x 3 1/4 in. (7 x 8.3 cm). Massachusetts Historical Society.

subject when he or she is absent. In this sense, the portrait is like a caricature that accents the telling features of an individual. Generally, the nineteenth-century photographic portrait was designed to affirm or underscore the white middle-class individual's right to personhood, a fact underlined by legal and social structures as well. Further, the portrait signaled an individual's place in society, which explains why so many daguerreotypes feature sitters posed with the tools of their trade or other attributes. As Sekula makes clear, "Every portrait implicitly took its place within a social and moral hierarchy. The *private* moment of sentimental individuation, the look at the frozen gaze-of-the-loved-one, was shadowed by two other more *public* looks: a look up, at one's 'betters,' and a look down, at one's 'inferiors.'"[25] Few slaves, however, had the luxury of projecting any look at all. That slaves were denied individual identity in the antebellum South is merely underscored by the near-total absence of photographs depicting them.

This process of social ranking was most apparent in the work of early criminologists, ethnologists, and medical photographers. In such fields, it was necessary to construct a standard, or mean, to establish deviance and thus identify and isolate the ultimate threat to the ideal. Trachtenberg has astutely noted the similarity between the slave daguerreotypes and a slightly earlier project (ca. 1846) by Mathew Brady to record images of inmates at mental institutions.[26] These images, now lost, are preserved in the line engravings published as illustrations to the American edition of Marmaduke Sampson's *Rationale of Crime* (1846), edited by penal reformer Eliza Farnham. Brady's images fortified Farnham's argument that criminals and cretins could be recognized by their outward appearance, that the mark of deviance was presumed to be emblazoned across the head and body like a stigmata. With the rise of urbanism and industrialization in the mid-nineteenth century, such typological readings were deemed practical to protect oneself from strangers by immediately assessing their character.

This process of identifying another person by superficial physical characteristics structured the logic of racial classification. Surprisingly, such distinctions did not really exist before the nineteenth century. To be sure, various forms of prejudice and subjugation had existed in many societies, but prior to 1800, none of the variety of discriminatory terms and attitudes employed were based on race. Racism, as it emerged in the early nineteenth century, was a heavily encoded and naturalized belief that racial characteristics and behaviors were grounded in biology and conformed to a qualitative hierarchy.[27] But, as historian George M. Fredrickson has argued, "for its full growth, intellectual and ideological, racism required a body of 'scientific' and

25. Sekula, "The Body and the Archive," p. 10.
26. See Madeleine B. Stern, "Mathew Brady and the *Rationale of Crime*: A Discovery in Daguerreotypes," *Quarterly Journal of the Library of Congress* 31 (July 1974): 127–35. This series is also discussed in Sekula, "The Body and the Archive," p. 20; and in Trachtenberg, *Reading American Photographs*, pp. 57–58.
27. Literary theorist Anthony Appiah makes a distinction between what he calls "racialist" and "racist" discourses. The first involves a distinction of difference that may have no moral or evaluative distinction attributed to it; the second involves the application of that distinction to a hierarchical evaluation that signals the inferiority of one group in relation to another. See Kwame Anthony Appiah, "Racisms," in *Anatomy of Racism*, ed. Gary David Goldberg (Minneapolis: University of Minnesota Press, 1990), pp. 4–5.

cultural thought which would give credence to the notion that the blacks were for unalterable reasons of race, morally and intellectually inferior to whites."[28] Agassiz's slave photographs constitute a perfect example of the conjunction of scientific and cultural thought in the formation of racist ideology.

In attempting to understand the origins of racism, it is important to avoid removing it to a historical past or displacing its sources onto the oppressed. Any investigation of representations of African American blackness, then, must actually take a critical look at Euro-American whiteness to understand the construction of race as a category. As critic Coco Fusco has insisted, "To ignore white ethnicity is to redouble its hegemony by naturalizing it."[29] In this regard, it is crucial to understand the arsenal of institutional means geared toward the enforcement of white male superiority. Photography, typologies, archives, and museums serve as disciplinary structures, socially constructed means of defining and regulating difference.

Like all representations of difference, Louis Agassiz's slave daguerreotypes exploit the familiar ethnographic convention of introducing the comfortable white viewer to that which is not only exotic and safely distant, but also generally and deliberately invisible. But not all designations of difference are the same. As Frederick Douglass noted in a review of the work of the American School of Ethnology in 1854:

> It is fashionable now, in our land, to exaggerate the differences between the negro and the European. If, for instance, a phrenologist or naturalist undertakes to represent in portraits, the difference between the two races—the negro and the European—he will invariably present the highest type of the European, and the lowest type of the negro.... If the very best type of the European is always presented, I insist that justice, in all such works, demands that the very best type of the negro should be taken. The importance of this criticism may not be apparent to all;—to the black man it is very apparent.[30]

As Douglass so pointedly noted, the meaning of representations is governed not only by who makes the image but also by who looks. If this view accords with much recent critical theory that acknowledges the role of the observer in constructing knowledge, it also points to the part that museums and archives play in fixing meanings. By adhering to immutable versions of historical truth, such institutions structure information according to ideologically inflected principles. But rather than dismissing or rejecting these institutions, it is important to

28. George M. Fredrickson, *The Black Image in the White Mind: The Debate on Afro-American Character and Destiny, 1817–1914* (Middletown, Conn.: Wesleyan University Press, 1988), p. 2.

29. Coco Fusco, "Fantasies of Oppositionality," *Afterimage* 16 (December 1988): 6–9.

30. Frederick Douglass, "The Claims of the Negro Ethnologically Considered: An Address Delivered in Hudson, Ohio, on 12 July 1854," in *The Frederick Douglass Papers*, ed. John W. Blassingame, vol. 2 (New Haven: Yale University Press, 1979), pp. 510, 514.

critically examine their practices and to recognize that their versions
of history are not absolute. Such critical methods will help foster
multiplicity, subjectivity, and relativity in the construction of histories.

In the case of the slave daguerreotypes, this suggests that their
meaning extends well beyond the empirical proof that Louis Agassiz
sought. Quite different—but no less valid—histories and personal
meanings can be connected with these images. If colonialism and
ethnographic exploitation depend on appropriation, one must acknowledge that what is taken can always be taken back. In 1991, for example,
the African American artist and photographer Carrie Mae Weems
journeyed to the Sea Islands off the coast of South Carolina to record
the remnants of the culture of the Gullah, the survivors of slaves from

Carrie Mae Weems, *From Here I Saw What Happened And I Cried*, 1995/96. Chromogenic prints with sandblasted text
on glass, two of four prints, each 14 3/8 x 11 in. (36.4 x 27.9 cm). International Center of Photography, purchased with funds
from the ICP Acquisitions Committee, 2000.

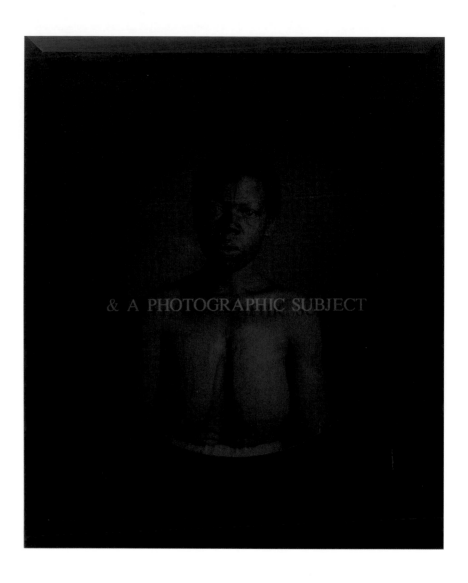

& A PHOTOGRAPHIC SUBJECT

31. See Andrea Kirsh and Susan Fisher Sterling, *Carrie Mae Weems* (Washington, D.C.: National Museum of Women in the Arts, 1994), pp. 102–9. In conjunction with the Getty Museum's "Hidden Witness" exhibition (28 February–18 June 1995) of early photography of African American subjects, Weems was invited to produce her own installation, "Carrie Mae Weems Reacts to 'Hidden Witness'," in an adjacent gallery. Using the format of her Sea Islands work, she rephotographed older images and added texts to comment on the photographs' hidden information and the changing representations of black subjects.

Africa. Weems photographed brick shelters and other surviving records of the Gullah, producing a series of works that combined texts, narratives, photographs, and plates. Among the images incorporated into Weems's works were old pictures of several slaves who had come from Africa—reproductions of Agassiz's slave daguerreotypes.[31] She did not alter or transform the images; she only selected, enlarged, and recontextualized them. By placing them beside pictures of remnants of the African culture the Gullah brought to America, Weems viewed their lives empathetically from a black point of view. She saw these men and women not as representatives of some typology but as living, breathing ancestors. She made them portraits.

Aleta M. Ringlero

PRAIRIE PINUPS

Reconsidering Historic Portraits of American Indian Women

I came across the photographs of Indian photographer Will Soule (1836–1908) in 1972 as an assignment for an undergraduate art history paper. The recent publication on Soule by Belous and Weinstein[1] was a rich source of several interesting images of Plains Indians decked out in feathers and buckskins, and sporting elaborate hair arrangements. The men of the Plains cultures appeared to be the epitome of Indian-ness, an archetypal appearance all photographs of Indians seemed to convey in period photography. Among the sepia prints, I was startled to discover six plates of images of Wichita women that would stay in my mind for over thirty years.[2] The images that so intrigued me in their stark realism were examples of erotic photographs of nude women, and all Indians. I discovered prairie pinups from 1870, and two were styled in the familiar poses of a Playboy centerfold! Except for the traditional forms of Plains-style buck-skin boots, disc belts, dangling necklaces, and the unmistakable faces of Plains people, they were all naked, or seminude to be precise. To my naive, 1972 pre-Women's Movement sensibilities, it was an astonishing identification of the presence of erotic photography with Indian women as the subject.

In the years since this revelation, I have come to understand the significance of the Soule photographs in other ways and couched in art-historical terms—on the nude, on the objectification of women, under the colonial gaze, and so forth. As years passed I waited for discussions on Soule's work to appear in the academic journals, certain they would engage me with theoretical issues of race and representation, with names like Marcus, Geertz, or Barthes thrown in to wrap around the Soule photographs. I waited in vain.

In hindsight, I arrived at my second big revelation about Soule's images. They make the viewer uncomfortable, and a general tone of reticence toward the prairie pinups—and more likely, toward the erotic photograph in general, and of course, pornography—surrounds the six photographs. Soule's images are, after all, visions of "amazons," "savages," and "barbarians," hardly the kind of subject the specialists of Plains ethnography and scholars of art history are anxious to pursue in the study of American Indians. The reluctance that surrounds the Wichita photographs is reflected in the lack of published work about them, beyond brief passing commentary.[3] In terms of discussions on the erotic photography that forms part of the historic visual portfolio of the Indian, the silence is deafening. Is it the nudity, the breasts, the Indian women posed in "come hither" attitudes, or the subject of pornographic intention permeating the nude images that the academic

1. Russell E. Belous and Robert A. Weinstein, *Will Soule: Indian Photographer at Fort Sill, Oklahoma 1869–74* (Los Angeles: Ward Ritchie Press, 1969) is the first work on Indian photographers I consulted for discussion of Plains photo-graphy and remains the single work to address Soule's oeuvre exclusively.
2. Ibid., pp. 67–72.
3. Joanna Cohen Scherer, "You Can't Believe Your Eyes: Inaccuracies in Photographs of North American Indians," *Studies in the Anthropology of Visual Communication* 2, no. 2 (1975): 77. Scherer's discussion of Soule's work includes a brief passing reference, "How-ever, he also liked to include Wichita 'cheesecake.'" Belous and Weinstein make no reference to the photographs, although they published six plates in their section on the Wichita, the largest number of plates dedicated to one specific genre. Wilbur S. Nye notes, "Wichita women were well dressed from the waist down.... Before these women learned that it was wrong to appear in public partly nude, Soule obtained a series of photographs which undoubt-edly sold well at Fort Sill as prairie pinups." *Plains Indian Raiders*, (Norman: University of Oklahoma Press, 1968), p. 404.

Will Soule, *Wichita Woman (Squaw 2)*, ca. 1867. Albumen print, 7 x 5 in. (17.8 x 12.7 cm). National Anthropological Archives, Smithsonian Insititution, Washington D.C.

183

world, with very few exceptions, shied away from? The subject of unclothed Indian women is extensively represented in the Western photography of Henry Buehman, Elias A. Bonine, Ben Whittick, and Carlo Gentile, to name a few, among the enormous corpus of Western photographers of the nineteenth century. In the wider scope of photography history, perhaps the acceptance of the nude is too familiar and mundane a subject today. Nevertheless, the Indian woman is unique in the history of pornography and worthy of further study. The images of seminude women staring blankly at the camera in variations of tribal costumes is not simply a record of Anglo-Indian encounters and documentation, but also one of manipulation, exploitation, and racism in the guise of science and knowledge. With my first glimpse of Soule's photographs many years ago, I immediately understood that I was not looking at objective, distanced, scientific records of natives.

Preparation for the exhibition *Only Skin Deep: Changing Visions of the American Self* has been an enlightening task of discovery. It has led from the mountain of digital images taped to the walls around my desk, to an odyssey of locating "naked Indian women photos" in

Unidentified photographer, *Ethnographic portrait–Indian woman*, ca. 1845. Quarter plate daguerreotype, 4¼ x 3¼ in. (10.8 x 8.3 cm). George Eastman House, Rochester, New York.

repositories in California, New Mexico, and Arizona, and to the personal discovery of my own tribe's significant presence as a subject before the lens. The numerous responses of archives, historical societies, and photographic libraries to my request for additional information about the nude studies—including "we like to forget those kinds of photographs are in our collection"[4]—did not deter me. As any researcher will understand, I had only scratched the surface.

The familiar tropes of the American Indian recorded in the photographs taken by adventurous photographers after 1860 continue to

4. This is not to say I was denied access to records, but considerable reluctance on the part of professional and volunteer staff on more than one occasion was not unique to any one facility. Curator Coco Fusco and I encountered this response but, after the first time, we simply found other ways to approach the enormous research task before us.

Elias A. Bonine, *Yuma, three unidentified women*, ca. 1880. Boudoir card, 7 ¹/₄ x 5 ¹/₂ in. (18.4 x 14.0 cm). Museum of New Mexico, Palace of the Governors, Santa Fe.

inform our knowledge of the American Indians. Attached to military campaigns, geographic expeditions, or as traveling entrepreneurs of the new photographic medium, photographers were agents through which the world saw the indigenous people of the Americas. Through formats rapidly developed in photography and print, the images reinforced public curiosity, fascination, and fear of the people they called "warriors, squaws, bucks, maidens, and braves."[5]

Photography in the aide of ethnography, a subdiscipline of anthropology, equaled Science; its task was the pursuit of Knowledge. Anthropology galvanized a belief in the truth and scientific accuracy of the image. Photographs were presumed to be objective evidence and to portray reality, the authentic image of native life. The salvage effort to construct the visual record of Indians viewed them as a doomed and vanishing race.

Ethnographic photography is no longer viewed as true or objective. Critical scholarship challenges the integrity of the images; records in journals, and/or accounts by sitters reveal the manipulation of photographs. The interest in profit from photography added other concerns about the role of the ethnographic image. Joanna Cohen Scherer, a curator and Native American specialist at the Smithsonian Institution, points out the distinction between photographers working

5. I use slang references to American Indians from the actual titles of historic images I came across in the course of my research. The titles of some photographs were handwritten on back or across the front. Often, the slang reference was added as a title at a later date by someone other than the photographer, possibly for sensationalism or to sell the image.

The Real Ramona.

George Wharton James, *Ramona Lubo (Cahuilla) as "The Real Ramona,"* ca. 1909. Postcard, 3 1/2 x 5 1/2 in. (9 x 14 cm). Courtesy of C. Ondine Chavoya.

in the West, "[T]he anthropology photographer was primarily interested in documenting how the Indian currently lived," [while the commercial photographer] "took pictures primarily to make money. These men often attempted to make their subjects look exotic, savage, or romantic to create more interest in their product—the Indian print they sold."[6]

Margaret Blackman, a cultural anthropologist pointed out that Franz Boas, "the father of American anthropology and meticulous chronicler of Northwest Coast Indian cultures, saw photography of Native Americans in commercial, as much as ethnographic terms."[7] Photographers recognized the value of their images, as did scientists. In addition, Blackman added "[w]ith expedition photographers and even I suspect, Boas, there was a strong motivation to photograph what would sell to the public; and the more exotic, the more salable. As far as many early photographers were concerned, the costume made the Indian."[8]

Photographers and anthropologists sold their work to a public eager for entertainment, hungry for information about other people and places, and able to afford the new technology.[9] Nevertheless, photographers, both commercial and anthropologist, also depicted Indians in staged settings of narratives constructed in a historic past. Photography, a powerful propaganda tool, could provide alternate messages against support for assimilation as the official policy toward Indians.

Ann Maxwell's study of colonial photography in national exhibitions and world's fairs identified how colonial photography's images of natives incorporated subtle forms of imperialism.[10] Maxwell demonstrated how antiassimilation supporters saw natives as doomed because the Indian could not compete with European technology; they could be

6. Scherer, "You Can't Believe Your Eyes," p. 68.

7. Margaret Blackman, "Posing the American Indian: Early Photographs Often Clothed Reality in Their Own Stereotypes," *Natural History* 89, no. 10 (1980): 70.

8. Ibid.

9. Ibid. Blackman points to John K. Hiller's stereoscope images of the John Wesley Powell 1873 Colorado River Expedition to the Ute and Paiute Great Basin region as netting $4,100 in sales over six months in 1874. The sets were sold by the U.S. Department of the Interior.

10. See Ann Maxwell, "Shifting focus: photographic representations of Native Americans and African Americans," in *Colonial Photography and Exhibitions: Representations of the 'Native' People and the Making of European Identities* (London and New York: Leicester University Press, 1999), pp. 96–127.

Unidentified photographer, *Student, Sylvenia Scott, at the Sherman Institute in Riverside*, ca. 1926. Gelatin silver print, 7 1/2 x 4 3/4 in. (19 x 12 cm); *Student, Sylvenia Scott, at the Sherman Institute in Riverside*, ca. 1926. Gelatin silver print, 7 1/2 x 4 1/2 in. (19 x 11.4 cm). Sherman Indian Museum, Riverside, California.

blamed for their own demise for failing to adjust under forced assimilation. The ideology of manifest destiny continued with this antiassimilation mindset; the goal was the removal of Indian from their lands.

As the popularity of staged images of Indians grew, tribal diversity was reduced to a formula of singular visual icons: bodies, clothing, and tribal identity became generalized Indianness. To the public, Indians appeared interchangeable, distinctive individuality was transformed; they appear timeless, ever clad in feathers, beads, and hide clothing. Cosmetic wardrobes and identifiable props supplied by photographers in the studio or field erased individuality and the unique attributes of distinction.[11] The representation of the Indian as noble overtook the reality of a devastated Indian culture and obscured individuality.

Today, discussions of historic photographs strip away the romanticized fantasy of Indians as mystical, egalitarian uberbeings in communion with Mother Nature. Instead, we must inquire whether visual records are the response of a photographer's desires. We are left with the impression of reluctant but cooperative "actors" revealed in costumes and tableaus in photography studios, or staged amid grand outdoor settings. The photographer directed a personal vision of Indian culture that was far from the reality of daily native life, and also provided the fainting couch on which comely starlets—the native women posed before the camera—emerged in the distinctive tropes of "squaw, belle, and princess."[12]

Native women who have been deliberately posed with aesthetic consideration to reveal their seminaked bodies are problematic. The numbers of photographs raise several questions surrounding the purpose of the images: who the target audience was (it was probably, but not exclusively, male), and, whether the photographs demonstrate an example of early erotica or pornography. Ethnographic photography of nonwhite subjects was a thin disguise for the sale of exotic subjects under the label of science. In this instance, their lack of clothing is central to the views of native women in sweltering areas of the Southwest and Plains regions. Together, the photographs provided a visual record, however problematic, of adaptation and innovation in response to Anglo contact. In this way, photographic records are the signs that marked the presence of crosscultural hybridity and cultural identities in transition at moments of convergence.

> These are Indians whom the white man justly feared.
> The portraits are not pacified, overdressed, "carnival"
> Indians with whom the white man could feel comfortable.
> These were warriors in every sense of the word, able and
> deadly. . . "savage" defenders of their families, their
> homes, their tribal rights, and their traditional lands.[13]

11. Blackman, "Posing the American Indian," p. 70. "Frontier studio photographers routinely kept a stock of Indian costumes with which to attire local native subjects. The result was that several natives were often photographed in the same outfit or one native might be photographed in two or more different outfits." See also, Paula Richardson Fleming and Judith Lusky, *The North American Indians in Early Photographs* (New York: Harper & Row, 1986), p. 24, for discussion of the authenticity of delegation photographs by Alexander Gardner. As cited, "It has been suggested that Mrs. Gardner had the unhappy task of assisting her husband in the posing of the Indians, and outfitting them in feathers and beads, and tribal garments from a smelly collection of native costumes maintained by the Gallery."
12. I use the terms identified from titles of actual photographs listed in archives and written or printed on the images themselves. I also use the self-referential term "Indian" as it is used in popular vernacular among tribal communities today.
13. Belous and Weinstein, *Will Soule*, p. 20.

The original photographs by Soule that drew my attention are six plates of Wichita women photographed at Fort Sill, Oklahoma, some time after 1870 (the date is the consensus of scholars of Soule's work). The Wichita, along with the Kiowa, Apache, and Commanche tribes, were a ready subject for the lens of the young photographer from Maine. At Fort Sill, his subjects were literally a captive audience at the Indian Agency and Military Control Headquarters, U.S. Army, which was under construction in 1869–70.[14] Two of the six photographs are the subject of this discussion in the clear presentation of the posed subject. Without observing the images, the description of the works is simply a straightforward observation of details and identification of the compositional elements of the image. In the process, the word and image are at opposite ends of the spectrum.

Squaw 1, ca. 1867

The sitter appears posed and reclines to the left of frame. She holds her right hand (to the viewer's left) with palm open against her cheek, supporting her head in one hand. She wears a ring on the middle finger and a single bracelet surrounds the wrist. Her body reclines against a buffalo hide drape; her left arm appears relaxed and falls at her side, the forearm bends at the elbow and across a blanket or fabric that covers her lap and hips. Her right hand is extended, fingers curved, and appears relaxed and flexed. A faint tan line is visible above the right wrist, possibly from a bracelet. Legs are tucked to the right and extend in the opposite angle from the torso. Both lower limbs are visible, her feet rest parallel at ankles. The sitter wears knee-high, hide boots covering her legs from knee to foot. The hide is folded at the top of the upper shank of the boot. Minimal beadwork is visible on the boot in a single strip; the pattern is indistinct but appears to be light-colored with a faint, dark alternating pattern. A side seam is visible on the outer shank of the boot. From the waist, the blanket or cloth drapery gathers in folds at the hips, which remain hidden. She is seminude, her torso and exposed left breast are partially covered with necklace strands. Her right breast is fully exposed. Around her neck dangle several layers of necklaces of pipebone and twisted strands of glass beads, possibly four or five necklaces. The sitter's hair is parted in the center and falls below the shoulder. One hair ornament is visible, fastened at the ear and pulling the hair back from her face. The backdrop, visible behind her, appears to be painted with elements of low shrubbery. Her facial expression is unsmiling and solemn. She appears to be in her late teens or twenties and looks directly into the camera.

14. Ibid., p. 18.

Will Soule, *Wichita Woman (Squaw 1)*, ca. 1867. Albumen print, 7 x 5 in. (17.8 x 12.7 cm). National Anthropological Archives, Smithsonian Insititution, Washington D.C.

Squaw 2, ca. 1867

The second variation of the reclining pose features the same Wichita woman covered by yards of cloth with a pattern of alternating bands of light and dark stripes, with a second pattern visible in the lighter stripes. The material, printed on one side, twines around her arm, over her head, and falls behind her back in a veil. The remainder of the loose fabric emerges behind and to the right of the exposed arm and rests across her lap, partially covering her waist and hips before draping off to the right where it terminates in a mass of folded yardage. The woman reclines in an upright position and leans slightly to the left. Her supporting left arm is bent at the elbow and rests against the support feature hidden by the drapery. One leg is obscured and tucked underneath the fabric. The second limb emerges from under the drapery, and a second drape or blanket appears to cover the hips and upper thigh, and is tucked at the waist. On the visible leg, she wears a knee-high boot of hide with a side seam and faint beadwork on the instep of the boot shoe. The boot ends at the knee and appears to be folded and secured by hide strips. No beading is visible on the upper boot shank. The exposed leg seems to dangle and is not weight bearing or touching the floor. The backdrop behind the figure is painted with a faint cloud formation and open sky. Shrubbery juts up in a small tuft behind the drapery. She holds her hand to her cheek, supporting her head. A ring is visible on the hand, and a single bracelet encircles each wrist. Both hands are closed and the left arm, held at her side falls across her lap. Her hand is partially hidden by fabric and appears to clutch fabric in her lap. Her hair is parted in the center, her head partially covered by the draped veil of fabric behind her. She wears no earrings or necklaces. Her back appears arched with both breasts fully exposed. Her facial expression is unsmiling, and she looks directly at the camera. She appears to be in her teens or early twenties.

Dated 1870, Soule's Wichita portraits are early in the photographic history of Indian materials.[15] Photography's brief history begins in 1839, with credit for its invention given to Louis Daguerre in France. Although Western painting is laden with depictions of the sleeping Venus, odalisque, and undraped goddess, it is unclear if an American precedent exists for the presentation of the Indian female in the convention of a reclining nude. Manet's important work, *Olympia* (1863), which was rejected by the French Salon, is one possible source. If Soule chose to recreate the format of paintings, he merely followed the already established practice of artists who relied on academic images that traveled from France and Europe to the United States. Nevertheless, while schools of French, British, and German erotic photography are documented, the transatlantic influence of these

15. Ibid., p. 14.

centers on the United States in terms of the adoption of the Indian as subject is unclear. Paris was the center for distribution of the bulk of printed erotic material from 1845 to1860,[16] and the fact that Soule's photographs were some of the very early examples of American erotic photography intended for commercial distribution and featuring Indian women, is a distinction of sorts.

The United States remained conservative toward the subject of obscenity and actively enforced the Customs Act of 1842 against importing pornography. In a discussion of American obscenity, Walter Kendrick noted "America's first antiobscenity legislation was directed at imports as if domestic manufacture were inconceivable."[17] In American art, prudish conventions and provincial themes were dominant subjects in the nineteenth century. With photography, studies of undraped nonWestern women manifested a double legitimization: as knowledge, and as science. Disguised as the pursuit of knowledge, ethnographic photography—images of the nonWestern subject—permitted scientific scrutiny of women's bodies without the taint of pornography.

Soule's images present women not in response to hot climates, but posed in reference to a vocabulary of postures that was adapted from the licensed academies in painting and repeated in European pornographic photographs. In these sources, models recline, stand against painted backdrops, sit on chairs, and face forward, upright and with genitals exposed. The formal frontal pose was the format favored by anthropologists and was also adopted by law enforcement agencies for criminal record keeping.[18]

Visceral nakedness, however, raised apprehensions about the savage, a notion never far from the Anglo imagination. The female Indian appears as the savage, albeit with elaborate adornment. Her hair, in disarray and uncombed, is thick, straight, often with detailed mud patterns. Her legs and feet are bare, breasts jut forward, exposed. Layers of beaded necklaces draw attention to the exposed breasts and her naked state. The depiction of the naked Indian female is threatening, unlike her counterpart, the noble Indian male. By contrast, she is ignoble, evidenced by her untamed appearance and ambiguous reference to a civilized state by means of the adaptation of Western garments such as skirts of printed fabrics, cummerbunds, and furniture, for example, Victorian chairs. If depicted without a male at her side, she has no master. In the images of men and women together, the pair bond is reinforced by hand holding, or their bodies are entwined in close physical contact. Pairs or groups of naked Indian women are defiant of the civilized male observer. Faced with this image of the indigenous savage woman, desire wilts.

16. Jorge Lewinski, *The Naked and the Nude* (New York: Harmony Books, 1987), p. 42.

17. Walter Kendrick, *The Secret Museum: Pornography in Modern Culture* (Berkeley: University of California Press): 126.

18. See John Tagg, *The Burden of Representation: Essays on Photographies and Histories* (Minneapolis: University of Minnesota Press, 1988), and James C. Faris, *Navajo and Photography: A Critical History of the Representation of an American People* (Albuquerque: University of New Mexico Press, 1996).

The naked Indian woman opposes the nude of Kenneth Clark's Western art. Her naked realism in photographs is the visual evidence of the challenge to the West's notion of its superiority. These images do not attempt to reference classical antiquity, myth, allegory, or heroic idealism. They negate poetic visions of Eden and the New World paradise inhabited by Rousseau's natural beings. In all the images, breasts receive the focus of attention, emphasized by the layers of necklaces wrapped at the throat, dangled in cleavage, or peaking from under elbow-length beaded capes.

In the objective records of human diversity, photographed bodies of dark-skinned women were mapped, charted, measured, diagrammed, and reproduced under the rationale of science. Targeted non-Western cultures became exotic subjects for photographers who recorded the breasts, genitals, and buttocks of tribal women. Publications like *The Secret Museum of Anthropology*, printed in 1935, leave a record of doubt as to the original intentions of the photographers.[19] The data reveals ethnography/anthropology was never distant, objective, or unbiased. Photography of exotic nonWestern cultures crossed boundaries that shifted notions of science closer to pornography than art.[20] Images recorded an intentional manipulation of the native body with posture, physical gesture, and minimal clothing that suggests sexual eroticism. The idea of natives who were incapable of rising above the level of savagery confirmed sexual excess and wantonness.

In all the photographs I surveyed, however, the sitters' genitals remain covered by clothing or drapery, unlike the French erotic photographs and postcards. Early examples of the French style of erotic photographs have an awkwardness about the figure. In some examples the posture of the model lacked graceful presentation of the body and overall symmetry in body lines. Art historian Anne McCaulley suggests that the vocabulary of erotic poses had not yet been created or assimilated by the models. She notes, "Sexuality had to be learned." The sexy pose had to be internalized by models until, in the late nineteenth century, erotic images became "professional looking, smoother," more like the contemporary poses of today.

The growing commercialization of photography involved the production of photographs to assist artists in rendering the human form, that is, licensed academic female nude studies. These became a cheap and accessible reference. However, the realism of the photograph necessitated crucial differences between the academic and pornographic image. The photograph recorded the rawness and imperfection of the human body. The artist confronted the realism of the body through the photographic medium. Unlike painting or sculpture, in which the ideal body is nude, the photograph captures naked realism.

19. See *The Secret Museum of Anthropology* (New York: 1935).
20. Scherer states, "[d]rawing, paintings, engravings, and even photographs are no more objective than written material." She further notes that the photograph, while a record of an exact historical moment is an intentional act of the photographer and limited by the data that accompany the image in its historical context. "You Can't Believe Your Eyes," p. 67.

The reality of the imperfect body is visible in the naked portraits of Indian women. The bodies are not ideal but reflect adolescence, motherhood, and maturity. Breasts sag, waists were never confined by corsets. Feet appear hard and are wide and callused. Hair is straight and hangs in their eyes, some display clay pigment. Faces are painted or tattooed in a painful process of body modification.

Of the group of photographs of Indians in the Southwest, a few others stand beside the unique images by Soule. Henry Buehman recorded two portraits of unique character, *Pima Beauty* and *Maricopa Squaw II*. With the inclusion of a third Buehman, *Apache Chief Geronimo's Wife*, a trio of metaphors completes a summary of the variation of imagery of the naked Indian woman. *Geronimo's Wife*, I suggest, is the same woman depicted in Buehman's *Maricopa Squaw*.[21] I share a tribal affiliation with the sitters of this trio, who are identified as Pima and are from the reservation communities where we continue to reside.[22]

21. Although the sitter wears different skirt styles in each photograph, and her body is posed seated in one and propped in the second, the necklaces, hair elaboration, and faint facial embellishment (painted or tattoos) appear strikingly similar. Other characteristics such as body type, breast size, hair length and style, and phenotypic features appear to match. More research needs to be carried out with the actual photographs, which I am unable to access for confirmation of my theory.

22. The Pima and Maricopa tribes have coexisted together for over two hundred years. The Maricopa (Λu'au-bop or Piposh), a Yuman-speaking group who resided near the lower Colorado River boundary between Arizona and California fled their traditional lands from the aggressive Mojave and Apache raids. They sought refuge among the Pima of Southern Arizona. The Pima (Ak'mul Au'Authum) continue to reside on lands surrounding the cities of Phoenix and Scottsdale. Pima are Uto-Aztecan speakers and the presumed ancestors of the prehistoric Hohokam, the original settlers of Southern Arizona. The closest relatives of the Pima are the Papago (Tohono O'Odham) who live in the region between Tucson and the border southward into Sonora, Mexico. The two tribes were recognized by the federal government in 1879, and formally incorporated as the Gila River Pima-Maricopa, and the Salt River Pima-Maricopa Indian Communities, respectively.

Henry Buehman, *Apache Chief Geronimo's Wife*, ca. 1883. Albumen print, 6 7/8 x 3 7/8 in. (17.5 x 9.8 cm). Collection of Jeremy Rowe Vintage Photography, Mesa, Arizona.

Pima Beauty

Henry Buehman's *Pima Beauty* is a striking portrait of a native woman. The photographer's aesthetic regard for this attractive young woman is apparent in the attention to detail. The sitter's appearance suggests she is in her teens. Her features are large and round with a full mouth, straight nose, with slender shoulders, arms, and frame. Her thick hair is parted in the center and arranged behind the ears falling down her back. She has a lovely, pleasant expression. She wears large distinctive earrings that appear to have multiple stones. She is lit by key light from the side and overhead creating delicate shading across her face. Her face and her gaze turn slightly toward the right. The portrait is a head-and-shoulders study, cropped just below her exposed breasts. *Pima Beauty* is a desert rose judging by the treatment and handling of the photographer. The artistic sense of femininity and youth conveyed in the gentle lighting and the appearance of the model is appreciated by the viewer and by the photographer who captured her beauty and charm.

Maricopa Squaw

Pima Beauty's stunning looks and feminine appeal are a stark contrast to the stiff pose of *Maricopa Squaw*. Dark skinned with a thick waist, the Maricopa stares directly into camera. She wears a three-strand necklace of white beads. Her upper body and breasts are exposed, and she sits stiffly upright. Her arms are at her sides with her hands resting in her lap. The straight face-forward position of the body, and solemn features convey a harsh appearance, particularly in contrast to the soft lighting and features of the elegant Pima. *Maricopa Squaw* lacks the graceful presentation of *Pima Beauty*. The sitter is older, perhaps in her twenties. She exhibits facial markings under each eye in parallel vertical lines that extend from the lower eyelid to the chin. Her hair falls to the front and is decorated with mud visible in overall light patches. She wears a patterned fabric skirt around her waist.

Maricopa Squaw is a coded visual and verbal reference that continues to offend modern Indians as a euphemism for prostitute or female genitalia. Although Henry Buehman photographed both women approximately five years apart, the treatment of one sitter is privileged. *Pima Beauty* glows with soft light while *Maricopa Squaw* appears hardened with dour expression and a stocky torso.

Finally, let me consider the motives and uses of two typical photographs of this genre. The first, *A Paiute Kaiar*, was recorded by photographer John K. Hillers during the John Wesley Powell Colorado River Expedition of 1873. The second, an anonymous snapshot titled *Pima Woman in Anglo Dress*, is an example of the overt image that

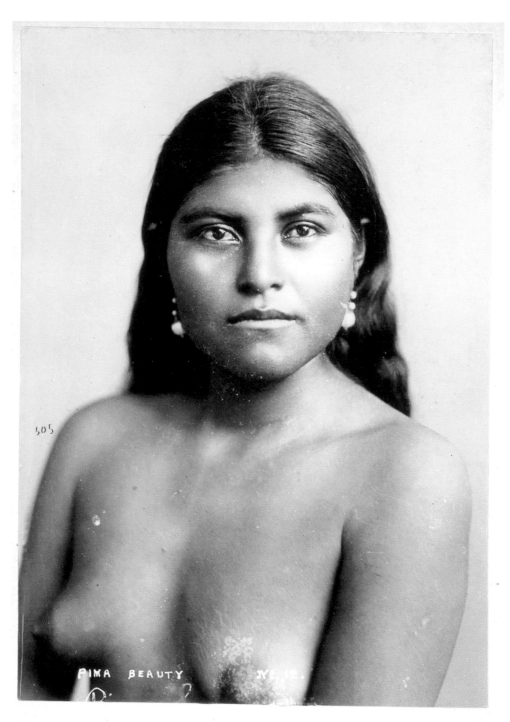

ARIZONA ILLUSTRATED

BY

H. BUEHMAN,   TUCSON, ARIZ.

Henry Buehman, *Pima Beauty*, ca. 1890. Cabinet card, 6 ¹/₂ x 4 ¹/₂ in. (16 x 12 cm). Denver Public Library, Western History Collection.

ARIZONA ILLUSTRATED

BY

H. BUEHMAN,   TUCSON, ARIZ.

Henry Buehman, *Maricopa Squaw*, ca. 1880. Albumen print, 5 1/2 x 4 in. (14 x 10 cm). Denver Public Library, Western History Collection.

questions the intention of the photographer. In each of these images clothing is arranged and the positioning of the model is intentional. One cannot disregard the deliberate attempts to convey an erotic impression by exposing the breasts or legs of the woman. Hillers' photograph would be for sale to the public, and the intention to create an image of erotic intention to arouse is one definition of pornography.

In Hillers' photograph of Kaiar she is shown in three-quarter profile, wearing a fringed hide dress adjusted to expose one breast and her bare leg from hip to ankle. Joanna Scherer quotes from a 1939 article by Julian Steward that mentioned Hillers and the photograph: "Art seems often to have outweighed realism in the selection of objects represented. 'A woman in semidress' probably indicates Powell's and Hillers' idea of photographic art rather than actual use of garments."[23] Scherer also notes the severe poverty of the Paiute and the excessive climate, "It is therefore doubtful that in summer women wore such dresses."[24] Margaret Blackman responded to Scherer about the unlikelihood that Paiute women wore buckskin after Memorial Day and added:

> While photographers often accompanied early ethno-graphic expeditions to Indian settlements, their motives were usually not strictly ethnographic. . . .Hillers' Ute and Paiute Indian photographs were used by Powell to illustrate. . .his publications. . .for viewing through parlor stereoscopes, [the photographs are] evidence that entertainment value governed the selection of subject matter..."[t]he bare-breasted 'Wu-naval gathering seeds" certainly was not viewed by Victorian gentlemen for its documentation of Great Basin seed gathering.[25]

The last image, a snapshot of *Pima Woman in Anglo Dress*, is an example of the impact of lightweight affordable cameras in the latter years of the century. An intentional attempt to expose the woman also raises serious questions about the photographer's motive as well as whether the image was for private or public viewing. Can we avoid this factor and ask if this is pornography? The snapshot, a popular form of photography around the turn of the century, was rapidly adopted by the American public and enabled anyone to become a photographer. Affordable and accessible camera equipment and film processing led to a democratizing of photography, as more and more cameras were available to a larger population. Informal, spontaneous, and mobile, the snapshot photograph was a personal record of travel, a souvenir, a trophy of encounters with people outside the range of the everyday experience. The format provided entertainment to share with others in the home or outside. For whose entertainment was *this* woman exposed?

23. Scherer, "You Can't Believe Your Eyes," p. 70.
24. Ibid.
25. Margaret Blackman, "Posing the American Indian," p. 70.

197

C. Ondine Chavoya

NO-MOVIES

The Art of False Documents

1. Max Benavidez, "Interview with Willie Herrón," radio broadcast, KPFK-FM Los Angeles, June 8, 1981, audiocassette (Gamboa Collection, Stanford University Libraries Special Collections).

2. Zaneta Kosiba-Vargas, "Harry Gamboa and ASCO: The Emergence and Development of a Chicano Art Group, 1971–1987" (Ph.D. diss., University of Michigan, 1988), p. 4.

3. Harry Gamboa, Jr., "Light at the End of Tunnel Vision," paper presented at Armand Hammer Museum, Los Angeles, April 26, 1994 (Gamboa Collection, Stanford University Libraries Department of Special Collections), p. 7.

4. Philip Brookman and Amy Brookman, "Interview with ASCO," *CALIFAS: Chicano Art and Culture in California, Transcripts*, Book 3, Colección Tlogque Nahuaque (University of California at Santa Barbara Davidson Library, 1983), pp. 7–8.

5. John Tagg, "The Discontinuous City: Picturing the Discursive Field," in *Visual Culture: Images and Interpretations*, ed. Norman Bryson, Michael Ann Holly, and Keith Moxey (Hanover, N.H.: University Press of New England, 1994), pp. 83–103.

6. Chon A. Noriega, "Talking Heads, Body Politic: The Plural Self of Chicano Experimental Video," in *Resolutions: Contemporary Video Practices*, ed. Michael Renov and Erika Suderburg (Minneapolis: University of Minnesota Press, 1992), p. 214.

In the early 1970s, the Los Angeles performance group ASCO staged a number of events that underscored the potentially explosive social and racial conditions in their city. ASCO sensed that the presence of violence in their environment was profoundly problematic, but the methods they chose to engender awareness of it were purposefully disruptive. ASCO Member Willie Herrón remembers, "We wanted to reach inside and pull people's guts out."[1] As scholar Zaneta Kosiba-Vargas suggests, "ASCO rendered new interpretations of the Chicano urban experience which emphasized the irrationality of an environment shaped by violence, racial oppression, and exploitation."[2] For the artists, such work was a means to combat the power of the stereotype as a system of subjection and its role in the promotion of violence.

ASCO's *Decoy Gang War Victim* (1974) was both a performance and media intervention "designed to provoke the viewer to commit acts of perceptual sabotage"[3] and then to question "objective" sources of information and meaning. After closing off a residential city block with flares in the Li'l Valley area of East L.A., founding member Gronk sprawled across the asphalt posing as the "victim" of a gang retribution killing with ketchup all over him. As another founding member Harry Gamboa, Jr. explains, "We would go around and whenever we heard of where there might be potential violence, we would set up these decoys so they would think someone had already been killed."[4]

The performance's status as media hoax and counter-spectacle depended upon the way that the documentation was put to use. ASCO distributed a photograph of the performance to various publications and television stations, which was accepted by the local media as a real scenario of violence. The image was broadcast on KHJ-TV LA Channel 9 as an "authentic" East L.A. Chicano gang murder and condemned as a prime example of rampant gang violence in the City of Angels.

The artists were all too familiar with the power of photographic documents "to structure belief and recruit consent; the power of conviction and the power to convict."[5] Not only did the mass media represent crime and violence as East Los Angeles's specialty but also Gamboa was the target of "internal subversives" surveillance sponsored by the FBI's COINTELPRO agency. This was possible, Gamboa argues, because "they had pictures and I didn't have pictures to prove my point."[6]

Thus, by inverting the documentary sign function of the photograph, the aesthetics of the image were mediated by an ethics of the image (as stereotype) intent on reversing the terms of everyday media manipulation. "So much death had been occurring and does

ASCO, Harry Gamboa, Jr., From *No-Movie announcement poster (1977) featuring A la Mode (1975)*, 1977. Offset lithography. Courtesy of the artist and the Harry Gamboa Collection, Stanford University Library.

occur in East L.A. without any meaning attached to it," Gamboa said in an interview, "we wanted to give people a certain kind of almost gastrointestinal response."[7] That the decoy restored peace to the barrio or effectively revealed the media's biases to all is unlikely; however, the artists became aware of the possible uses of mainstream media to communicate their messages. The group did not seek to create spectacles for spectacle's sake but to bring attention to the spectacular condition of everyday life in the barrio and, through counter-spectacles, to destabilize the power of the media to represent it as such.

The "No-Movie" was ASCO's signature invented medium—conceptual performances that invoked cinematic codes but were created for a still camera. The "No-Movies" were staged events in which performance artists played the parts of film stars in photographs that were distributed as film stills from "authentic" Chicano motion pictures. "No-Movies" alluded to two models of presentation: the Latin American *fotonovela* and the Hollywood film still. Bearing the signature red stamp "ASCO/ Chicano Cinema," "No-Movies" were distributed to local and national press and media, and to film distributors, and reached an international audience through mail-art circuits. Chon Noriega has succinctly described the "No-Movie" format as an "intermedia synesthesia" that uses one affordable medium (the still 35mm camera) as another more expensive medium (a 16mm or 35mm motion picture camera).[8] The "No-Movies" circulated as examples of "authentic" Chicano-produced motion pictures, creating the specious illusion of an active body of Chicano cinema being produced from the periphery of Hollywood.

The "No-Movie" operated as ideological "rebuff to celluloidic capitalism of contemporary cinema."[9] "No-Movies" were both a critical assault and evasion of the Hollywood studio system, foregrounding the absence of Chicano access to and participation in mass media. The "No-Movies" were not only critically satirizing Hollywood cinema but also parodied the utopian nationalism of the Chicano Art Movement.[10] In a mock interview that Gronk and Gamboa wrote for the magazine *Chismearte*, they sarcastically critiqued nationalist Chicano filmmakers.

> *Chismearte: At what point did you reject the celluloid format of cinema?*
> *Gronk: When I realized Chicano filmmakers were making the same movie over and over again.*
> *Gamboa: When I discovered for myself that a multi-million dollar project could be accomplished for less than 10 dollars and have more than 300 copies in circulation around the world.*[11]

The "No-Movie" that most clearly addresses this issue is appropriately titled *Chicano Cinema* (1976). The image of a gunshot victim fallen

7. Alicia Sandoval, *Let's Rap with Alicia Sandoval*, television broadcast interview with Harry Gamboa, KTLA Channel 5, Los Angeles, April 1978, audiorecording (Gamboa Collection, Stanford University Libraries Special Collections).

8. Chon A. Noriega "Road to Aztlán: Chicanos and Narrative Cinema" (Ph.D. diss., Stanford University, 1991), p. 192.

9. Harry Gamboa, Jr. and Gronk, "Interview: Gronk and Gamboa," *Chismearte*, no. 1 (1976): 31.

10. "No-Movies" appropriated the spectacle of Hollywood even as they critiqued the absence of Chicano access and participation in the mass media; moreover, albeit somewhat ironically, "No-Movies" fulfilled the goals of the nationalist Chicano cinema movement to gain control of the means of production by inverting its methods. See Cine-Aztlan "Ya Basta con Yankee Imperialist Documentaries" (1974) and Francisco X. Camplis "Towards the Development of a Raza Cinema" (1975), both reprinted in *Chicanos and Film: Representations and Resistance*, ed. Chon Noriega (Minneapolis: University of Minnesota Press, 1992).

11. Gamboa and Gronk interview, *Chismearte*, pp. 30–33.

to the floor resembles those from the sensationalist Mexican true crime magazine *Alarma!*. His white tank-top T-shirt is saturated with blood, but he remains propped up in the corner of the room. Fiercely yet blankly staring ahead, his eyes confront the viewer. The cinematic mise-en-scéne suggests a cheap motel room. The words "Chicano Cinema" have been painted on brown butcher paper above the fallen casualty. However, the final letter of the title drips off the paper on to the floor, indicating that perhaps the bullet penetrated the author while in process. Cryptically scrawled out on the wall below is a signature—"Gamboa," and opposite him a pile of bank notes is aflame. One hand is placed inside his unbuttoned trousers, the other holding a gun pointed at the viewer; it is unclear whether this figure is a rebel with a cause or a victim of his own art and ideology. Regardless, "Chicano Cinema" has become his final rite and epitaph.

Gamboa notes that ASCO's theories of performance crystallized with the "No-Movies." The "No-Movie" format facilitated the circulation of their performances by taking "the barrier out of the barrio."[12] Gronk has described the "No-Movie" concept as follows: "We were using Hollywood by mimicking it—we became its characters," as well as its technical staff, producers, directors; "L.A., the city, became our canvas and we became the pigment."[13]

12. Harry Gamboa, Jr., Willie Herrón, and Gronk, transcript of interview by Shifra M. Goldman, January 16, 1980 (Collection of Shifra M. Goldman, used with permission).
13. Gronk, "Artist's Talk," Cornell University, October 28, 1993, audio-cassette (Collection of author).

ASCO, Harry Gamboa, Jr., *Decoy Gang War Victim*, 1976. Chromogenic print, 16 x 20 in. (40.6 x 50.8 cm). Courtesy of the artist.

ASCO's spatially politicized aesthetics embodied resistant meanings in order to mobilize resistant readings. The frequent object of their critical investigations was the normative landscape and official culture of Los Angeles. In one series of performances, ASCO appointed themselves municipal officials to East L.A., a predominantly Mexican-American populated, unincorporated county territory. (To this day, East L.A. remains unincorporated and, thus, does not have a City Hall.) ASCO toured their municipality on random site-visits, designating various spaces and objects to be civic landmarks, monuments, and preservation zones. In one such "No-Movie" performance, a storm drain was anointed the illustrious title *Asshole Mural* (1975). Traditionally, monuments mark, embody, and make visible power relations. Steve Pile describes this process as making space incontestable "both by closing off alternative readings and by drawing people into the presumption that the values they represent are shared."[14] ASCO's spatial aesthetic is an example of an enacted heterotopia that embodies and actualizes alternative readings.[15] Their ephemeral performance challenges the sanctioned durable autonomy of monuments as grids of social meaning and state power and intervenes in the control and manipulation of space (both real and metaphorical) exerted in the production of monuments.

Asshole Mural is a performative subversion of the historical process that has produced Chicanas/os as the categorical blind spot—the "disposable phantom culture"[16]—of dominant media as well as political and cultural institutions. The tactic utilized is to usurp the authority and power invested in the civic heritage industry as spectacle. Jonathan Crary has described similar strategies employed by the surrealists and other Euro-American avant-garde artists as "turning the spectacle of the city inside out through counter-memory and counter-itineraries," arguing that this strategy incarnates "a refusal of the imposed present."[17] But whereas such Euro-American avant-garde artists may have attempted to refuse an imposed present by reclaiming fragments of a demolished past in order to implicitly figure an alternative future, ASCO's performance is clearly not one of cultural reclaiming; instead it marks an absence.[18] ASCO's aesthetic strategies and interventionist tactics emanate from neither the fragment nor the ruin, but from the absence.

As non-celluloid dramas, "No-Movies" produce the affect of cinematic reality. As barrio-star vehicles, "No-Movies" explored and exploited the power of the image. *Vogue* (1978), featuring Billy Estrada and Patssi Valdez (looking remarkably like Sophia Loren), appropriates the aura of stardom by referencing the photographic conventions of fashion advertising. Occasionally "No-Movies" were far more explicit in their cinematic references, such as *Fountain of Aloof* (1978), the

14. Steve Pile, *The Body and the City* (London: Routledge, 1996), p. 213.
15. On the heterotopia, please see Michel Foucault, "Of Other Spaces," trans. Jay Miskowiec, *Diacritics* (Spring 1986): 22–27; Edward W. Soja, "Heterotopologies: Foucault and the Geohistory of Otherness," *Thirdspace: Journeys to Los Angeles and other real-and-imagined Places* (Oxford: Blackwell, 1996), pp. 145–63; Jennifer A. González and Michelle Habell-Pallan, "Heterotopias and Shared Methods of Resistance: Navigating Social Spaces and Spaces of Identity," *Inscriptions* 7 (1994): 80–104.
16. Harry Gamboa, Jr., "No Phantoms," *High Performance*, no. 2 (1981): 15.
17. Jonathan Crary, "Spectacle, Attention, Counter-Memory," *October*, no. 50 (1989): 107.
18. For recent art historical accounts on flânerie to dérive in such Euro-American movements as dada, surrealism, Situationist International, and their contemporary influences, see: Mirella Bandini, "Surrealist References in the Notions of Dérive and Psychogeography of the Situationist Urban Environment, in *Situationists: Art, Politics, Urbanism*, ed. Libero Andraotti and Xavier Costa (Barcelona: ACTAR/Museu d'Art Contemporani de Barcelona, 1996) pp. 40–51; A. Bonnett, "Art, Ideology, and Everyday Space: Subversive Tendencies from Dada to Postmodernism," *Environment and Planning D: Society and Space* 10 (1992): 69–86; Christel Hollevoet, "Wandering in the City: Flânerie to Dérive and After: The Cognitive Mapping of Urban Space," *The Power of the City/The City of Power*, ed. Christel Hollevoet, Karen Jones, and Timothy Nye, Whitney Independent Study Program Papers, No. 1 (New York: Whitney Museum of American Art, 1992) pp. 25–57.

Patssi Valdez and Billy Estrada remake of the Anita Ekberg and Marcello Mastroianni fountain scene in *La Dolce Vita* (1960). Concepts for still other "No-Movies" included: *ASCO Goes to the Universe* (1975); *The Gore Family* (1975), a cannibalistic sci-fi thriller, in which descendants of Lesley Gore are mugged while attempting to pawn a camera, and transformed into city terrorists from City Terrace; the *Hollywood Slasher Victim* interview and press conference (1978); and *Stranglers in the Night* (1978), a domestic mass-murder plot that unfolds in a shower stall.

Gronk often invokes the celebrated postmodern photographer Cindy Sherman in discussion of the "No-Movies." In his influential essay "The Photographic Activity of Postmodernism," Douglas Crimp surveys the history of technological challenges to aura, and identifies the work of a group of young (at the time of the essay) artists that reflexively contest the auratic fetishization of the original. These artists, of which Sherman is a stellar example, demonstrate how the photographic medium is primarily and always "a representation, always-already seen,"[19] and do so by turning the medium's axiomatic claim to originality against itself. The aura is thus only an aspect of the copy.

Although there is a formal and conceptual convergence in ASCO's "No-Movies" and Sherman's "Film Stills" through their "rhetoric of the pose,"[20] there is a crucial distinction to be made. For Sherman, the rhetoric of the pose is utilized to effect a sense of cinematic unreality. Working within an established, if entrenched, series of signifiers and overdetermined narratives, the effect of cinematic unreality is a strategy to destabilize or denaturalize normative gender codes. As Crimp describes, Sherman's "Film Stills" function to expose an unwanted dimension of fiction. Created in the images of "already known feminine stereotypes," Sherman's photographs "show that the supposed autonomous and unitary self out of which other 'directors' would create their fictions is itself nothing other than a discontinuous series of representations, copies, fakes."[21]

"No-Movies," in contrast, were "designed to create an impression of factuality,"[22] to produce the affect of cinematic reality. In their impersonating an institution they wish to see themselves in, the strategy employed is to construct a series of signifiers and narratives. While Sherman's "Film Stills" constitute a simulation of overdetermined signifiers, the "No-Movie" is a simulacrum for which there is no original.[23] As Gronk coyly proclaims, "It is projecting the real by rejecting the reel."[24]

19. Douglas Crimp, "The Photographic Activity of Postmodernism [1980]," in Crimp, *On the Museum's Ruins*, (Cambridge, Mass.: MIT Press, 1993) pp. 108–24.
20. On the "rhetoric of the pose," see Craig Owens, "The Medusa Effect, or, The Specular Ruse," and "Posing," in *Beyond Recognition: Representation, Power, Culture*, ed. Scott Bryson, Barbara Kruger, Lynne Tillman, and Jane Weinstock (Berkeley: University of California Press, 1992), pp. 191–217; and Henry Sayre, "The Rhetoric of the Pose: Photography and the Portrait as Performance," in *The Object of Performance: The American Avant-Garde Since 1970* (Chicago: University of Chicago Press, 1989), pp. 35–65.
21. Crimp, "The Photographic Activity of Postmodernism," p. 122.
22. Marisela Norte, "Harry Gamboa, Jr.: No Movie Maker," *Revista Literaria de El Tecolote* 4, no. 2 (July 1983): 3, 12.
23. For a different interpretation of the simulacral structure in Sherman's "Film Stills," see Rosalind Krauss's essay in *Cindy Sherman 1975–1993* (New York: Rizzoli, 1993). Perhaps another way to approach this debate would be through Barthes's discussion of the "third" or "obtuse" meaning—the signifier without a signified—and the specifically filmic existing not in the moving image but in the still; see "Third Meaning: Research Notes on Some Einstein Film Stills," in his *Image-Music-Text*, trans. Stephen Heath (New York: Hill and Wang, 1977), pp. 152–68.
24. Gamboa and Gronk interview, *Chismearte*, p. 31.

III.
HUMANIZE/
FETISHIZE

Gordon Parks, *Emerging Man, Harlem*, 1952. Gelatin silver print, 16 ¹/₈ x 19 ⁷/₈ in. (40.9 x 50.4 cm). International Center of Photography, purchased by the ICP Acquisitions Committee, 2003.

Walker Evans, *Mask; Africa, Cameroon, Bandjoun, Bamendjo Kingdom, #271, from African Negro Art portfolio*, 1935.

Gelatin silver print, 8 ⁷/₈ x 7 in. (22.5 x 18.8 cm). New York University, Institute of Fine Arts, Visual Resource Collection Photography.

Vik Muniz, *Frederick Douglass*, from "Pictures of Ink" series, 2000. Cibachrome print, 60 x 48 in. (144 x 115.2 cm). International Center of Photography, purchased by the ICP Acquisitions Committee, 2003.

Walter S. Ferguson, *Geronimo, Apache Warrior, rides in automobile with three other members of his tribe*, 1904, Gelatin silver print from original negative, 14 $^{5}/_{16}$ x 17 $^{7}/_{8}$ in. (36.4 x 45.4 cm). National Archives, Washington D.C.

Andy Warhol, *Cowboys and Indians: Geronimo*, 1986. Screenprint on Lenox Museum Board, 36 x 36 in. (86.4 x 86.4 cm).
The Andy Warhol Museum, Pittsburgh/ARS, NY.

Horace Poolaw, *Trecil Poolaw Unap, Mountain View, Oklahoma*, 1929. Gelatin silver print, 11 7/8 x 8 1/2 in. (30.1 x 21.6 cm).
Courtesy of Charles Junkerman.

Unidentified photographer, *Outside Tule Lake Internment Camp, Tule Lake, Calif*, 1942. Gelatin silver print, 6 x 4 in. (15.2 x 10.1 cm). International Center of Photography, Museum purchase, 2001.

James VanDerZee, *Beau of the Ball*, 1926. Gelatin silver print, 10 x 8 in. (25.4 x 20.3 cm). Collection of Donna Mussenden VanDerZee.

Paul Outerbridge, *Asian Nude with Ornament*, ca. 1936. Color carbro print, 16 x 12 in. (40.6 x 30.5 cm). Private collection.
Courtesy of G. Ray Hawkins Gallery, Los Angeles.

Lee Marmon, *White Man's Moccasins (Jeff Sousea)*, 1954. Gelatin silver print, 20 x 16 in. (50.8 x 40.6 cm).
Courtesy of the artist.

Victor Masayesva, Jr., *Cold Moon*, 1996. Digital chromogenic print, 20 x 24 in. (50.8 x 60.9 cm).
Courtesy of the artist.

Prentice H. Polk, *The Boss*, 1932. Gelatin silver print, 14 x 11 in. (35.5 x 27.9 cm). International Center of Photography, gift of P. H. Polk and Southlight.

Bruce Davidson, *New York City*, 1961–65. Gelatin silver print, 14 x 11 in. (35.5 x 27.9 cm). Courtesy of the artist and
Magnum Photos, Inc.

Ben Shahn, *A Medicine Show, Huntingdon, Tennessee*, 1935. Gelatin silver print, 6 ¹/₂ x 9 ³/₄ in. (15.6 x 23.4 cm). International Center of Photography, anonymous gift.

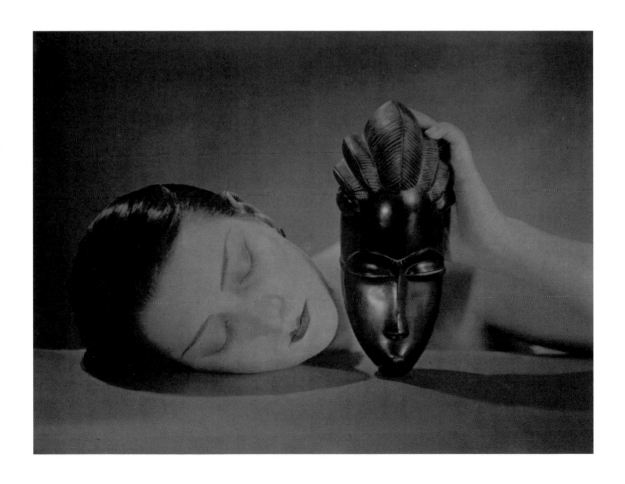

Man Ray, *Noire et Blanche*, 1926. Gelatin silver print, 6 3/4 x 8 3/4 in. (16.2 x 21 cm). Private collection.

Thomas Eakins, *African-American Girl Nude Reclining on a Couch*, ca. 1880. Gelatin silver print, 10 $^1/_2$ x 12 $^1/_2$ in. (26.6 x 31.7 cm). Museum of the Pennsylvania Academy of the Fine Arts, Charles Bregler's Thomas Eakins Collection, purchased with the partial support of the Pew Memorial Trust.

220

Coreen Simpson, *Masqued Nude*, 1999. Gelatin silver print, 20 x 24 in. (50.8 x 60.9 cm). Courtesy of the artist.

Unidentified photographer, *Hawaiian woman posed in photo studio*, ca. 1890. Postcard, 5 ¹/₂ x 3 ¹/₂ in. (14 x 9 cm).
Bishop Museum, Honolulu, Hawaii.

Carl Van Vechten, *Pearl Bailey*, 1946. Gelatin silver print, 9 1/2 x 7 1/8 in. (24.1 x 18 cm). Yale University, Beinecke Rare Book and Manuscript Library, American Literature Collection.

Richard Throssel, *Unidentified Crow Couple Sitting in Tipi*, ca. 1905. Modern gelatin silver print from the original glass plate negative, 8 x 10 in. (20.3 x 25.4 cm). American Heritage Center, University of Wyoming, Richard Throssel Collection.

Zig Jackson, *Indian Man on the Bus*, from the "Indian in San Francisco" series, 1994. Gelatin silver print, 16 x 20 in. (40.6 x 50.8 cm). Courtesy of the artist.

Bently Spang, *Modern Warrior Series: War Shirt #1*, 1998. Mixed mediums, 36 x 56 x 10 in. (91.4 x 142.2 x 25.4 cm).
Collection of Sandra Spang.

Delilah Montoya, *La Guadalupana*, 1998. Kodacolor photo mural with mixed mediums, 120 x 36 in. (304.8 x 91.4 cm). Museum of New Mexico, Palace of the Governors, Santa Fe, museum purchase with funds donated by J. Michael O'Shaughnessy, 1999.

Frank Kunishige, *Aida Kawakami*, ca. 1927. Gelatin silver print, 13 ³/₄ x 9 ¹/₄ in. (34.9 x 23.6 cm). University of Washington Libraries, Manuscripts, Special Collections, University Archives Division, Kunishige Collection.

Nan Goldin, *At the Bar: Toon, C. and So, Bangkok*, 1992. Cibachrome print, 30 x 40 in. (76.2 x 101.6 cm). Courtesy of the artist and Matthew Marks Gallery, New York.

Robert C. Buitron, *Ixta Dates a Nazi Skinhead*, from "The Legend of Ixtaccihuatl y Popcatepetl" series, 1989. Gelatin silver print, 13 3/4 x 17 3/4 in. (34.9 x 45 cm). Courtesy of the artist.

230

Alex Harris, *Rodarte, New Mexico, Looking South from Fred Martinez's Chevrolet Impala*, 1987. Ink jet print, 20 x 24 in. (50.8 x 60.9 cm). Courtesy of the artist.

Soon Mi Yoo, *Seeking saf (single asian female)*, 2003. Mixed medium installation, wall paper, and gelatin silver prints, dimensions variable. Courtesy of the artist.

Charlene Teters, *Mound to the Heroes*, 1999. Mixed medium installation, dimensions variable. Image courtesy of SITE Santa Fe.

Edward Steichen, *Portrait of Hawaiian Model Kaaloalaikini "Toots" Notley*, 1937. Chromogenic print, 8 x 9 ³/₄ in. (20.4 x 25.1 cm). George Eastman House, Rochester, New York, bequest of Edward Steichen by direction of Joanna T. Steichen, with permission of Joanna T. Steichen.

Facing page:
Ed Greevy, *Haunani-Kay, nationalist and leader of the Hawaiian sovereignty movement, speaking before 15,000 people on the 1993 commemoration of the 1893 overthrow of the Hawaiian Kingdom by the American military in support of American businessmen*, 1993. Gelatin silver print, 20 x 16 in. (50.8 x 40.6 cm). Courtesy of the artist.

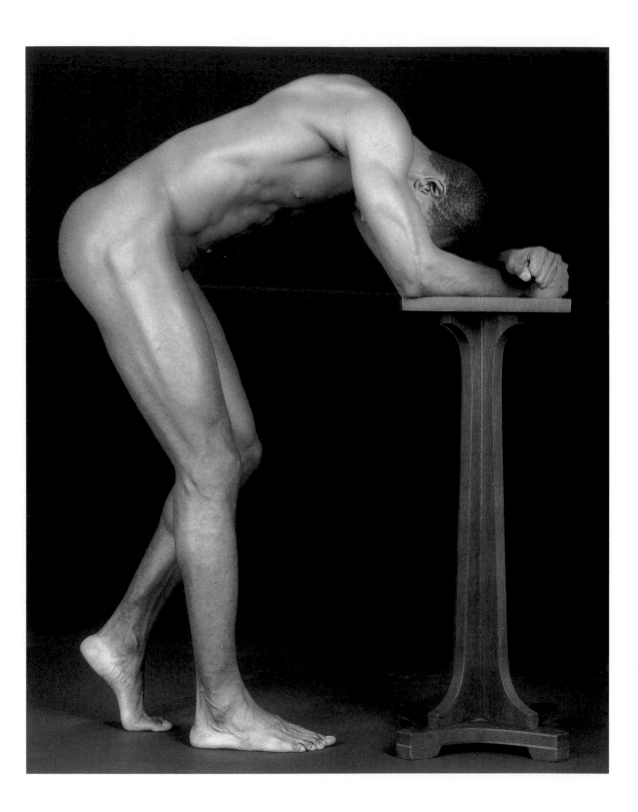

Kobena Mercer

In this article I want to explore the experience of aesthetic ambivalence in visual representations of the black male nude. The photographs of Robert Mapplethorpe provide a salient point of entry into this complex "structure of feeling" as they embody such ambivalence experienced at its most intense.[1]

My interest in this aspect of Mapplethorpe's work began in 1982, when a friend lent me his copy of *Black Males.* It circulated between us as a kind of illicit object of desire, albeit a highly problematic one. We were fascinated by the beautiful bodies, as we went over the repertoire of images again and again, drawn in by the desire to look and enjoy what was given to be seen. We wanted to look, but we didn't always find what we wanted to see: we were shocked and disturbed by the racial discourse of the imagery,

SKIN HEAD SEX THING
Racial Difference and the Homoerotic Imaginary

and above all, we were angered by the aesthetic equation that reduced these black male bodies to abstract visual "things," silenced in their own right as subjects, serving only to enhance the name and reputation of the author in the rarefied world of art photography. But still we were stuck, unable to make sense of our own implication in the emotions brought into play by Mapplethorpe's imaginary.

I've chosen to situate the issue of ambivalence in relation to these experiences because I am now involved in a partial revision of arguments made in an earlier reading of Mapplethorpe's work.[2] This revision arises not because those arguments were wrong, but because I've changed my mind, or rather I should say that I still can't make up my mind about Mapplethorpe. In returning to my earlier essay I want to suggest an approach to ambivalence not as something that occurs "inside" the text (as if cultural texts were hermetically sealed or self-sufficient), but as something that is experienced across the relations between authors, texts, and readers, relations that are always contingent, context-bound, and historically specific.

Posing the problem of ambivalence and undecidability in this way not only underlines the role of the reader, but also draws attention to the important, and equally undecidable, role of context in determining the range of different readings that can be produced from the same text. In this respect, it is impossible to ignore the crucial changes in context that frame the readings currently negotiated around Mapplethorpe and his work. Mapplethorpe's death in 1989 from AIDS, a major retrospective of his work at the Whitney Museum in New York, the political "controversy" over federal arts policy initiated by the fundamentalist right in response to a second Mapplethorpe exhibition organized by the Institute of Contemporary Art in Philadelphia—these

1. References are made primarily to *Black Males*, with introduction by Edmund White (Amsterdam: Gallerie Jurka, 1982) and *The Black Book*, with foreword by Ntozake Shange (New York: St. Martin's Press, 1986).
2. Kobena Mercer, "Imagine the Black Man's Sex," in *Photography/Politics: Two*, ed. Pat Holland, Jo Spence, and Simon Watney (London: Comedia/ Methuen, 1987), pp. 61–69.

Robert Mapplethorpe, *Thomas*, 1986. Gelatin silver print, 24 x 20 in. (60.9 x 50.8 cm). The Robert Mapplethorpe Foundation, Inc., New York.

events have irrevocably altered the context in which we perceive, argue about, and evaluate Mapplethorpe's most explicitly homoerotic work.

The context has also changed as a result of another set of contemporary developments: the emergence of new aesthetic practices among black lesbian and gay artists in Britain and the United States. Across a range of media, such work problematizes earlier conceptions of identity in black cultural practices. This is accomplished by entering into the ambivalent and over-determined spaces where race, class, gender, sexuality, and ethnicity intersect in the social construction and lived experiences of individual and collective subjectivities. Such developments demand acknowldgement of the historical contingency of context and in turn raise significant questions about the universalist character of some of the grand aesthetic and political claims once made in the name of cultural theory. Beginning with a summary of my earlier argument, I want to identify some of the uses and limitations of psychoanalytic concepts in cultural theory before mapping a more historical trajectory within which to examine the constitutive ambivalence of the identifications we actually inhabit in living with difference.

Revising

The overriding theme of my earlier reading of Mapplethorpe's photographs was that they inscribe a process of objectification in which individual black male bodies are aestheticized and eroticized as objects of the gaze. Framed within the artistic conventions of the nude, the bodies are sculpted and shaped into artifacts that offer an erotic source of pleasure in the act of looking. Insofar as what is represented in the pictorial space of the photograph is a "look," or a certain "way of looking," the pictures say more about the white male subject behind the camera than they do about the black men whose beautiful bodies we see depicted. This is because the invisible or absent subject is the actual agent of the look, at the center and in control of the apparatus of representation, the I/eye at the imaginary origin of the perspective that marks out the empty space to which the viewer is invited as spectator. This argument was based on a formal analysis of the codes and conventions brought to bear on the pictorial space of the photographs, and equally important, on an analogy with feminist analyses of the erotic objectification of the image of women in Western traditions of visual representation.

Three formal conventions interweave across the photographic text to organize and direct the viewer's gaze into its pictorial space: a sculptural code, concerning the posing and posture of the body in the studio enclosure; a code of portraiture concentrated on the face; and a code of lighting and framing, fragmenting bodies in textured formal abstractions. All of these help to construct the mise-en-scène of fantasy and desire that structures the spectator's disposition toward the image. As all references to a social or historical context are effaced by the cool distance of the detached gaze, the text enables the projection of a fantasy that saturates the black male body in sexual predicates.

These codes draw from aspects of Mapplethorpe's oeuvre as a whole and have become the signs by which we recognize his authorial signature. Their specific combination, moreover, is punctuated by the technical perfection—especially marked in the printing process—that also distinguishes Mapplethorpe's presence as an author. Considering the way in which the glossy allure of the photographic print becomes cosubstantial with the shiny texture of black skin, I argued that a significant element in the pleasures the photographs make available consists in the fetishism they bring into play. Such fetishism not only eroticizes the visible difference the black male nude embodies, it also

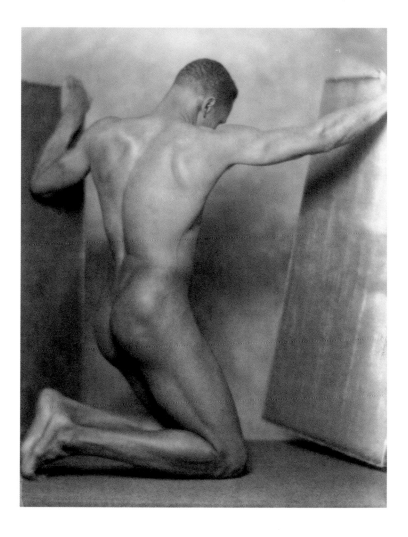

Nickolas Muray, *Paul Robeson*, ca. 1925. Gelatin silver print, 9 ¹/₄ x 7 in. (23.4 x 18 cm). George Eastman House, Rochester, New York.

lubricates the ideological reproduction of racial otherness as the fascination of the image articulates a fantasy of power and mastery over the other.

Before introducing a revision of this view of racial fetishism in Mapplethorpe's photographs, I want to emphasize its dependence on the framework of feminist theory initially developed in relation to cinematic representation by Laura Mulvey.[3] Crudely put, Mulvey showed that men look and women are looked at. The position of "woman" in the dominant regimes of visual representation says little or nothing about the historical experiences of women as such, because the female subject functions predominantly as a mirror image of what the masculine subject wants to see. The visual depiction of women in the mise-en-scène of heterosexual desire serves to stabilize and reproduce the narcissistic scenario of a phallocentric fantasy in which the omnipotent male gaze sees but is never seen. What is important about this framework of analysis is the way it reveals the symbolic relations of power and subordination at work in the binary relations that structure dominant codes and conventions of visual representations of the body. The field of visibility is thus organized by the subject-object dichotomy

3. Laura Mulvey, "Visual Pleasure and Narrative Cinema," in *Feminism and Film Theory*, ed. Constance Penley (New York: Routledge, 1988), pp. 57–68.

Robert Mapplethorpe, *Isaiah*, 1981. Gelatin silver print, 20 x 16 in. (50.8 x 40.6 cm). The Robert Mapplethorpe Foundation, Inc., New York.

that associates masculinity with the activity of looking and femininity with the subordinate, passive role of being that which is looked at.

In extrapolating such terms to Mapplethorpe's black nudes, I suggested that because both artist and models are male, a tension arises that transfers the frisson of difference to the metaphorically polarized terms of racial identity. The black-white duality overdetermines the subject-object dichotomy of seeing and being seen. This metaphorical transfer underlines the erotic investment of the gaze in the most visible element of racial difference—the fetishization of black skin. The dynamics of this tension are apparently stabilized within the pictorial space of the photographs by the ironic appropriation of commonplace stereotypes—the black man as athlete, as savage, as mugger. These stereotypes in turn serve to regulate and fix the representational presence of the black subject, who is thereby "put into his place" by the power of Mapplethorpe's gaze.

F. Holland Day, *Menelek*, 1896. Platinum print, 9 5/8 x 7 11/16 in. (24.4 x 19.2 cm). The Metropolitan Museum of Art, New York, The Alfred Stieglitz Collection, 1933.

The formal work of the codes essentializes each model into the homogenized embodiment of an ideal type. This logic of typification in dominant regimes of racial representation has been emphasized by Homi Bhabha, who argues that "an important feature of colonial discourse is its dependence on the concept of 'fixity' in the ideological construction of otherness."[4] The scopic fixation on black skin thus implies a kind of "negrophilia," an aesthetic idealization and eroticized investment in the racial other that inverts and reverses the binary axis of the fears and anxieties invested in or projected onto the other in "negrophobia." Both positions, whether they devalue or overvalue the signs of racial difference, inhabit the representational space of what Bhabha calls colonial fantasy. Although I would now qualify the theoretical analogies on which this analysis of Mapplethorpe's work was based, I would still want to defend the terms of a psychoanalytic reading of racial fetishism, a fetishism that can be most tangibly grasped in a photograph such as *Man in a Polyester Suit* (1980).

The scale and framing of this picture emphasizes the sheer size of the black dick. Apart from the hands, the penis and the penis alone identifies the model as a black man. As Frantz Fanon said, diagnosing the figure of "the Negro" in the fantasies of his white psychiatric patients, "One is no longer aware of the Negro, but only of a penis: the Negro is eclipsed. He is turned into a penis. He *is* a penis."[5] The element of scale thus summons up one of the deepest mythological fears and anxieties in the racist imagination, namely that all black men have huge willies. In the fantasmatic space of the supremacist imaginary, the big black phallus is a threat not only to the white master (who shrinks in impotence from the thought that the subordinate black male is more potent and sexually powerful than he) but also to civilization itself, since the "bad object" represents a danger to white womanhood and therefore miscegenation and racial degeneration.

The binarisms of classical racial discourse are emphasized in Mapplethorpe's photograph by the jokey irony of the contrast between the black man's private parts and the public respectability signified by the business suit. The oppositions exposed/hidden and denuded/clothed play upon the binary oppositions nature/culture and savage/civilized to bring about a condensation of libidinal investment, fear, and wish-fulfillment in the fantasmatic presence of the other. The binarisms repeat the assumption that sex is the essential "nature" of black masculinity, while the cheap, tacky polyester suit confirms the black man's failure to gain access to "culture." The camouflage of respectability cannot conceal the fact that, in essence, he originates, like his prick, from somewhere anterior to civilization. What is dramatized in the picture is the splitting of levels of belief, which Freud

4. Homi Bhabha, "The Other Question: The Stereotype and Colonial Discourse," *Screen 24*, no. 6 (November-December 1985): 18–36.
5. Frantz Fanon, *Black Skin, White Masks* (London: Paladin, 1970), p. 120.

Robert Mapplethorpe, *Man in a Polyester Suit*, 1980. Gelatin silver print, 20 x 16 in. (50.8 x 40.6 cm). The Robert Mapplethorpe Foundation, Inc., New York.

regarded as the key feature of the logic of disavowal in fetishism.[6] Hence, the implication: "I *know* it's not true that all black men have big penises, *but still,* in my photographs they do."

It is precisely at this point, however, that the concept of fetishism threatens to conceal more than it reveals about the ambivalence the spectator experiences in relation to the "shock effect" of Mapplethorpe's work. Freud saw the castration anxiety in the little boy's shock at discovering the absence of a penis in the little girl (acknowledged and disavowed in the fetish) as constitutive of sexual difference. The clinical pathology or perversion of the fetishist, like a neurotic symptom, unravels for classical psychoanalysis the "normal" development path of oedipal heterosexual identity: it is the point at which the norm is rendered visible by the pathological. The concept of fetishism was profoundly enabling for feminist film theory because it uncovered the logic of substitution at work in all regimes of representation, which make present for the subject what is absent in the real. But although analogies facilitate cognitive connections with important cultural and political implications, there is also the risk that they repress and flatten out the messy spaces in between. As Jane Gaines has pointed out concerning feminist film theory, the inadvertent reproduction of the heterosexual presumption in the orthodox theorization of sexual difference also assumed a homogeneous racial and ethnic context, with the result that racial and ethnic differences were erased from or marginalized within the analysis.[7] Analogies between race and gender in representation reveal similar ideological patterns of objectification, exclusion, and "othering." In Mapplethorpe's nudes, however, there is a subversive homoerotic dimension in the substitution of the black male subject for the traditional female archetype. This subversive dimension was underplayed in my earlier analysis: my use of the theoretical analogy minimized the homosexual specificity of Mapplethorpe's eroticism, which rubs against the grain of the generic high-art status of the traditional female nude.

To pose the problem in another way, one could approach the issue of ambivalence by simply asking: do photographs like *Man in a Polyester Suit* reinscribe the fixed beliefs of racist ideology, or do they problematize them by foregrounding the intersections of difference where race and gender cut across the representation of sexuality? An unequivocal answer is impossible or undecidable, it seems to me, because the image throws the question back onto the spectator, for whom it is experienced precisely as the shock effect. What is at issue is not primarily whether the question can be decided by appealing to authorial intentions, but rather the equally important question of the role of the reader and how he or she attributes intentionality to the

6. Sigmund Freud, "Fetishism" (1927), *The Standard Edition of the Complete Psychological Works of Sigmund Freud,* ed. James Strachey (London: Hogarth Press, 1953–74), vol. 21 (1961), pp. 147–57.
7. Jane Gaines, "White Privilege and Looking Relations: Race and Gender in Feminist Film Theory," *Screen* 29, No. 4 (Autumn 1988): 12–27.

Unidentified photographer, *Everything you ever hear about black men...*, ca. 1975. Greeting card.

author. The elision of homoerotic specificity in my earlier reading thus refracts an ambivalence not so much on the part of Mapplethorpe the author, or on the part of the text, but on my part as a reader. More specifically, it refracted the ambivalent "structure of feeling" that I inhabit as a black gay male reader in relation to the text. Indeed, I've only recently become aware of the logical slippage in my earlier reading, which assumed an equivalence between Mapplethorpe as the individual agent of the image and the empty, anonymous, and impersonal ideological category I described as "the white male subject" to which the spectator is interpellated. Paradoxically, this conflation undermined the very distinction between author-function and ideological subject-position that I drew from Michel Foucault's antinaturalist account of authorship.[8]

In retrospect I feel this logical flaw arose as a result of my own ambivalent positioning as a black gay spectator. To call something fetishistic implies a negative judgment, to say the least. I want to take back the unavoidably moralistic connotation of the term, because I think what was at issue in the rhetoric of my previous argument was the encoding of an ambivalent structure of feeling, in which anger and envy divided the identifications that placed me somewhere always already inside the text. On the one hand, I emphasized objectification because I felt identified with the black males in the field of vision, an identification with the other that might best be described in Fanon's terms as a feeling that "I am laid bare. I am overdetermined from without. I am a slave not of the 'idea' that others have of me but of my own appearance. I am being dissected under white eyes. I am *fixed*... Look, it's a Negro."[9] But on the other hand, and more difficult to disclose, I was also implicated in the fantasy scenario as a gay subject. That is to say, I was identified with the author insofar as the objectified black male was also an image of the object chosen by my own fantasies and erotic investments. Thus, sharing the same desire to look as the author-agent of the gaze, I would actually occupy the position that I said was that of the "white male subject."

I now wonder whether the anger in that earlier reading was not also the expression and projection of a certain envy. Was it not, in this sense, an effect of a homosexual identification on the basis of a similar object-choice that invoked an aggressive rivalry over the same unattainable object of desire, depicted and represented in the visual field of the other? According to Jacques Lacan, the mirror-stage constitutes the "I" in an alienated relation to its own image, as the image of the infant's body is "unified" by the prior investment that comes from the look of the mother, always already in the field of the other.[10] In this sense, the element of aggressivity involved in textual analysis—the act

8. Michel Foucalt, "What Is an Author?" in *Language, Counter-Memory, Practice*, ed. Donald F. Bouchard (Ithaca, N.Y.: Cornell University Press, 1977), pp. 113–38; see also Roland Barthes, "The Death of the Author," in *Image-Music-Text* (New York: Hill and Wang, 1977), pp. 142–48.
9. Fanon, *Black Skin, White Masks*, p. 82.
10. Jacques Lacan, "The mirror stage as formative of the function of the I," in *Ecrits: A Selection* (London: Tavistock, 1977), pp. 1–7.

of taking things apart—might merely have concealed my own narcissistic participation in the pleasures of Mapplethorpe's texts. Taking the two elements together, I would say that my ambivalent positioning as a black gay male reader stemmed from the way in which I inhabited two contradictory identifications at one and the same time. Insofar as the anger and envy were an effect of my identifications with both object and subject of the gaze, the rhetorical closure of my earlier reading simply displaced the ambivalence onto the text by attributing it to the author.

If this brings us to the threshold of the kind of ambivalence that is historically specific to the context, positions, and experiences of the reader, it also demonstrates the radically polyvocal quality of Mapplethorpe's photographs and the way in which contradictory readings can be derived from the same body of work. I want to suggest, therefore, an alternative reading that demonstrates this textual reversibility by revising that assumption that fetishism is necessarily a bad thing.

By making a 180-degree turn, I want to suggest that the articulation of ambivalence in Mapplethorpe's work can be seen as a subversive deconstruction of the hidden racial and gendered axioms of the nude in dominant traditions of representation. This alternative reading also arises out of a reconsideration of poststructuralist theories of authorship. Although Romantic notions of authorial creativity cannot be returned to the central role they once played in criticism and interpretation, the question of agency in cultural practices that contest the canon and its cultural dominance suggests that it really *does* matter who is speaking.

The question of enunciation—who is speaking, who is spoken to, what codes do they share to communicate?—implies a whole range of important political issues about who is empowered and who is disempowered in the representation of difference. It is enunciation that circumscribes the marginalized positions of subjects historically misrepresented or underrepresented in dominant systems of representation. To be marginalized is to have no place from which to speak, since the subject positioned in the margins is silenced and invisible. The contestation of marginality in black, gay, and feminist politics thus inevitably brings the issue of authorship back into play, not as the centered origin that determines or guarantees the aesthetic and political value of a text, but as a question about agency in the cultural struggle to "find a voice" and "give voice" to subordinate experiences, identities, and subjectivities. A relativization of authoritative poststructuralist claims about decentering the subject means making sense of the biographical and autobiographical dimension of the context-bound relations between authors, texts, and readers without falling back on liberal humanist or empiricist common sense. Quite specifically, the "death of the author" thesis demands revision because the death of the author in *our* case inevitably makes a difference to the kinds of readings we make.

Comments by Mapplethorpe, and by some of the black models with whom he collaborated, offer a perspective on the questions of authorship, identification, and enunciation. The first of these concerns the specificity of Mapplethorpe's authorial identity as a gay artist and the importance of a metropolitan gay male culture as a context for the homoeroticism of the black male nudes.

In a British Broadcasting Corporation documentary in 1988, Lynne Franks pointed out that Mapplethorpe's work is remarkable for its absence of voyeurism. A brief comparison with the avowedly heterosexual scenario in the work of photographers such as Edward Weston and Helmut Newton would suggest similar aesthetic conventions at the level of visual fetishization; but it would also highlight the significant differences that arise in Mapplethorpe's homoeroticism. Under Mapplethorpe's authorial gaze there is a tension within the cool distance between subject and object. The gaze certainly involves an element of erotic objectification, but like a point-of-view shot in gay male pornography, it is reversible. The gendered hierarchy of seeing/being seen is not so rigidly coded in homoerotic representations, since sexual sameness liquidates the associative opposition between active subject and passive object. This element of reversibility at the level of the gaze is marked elsewhere in Mapplethorpe's oeuvre, most notably in the numerous self-portraits, including the one of him with a bullwhip up his bum, in which the artist posits himself as the object of the look. In relation to the black male nudes and the s&m pictures that preceded them, this reversibility creates an ambivalent distance measured by the direct look of the models, which is another salient feature of gay male pornography. In effect, Mapplethorpe implicates himself in his field of vision by a kind of participatory observation, an ironic ethnography whose descriptive clarity suggests a reversible relation of equivalence, or identification, between the author and the social actors whose world is described. In this view, Mapplethorpe's homoeroticism can be read as a form of stylized reportage that documented aspects of the urban gay subcultural milieu of the 1970s. One can reread Mapplethorpe's homoerotica as a kind of photographic documentary of a world that has profoundly changed as a result of AIDS. This reinterpretation is something Mapplethorpe drew attention to in the BBC television interview:

> *I was part of it. And that's where most of the photographers who move in that direction are at a disadvantage,*

in that they're not part of it. They're voyeurs moving in.
With me it was quite different. Often I had experienced
some of those experiences which I later recorded,
myself, firsthand, without a camera.... It was a certain
moment, and I was in a perfect situation in that most
of the people in the photographs were friends of mine
and they trusted me. I felt almost an obligation to record
those things. It was an obligation for me to do it, to
make images that nobody's seen before and to do it in
a way that's aesthetic.

In this respect, especially in the light of the moral and ethical emphasis by which Mapplethorpe locates himself as a member of an elective community, it is important to acknowledge the ambivalence of authorial motivation suggested in his rationale for the black male nude studies:

At some point I started photographing black men. It
was an area that hadn't been explored intensively. If you
went through the history of nude male photography,
there were very few black subjects. I found that I could
take pictures of black men that were so subtle, and the
form was so photographical.

On the one hand, this could be interpreted as the discovery and conquest of "virgin territory" in the field of art history; but alternatively, Mapplethorpe's acknowledgement of the exclusion and absence of the black subject from the canonical realm of the fine art nude can be interpreted as the elementary starting point of an implicit critique of racism and ethnocentrism in Western aesthetics.

Once we consider Mapplethorpe's own marginality as a gay artist, placed in a subordinate relation to the canonical tradition of the nude, his implicitly critical position on the presence/absence of the race in dominant regimes of representation enables a reappraisal of the inter-subjective collaboration between artist and model. Whereas my previous reading emphasized the apparent inequality between the famous, author-named white artist and the anonymous and interchangeable black models, the biographical dimension reveals an important element of mutuality. In a magazine interview that appeared after his death in 1989, Mapplethorpe's comments about the models suggest an inter-subjective relation based on a shared social identity: "Most of the blacks don't have health insurance and therefore can't afford AZT. They all died quickly, the blacks. If I go through my *Black Book*, half of them are dead."[11] In his mourning, there is something horribly accurate about the truism that death is the great leveler, because his pictures have now become *memento mori*, documentary evidence of a style of

11. "The Long Goodbye," interview by Dominick Dunne, *Blitz* (London) May 1989, pp. 67–68.

life and a sexual ethics in the metropolitan gay culture of the 1970s and early 1980s that no longer exist in the way they used to. As a contribution to the historical formation of urban gay culture, Mapplethorpe's homoeroticism is invested with memory, with the intense emotional residue Barthes described when he wrote about the photographs of his mother.[12]

The element of mutual identification between artist and models undermines the view that the relation was necessarily exploitative simply because it was interracial. Comments by Ken Moody, one of the models in the *Black Book*, suggest a degree of reciprocity. When asked in the BBC television interview whether he recognized himself in Mapplethorpe's pictures, he said, "Not always, not most of the time.... When I look at it as me, and not just a piece of art, I think I look like a freak. I don't find that person in the photograph necessarily attractive, and it's not something I would like to own." The alienation of not even

12. Roland Barthes, *Camera Lucida* (New York: Hill and Wang, 1981).

F. Holland Day, *Ebony and Ivory*, 1897. Platinum print, 7 3/16 x 7 7/8 in. (18.2 x 19.9 cm). The Metropolitan Museum of Art, New York, The Alfred Stieglitz Collection, 1933.

owning your own image might be taken as evidence of objectification, of being reduced to a "piece of art"; but at the same time Moody rejects the view that it was an unequivocal relation, suggesting instead a reciprocal gift relationship that further underlines the theme of mutuality:

> *I don't honestly think of it as exploitation.... It's almost*
> *as if—and this is the conclusion I've come to now,*
> *because I really haven't thought about it up to now—*
> *it's almost as if he wants to give a gift to this particular*
> *group. He wants to create something very beautiful*
> *and give it to them.... And he is actually very giving.*

I don't want to over- or underinterpret such evidence, but I do think this biographical dimension to the issues of authorship and enunciation enables a rereading of the textual ambivalence in Mapplethorpe's artistic practice. Taking the question of identification into account, as that which inscribes ambivalent relations of mutuality and reversibility in the gaze, enables a reconsideration of the cultural politics of Mapplethorpe's black male nudes.

Once grounded in the context of contemporary urban gay male culture in the United States, the shocking modernism that informs the ironic juxtaposition of elements drawn from the repository of high culture—where the nude is indeed one of the most valued genres in Western art history—can be read as a subversive recording of the normative aesthetic ideal. In this view, it becomes possible to reverse the reading of racial fetishism in Mapplethorpe's work, not as a repetition of racist fantasies but as a deconstructive strategy that lays bare psychic and social relations of ambivalence in the representation of race and sexuality. This deconstructive aspect of his homoeroticism is experienced, at the level of audience reception, as the disturbing shock effect.

The Eurocentric character of the liberal humanist values invested in classical Greek sculpture as the originary model of human beauty in Western aesthetics is paradoxically revealed by the promiscuous intertextuality whereby the filthy and degraded form of the commonplace racist stereotype is brought into the domain of aesthetic purity circumscribed by the privileged place of the fine-art nude. This doubling within the pictorial space of Mapplethorpe's black nudes does not reproduce either term of the binary relation between "high culture" and "low culture" as it is: it radically decenters and destabilizes the hierarchy of racial and sexual difference in dominant systems of representation by folding the two together within the same frame. It is this ambivalent intermixing of textual references, achieved through the appropriation and articulation of elements from the "purified" realm of the transcendental aesthetic idea and from the debased and "polluted" world of the commonplace racist stereotype, that disturbs the fixed positioning of the spectator. One might say that what is staged in Mapplethorpe's black male nudes is the return of the repressed in the ethnocentric imaginary. The psychic-social boundary that separates "high culture" and "low culture" is transgressed, crossed and disrupted precisely by the superimposition of two ways of seeing, which thus throws the spectator into uncertainty and undecidability, precisely the experience of ambivalence as a structure of feeling in which one's subject-position is called into question.

In my previous argument, I suggested that the regulative function of the stereotype had the upper hand, as it were, and helped to "fix" the spectator in the ideological subject-position of the "white male subject." Now I'm not so sure. Once we recognize the historical and political specificity of Mapplethorpe's practice as contemporary gay artist, the aesthetic irony that informs the juxtaposition of elements in his work can be seen as the trace of a subversive strategy that disrupts the stability of the binary oppositions into which difference is coded. In social, economic, and political terms, black men in the United States constitute one of the "lowest" social classes: disenfranchised, disadvantaged, and disempowered as a distinct collective subject in the late capitalist underclass. Yet in Mapplethorpe's photographs, men who in all probability came from this class are elevated onto the pedestal of the transcendental Western aesthetic ideal. Far from reinforcing the fixed beliefs of the white supremacist imaginary, such a deconstructive move begins to undermine the foundational myths of the pedestal itself.

The subaltern black social subject, who was historically excluded from dominant regimes of representation—an "invisible man" in Ralph Ellison's phrase—is made visible within the codes and conventions of the dominant culture whose ethnocentrism is thereby exposed as a result. The mythological figure of "the Negro," who was always excluded from the good, the true, and the beautiful in Western aesthetics on account of his otherness, comes to embody the image of physical per-fection and aesthetic idealization in which, in the canonical figure of the nude, Western culture constructed its own self-image. Far from confirming the hegemonic white, heterosexual subject in his centered position of mastery and power, the deconstructive aspects of Mapplethorpe's black male nude photographs loosen up and unfix the common-sense sensibilities of the spectator, who thereby experiences the shock effect precisely as the affective displacement of given ideological subject-positions.

To shock was always the key verb of the avant-garde in modernist art history. In Mapplethorpe's work, the shock effected by the promiscuous textual intercourse between elements drawn from opposite ends of the hierarchy of cultural value decenters and destabilizes the ideological fixity of the spectator. In this sense, his work begins to reveal the political unconscious of white ethnicity. It lays bare the constitutive ambivalence that structures whiteness as a cultural identity whose hegemony lies, as Richard Dyer suggests, precisely in its "invisibility."[13]

The splitting of the subject in the construction of white identity, entailed in the affirmation and denial of racial difference in Western humanism, is traced in racist perception. Blacks are looked down upon and despised as worthless, ugly, and ultimately unhuman creatures. But in the blink of an eye, whites look up to and revere the black body, lost in awe and envy as the black subject is idolized as the embodiment of the whites' ideal. This schism in white subjectivity is replayed daily in the different ways black men become visible on the front and back

13. Richard Dyer, "White," *Screen* 29, no. 4 (Autumn 1988): 44–64.

George Platt Lynes, *Untitled*, ca. 1952. Gelatin silver print, 8 x 10 in. (20.3 x 25.4 cm). Courtesy of Kinsey Institute for Research in Sex, Gender, and Reproduction, Bloomington, Indiana.

pages of tabloid newspapers, seen as undesirable in one frame—the mugger, the terrorist, the rapist—and highly desirable in the other—the athlete, the sports hero, the entertainer. Mapplethorpe undercuts this conventional separation to show the recto-verso relation between these contradictory "ways of seeing" as constitutive aspects of white identity. Like a mark that is legible on both sides of a sheet of paper, Mapplethorpe's aesthetic strategy places the splitting in white subjectivity under erasure: it is crossed out but still visible. In this sense, the anxieties aroused in the exhibition history of Mapplethorpe's homoerotica not only demonstrate the disturbance and decentering of dominant versions of white identity, but also confront whiteness with the otherness that enables it to be constituted as an identity as such.

In suggesting that this ambivalent racial fetishization of difference actually enables a potential deconstruction of whiteness, I think Mapplethorpe's use of irony can be recontextualized in relation to pop art practices of the 1960s. The undecidable question that is thrown back on the spectator—do the images undermine or reinforce racial stereotypes?—can be compared to the highly ambivalent aura of fetishism that frames the female body in the paintings of Allen Jones. Considering the issues of sexism and misogyny at stake, Laura Mulvey's reading, from 1972, suggests a contextual approach to the political analysis of fetishism's "shocking" undecidabilty:

> By revealing the way in which fetishistic images pervade not just specialist publications but the whole of mass media, Allen Jones throws a new light on woman as spectacle. Women are constantly confronted with their own image… yet, in a real sense, women are not there at all. The parade has nothing to do with woman, everything to do with man. The true exhibit is always the phallus…. The time has come for us to take over the show and exhibit our own fears and desires.[14]

This reading has a salutary resonance in the renewal of debates on black aesthetics insofar as contemporary practices that contest the marginality of the black subject in dominant regimes of representation have gone beyond the unhelpful binarism of so-called positive and negative images. We are now more aware of the identities, fantasies, and desires that are coerced, simplified, and reduced by the rhetorical closure that flows from that kind of critique. But Mulvey's reading also entails a clarification of what we need from theory as black artists and intellectuals. The critique of stereotypes was crucial in the women's and gay movements of the 1960s and 1970s, just as it was in the black movements that produced aesthetic-political perfor-

14. Laura Mulvey, "Fears, Fantasies and the Male Unconscious, or 'You don't know what is happening, do you, Mr. Jones'" in *Visual and other Pleasures* (London: Macmillan, 1989), p. 13.

mative statements such as Black is Beautiful. As the various movements have fragmented politically, however, their combined and uneven development suggests that analogies across race, gender, and sexuality may be useful only insofar as we historicize them and what they make possible. Appropriations of psychoanalytic theory arose at a turning point in the cultural politics of feminism; in thinking about the enabling possibilities this has opened up for the study of black representation, I feel we also need to acknowledge the other side of ambivalence in contemporary cultural struggles, the dark side of the political predicament that ambivalence engenders.

In contrast to the claims of academic deconstruction, the moment of undecidability is rarely experienced as a purely textual event; rather it is the point where politics and the contestation of power are felt to be at their most intense. According to V. N. Volosinov, the social multi-accentuality of the ideological sign has an "inner dialectical quality [that] comes out only in times of social crises or revolutionary changes," because "in ordinary circumstances… an established dominant ideology… always tries, as it were, to stabilize the dialectical flux."[15] Indeterminacy means that multiaccentual or polyvalent signs have no necessary belonging and can be articulated and appropriated into the political discourse of the right as easily as they can into that of the left. Antagonistic efforts to fix the multiple connotations arising from the ambivalence of the key signs of ideological struggle demonstrate what in Gramsci's terms would be described as a war of position whose outcome is never guaranteed in advance one way or the other.

We have seen how, despite their emancipatory objectives, certain radical feminist antipornography arguments have been taken up and translated into the neoconservative cultural and political agenda of the right. For my part, I want to emphasize that I've reversed my reading of racial signification in Mapplethorpe not for the fun of it, but because I do *not* want a black gay critique to be appropriated to the purposes of the right's antidemocratic cultural offensive. Jesse Helms's amendment to public funding policies in the arts—which was orchestrated in relation to Mapplethorpe's homoerotic work—forbids the public funding of art deemed "obscene or indecent." But it is crucial to note that a broader remit for censorship was originally articulated on the grounds of a moral objection to art that "denigrates, debases, or reviles a person, group, or class of citizens on the basis of race, creed, sex, handicap, or national origin."[16] In other words, the discourse of liberal and social democratic antidiscrimination legislation is being appropriated and rearticulated into a right-wing position that promotes a discriminatory politics of cultural censorship and ideological coercion.

15. V. N. Volosinov, *Marxism and the Philosophy of Language*, Cambridge, Mass.: Harvard University Press, 1973), p. 24.
16. *The New York Times*, 27 July 1989, A1.

Without a degree of self-reflexivity, black critiques of Mapplethorpe's work can be easily assimilated into a politics of homophobia. Which is to say, coming back to the photographs, that precisely on account of their ambivalence, Mapplethorpe's photographs are open to a range of contradictory readings whose political character depends on the social identity that different audiences bring to bear on them. The photographs can confirm a racist reading as easily as they can produce an antiracist one. Or again, they can elicit a homophobic reading as easily as they can confirm a homoerotic one. Once ambivalence and undecidability are situated in the contextual relations between author, text, and readers, a cultural struggle ensues in which antagonistic efforts seek to articulate the meaning and value of Mapplethorpe's work.

What is at issue in this "politics of enunciation" can be clarified by a linguistic analogy, since certain kinds of performative statements produce different meanings not so much because of what is said but because of who is saying it. As a verbal equivalent of Mapplethorpe's visual image, the statement "the black man is beautiful" takes on a different meanings depending on the identity of the social subject who enunciates it. Does the same statement mean the same thing when uttered by a white woman, a black woman, a white man, or a black man? Does it mean the same thing whether the speaker is straight or gay? In my view, it cannot possibly mean the same thing in each instance because the racial and gendered identity of the enunciator inevitably "makes a difference" to the social construction of meaning and value. Today we are adept at the all-too-familiar concatenation of identity politics, as if by merely rehearsing the mantra of "race, class, gender" (and all other intervening variables) we have somehow acknowledged the diversified and pluralized differences at work in contemporary culture, politics, and society. Yet the complexity of what actually happens "between" the contingent spaces where each variable intersects with the others is something only now coming into view theoretically, and this is partly the result of the new antagonistic cultural practices by hitherto marginalized artists. Instead of analogies, which tend to flatten out these intermediate spaces, I think we need to explore theories that enable new forms of dialogue. In this way we might be able to imagine a dialogic or relational conception of the differences we actually inhabit in our lived experiences of identity and identification. The observation that different readers produce different readings of the same cultural texts is not as circular as it seems: I want to suggest that it provides an outlet onto the dialogic character of the political imaginary of difference. To open up this area for theoretical investigation, I want to point to two ways in which such relational differences of race, gender, and sexuality do indeed "make a difference."

Different readers make different readings

Here, I simply want to itemize a range of issues concerning readership and authorship that arise across the intertextual field in which
Mapplethorpe "plays." To return to *Man in a Polyester Suit*, one can see
that an anonymous greeting card produced and marketed in a specifically gay cultural context works on similar fantasies of black sexuality.
The greeting card depicts a black man in a business suit alongside the
caption "Everything you ever heard about black men ... is true"—at
which point one unfolds the card to reveal the black man's penis. The
same savage-civilized binarism that I noted in Mapplethorpe's photograph is signified here by the contrast between the body clothed in
a business suit, then denuded to reveal the penis (with some potted
plants in the background to emphasize the point about the nature-
culture distinction). Indeed, the card replays the fetishistic splitting of
levels of belief as it is opened: the image of the big back penis serves
as the punchline of the little joke. But because the card is authorless,

George Platt Lynes, *Untitled (Francisco Moncion with Medallion)*, 1948. Gelatin silver print, 10 x 8 in. (25.4 x 20.3 cm). Courtesy of
Robert Miller Gallery, New York.

the issue of attributing racist or antiracist intentions is effectively secondary to the context in which it is exchanged and circulated, the context of an urban, commercial, gay male subculture. My point is that gay readers in this vernacular sign-community may share access to a range of intertextual references in Mapplethorpe's work that other readers may not be aware of.

Returning to the "enigma" of the black models in Mapplethorpe's work: the appearance of black gay video porn star Joe Simmons (referred to as Thomas in *The Black Book*) on magazine covers from *Artscribe* to *Advocate Men* offers a source of intertextual pleasure to those "in the know" that accentuates and inflects Mapplethorpes depiction of the same person. Repetition has become one of the salient pleasures of gay male pornography, as photographic reproduction and video piracy encourage the accelerated flow by which models and scenarios constantly reappear in new intertextual combinations. By extending this process into "high art," circulating imagery between the streets and the galleries, Mapplethorpe's promiscuous textuality has a sense of humor that might otherwise escape the sensibilities of nongay or antigay viewers.

The mobility of such intertextual moves cannot be arrested by recourse to binary oppositions. The sculpted pose of Joe Simmons in one frame immediately recalls the celebrated nude studies of Paul Robeson by Nickolas Muray in 1926. Once the photograph is situated in this historical context, which may or may not be familiar to black readers in particular, one might compare Mapplethorpe to Carl Van Vechten, the white photographer of black literati in the Harlem Renaissance. In this context, Richard Dyer has retrieved a revealing instance of overwhelming ambivalence in racial-sexual representations. In the 1920s, wealthy white patrons in the Philadelphia Art Alliance commissioned a sculpture of Robeson by Antonio Salemme. Although they wanted it to embody Robeson's "pure" beauty in bronze, they rejected the sculpture because its aesthetic sensuality overpowered their moral preconceptions.[17]

The historical specificity of this reference has a particular relevance in the light of renewed interest in the Harlem Renaissance in contemporary black cultural practices. This rediscovery of the past has served to thematize questions of identity and desire in the work of black gay artists such as Isaac Julien. In *Looking for Langston* (1988), Julien undertakes an archeological inquiry into the enigma of Langston Hughes's sexual identity. Insofar as the aesthetic strategy of the film eschews the conventions of documentary realism in favor of a dialogic combination of poetry, music, and archival imagery, it does not claim to discover an authentic or essential homosexual identity

17. Richard Dyer, "Paul Robeson: Crossing Over," in *Heavenly Bodies: Film Stars and Society* (New York: St. Martin's Press, 1986), pp. 67–139.

(for Langston Hughes or anyone else). Rather, the issue of authorial identity is invested with fantasy, memory, and desire, and serves as an imaginative point of departure for speculation and reflection on the social and historical relations in which black gay male identity is lived and experienced in diaspora societies such as Britain and the United States. In this sense, the criticism that the film is not about Langston Hughes misses the point. By showing the extent to which our identities as black gay men are historically constructed in and through representations, Julien's film interrogates aspects of social relations that silence and repress the representability of black gay identities and desires. The search for iconic heroes and heroines has been an important element in lesbian, gay, and feminist cultural politics, and the process of uncovering identities previously "hidden from history" has had empowering effects in culture and society at large. Julien is involved in a similar project, but his film refuses, through its dialogic strategy, to essentialize Hughes into a black gay cultural icon. This strategy focuses on the question of power at issue in the ability to make and wield representations. Above all, it focuses on who has the "right to look" by emphasizing both interracial and intraracial looking relations that complicate the subject-object dichotomy of seeing and being seen.

Hence, in one key scene, we see the white male protagonist leisurely leafing through *The Black Book*. Issues of voyeurism, objectification, and fetishization are brought into view not in a didactic confrontation with Mapplethorpe, but through a seductive invitation into the messy spaces in between the binary oppositions that dominate the representation of difference. Alongside visual quotations from Jean Cocteau, Jean Genet, and Derek Jarman, the voices of James Baldwin, Toni Morrison, and Amiri Baraka combine to emphasize the relational conception of "identity" that Julien's dialogic strategy makes possible. It is through this relational approach that the film reopens the issue of racial fetishism. An exchange of looks between "Langston" and his mythic object of desire, a black man called "Beauty," provokes a hostile glare from Beauty's white partner. In the daydream that follows, Langston imagines himself coupled with Beauty, their bodies inter twined on a bed in an image reappropriated and reaccentuated from the homoerotic photography of George Platt Lynes. It is here that the trope of visual fetishization makes a subversive return. Close-up sequences lovingly linger on the sensuous mouth of the actor portraying Beauty, with the rest of his face cast in shadow. As in Mapplethorpe's photographs, the strong emphasis on chiaroscuro lighting invests the fetishized fragment with a powerful erotic charge in which the "thick lips" of the Negro are hypervalorized as the emblem of Beauty's impossible desirability. In other words, Julien takes the artistic risk of replicating the stereotype of the "thick-lipped Negro" in order to revalorize that which has historically been devalorized as emblematic of the other's ugliness. It is only by operating "in and against" such tropes of racial fetishism that Julien lays bare the ambivalence of the psychic and social relations at stake in the relay of looks between the three men.

Historically, black people have been the objects of representation rather than its subjects and creators because racism often determines who gets access to the means of representation in the first place. Through his dialogic textual strategy, Julien overturns this double-bind as the black subject "looks back" to ask the audience who or what *they* are looking for. The motif of the "direct look" appeared in Julien's first film with the Sankofa Collective, *Territories* (1984), which involved an "epistemological break" with the realist documentary tradition in black art. Similarly, what distinguishes current work by black lesbian and gay artists—such as the film and video of Pratibha Parmar or the photography of Rotimi Fani-Kayode—is the break with static and essentialist conceptions of identity. The salient feature of such work is its hybridity; it operates on the borderlines of race, class, gender, nationality, and sexuality, investigating the complex overdetermination of subjective experience and desires as they are historically constituted in the ambivalent spaces in between.

Elsewhere I suggested that, in relation to black British film, such hybridized practices articulate a critical dialogue about the constructed character of black British identities and experiences.[18] Something similar informs the hybridized homoerotica of Nigerian British photographer Rotimi Fani-Kayode. The very title of his first publication, *Black Male/White Male*,[19] suggests an explicitly intertextual relationship with Mapplethorpe. However, salient similarities in Fani-Kayode's construction of pictorial space—the elaborate body postures enclosed within the studio space, the use of visual props to stage theatrical effects, and the glossy monochrome texture of the photographic print—underline the important differences in his refiguration of the black male nude. In contrast to Mapplethorpe's isolation-effect, whereby only one black man occupies the field of vision at any one time, in Fani-Kayode's photographs bodies are coupled and contextualized. In pictures such as *Technique of Ecstasy*, the erotic conjunction of two black men suggests an Afrocentric imaginary in which the implied power relations of the subject-object dichotomy are complicated by racial sameness. In *Bronze Head*, what looks like a Benin mask appears beneath a black man's splayed buttocks. This shocking contextualization places the image in an ambivalent space, at once an instance of contemporary African art, referring specifically to Yoruba iconography, and an example

18. Kobena Mercer, "Diaspora Culture and the Dialogic Imagination: The Aesthetics of Black Independent film in Britain," in *Blackframes: Critical Perspectives on Black Independent Cinema*, ed. Mybe B. Cham and Clarie Andrade-Watkins (Cambridge: MIT Press, 1988), pp. 50–61.
19. Rotimi Fani-Kayode, *Black Male/White Male* (London: Gay Men's Press, 1987); see also Rotimi Fani-Kayode, "Traces of Ecstasy," *Ten.8*, no. 28 (Summer 1988): 36–43.

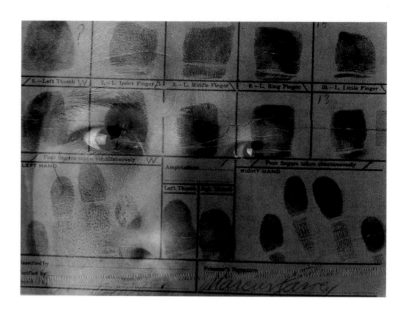

of homoerotic art photography that recalls Mapplethorpe's portrait of Derrick Cross, in which the black man's bum resembles a Brancusi.

If such dialogic strategies do indeed "make a difference" to our understanding of the cultural politics of identity and diversity, does this mean the work is different *because* its authors are black? No, not necessarily. What is at issue is not an essentialist argument that the ethnic identity of the artist guarantees the aesthetic or political value of the text, but on the contrary, how common sense conceptions of authorship and readership are challenged by practices that acknowledge the diversity and heterogeneity of the relations in which identities are socially constructed. Stuart Hall helped to clarify what is at stake in this shift when he argued that such acknowledgment of difference and diversity in black cultural practices has brought the innocent notion of the essential black subject to an end. Once we recognize blackness as a category of social, psychic, and political relations that have no fixed guarantees in nature but only the contingent forms in which they are constructed in culture, the questions of value cannot be decided by recourse to empirical common sense about "color" or melanin. As Stuart Hall put it, "Films are not necessarily good because black people make them. They are not necessarily 'right on' by virtue of the fact that they deal with the black experience.[20]

In this view, I would argue that black gay and lesbian artists are producing exciting and important work not because they happen to be black lesbians and gay men but because they have made cultural and political choices out of their experiences of marginality that situate them at the interface between different traditions. Insofar as they

20. Stuart Hall, "New Ethnicities," in *Black Film/British Cinema*, ICA Document 7 (London: Institute of Contemporary Art/British Film Institute, 1988), p. 28.

Albert Chong, *Self-Portrait with Garvey's Prison Docket*, 1995. Gelatin silver print, 14 3/8 x 11 in. (36.5 x 27.9 cm). International Center of Photography, Museum purchase, 2003.

speak *from* the specificity of such experiences, they overturn the assumption that minority artists speak *for* the entire community from which they come. This is an important distinction in the relations of enunciation because it bears upon the politics of representation that pertain to all subjects in marginalized or minoritized situations, whether black, feminist, lesbian, or gay. In a material context of

Lyle Ashton Harris, *Americas Triptych*, 1987–88. Gelatin silver print, one of three panels, each 30 x 20 in. (76.2 x 50.8 cm). Private collection.

restricted access to the means of representation, minoritized subjects are charged with an impossible "burden of representation." Where subordinate subjects acquire the right to speak only one at a time, their discourse is circumscribed by the assumption that they speak as "representatives" of the entire community from which they come.

It is logically impossible for any one individual to bear such a burden, not only because it denies variety and heterogeneity within minority communities but also because it demands an intolerable submission to the iron law of the stereotype, namely the view from the majority culture that every minority subject is "the same." In the master codes of the dominant culture, the assumption that "all black people are the same" reinforces the view that black communities are monolithic and homogeneous and that black subjectivity is defined exclusively by race and nothing but race. The dialogic element in contemporary black artistic practices begins to interrupt this restricted economy of representation by making it possible to imagine a democratic politics of difference and diversity. The work of black gay and lesbian artists participates in what has been called "postmodernism" in terms of practices that pluralize available representations in the public sphere. To the extent that their aesthetic of critical dialogism underline their contribution to the "new cultural politics of difference," as Cornel West has put it,[21] it seems to me that rather than mere "celebration," their work calls for a critical response that reopens issues and questions we thought had been closed.

As I suggested in rereading Mapplethorpe, one of the key questions on the contemporary agenda concerns the cultural construction of whiteness. One of the signs of the times is that we really don't know what "white" is. The implicitly ethnocentric agenda of cultural criticism, since the proliferation of poststructuralist theories in the 1970s, not only obscured the range of issues concerning black authorship, black spectatorship, and black intertextuality that black artists have been grappling with but also served to render invisible the constructed, and contested, character of "whiteness" as a racial/ethnic identity. Richard Dyer has shown how difficult it is to theorize whiteness, precisely because it is so thoroughly naturalized in dominant ideologies as to be invisible as an ethnic identity: it simply goes without saying. Paradoxically, then, for all our rhetoric about "making ourselves visible," the real challenge in the new cultural politics of difference is to make "whiteness" visible for the first time, as a culturally constructed ethnic identity historically contingent upon the disavowal and violent denial of difference. Gayatri Spivak has shown that it was only through the "epistemic violence" of such denial that the centered subject of Western philosophy posited itself as the universalized subject—

21. Cornel West, "The New Cultural Politics of Difference," in *Out there: Marginalization and Contemporary Cultures*, ed. Russell Ferguson, Martha Gever, Trinh T. Minh-ha, and Cornel West (Cambridge, Mass.: MIT Press, 1990), pp. 19–36.

"Man"—in relation to whom others were not simply different but somehow less than human, dehumanized objects of oppression. Women, children, savages, slaves, and criminals were all alike insofar as their otherness affirmed "his" identity as the subject at the center of logocentrism and indeed all the other centrisms—ethnocentrism and phallocentrism—in which "he" constructed his representations of reality.[22] But who is "he"? The identity of the hegemonic white male subject is an enigma in contemporary cultural politics.

Different degrees of othering

Coming back to Mapplethorpe's photographs, in the light of this task of making "whiteness" visible as a problem for cultural theory, I want to suggest that the positioning of gay (white) people in the margins of Western culture may serve as a perversely privileged place from which to reexamine the political unconscious of modernity. By negotiating an alternative interpretation of Mapplethorpe's authorial position, I argued that his aesthetic strategy lays bare and makes visible the "splitting" in white subjectivity that is anchored by homology, in the split between "high culture" and "low culture." The perverse interaction between visual elements drawn from both sources begins to subvert the hierarchy of cultural value, and such subversion of fixed categories is experienced precisely as the characteristic shock effect.

Broadening this theme, one can see that representations of race in Western culture entail different degrees of othering. Or, to put it the other way around: practices of racial representation imply different positions of identification on the part of the white subject. Hollywood's iconic image of the "nigger minstrel" in cinema history, for example, concerns a deeply ambivalent mixture of othering and identification. The creation of the minstrel mask in cinema, and in popular theater and the music hall before it, was really the work of white men in black-face. What is taking place in the psychic structures of such historical representations? What is going on when whites assimilate and introject the degraded and devalorized signifiers of racial otherness into the cultural construction of their own identity? If imitation implies identification, in the psychoanalytic sense of the word, then what is it about whiteness that makes the white subject want to be black?

"I Wanna Be Black," sang Lou Reed on the album *Street Hassle* (1979), which was a parody of a certain attitude in postwar youth culture in which the cultural signs of blackness—in music, clothes, and idioms of speech—were the mark of "cool." In the American context, such a sensibility, predicated on the ambivalent identification with the other, was enacted in the bohemian beatnik subculture and became embodied in Norman Mailer's literary image of "the White

22. Gayatri Chakravorty Spivak, "Feminism and Critical Theory," in *In Other Worlds: Essays in Cultural Politics* (New York and London: Methuen, 1987), pp. 77–92.

Negro" stalking the jazz clubs in search of sex, speed, and psychosis. Like a photographic negative, the white negro was an inverted image of otherness, in which attributes devalorized by the dominant culture were simply revalorized or hypervalorized as emblems of alienation and outsiderness, a kind of strategic self-othering in relation to dominant cultural norms. In the museum without walls, Mailer's white negro, who went in search of the systematic derangement of the senses, merely retraced an imaginary pathway in the cultural history of modernity previously traveled by Arthur Rimbaud and Eugene Delacroix in nineteenth-century Europe. There is a whole modernist position of "racial romanticism" that involves a fundamental ambivalence of identifications. At what point do such identifications result in an imitative masquerade of white ethnicity? At what point do they result in ethical and political alliances? How can we tell the difference?[23]

My point is that white ethnicity constitutes an "unknown" in contemporary cultural theory: a dark continent that has not yet been explored. One way of opening it up is to look at the ambivalent coexistence of the two types of identification, as they figure in the work of

23. See Norman Mailer, "The White Negro: Superficial Reflections on the Hipster," in *Advertisements for Myself* (New York: Putnam 1959), pp. 337–58. The fantasy of wanting to be black is discussed as a masculinist fantasy in Suzanne Moore, "Getting a Bit of the Other: The Pimps of Postmodernism," in *Male Order: Untrapping Masculinity,* ed. Rowene Chapman and Jonathan Rutherford, (London: Lawrence and Whisart, 1988), pp. 165–92.

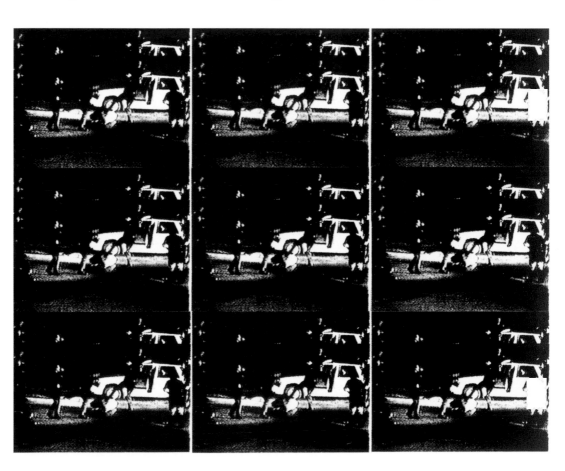

Daniel Tisdale, *Rodney King Police Beating*, from "The Disaster Series," 1991. Screenprint on canvas, 24 x 33 in. (60.9 x 83.8 cm). Courtesy of the artist.

(white) gay artists such as Mapplethorpe and Jean Genet. In *Un Chant d'amour* (1950), Genet's only foray into cinema, there is a great deal of ambivalence, to say the least, about the black man, the frenzied and maniacal negro seen in the masturbatory dance through the scopophilic gaze of the prison guard. In another context, I wrote, "The black man in Genet's film is fixed like a stereotype in the fetishistic axis of the look … subjected to a pornographic exercise of colonial power."[24] Yes, I know… but. There is something else going on as well, not on the margins but at the very center of Genet's film. The romantic escape into the woods, which is the liberated zone of freedom in which the lover's utopian fantasy of coupling is enacted, is organized around the role of the "dark" actor, the Tunisian, the one who is not quite white. In this view, the ambivalence of ethnicity has a central role to play in the way that Genet uses race to figure the desire for political freedom beyond the prisonhouse of marginality. Once located in relation to his plays, such as *The Balcony* and *The Blacks*, Genet's textual practice must be seen as his mode of participation in the "liberation" struggles of the postwar era.

The word *liberation* tends to stick in our throats these days because it sounds so deeply unfashionable; but we might also recall that in the 1950s and the 1960s it was precisely the connections between movements for the liberation from colonialism and movements for the liberation from the dominant sex and gender system that underlined their radical democratic character. In the contemporary situation, the essentialist rhetoric of categorical identity politics threatens to erase the connectedness of our different struggles. At its worst, such forms of identity politics play into the hands of the right as the fundamental-ist belief in the essential and immutable character of identify keeps us locked into the prisonhouse of marginality in which oppression of race, class, and gender would have us live. By historicizing the imaginary identifications that enable democratic agency, we might rather find a way of escaping this ideological bantustan.

Instead of giving an answer to the questions that have been raised about the ambivalence of ethnicity as a site of identification and enun-ciation, I conclude by recalling Genet's wild and adventurous story about being smuggled across the Canadian border by David Hilliard and other members of the Black Panther Party in 1968. He arrived at Yale University to give a May Day speech, along with Allen Ginsberg and others, in defense of imprisoned activist Bobby Seale. Genet talks about this episode in *Prisoner of Love* (1989), where it appears as a memory brought to consciousness by the narration of another memory, about the beautiful *fedayeen*, in whose desert camps Genet lived between 1969 and 1972. The memory of his participation in the elective

24. See "Sexual Identities: Questions of Difference," a panel discussion with Kobena Mercer, Gayatri Spivak, Jacqueline Rose, and Angela McRobbie, *Undercut*, no. 17 (Spring 1988): 19–30.

community of the Palestinian freedom fighters precipitates the memory of the Black Panther "brotherhood," into which he was adopted—this wretched, orphaned, nomadic homosexual thief. I am drawn to this kind of ambivalence, sexual, and political, that shows through, like a stain, in his telling:

> In white America the Blacks are the characters in which history is written. They are the ink that gives the white page its meaning…. [The Black Panthers' Party] built the black race on a white America that was splitting…. The Black Panthers' Party wasn't an isolated phenomenon. It was one of many revolutionary outcrops. What made it stand out in white America was its black skin, its frizzy hair, and despite a kind of uniform black leather jacket, an extravagant but elegant way of dressing. They wore multicolored caps only just resting on their springy hair; scraggy moustaches, sometimes beards; blue or pink or gold trousers made of satin or velvet, and cut so that even the most nearsighted passerby couldn't miss their manly vigour.[25]

Under what conditions does eroticism mingle with political solidarity? When does it produce an effect of empowerment? And when does it produce an effect of disempowerment? When does the identification imply objectification, and when does it imply equality? I am intrigued by the ambivalent but quite happy coexistence of the fetishized big black dick beneath the satin trousers and the ethical equivalence in the struggle for postcolonial subjectivity. Genet's affective participation in the political construction of imagined communities suggests that the struggle for democratic agency and subjectivity always entails the negotiation of ambivalence. Mapplethorpe worked in a different context, albeit one shaped by the democratic revolutions of the 1960s, but his work similarly draws us back into the difficult questions that Genet chose to explore, on the "dark side" of the political unconscious of the postcolonial world. The death of the author doesn't necessarily mean mourning and melancholia, but rather mobilizing a commitment to countermemory. In the dialogue that black gay and lesbian artists have created in contemporary cultural politics, the exemplary political modernism of Mapplethorpe and Genet, "niggers with attitude" if there ever were, is certainly worth remembering as we begin thinking abut our pitiful "postmodern" condition.

25. Jean Genet, *Prisoner of Love* (London: Picador, 1989), p. 215.

Leigh Raiford

Lynching photographs, like the macabre spectacles they depict, have occupied a crucial if unacknowledged place in the "shadow archive" of black representation.[1] Along with images of African Americans as slave caricatures, criminal types, sexual predators, and objects of scientific study, lynching photography has long been engaged in a complex dialectic with portraits of uplift and self-possession. This essay focuses attention on the dark and disquieting corpus of lynching photography and the myriad ways these images have been made to signify and testify from the late nineteenth century into the twenty-first. Only by recognizing post–Civil War lynching as a peculiarly modern phenomenon, reliant on various communication, transportation, and especially media and consumer technolo-

THE CONSUMPTION OF LYNCHING IMAGES

gies, rather than as a Southern anachronism, can the cultural work of photography in both the making and unmaking of racial identities and subjectivities be revealed.

In the hands of whites, photographs of lynchings, circulated as postcards in the late nineteenth and early twentieth centuries, served to extend and redefine the boundaries of white community beyond the localities in which lynchings occurred to a larger "imagined community." In the hands of blacks during the same time period, these photographs were recast as a call to arms against a seeming never-ending tide of violent coercion, and transformed into tools for the making of a new African American national identity. Similar, if not the same images of tortured black bodies were used to articulate and assert specifically racialized identities in the Progressive Era, a period marked by the expansion of corporate capitalism, the rise of the middle classes, and the birth of consumer culture.

By uncovering and pulling apart the threads of white supremacy and black resistance embedded in, or perhaps more accurately, read into these photographs, we can begin to understand how lynching photography simultaneously makes and unmakes racial identity. Indeed, the very need to use photographs in campaigns for racial domination or racial justice points to cracks and fissures in these identities. Exposed are the social, sexual, and political anxieties that the framing of these images attempt to deny. The photographs them-selves offer up a different sort of evidence of the complexities of racial formation, whether by scrutinizing the disgusted look on the face of a white mob member, or acknowledging the quiet yet visible presence of a black man in the crowd. Because of its "spectacularness," lynching reminded everyone who looked that in the end one was either black or white, either wrong or right. It returned everyone to his or her corpo-real essence, to the (racial) truth that is "only skin deep." But in their

1. "Shadow archive" is photographer and critic Allan Sekula's term that describes an all-inclusive corpus of images that situates individuals accord-ing to a socially proscribed hierarchy. See Sekula, "The Body and the Archive," in *The Contest of Meaning: Critical Histories of Photography*, ed. Richard Bolton (Cambridge, Mass.: MIT Press, 1989).

Vivian Cherry, *Untitled*, from "The Game of Lynching, Yorkville, East Harlem" series, 1947. Gelatin silver print, 14 3/8 x 11 in. (36.5 x 27.9 cm). International Center of Photography, purchased by the ICP Acquisitions Committee, 2003.

various contexts and incarnations, we can discern how lynching photographs both create and coerce the image of unified racial identities, black and white, across the clefts of gender and class, location and circumstance.

Spectacles of white supremacy

The history of lynching in the United States is a long and brutal one. At its apex, between 1882 and 1930, this strain of extra-legal violence claimed over three thousand lives, approximately 88 percent of which were African American.[2] White on black lynching, which saw its peak in 1892, can best be understood as the cruel physical manifestations of white patriarchal anxiety over a perceived loss of power in the years following Emancipation; as a communal and ritual act in response to the threat of social, political, economic, and sexual displacement by African Americans, particularly African American men; and a performance of white racial identity that placed black bodies center stage as it attempted to exorcise those bodies, and their perceived threat to the future of white civilization, from white communities. The reality and threat of lynching—lynching as both concrete act and shared narrative—worked to hold African Americans in their (subordinate) place, and help imagine and construct a unified white identity.

Lynching also needs to be considered a leisure activity deeply embedded in the rise of consumer culture in the South in the late nineteenth and twentieth centuries. As historian Grace Hale has argued, lynchings helped ease white anxiety about a new culture of consumption that exposed holes in the blanket segregation of the New South. This new mass society signaled a "raceless" consumer culture, one in which any person, of any race, gender, or class, could purchase goods in any number of mixed public spaces. Not only did lynchings "reverse the decommodification of black bodies begun with emancipation," writes Hale, but they enforced a segregated consumer society, a commodity culture in which only whites could experience or consume the "amusement" of lynching, and only blacks could be lynched and consumed, often literally by fire.[3]

Lynching remanded African Americans, cloaked in newly granted post-Emancipation citizenship, back to black bodies, vessels suitable for physical and ideological labor. This is seen most clearly in the post-lynching scramble for fetishistic mementos of the event, such as scraps of victims' clothing, charred bits of bone, locks of hair. These gruesome trophies, these relics, were sources of pride for those who had participated in the murder, or for those who were able to get to the corpse before it was finally buried. Indeed, a framed photograph of the 1930 lynching of Thomas Shipp and Abram Smith contains a tuft

2. Robert L. Zangrando, *The NAACP Crusade Against Lynching, 1909–1950* (Philadelphia: Temple University Press, 1980).
3. Grace Elizabeth Hale, *Making Whiteness: The Culture of Segregation in the South, 1890–1940.* (New York: Vintage Books, 1998).

of hair attached to the matte board.[4] Such souvenirs also could provide a source of income for those who got to the body first. In her report to the NAACP about the 1915 lynching of young Jesse Washington in Waco, Texas, investigator Elizabeth Freeman writes, "Some little boys pulled out the teeth and sold them to some men for five dollars apiece. The chain was sold for twenty-five cents a link." The collection of relics as religious fetishes is a practice that dates back to ancient and medieval times when the devoted would gather, trade, and keep close the remnants of saints' lives or their bodies. Indeed, in a complex manner, lynchings incorporated elements of ancient traditions and antebellum nostalgia.[5]

Yet lynchings are also a peculiarly modern phenomenon. As the New South grew and industrialized rapidly, lynching made use of some of the most modern technologies available: the telephone and telegraph to announce and advertise the event; print media to carry the message; and cars and trains to carry participants to the designated location. The specificity of lynching's modernity lies in the prevalence and pervasiveness of photographers, both amateur and professional. Indeed, photography emerged as integral to the lynching spectacle. For those not close enough to the scene or for those not lucky enough to obtain clothing or body parts, photographs proved the next best things. As postcards, trade cards, and stereographs, lynching images held a strong popular commercial appeal. For professional photographers, lynchings spawned a cottage industry in which picture makers conspired with mob members and even local officials for the best vantage point, constructed portable darkrooms for quick

4. See James Allen et al., *Without Sanctuary: Lynching Photography in America* (Santa Fe: Twin Palms Publishers, 2000).
5. NAACP Anti-Lynching Campaign Files, Series A, Group I, Container C, box 370 (Washington, D.C.: Library of Congress).

J. P. Ball & Son/James Presley Ball, *Portrait of William Biggerstaff seated in a chair with a hand on his face, wearing a flower in his lapel*, 1896; *Photograph of the Execution of William Biggerstaff, hanged for the murder of "Dick" Johnson, flanked by Rev. Victor Day and Henry Jurgens, sheriff*, 1896; *Photograph of William Biggerstaff, former slave, born in Lexington, Kentucky, in 1854*, 1896. Cabinet cards, each 6 1/4 x 4 1/2 in. (15.9 x 11.4 cm). Courtesy of the Montana Historical Society, Helena.

turnaround, and pedaled their product "through newspapers, in drug-stores, on the street—even…door to door."[6] If lynching was a return to the slave block, a reinscribing of the black body as commodity, then lynching photographs functioned as the bill of sale and receipt of ownership. If lynchings helped construct a unified white identity among those whites present and in the surrounding areas, then photographs of lynchings helped extend that community far beyond the town, the county, the state, the South, to include whites nationwide and even internationally. Now all whites, rich or poor, male or female, Northern or Southern, could imagine themselves to be master. This is true not only of the images made professionally and sold commercially, but also of those amateur photographs taken by everyday folk with cameras readily available through a burgeoning photographic industry.

From lynching photography to antilynching photography

Antilynching activists, beginning with the pioneer Ida B. Wells and continuing with the interracial NAACP, would not always be frightened into submission by either the threat of lynching or the recounting of the tale as framed by lynchers and their proponents or apologists. Antilynching activists chose to tell the story in a different manner, indeed to subvert the common tale of black bestiality resulting in swift white justice that culminated in, and forever echoed through the frozen

6. Text from the *Without Sanctuary* exhibition at the New-York Historical Society, May 12, 2000.

Unidentified photographer, *Lynching*, ca. 1900. Gelatin silver print on board, 5 3/4 x 4 in. (14.6 x 10.2 cm). International Center of Photography, Daniel Cowin Collection, 1990.
Frank Hudson, *The Avengers of Little Myrtle Vance, and the Villian brought to Justice,* ca. 1900. Gelatin silver print, 6 5/16 x 9 1/4 in. (16.5 x 23.5 cm). International Center of Photography, Daniel Cowin Collection, 1990.

black and white still photograph. Photographs of lynchings appeared in antilynching propaganda and pamphlets, Wells's *A Red Record* (1895) being the first, as well as in reports of mob violence in the black press. In such contexts, these images reframed the received narrative of black savagery as one of black vulnerability; white victimization was recast as white terrorization. Though actors and the fundamental story of crimes remained the same, in this new forum photography changed the roles and the ultimate moral.

Indeed, we must consider the use of lynching photographs an effort to reverse or subvert the lynching ritual. Trudier Harris notes that African American writers have restaged lynchings in their literature as a political statement regarding the "oppression of a people."[7] Such a tradition serves to keep the past alive as a force that daily shapes the way communities remember and organize for the future. Through literary or performative or, in this case, visual recreations or recontextualizations of the lynching spectacle, political and cultural workers wield power to represent a symbol of degradation as such, or to transform it into an embodiment of the possibilities of freedom.

By entering in and engaging with a space of death framed by the lynching photograph, African American activists recognized these painful images as part of the larger shadow archive of black representation. By claiming them, antilynching crusaders began the work of repossessing lynching victims from their commodified consignment to the black and white photograph previously "owned" by white individuals and communities. These activists effectively entered into a debate about ownership and citizenship that focused on the right to represent, and indeed possess, black bodies. They challenged the enforced segregation and return to the slave block that the circulation of these images signaled within white communities. By "integrating" the consumption of lynching photographs, antilynching activists announced that the shame and terror that lynching wrought would also have to be shared and consumed by white communities. Within this expanded and contested public arena, and imbued with a different set of meanings, lynching photographs reemerged as antilynching photographs. They visually marked an effort to bring an end to the destruction and dispossession of African Americans that occurred outside of the public eye.

The antinomies of antilynching photography

7. Trudier Harris, *Exorcising Blackness: Historical and Literary Lynching and Burning Rituals* (Bloomington: Indiana University Press, 1984).

Lynchings were often spectacles, and the retelling of the lynching story, either as written text or by visual image, continues to spectacularize racial violence. Such repetition both compounded the violence of

lynching and served to anesthetize audiences, in turn making people
want more and more graphic accounts. The public's seeming insatia-
bility for tales of racial violence and transgression has kept the tale
of the black male rapist/criminal (read: O. J. Simpson, racial profiling)
alive and well and circulating in our cultural and political imaginary.
This narrative finds its "antithesis" in the image of "the lynched black
man," which has emerged and evolved as visual shorthand, as a powerful icon paradigmatic of the suffering of all African Americans and
understood only through the abject black male body.

Moreover, the lynching icon has been made to conjure, figuratively
and aesthetically, the Crucifixion. In 1965, SNCC reproduced a lynching
photograph by Mississippian O. N. Pruitt, adding the statement and
accusation: "MISSISSIPPI" to the original image. Somewhat more ambig-
uously, one of the images in Vivian Cherry's "The Game of Lynching"
series (1948) depicts a young black boy whose arms are forcibly out-
stretched by the white boys who surround him. Though we cannot be
sure of the precise event occurring—are they playing or bullying?—
the image is laden with tension, recalling the black body on the auction
block, the black body readied for the lynching stage. In both instances,
viewers are encouraged to link Christ's sacrifice with a legacy of
lynching and racial violence, an offering up of African American males
as Eucharist for visual consumption.

R.C. Holmes, *Wilmington, Delaware*, 1900. Gelatin silver print on board, 4 ¹⁵/₁₆ x 6 ⁹/₁₆ in. (12.5 x 16.7 cm).
International Center of Photography, Daniel Cowin Collection, 1990.

Lynching imagery has provided a different sort of capital for more contemporary artists, curators, and activists. Paul Gilroy has argued that slavery and the Middle Passage have aided in "configuring modern black political" and artistic cultures. In the U.S. context, lynching constitutes a third moment of regenerative terror. African American artists have employed lynching photographs as both backdrops and centerpieces for their dialogues with and about mass consumer culture, police brutality, and the politics of looking at the black body. Artists like Pat Ward Williams, Dread Scott, Renee Cox, and Daniel Tisdale use lynching photography to continue to remake, reclaim, and recontextualize lynching's meaning for all who dare or care to look.

There's SOMETHING going on here. I didn't understand it right away. I just saw that he looked so HELPLESS. He didn't look tortured he didn't look lynched WHAT is that? How long has he been LOCKED to that tree? Can you be black and look at this without fear? Life mag. WHO took this picture? published this photo Could Hitler show pics of the Holocaust to keep the Couldn't he just as easily let the man go? Did he take his camera home JEWS in line? and bring back a BLOWTORCH? And where do you torture someone with a blowtorch BURN off an ear Melt an eye a screaming mouth Oh God WHO took this picture? HOW can this photograph EXIST? somebody Life answers — Page 141 — no credit do something

Pat Ward Williams, *Accused/Blowtorch/Padlock*, 1986. Mixed mediums, 59 ½ x 107 x 4 ½ in. (151.1 x 271.8 x 11.4 cm). Whitney Museum of Art, New York, purchased with funds from The Audrey and Sydney Irmas Charitable Foundation.

Deborah Willis

I find it difficult to look at these photographs without flinching from the memories and from the anger they invoke. But I must look. I must remember, as you must. For this was history in the making. Like it or not, you cannot hide from the camera's eye.
—Myrlie Evers-Williams[1]

EXPOSURE

I begin my essay with this epigraph in order to situate the Civil Rights photographs in *Only Skin Deep: Changing Visions of the American Self*. Just as Evers-Williams, widow of slain civil rights leader Medgar Evers, imagines "you cannot hide from the camera's eye," the curators of *Only Skin Deep* argue "photography has played a key role in shaping our ideas about nationalism and selfhood." The images I have selected to discuss reflect life in America between 1942 and 1968, a time of racial strife and new social awareness. Some of the photographs are widely known, while others are familiar to the neighborhoods and communities they represent. Some of the photographers are black, some white, both male and female. Photographers including Gordon Parks, Danny Lyon, Ernest Withers, Pirkle Jones, Roz Payne, and Charles Moore played crucial roles documenting and reinterpreting the varied experiences of living in a segregated society. What we imagine about this period is mediated through the insights of the photographers. This essay explores the social conditions governing the act of being photographed and the decoding of the photographs.

From its beginnings, photography was used to define, oppress, and subjugate, but it also was used in positive ways: a close examination of private family photographs indicates that photography was also used to document and celebrate. During the first decades of the twentieth century, photography as an art form and as a vehicle of popular culture moved more directly into the national psyche. Documenting family activities as well as the faces of young children was an important role for many American photographers. Baby and beauty contests were among the types of images offering a new paradigm in which to express black culture.

Contending "all art is propaganda,"[2] W. E. B. DuBois used the photographic image to promote positive aspects of the black race. With the introduction of photographs in 1910, *Crisis*, the journal of the National Association for the Advancement of Colored People (NAACP), "doubled the size of the tiny first issue." As evidenced in Daylanne English's essay "DuBois's Family *Crisis*," DuBois created a visual taxonomy in which to read photographs of black people. English argues that:

1. Myrlie Evers-Williams, foreword to Steven Kasher, *The Civil Rights Movement: A Photographic History, 1954–68* (New York: Abbeville Press, 2000).
2. Ibid., Stephen Kasher, "Criteria of Negro Art," p. 323.

Pirkle Jones, *Window of the Black Panthers Party National Headquarters*, 1968. Gelatin silver print, 14 3/8 x 11 in. (36.4 x 27.9 cm). International Center of Photography, purchased by the ICP Acquisitions Committee, 2003.

[U]nder DuBois's editorship, the Crisis *comprises a kind of eugenic "family album," a visual and literary blueprint for the ideal, modern black individual....[His] column functions to counter racist representations of African Americans by the white press; but given the predominantly black readership of the* Crisis, *such compulsive cataloging also serves to keep the "family" updated on its members' activities.*[3]

Throughout his early years as editor, DuBois published hundreds of photographs of "Prize Babies." As historians Shane White and Graham White observed, "There were babies on the cover, pages with sixteen photographs of babies, half-page shots of babies, babies in cute outfits, and even naked babies artistically arrayed on rugs."[4] The photograph of the 1946 NAACP Baby Contest is rooted in the DuBoisian construction. The photographs showed black children as the pride of the race as a whole. DuBois wrote: "These are selected children; but careful consideration of the total pictures received by the *Crisis*... makes it seem certain that there is growing up in the United States a large and larger class of well-nourished, healthy, beautiful children among the colored people."[5]

Immediately following World War II, a large number of black Americans found work as preachers, tenant farmers, factory and domestic workers, teachers, and cooks throughout the rural South. Many moved to urban centers like Detroit, Chicago, Oakland, New York, and Los Angeles, hoping for a new life outside of poverty and discrimination. The photographs of this era create a new historical consciousness that has the power to rewrite history itself. Central to this new visualization were images that depicted life within the margins, images of beauty, advertising, and work, representing a vibrant community of men, women, and their sons and daughters who fought to achieve their rights. No doubt this informed consciousness possessed an undeniable and collective power. Family and community life were important, and protecting the family was paramount. This changing attitude was captured most evocatively through the photographic medium.

With the postwar migration, more and more black men and women also experienced racial discrimination, physical and emotional abuses, economic rejection, and too often, death. As I began to select images I noted the smiling face of Emmett Till and was reminded of the photograph of the brutally beaten and swollen body of the young Till published in *Jet* magazine in 1955. Photography had played a significant role in Till's life prior to his murder that summer of 1955, "He had brought with him photos from his junior high school graduation in Chicago, which

3. Daylanne English, "W. E. B. DuBois's Family *Crisis,*" *American Literature,* 72, no. 2 (June 2000): 300.
4. Shane White and Graham White, *Stylin': African American Expressive Culture from Its Beginnings to the Zoot Suit* (Ithaca: Cornell University Press, 1998), p. 195.
5. "Our Baby Pictures," *Crisis,* October 1914, p. 298.

showed both black and white students. Seeing that the Southern children were impressed, Emmett commented that one of the white girls in the photographs was his girlfriend. This prompted one of the local boys to say, 'Hey, there's a white girl in that store there. I bet you won't go in there and talk to her.' Calling the boy's bluff, Emmett went in, bought some candy, and as he was leaving the store, said to the woman, 'Bye, baby.'"[6]

Memphis-born Ernest Withers was hired as photographer for the Emmett Till murder trial, which lasted a week. The all-white, all-male jury found the white male defendants *not guilty*.[7] After the trial, Withers returned to Memphis where he copublished and distributed a pamphlet on the murder trial of young Emmett Till, titled *Complete Photo Story of Till Murder Case*. It was sold for one dollar a copy. This act revealed Withers's concern for preserving the memory of this horrific experience. As he wrote in the circular, "... we are not only depicting

6. Brenda Wilkinson, *The Civil Rights Movement: An Illustrated History* (New York: Crescent Books, 1997), p. 84.
7. Ernest C. Withers, *Pictures Tell the Story: Ernest C. Withers Reflections in History* (Norfolk, VA: Chrysler Museum of Art, 2000), p. 60.

Charles Moore, *Birmingham Riots. Demonstrators attacked by water cannons, Birmingham, Alabama*, 1963. Gelatin silver print, 16 x 19 ⁷/₈ in. (38.4 x 47.2 cm). International Center of Photography, gift of the Professional Division, Eastman Kodak Company.

the plight of an individual Negro, but rather of life as it affects all Negroes in the United States....In brief we are presenting this photo story not in an attempt to stir up racial animosities or to question the verdict in the Till Murder Case, but in the hope that this booklet might serve to help our nation decide itself to seeing that such incidents need not occur again."[8]

Many families experienced episodes of hostile confrontation that intensified during the years of the social protest movements. Blacks were being killed, hosed, jailed, and subjected to Jim Crow laws throughout the American landscape. Photographers witnessing assaults both brutal and social, created a new visual consciousness for the American public, and established a visual language of "testifying" about their individual and collective experience. As Danny Lyon recounts about his experience in Albany, Georgia:

8. Ibid., p. 60.

Charles Moore, *Martin Luther King, Jr., Arrested on a Loitering Charge, Montgomery, September 3, 1958*, 1958. Gelatin silver print, 14 x 11 in. (35.5 x 27.9 cm). Courtesy of the artist.

Smoking a corncob pipe, drifting in and out of the southern accent he had picked up in Mississippi, [SNCC executive secretary James Forman] was serious, extremely polite, and always under pressure. Forman treated me like he treated most newcomers. He put me to work. "You got a camera? Go inside the courthouse. Down at the back they have a big water cooler for whites and next to it a little bowl for Negroes. Go in there and take a picture of that." With Forman's blessing, I had a place in the civil rights movement that I would occupy for the next two years. James Forman would direct me, protect me, and at times fight for a place for me in the movement. He is directly responsible for my pictures existing at all.[9]

9. Danny Lyon, *Memories of the Southern Civil Rights Movement*, (Chapel Hill, NC: Center for Documentary Studies, Duke University/The University of North Carolina Press, 1992), p. 30.

Danny Lyon, *Atlanta, Georgia. Segregated water fountains*, 1962. Gelatin silver print, 14 x 11 in. (35.5 x 27.9 cm). Courtesy of the artist and Magnum Photos, Inc.

Lyon's photograph plainly depicts the horrific reality of black people in Albany. As the perfect visual metaphor for "Jim Crow," this photograph, like many others of its type, mobilized the protest movement. The segregated signs—one marked "colored" and the other "white"—simply demonstrate what it meant to be a member of the privileged class. The "white" water fountain was larger, free flowing with a quick switch of the dial; while the drinking water fountain for the black man, woman, or child, short or tall, was anything but equal—theirs was the size of a small bowl that appears to be not even three feet from the floor.

On June 19, 1963, seven days after the murder of NAACP leader Medgar Evers in Jackson, Mississippi, a civil rights bill was introduced in the U.S. Senate. That year was a pivotal one in the visualization of racial discontent: Charles Moore photographed the Birmingham Riots, and hundreds of photographers witnessed the March on Washington. Photography was instrumental in galvanizing young people, motivating cultural change and defining the significance of the struggle for human and civil rights that eventually forced the Federal government into creating laws against racial domination and discrimination. Photographs of anonymous Americans and leading figures such as Martin Luther King, Jr. and Malcolm X marching, protesting, participating in sit-ins, and attending rallies showed the world that blacks were indeed fighting back and depicted the new Southern black as rebellious and deviant. Moore's photographs of Martin Luther King's arrest are graphic evidence of this new black citizen. Dr. King, wearing a hat and suit, is jostled by police officers. The underlying tension in the image can be found in King's own words:

> The tension, which we are witnessing in race relations in the South today, is to be explained in part by the revolutionary change in the Negro's evaluation of himself.... You cannot understand the bus protest in Montgomery without understanding that there is a New Negro in the South.[10]

By the early 1960s, the protest movements had become a national crusade for human rights for all oppressed people. Newspapers and magazines throughout the world had published gripping images of racial hatred and police brutality in Birmingham, Selma, Montgomery, Oakland, and Los Angeles. The most brutalizing events caused photographers to speak out en masse. On April 27, 1962, there was a shootout between the Los Angeles police and members of the Nation of Islam; Ronald Stokes, a member of the Nation of Islam, was killed. Fourteen Muslims were arrested; one was charged with assault with intent to kill and the others with assault and interference with police

10. Quoted in Aldon Morris, *The Origins of the Civil Rights Movement: Black Communities Organizing for Change* (New York: Free Press, 1984), p. 106.

officers. A year later Elijah Muhammad sent Malcolm X to investigate the incident and the trial. Gordon Parks's photograph of Malcolm X holding a photograph of a brutally beaten Nation of Islam member was remembered in this way:

> I remember the night Malcolm spoke after this brother Stokes was killed in Los Angeles, and he was holding up a huge photo showing the autopsy with a bullet hole at the back of the head. He was angry then, he was dead angry. It was a huge rally. But he was never out of control. The press tried to project his militancy as wild, unthoughtful, and out of control. But Malcolm was always controlled, always thinking what to do in political terms.[11]

The Civil Rights Movement was unfolding on the streets in virtually every rural and urban city in America. Reporters, photographers, and students from television stations, newspapers, and magazines were on hand to document the conscience of this country. The small triumphs in local communities and the disappointments in the larger cities are forever etched into our memories because of the camera. During this dangerous yet invigorating time, photographers sought to create a collective visual memory that would empower communities while at the same time provide evidence of the struggles, defeats, goals, and victories.

11. James Turner quoted in *Malcolm X: The Great Photographs*, ed. Howard Chapnick and Thulani Davis (New York: Stewart, Tabori and Chang, 1992), p. 83.

Bruce Davidson, *Voter Registration*, 1965. Gelatin silver print, 11 x 14 in. (27.9 x 35.5 cm). Courtesy of the artist and Magnum Photos, Inc.

IV.
ALL FOR ONE /
ONE FOR ALL

Andres Serrano, *Klanswoman (Grand Kaliff II)*, 1990. Cibachrome print, 60 x 49 ¹/₂ in. (152.4 x 125.7 cm). Courtesy of Paula Cooper Gallery, New York.

George Ballis, *Cesar Chavez, leader of United Farm Workers, confronts Delano policeman during rally and march through city*, 1965. Gelatin silver print, 10 x 8 in. (25.4 x 20.3 cm). Courtesy of the artist.

Dorothea Lange, *First Braceros*, 1942. Gelatin silver print, 11 ¼ x 8 ¼ in. (28.5 x 20.6 cm). Oakland Museum of California,
City of Oakland, the Dorothea Lange Collection, gift of Paul S. Taylor.

J. Shimon & J. Lindemann, *R. J. as Glade Boy in an abandoned K-mart parking lot, Manitowoc, Wisconsin*, 1996. Gelatin silver contact print, 10 x 8 in. (25.4 x 20.3 cm). Courtesy of the artists.

Clarence G. Morledge, *In My Fighting Clothes [Portrait of Nat Love, Buffalo Soldier]*, from *Nat Love, Life and Adventures of Nat Love...*, 1907. Gelatin silver print mounted in book, 7 x 5 in. (17.8 x 12.7 cm). Denver Public Library, Western History and Geneaology Collection.

Typical Revolutionist

Unidentified photographer, *Typical Revolutionist*, ca. 1916. Real photo postcard, 5 1/2 x 3 1/2 in. (14 x 9 cm). Research Library, The Getty Research Institute, Los Angeles.

Richard Prince, *Untitled (Cowboy)*, 1991–92. Chromogenic print, 48 x 72 in. (122 x 182.9 cm). San Francisco Museum of Modern Art,
Photo Ben Blackwell, Courtesy of Barbara Gladstone Gallery, New York.

Michael Abramson, *March to the United Nations, October 30, 1970*, 1970. Gelatin silver print, 16 x 20 in. (40.6 x 50.8 cm).
Courtesy of the artist.

Roz Payne, *Yellow Peril Supports Black Power*, 1968. Gelatin silver print, 14 3/8 x 11 in. (36.4 x 27.9 cm). International Center of Photography, purchased by the ICP Acquisitions Committee, 2003.

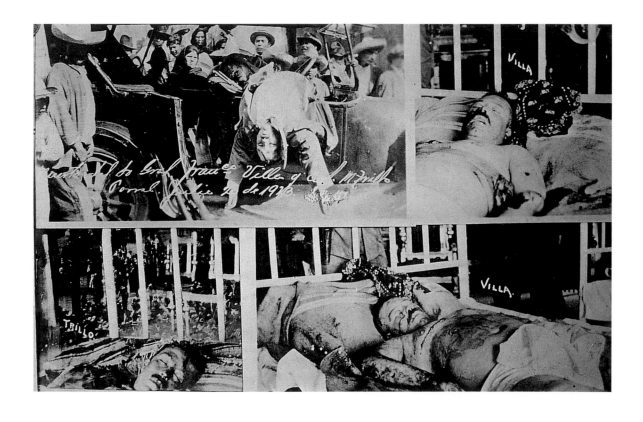

Unidentified photographer, *Assassination of Pancho Villa*, 1923. Real photo postcard, 3 $\frac{1}{2}$ x 5 $\frac{1}{2}$ in. (9 x 14 cm).
Research Library, The Getty Research Institute, Los Angeles.

George Trager, *Big Foot Lying Dead in the Snow at Wounded Knee, South Dakota*, 1891/ca. 1920. Real photo postcard, 3 x 4 ⁷/₈ in. (7.6 x 12.3 cm). International Center of Photography, purchased by the ICP Acqusitions Committee, 2001.

Louise Dahl-Wolfe, *Night Bathing*, 1939. Gelatin silver print, 14 x 10 in. (35.5 x 25.4 cm). International Center of Photography, gift of the photographer, 1982.

Bruce Nauman, *Self-Portrait as a Fountain*, 1966–67/1970. Chromogenic print, 20 ¹/₁₆ x 23 ¹⁵/₁₆ in. (50.9 x 60.8 cm).
Whitney Museum of American Art, New York.

Ralph Bartholomew, *Untitled*, 1947. Gelatin silver print, 10 ¹/₈ x 14 ¹/₈ in. (25.7 x 35.9 cm). Los Angeles County Museum of Art, gift of the Bartholomew Family. Courtesy of Keith deLellis Gallery.

Tina Barney, *The Westwater Family*, 1999. Chromogenic print, 48 x 60 in. (121.9 x 152.4 cm). Courtesy of Janet Bordon, Inc., New York.

Roy DeCarava, *Graduation Dress*, 1949. Gelatin silver print, 9 ¹/₂ x 13 ⁷/₁₆ in. (24.1 x 34.1 cm). George Eastman House, Rochester, New York.

Margaret Bourke-White, *At the Time of the Louisville Flood*, 1937. Gelatin silver print, 10 x 13 ⁵/₁₆ in. (25.4 x 33.8 cm).
George Eastman House, Rochester, New York.

Richard Dyer

ON THE MATTER OF WHITENESS

Racial imagery is central to the organization of the modern world. At what cost regions and countries export their goods, whose voices are listened to at international gatherings, who bombs and who is bombed, who gets what jobs, housing, access to health care and education, what cultural activities are subsidized and sold, in what terms they are validated—these are all largely inextricable from racial imagery.[1] The myriad minute decisions that constitute the practices of the world are at every point informed by judgments about people's capacities and worth, judgments based on what they look like, where they come from, how they speak, even what they eat, that is, racial judgments. Race is not the only factor governing these things and people of goodwill everywhere struggle to overcome the prejudices and barriers of race, but it is never not a factor, never not in play. And since race in itself—insofar as it is anything in itself—refers to some intrinsically insignificant geographical/physical differences between people, it is the imagery of race that is in play.

There has been an enormous amount of analysis of racial imagery in the past decades, ranging from studies of images of, say, blacks or American Indians in the media to the deconstruction of the fetish of the racial Other in the texts of colonialism and postcolonialism. Yet until recently a notable absence from such work has been the study of images of white people. Indeed, to say that one is interested in race has come to mean that one is interested in any racial imagery other than that of white people. Yet race is not only attributable to people who are not white, nor is imagery of nonwhite people the only racial imagery.

[...] There is no more powerful position than that of being "just" human. The claim to power is the claim to speak for the commonality of humanity. Raced people can't do that—they can only speak for their race.[2] But nonraced people can, for they do not represent the interests of a race. The point of seeing the racing of whites is to dislodge them/us from the position of power, with all the inequities, oppression, privileges, and sufferings in its train, dislodging them/us by undercutting the authority with which they/we speak and act in and on the world.

The sense of whites as nonraced is most evident in the absence of reference to whiteness in the habitual speech and writing of white people in the West. We (whites) will speak of, say, the blackness or Chineseness of friends, neighbors, colleagues, customers, or clients, and it may be in the most genuinely friendly and accepting manner, but we don't mention the whiteness of the white people we know. An old-style white comedian will often start a joke: "There's this bloke walking down the street and he meets this black geezer," never thinking to race the bloke as well as the geezer. Synopses in listing of films on

1. I use the terms "race" and "racial" in this opening section in the most common though problematic sense, referring to supposedly visibly differentiable, supposedly discrete social groups.
2. In their discussion of the extraordinarily successful TV sitcom about a middle-class African American family, *The Cosby Show*, Sut Jhally and Justin Lewis note the way that viewers repeatedly recognize the characters' blackness but also feel the way that "you just think of them as people," in other words, they don't only speak for their race. Jhally and Lewis argue that this is achieved by the ways the family conforms to the "everyday, generic world of white television," an essentially middle-class world. The family is "ordinary" *despite* being black; because it is upwardly mobile, it can be accepted as "ordinary," in a way that marginalizes most actual African Americans. If the realities of African American experience were included, then the characters would not be perceived as "just people." Sut Jhally and Justin Lewis, *Enlightened Racism: The Cosby Show, Audiences and the Myth of the American Dream* (Boulder: Westview Press, 1992), p. 100.

Aaron Siskind, *Harlem*, ca. 1936. Gelatin silver print, 10 3/8 x 7 1/2 in. (26.3 x 19 cm). International Center of Photography, gift of Roger P. Smith, 1984, Courtesy of Robert Mann Gallery, New York.

TV, where wordage is tight, nonetheless squander words with things like: "Comedy in which a cop and his black sidekick investigate a robbery," "Skinhead Johnny and his Asian lover Omar set up a launderette," "Feature film from a promising Native American director," and so on. Since all white people in the West do this all the time, it would be invidious to quote actual examples, and so I shall confine myself to one from my own writing. In an article on lesbian and gay stereotypes,[3] I discuss the fact there can be variations on a type such as the queen or dyke. In the illustrations which accompany this point, I compare a "fashion queen" from the film *Irene* with a "black queen" from *Car Wash*—the former, white image is not raced, whereas all the variation of the latter is reduced to his race. Moreover, this is the only nonwhite image referred to in this article, which does not however point out that all the other images discussed are white. In this, as in the other white examples in this paragraph, the fashion queen is, racially speaking, taken as being just human.

This assumption that white people are just people, which is not far off saying that whites are people whereas other colors are something else, is endemic to white culture. Some of the sharpest criticism of it has been aimed at those who would think themselves the least racist or white supremacist. bell hooks, for instance, has noted how amazed and angry white liberals become when attention is drawn to their whiteness, when they are seen by nonwhite people as white.

> Often their rage erupts because they believe that all ways of looking that highlight difference subvert the liberal belief in a universal subjectivity (we are all just people) that they think will make racism disappear. They have a deep emotional investment in the myth of "sameness," even as their actions reflect the primacy of whiteness as a sign informing who they are and how they think.[4]

Similarly, Hazel Carby discusses the use of black texts in white classrooms, under the sign of multiculturalism, in a way that winds up focusing "on the complexity of response in the (white) reader/student's construction of self in relation to a (black) perceived 'other.'" We should, she argues, recognize that "everyone in this social order has been constructed in our political imagination as a racialized subject" and thus that we should consider whiteness as well as blackness, in order "to make visible what is rendered invisible when viewed as the normative state of existence: the (white) point in space from which we tend to identify difference."[5]

The invisibility of whiteness as racial position in white (which is to say dominant) discourse is of a piece with its ubiquity. When I said

3. Richard Dyer, "Seen to Be Believed: Problems in the Representation of Gay People as Typical" in Dyer, *The Matter of Images: Essays on Representations* (London: Routledge, 1993), pp. 19–51.
4. bell hooks, "Representations of Whiteness in the Black Imagination," in *Black Looks: Race and Representation* (Boston: South End Press, 1992), p. 167.
5. Hazel V. Carby, "The Multicultural Wars" in *Black Popular Culture*, ed. Gina Dent (Seattle: Bay Press, 1992), p. 193.

6. See, for instance, Donald Bogle, *Toms, Coons, Mulattoes, Mammies and Bucks: An Interpretive History of Blacks in America Films* (New York: Viking Press, 1973); Paul Hartmann and Charles Husband, *Racism and the Mass Media* (London: Davis-Poynter, 1974); Barry Troyna, "Images of Race and Racist Images in the British News Media" in *Mass Media and Mass Communications*, ed. J. D. Halloran (Leicester: Leicester University Press, 1981); J. F. MacDonald, *Blacks and White TV: Afro-Americans in Television since 1948* (Chicago: Nelson-Hall, 1983); C. J. Wilson and F. Gutierez, *Minorities and Media* (Beverly Hills: Sage, 1985); T. A. van Dijk, *Communicating Racism*

above that this book wasn't merely seeking to fill a gap in the analysis of racial imagery, I reproduced the idea that there is no discussion of white people. In fact for most of the time white people speak about nothing but white people, it's just that we couch it in terms of "people" in general. Research—into books, museums, the press, advertising, films, television, software—repeatedly shows that in Western representation whites are overwhelmingly and disproportionately predominant, have the central and elaborated roles, and above all are placed as the norm, the ordinary, the standard.[6] Whites are everywhere in representation. Yet precisely because of this and their placing as norm, they seem not be represented to themselves *as* white, but as people who are variously gendered, classed, sexualized, and abled. At the level of racial representation, in other words, whites are not of a certain race, they're just the human race.

We are often told that we are living now in a world of multiple identities, of hybridity, of decenteredness, and fragmentation. The old illusory unified identities of class, gender, race, sexuality are breaking up; someone may be black *and* gay *and* middle class *and* female; we may be bi-, poly- or nonsexual, of mixed race, indeterminate gender, and heaven knows what class. Yet we have not yet reached a situation

Frank Wendt, *Little Levey Sisters*, ca. 1880. Cabinet cards, each 6 ¹/₂ x 4 ¹/₂ in. (16.5 x 11.4 cm). Syracuse University Library, Syracuse, New York, Becker Collection.

in which white people and white cultural agendas are no longer in the ascendant. The media, politics, education are still in the hands of white people, still speak for whites while claiming—and sometimes sincerely aiming—to speak for humanity. Against the flowering of a myriad of postmodern voices, we must also see the countervailing tendency toward a homogenization of world culture, in the continued dominance of U.S. news dissemination, popular TV programs, and Hollywood movies. Postmodern multiculturalism may have genuinely opened up a space for the voices of the other, challenging the authority of the white West,[7] but it may also simultaneously function as a side-show for white people who look on with delight at all the differences that surround them.[8] We may be on our way to a genuine hybridity, multiplicity without (white) hegemony, and it may be where we want to get to—but we aren't there yet, and we won't get there until we see whiteness, see its power, its particularity and limitedness, put it in its place and end its rule. This is why studying whiteness matters.

It is studying whiteness *qua* whiteness. Attention is sometimes paid to "white ethnicity,"[9] but this always means an identity based on cultural origins such as British, Italian, or Polish, or Catholic or Jewish, or Polish American, Irish American, Catholic American, and so on. These however are variations on white ethnicity (though as I suggest below, some are more securely white than others), and the examination of them tends to lead away from a consideration of whiteness itself. John Ibson, in a discussion of research on white U.S. ethnicity, concludes that being, say, Polish, Catholic, or Irish, may not be as important to white Americans as some might wish.[10] But being white is [....] White people need to learn to see themselves as white, to see their particularity. In other words, whiteness needs to be made strange.

There is a political need to do this, but there are also problematic political feelings attendant on it, which need to be briefly signaled in order to be guarded against. The first of these is the green light problem. Writing about whiteness gives white people the go-ahead to write and talk about what in any case we have always talked about: ourselves. In, at any rate, intellectual and education life in the West in recent years there have been challenges to the dominance of white concerns and a concomitant move towards inclusion of nonwhite cultures and issues. Putting whiteness on the agenda now might permit a sigh of relief that we white people don't after all any longer have to take on all this nonwhite stuff.

Related to this is the problem of "me-too-ism," a feeling that, amid all this (*all* this?) attention being given to nonwhite subjects, white people are being left out. One version of this is simply the desire to have attention paid to one, which for whites is really only the wish

(note 6, cont'd)
(London: Sage, 1987); Jhally and Lewis, *Enlightened Racism*, 1992; and Karen Ross, *Black and White Media* (Oxford: Polity, 1995). The research findings are generally cast the other way round in terms of nonwhite underrepresentation, textual marginalization and positioning as deviant or a problem. Recent research in the U. S. does suggest that African Americans (but not other racially marginalized groups) have become more represented in the media, even in excess of their proportion of the population. However, this number still falls off if one focuses on central characters.
7. Craig Owens, "The Discourse of Others: Feminists and Postmodernism," in *The Anti-Aesthetic: Essays on Post-modern Culture*, ed. Hal Foster (Port Townsend, Wash.: Bay Press, 1983), pp. 57–82.
8. *The Crying Game* (G.B. 1992) seems to me to be an example of this. It explores, with fascination and generosity, the hybrid and fluid nature of identity; gender, race, national belonging, sexuality. Yet all of this revolves around a bemused but ultimately unchallenged straight white man—it reinscribes the position of those at the intersection of hetero-sexuality, maleness, and whiteness as that of the one group which does not need to be hybrid and fluid.
9. Richard D. Alba, *Ethnic Identity: The Transformation of White America* (New Haven: Yale University Press, 1990).
10. John Ibson, "Virgin Land or Virgin Mary? Studying the Ethnicity of White Americans," *American Quarterly,* 33, no. 3 (1981): 284–303.

to have all the attention once again. Another is the sense that being white is no great advantage, what with being so uptight, out of touch with our bodies, burdened with responsibilities we didn't ask for. Poor us. A third variant is the notion of white men, specifically, as a new victim group, oppressed by the gigantic strides taken by affirmative action policies, can't get jobs, can't keep women, a view identified and thus hardened up by a *Newsweek* cover story on March 29, 1993 on white male paranoia.

The green light and me-too-ism echo the reaction of some men to feminism. There is a lesson here. My blood runs cold at the thought that talking about whiteness could lead to the development of something called "White Studies," that studying whiteness might become a part of what Mike Phillips suspects is "a new assertiveness… amounting to a statement of 'white ethnicity,' the acceptable face of white nationalism,"[11] or what Philip Norman identifies as a 1990s fascist chic observable in Calvin Klein and Häagen-Dazs ads as well as the rise of neofascist parties in Europe and North America.[12] I dread to think that paying attention to whiteness might lead to white people saying that they need to get in touch with their whiteness, that we might end up with the white equivalent of "Iron John" and company, the "men's movement" embrace of hairiness replaced with strangled vowels and rigid salutes. The point of looking at whiteness is to dislodge it from its centrality and authority, not to reinstate it (and much less, to make a show of reinstating it, when, like male power, it doesn't actually need reinstating).

A third problem about talking about whiteness is guilt. The kind of white people who are going to talk about being white, apart from the

11. Mike Phillips, "White Heroes in the Hall of Fame," *Black Film Bulletin* 1, no. 4 (1993): 30. He makes this point in the context of both a TV documentary about D. W. Griffith and an article by me on Lillian Gish; though I think it is inaccurate to call the latter a "celebration" (as opposed to a recognition) of the whiteness of her stardom, the general tenor of his remarks is salutary.
12. Philip Norman, "The Shock of the Neo," *Weekend Guardian*, May 30–31, 1992, pp. 4–6.

Adrian Piper, *It Doesn't Matter #1 ("It doesn't matter who you are"); It Doesn't Matter #2 ("If what you want to do to me"); It Doesn't Matter #3 ("Is what I want you to do to me"),* 1975. Crayon oil drawing on gelatin silver prints, each 24 x 18 in. (60.9 x 45.7 cm). Spencer Museum of Art, University of Kansas, Museum purchase, Helen Foresmen Spencer Art Acquisition Fund.

conscious racists who have always done so, are liable to be those sensitized to racism and the history of what white people have done to nonwhite peoples. Accepting ourselves as white and knowing that history, we are likely to feel overwhelmed with guilt at what we have done and are still doing.[13] Guilt tends to be a blocking emotion. One wants to acknowledge so much how awful white people have been that one may never get around to examining what exactly they have been, and in particular, how exactly their image has been constructed, its complexities and contradictions. This problem—common to all "images of" analyses—is a special temptation for white people. We may lacerate ourselves with admission of our guilt, but that bears witness to the fineness of a moral spirit that can feel such guilt—the display of our guilt is our calvary.[14]

A political problem of a different order has to do with what term to use to refer to (images of) people who are not white. In most contexts, one would not want to make such sweeping reference to so generalized a category, but in the present context of trying to see the specificity of whiteness it is sometimes necessary. I have opted for the term "nonwhite." This is problematic because of its negativity, as if people who are not white only have identity by virtue of what they are not; it is not a term that I would want to see used in other contexts. However, the two common alternatives pose greater problems for my purposes. "Black," the term preferred by many theorists and activists, has two drawbacks. First, it excludes a huge range of people who are neither white nor black, Asians, Native Americans (North and South), Chicanos, Jews, and so on. Second, it reinforces the dichotomy of black : white that underpins racial thought but which it should be our aim to dislodge. "Black" is a privileged term in the construction of white racial imagery and I shall examine it as such, but where I need to see whiteness in relation to all peoples who are not white, "black" will not do. The other option would be "people of color," the preferred U.S. term (though with little currency in Britain). While I have always appreciated this term's generosity, including in it all those people that "black" excludes, it nonetheless reiterates the notion that some people have color and others, whites, do not. We need to recognize white as a color, too, and just one among many, and we cannot do that if we keep using a term that reserves color for anyone other than white people. Reluctantly, I am forced back on "nonwhite."

Politics also inform more evidently methodological questions. When I first started thinking about studying the representation of whiteness, I soon realized what one could not do was the kind of taxonomy of typifications that had been done for nonwhite peoples. One

13. Pascal Bruckner discusses liberal guilt and "Third Worldism" in his *Le sanglot de l'homme blanc* (*The White Man's Tears*) (Paris: Editions du Seuil, 1983).

14. Alastair Bonnett makes a related point about the discourse of blame in recent studies of whiteness by white people. "[A]lthough whiteness is subjected to a barrage of unsentimental critique, it emerges from this process as an omnipresent and all-powerful historical force. Whiteness is seen to be responsible for the failure of socialism to develop in America, for racism, for the impoverishment of humanity. With this 'blame' comes a new kind of centering: Whiteness, and White people, are tuned into the key agents of historical change, the shapers of contemporary America." Bonnett, "White Studies: The Problems and Projects of a New Research Agenda," *Theory, Culture and Society* 13, no. 2 (1996): 145–55.

15. On the whiteness of queers, see Lynda Hart, *Fatal Women: Lesbian Sexuality and the Mark of Aggression* (London: Routledge, 1994); and of disabled people, see Guy Cumberbatch and Ralph Negrine, *Images of Disability on Television* (London: Routledge, 1992), p. 74. Paul Darke argues (in a personal communication) that the overwhelming prevalence of whites in the representation of disability is due not only to the assumption of white as a human norm but also to two other factors specific to disability—that it is to be imagined as the "worst quality of life on earth," which must be the most tragic for the most privileged, and that in the overriding representation of whites as individuals, the fact of the social construction of disability is hidden.

cannot come up with a limited range of endlessly repeated images, because the privilege of being white in white culture is not to be subjected to stereotyping in relation to one's whiteness. White people are stereotyped in terms of gender, nation, class, sexuality, ability, and so on, but the overt point of such typification is gender, nation, etc. Whiteness generally colonizes the stereotypical definition of all social categories other than those of race. To be normal, even to be normally deviant (queer, crippled),[15] is to be white. White people in their whiteness, however, are imaged as individual and/or endlessly diverse, complex and changing. There are also gradations of whiteness: some people are whiter than others. Latins, the Irish, and Jews, for instance, are rather less securely white than Anglos, Teutons, and Nordics; indeed, if Jews are white at all, it is only Ashkenazi Jews, since the Holocaust, in a few places.

Ernest C. Withers, *Bilbo Brown, Brown Skin Follies, Memphis*, 1949–50. Gelatin silver print, 20 x 16 in. (50.8 x 40.6 cm). Courtesy of Panopticon Gallery, Waltham, Massachusetts.

The individuated, multifarious, and graded character of white representation does not mean that white culture has succeeded in imagining in white people the plentitude of human potential and is only at fault for denying this representational range to nonwhite people. There is a specificity to white representation, but it does not reside in a set of stereotypes so much as in narrative structural positions, rhetorical tropes, and habits of perception. The same is true of all representation—the taxonomic study of stereotypes was only ever an initial step in the study of nonwhite representation. However, stereotyping—complex and contradictory though it is—does not characterize the representation of subordinated social groups and is one of the means by which they are categorized and kept in their place, whereas white people in white culture are given the illusion of their own infinite variety.[16]

[...] Equally, given the variety of whiteness, I have sometimes thought that what I am really writing about is the whiteness of the English, Anglo-Saxons, or North Europeans (and their descendants), that this whiteness would be unrecognizable to Southern or Eastern Europeans (and their descendants). For much of the past two centuries, North European whiteness has been hegemonic within a whiteness that has nonetheless been assumed to include Southern and Eastern

16. See, for example, T. E. Perkins, "Rethinking Stereotypes" in *Ideology and Cultural Production*, ed. Michèle Barrett, Philip Corrigan, Annette Kuhn, and Janet Wolff (London: Croom Helm, 1979), pp. 135–59. See also, Homi Bhabha, "The Other Question: the Stereotype and Colonial Discourse," *Screen* 24, no. 6 (1983): 18–36; and Dyer, *The Matter of Images*.

Pok-Chi Lau, *Room for Chinese Bachelor Chef with Marlboro, Pittsburgh, PA*, 1977. Gelatin silver print, 20 x 16 in. (50.8 x 40.6 cm). Courtesy of the artist.

European peoples (albeit sometimes grudgingly within Europe[17] and less assuredly without it, in, for instance, the Latin diaspora of the Americas). It is this overarching hegemonic whiteness which concerns me, one to which Northern Europeans most easily lay claim but which is not to be conflated with distinctive North European identities.

As others have found, it often seems that the only way to see the structures, tropes, and perceptual habits of whiteness, to see past the illusion of infinite variety, to recognize white *qua* white, is when nonwhite (and above all black) people are also represented. My initial stab at the topic of whiteness[18] approached it through three films, which were centrally about white-black interactions, and my account [...] of how I may have gotten into thinking about the topic at all also emphasizes the role of nonwhite people in my life. Similarly, Toni Morrison in her study of whiteness in American literature, *Playing in the Dark* (1992), focuses on the centrality, indeed inescapability, of black representation to the construction of white identity, a perception shared by the very influential work of Edward Said on the West's construction of an "Orient" by means of which to make sense of itself.[19] This is more than saying that one can only really see the specificity of one's culture by realizing that it could be otherwise, in itself an objectionable human process. What the work of Morrison, Said, and others

17. A schoolboy phrase I remember being taught was that "wogs begin at Calais"; even the French were not white enough for little Englanders. ("Wog" is British slang for "nigger.")
18. Richard Dyer, "White," reprinted in Dyer, *The Matter of Images*, pp. 141–63.
19. Edward Said, *Orientalism* (London: Routledge & Kegan Paul, 1978).

Louis Carlos Bernal, *Recamara de Mis Padres/My Parents' Bedroom*, 1980. Gelatin silver print, 8 7/8 x 11 5/8 in. (22.5 x 29.5 cm). Center for Creative Photography, The University of Arizona, Tuscon.

suggests is that white discourse implacably reduces the nonwhite subject to being a function of the white subject, not allowing her/him space or autonomy, permitting neither the recognition of similarities nor the acceptance of differences except as a means for knowing the white self. This cultural process justifies the emphasis, in work on the representation of white people, on the role of images of nonwhite people in it.

Yet this emphasis has also worried me, writing from a white position. If I continue to see whiteness only in texts in which there are also non-white people, am I not reproducing the relegation of nonwhite people to the function of enabling me to understand myself? Do I not do ana-lytically what the text themselves do? Moreover, while this is certainly the usual function of black images in white texts,[20] to focus exclusively on those texts that are "about" racial difference and interaction risks giving the impression that whiteness is only white, or only matters, when it is explicitly set against nonwhite, whereas whiteness repro-duces itself as whiteness in all texts all of the time. As a product of enterprise and imperialism, whiteness is of course always already

20. An insight explored in a film con-text in Cameron Bailey's analysis of *Something Wild* (USA 1986), where nonwhite culture is used as marker of authenticity and wildness that will give vitality and essence to the garish empti-ness of middle-American mass culture, to the point that the "wild" white woman (played by Melanie Griffiths) who dis-tracts the hero (Jeff Daniels) from the straight and narrow is entirely coded in terms of black culture. See Bailey, "Nigger/Lover: the Thin Sheen of Race in *Something Wild*," *Screen* 29, no. 4 (1988): 28–42.

Allora y Calzadilla, *Landmark (Footprints)*, 2002. Photo-based installation with text; four chromogenic prints, each 16 x 20 in. (40.6 x 50.8 cm); overall 32 x 40 in. (81.3 x 101.6 cm). Courtesy of the artists.

predicated on racial difference, interaction, and domination, but that is true of all texts, not just those that take such matters as their explicit subject matter. Similarly, [...] there is implicit racial resonance to the idea, endemic to the representation of white heterosexuality, of sexual desire as itself dark [...]. The point is to see the specificity of whiteness, even when the text itself is not trying to show it to you, doesn't even know that it is there to be shown.[21] I do make reference to nonwhite in my analyses to clarify the specificity of white, and I do look at texts with implicit (the peplum) or explicit (*The Jewel in the Crown*) colonial structures, since colonialism is one of the elements that subtends the construction of white identity. But I have eschewed a focus on nonwhite characters as projections of white imaginings, as the Other to the white person who is really the latter's unknown or forbidden self. This function, as the work of Morrison and others makes abundantly clear, is indeed characteristic of white culture, but it is not the whole story and may reinforce the notion that whiteness is only racial when it is "marked" by the presence of the truly raced, that is, nonwhite subject.

[...] White identity is founded on compelling paradoxes: a vividly corporeal cosmology that most values transcendence of the body; a notion of being at once a sort of race and the human race, an individual and a universal subject; a commitment to heterosexuality that, for whiteness to be affirmed, entails men fighting against sexual desires and women having none; a stress on the display of spirit while maintaining a position of invisibility; in short, a need always to be everything and nothing, literally overwhelmingly present and yet apparently absent, both alive and dead. Paradoxes are fascinating, endlessly drawing us back to them, either in awe of their unfathomability or else out of a wish to fathom them. Paradoxes provide the instabilities that generate stories, millions of engrossing attempts to find resolution. The dynamism of white instability, especially in its claims to universality, is also what entices those outside to seek to cross its borders and those inside to aspire ever upwards within it. Thus it is that the paradoxes and instabilities of whiteness also constitute its flexibility and productivity, in short, its representational power.

21. Linda Hart's discussion of *Attack of the 50-Ft. Woman* and *Single White Female* in Hart, *Fatal Women*, pp. 104–23, is an example of an analysis in these terms that I read too late to integrate into the discussion.

Rashid Johnson, *Manumission Papers*, 2000. Calotype, 55 x 44 in. (132 x 105.6 cm). Smith College Museum of Art Collection, Northampton, Massachusetts.

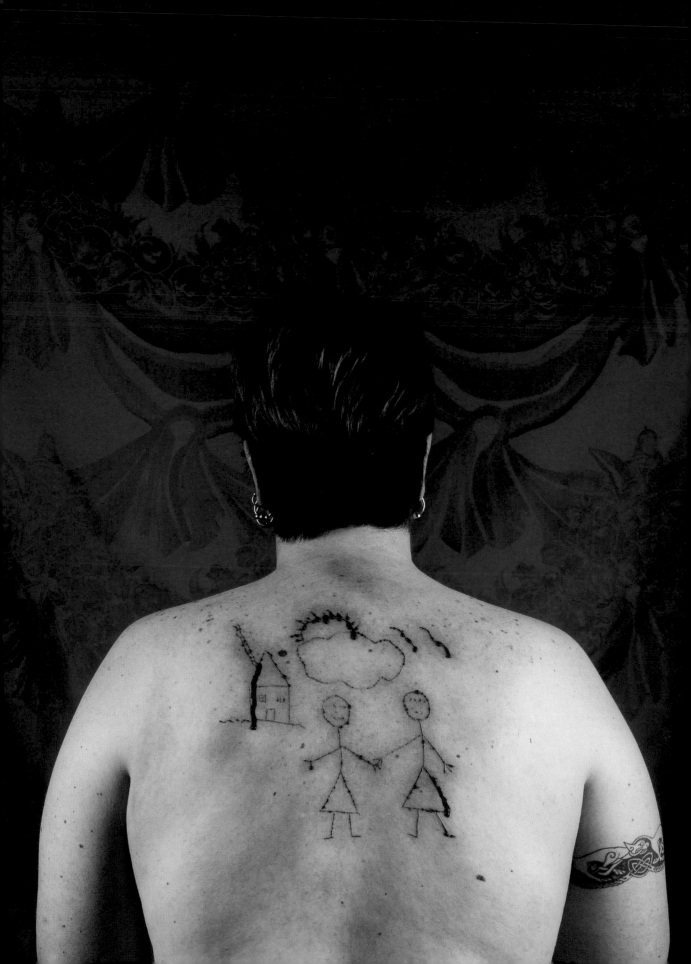

Lauri Firstenberg

AUTONOMY AND THE ARCHIVE IN AMERICA

Reexamining the Intersection of Photography and Stereotype

Visual anthropology and photography

In the context of *Only Skin Deep: Changing Visions of the American Self*, an undeniable dialogue between historical material and contemporary photographic practices surfaces that is fundamental to the design of the exhibition. Internationally, contemporary artists have unearthed the cultural and political narratives residing in institutional archives and historical collections of photographic images and have mined these sources for visual material and conceptual strategies. The photographic archive as such, serves as a repository for meaning relative to personal and historical memory. The work in this exhibition takes various forms from archival, documentary, and social realist to popular and contemporary art photography. In mapping a trajectory of photographic portraiture in America, one can begin with the historical legacies of the archive and the studio portrait and move forward to contemporary corollaries such as the reappropriated archival photograph, the self-portrait, and the performance-based photograph.

The photograph represented the product of an unmediated and objective recording process. Particularly in the context of national pavilions, world's fairs, and colonial expositions, a set of equivalencies was established between live exhibitions, wax models, taxidermy, and photography.[1] Both exhibitions and photography aided in popularizing racial science. As discussed by Victor Burgin in *Thinking Photography*[2] the photograph functions as a sociological text, as evidence. The "society effect" of the medium's role identifies photography as a practice of signification—in the service of producing and disseminating meaning. The myth of photographic verity[3] and its concomitant assertion of neutrality served as an instrument of the stereotypy that lies at the root of photography's relation to race. Photography's role in the hegemonic production of a standardized normative subjectivity also necessarily spawned a taxonomy of "others," that is, of identifiable, controllable, and decipherable archetypes conventionalized and archived into an infinite set of documents from the material to the imaginary.

The archive in America is distinctly colonial, and is based on a European model. It has been constituted and utilized for the political purposes of maintaining hierarchies of peoples, races, ethnicities, and sexes in the production of a proscriptive ideal of an American identity rooted in whiteness and heterogeneity. This exhibition examines the construction of race via photography, including the fabrication of whiteness through the framing devices of the camera. The notion of whiteness, manifested in the popular imagination as a dichotomous

1. Among the principal examples are these: 1893 Columbia Exposition, Chicago; 1915 Panama-Pacific International Exhibit, San Francisco; 1931 Exposition Coloniale Paris; 1933 Century of Progress Exposition, Chicago.
2. Victor Burgin, *Thinking Photography* (London: Macmillan Press, 1982), p. 2.
3. Cf., Roland Barthes, *Mythologies* (Paris: Editions Seuil, 1970).

Catherine Opie, *Self-Portrait*, 1993. Chromogenic print, 40 x 30 in. (101.6 x 76.2 cm). Los Angeles County Museum of Art, the Audrey and Sydney Irmas Collection. Courtesy of Regen Projects, Los Angeles.

and hierarchical relation to the other, was reliant on the tool of photography for maintaining, evidencing, and institutionalizing racial logic and policy. The photograph represented a product of unmediated and objective processes and thus sustained the medium in the service of political propaganda.

Our examination of contemporary meditations on the archive will create a relationship between postmodern engagements with the photographic archive and performance-based photography. Readings of archival photographs as documents of scientific verity are counteracted by contemporary readings of the archive as having been determined by a regime of domination and marginalization. The archive is scrutinized through a series of constructions or performances. By means of the devices of framing, excess, and estrangement, various artists undermine the official aura of documentary reality within the archive and reveal its utility as an instrument of engineered spectacle. Strategies of self-framing, self-staging, reobjectification, refetishization, and reversal are engaged to reinvent the authorship of the photograph and the politics of the camera's gaze. In turning the ethnographic lens back upon itself, these artists photographically restructure the staging of subjectivity.

In his canonical essay of 1986 titled "The Body and the Archive," Allan Sekula examines the nineteenth-century advent of photography and conterminous institutional policies that hinged on discourses of difference. The apparatus of the camera established practices of social categorization that ranged from criminology to ethnography to bourgeois normativity. The resulting visual and discursive cataloguing and surveying of bodies fueled ideological investments in colonialism and nation building. Sekula's overarching definition of the archive is rooted in the culture of realism and representation in late nineteenth- and early twentieth-century France, wherein the operations of the archive—denoting both class and classification—served as the basis for photographic meaning. In Sekula's terms, "photography came to establish and delimit the terrain of the other, to define…the generalized look—the typology."[4]

Photography served as a tool for recording populations, asserting an institutional network of gazes and controls,[5] thus translating the logic of Social Darwinism of the 1850s into racial eugenics. Anthropometric photography developed as a principal apparatus for the measuring of race, aberrance, and pathology. In the 1860s, British anthropologist Francis Galton's system of phrenology based on eugenics utilized composite photography to fabricate archetypal models, and social and cultural specimens. In 1869, British theorist Thomas Huxley based his system of naked frontal and profile photographs on evolu-

4. Allan Sekula, "The Body and the Archive," October, no. 39 (Winter 1986): 17. Sekula says, "In structural terms, the archive is both an abstract paradigmatic entity and a concrete institution… the archive is a vast substitution set, providing for a relation of general equivalence between images."
5. Charles Darwin, On the Origin of the Species by means of natural selection, or the preservation of favored races in the struggle for life (London: J. Murray, 1859).

tionary theory, seeking to document contemporary peoples along the axis of primitive to modern. In the 1880s, French bureaucrat Alphonse Bertillon produced an archive of criminality that was a system of profiling, or measuring moral degeneracy and corresponded to features of class and ethnicity. During the nineteenth century, photography was valued for its claim to scientific objectivity and was used to justify the civilizing mission of imperialism. The development of photographic anthropometry, which sought to classify phenotypic distinctions by depicting the faces and bodies of colonized subjects against a measured grid, gave credence to biological notions of race. As an entity of institutional authority, the archival photograph could be considered an anthropological fact and a scientific document.[6] This alliance of visual and scientific conventions in the production of a photographic genre of racial portraiture, what John Tagg has termed "ethnographic theatre,"[7] is taken up time and again by contemporary artists in their own negotiation of race as spectacle in the visual field.

Contemporary artistic engagements with recovering the apparatus of the archive rely on the familiarity of its structures. A formal re-enactment of the visual tropes of the archival portrait—the headshot, mugshot, anthropometric study, or phrenological inquiry—are rearticulated by contemporary artists in an effort to restage and resignify those encounters of domination and degradation as scenes of subversion and agency. Revisiting the historical construction of bodies and subjectivities vis-à-vis the photographic record serves to reimagine both the historical and current boundaries of identity.

Portraiture and the archive / Material appropriation and resignification

Carrie Mae Weems's *From Here I Saw What Happened And I Cried* (1995–96) consists of thirty-two images. The work was originally part of a project commissioned by the J. Paul Getty Museum to create a dialogue with an exhibition of mid-nineteenth-century photographs titled *Hidden Witness: African Americans in Early Photography*. This collection of daguerreotypes, ambrotypes, and tintypes primarily consisted of anonymous portraits of slaves and freedmen from the 1840s to 1860s, that is, prior to emancipation. Weems's intervention appropriates the archival photographs, enlarges them, and finally tints the images a deep red hue. Weems then inserts text, literally emblazoned onto the glass frames of the pictures. These inscriptions serve to activate dialogue between subject and spectator. The text reads, "You became a scientific profile…A Negroid Type…An anthropological debate…and a photographic subject."

This powerful repossession of archive imagery desublimates the

6. Sir Arthur Keith, introduction in Henry Field, *The Races of Mankind: An introduction to Chauncey Keep Memorial Hall* (Chicago: Field Museum of Natural History, 1937), pp 8–9. Keith defines "three main types of humanity—the white or European, the yellow or Mongolian, the black or Negro. The recognition of these three prevailing types and the perception of the differences which separate them, as well as the similarities which unite them, represent the central crux of modern anthropology." See Elizabeth Edwards, *Anthropology and Photography 1860–1920*, (New Haven: Yale University Press, 1992).
7. John Tagg, *Burden of Representation: Essays on Photographies and Histories* (Minneapolis: University of Minnesota Press, 1993), p. 12.

historical terms of black stereotype in an act of both recovery and accusation. Embedding the texts onto the surface of the glass frame creates a level of distancing, inhibiting the viewer's ability to apprehend the photographic subject. The glass, although transparent, functions as a barrier. The photographed body cannot be fetishized, as it is obstructed by the text, an impediment to the gaze of objectification. In Weems's images the conventions of the archive are subversively literalized, the unspoken message of domination spelled out. Weems's images, which speak directly to the historical function of the photographs, articulate Victor Burgin's observation that "vision is structured in such a way that the look always-already includes a history of the subject."[8] Whereas Weems's contemporaries such, as Glenn Ligon and Lorna Simpson, restage or mimic the photographic conventions of the mugshot or phrenological document, *From Here I Saw What Happened And I Cried* turns to the visual logic of a concrete archive in an act of recuperation, visually altering the primary material in significant ways and thereby dramatically derailing the process of repetition through which the construction of stereotypes operates, and that the colonial archive is designed to maintain.

Weems's series is punctuated by her appropriation of Robert Mapplethorpe's infamous *Man in a Polyester Suit* from his *Black Book* (1988). The insertion of this image in the context of recovered historical imagery sets up a logic of equivalency within the work. Weems places Mapplethorpe in line with a history of photographing racial types. By demonstrating the function of the dominant, colonial gaze on the black body as a site for sexual and racial fetishization, Weems traces the history of the photographed black body through to Mapplethorpe. In Weems's work, Mapplethorpe serves as a contemporary example of photography's categorization and classification of subjects by stereotype; his images of a sexualized black body can be read as a kind of postmodern extension of the colonial archive.

In this way, Glenn Ligon's multimedia practice is also involved in a critical dialogue with Mapplethorpe's *Black Book*. Ligon's *Notes on the Margin of the Black Book* (1991–93) was originally exhibited at the Whitney Biennial in 1993 and includes ninety-two images appropriated from Mapplethorpe, and seventy-eight texts. The work marks the artist's interest in giving voice to those imaged by Mapplethorpe as well as in reiterating various texts surrounding the notorious *Black Book*, from the memories of Mapplethorpe's models to the utterances of museum spectators and the critical comments of Jesse Helms:

> *"Mapplethorpe's relation to Warhol includes an ability to mirror the desires and prejudices of his spectators, to make them see what they do not want to see."*

8. Victor Burgin, "Photography, Phantasy, Function," *Screen* 21, no. 1 (Spring 1980): 43–80.

*"People looking at these kind of pictures become addicts
and spread AIDS."*
"Lord have mercy, Jesse, I'm not believing this."
"My lover."
*"I'm embarrassed to talk to you about this. I'm embarrassed
to talk to my wife."*
*"I hadn't seen one of those in so long I almost forgot what
they looked like."*

The framed captions juxtaposed to Mapplethorpe's pictures stand
in for wall labels and compete with the original photographs. The
textual commentary is set off by a white background and interrupts
the primacy of the images. Ligon's production of and emphasis on
the textual effects a distancing from the overburdened black body
as the object of excessive "othering" in the visual field. His linguistic
intervention provides an alternative to an exhausted mode of representation linked to racial and sexual difference.

Ligon's *Self-Portrait Exaggerating My Black Features/Self-Portrait
Exaggerating My White Features* (1997) annuls the standard lexicon
of photographing black subjects as archivally inscribed subjects. In
doubling his portrait in a Warholian way, he refutes the notion of an
authentic, primary subject. The photographed body can be incessantly
replicated and renamed. The disconnected process of repeating his
identical image and relocating it linguistically exposes the elusiveness
of identity. In *Self-Portrait* (1996), Ligon records the back of his head. He
unrelentingly refutes contact with the photographic gaze. This gesture
echoes Catherine Opie's strategy in her own *Self-Portrait* (1993). Back
to the camera, the artist's body is literally inscribed with a child-like
drawing, a generic stick-figure scene incised on Opie's back in blood.
Part of a series that includes another antiportrait of a back with a
tattoo of the word *Dyke*, Opie's picture attempts a play between photographically obscuring queer identity and asserting its stereotype
through the concrete signs and bodily marks of "butch" haircut and
tattooing. The images play between legibility and uncertainty of identification. The back, or rather skin, serves as a screen for the projection
of photographic memory, specifically that rooted in the archive.

Portraiture and the archive/formalization of the fetish

The photographic corpus of Lorna Simpson, a contemporary of Weems,
Ligon, and Opie, interrupts the seamless field of the imperialist gaze
by means of three distinct strategies—corporeal fragmentation; the
intersection of disjunctive image and text; and her signature antiportrait
convention.[9] In the latter, the sitter presents the back of a head or
reversed torso to the camera. Turned away from the viewer, Simpson's

9. Simpson's antiportrait gesture has
been rearticulated by contemporaries
such as Lyle Ashton Harris whose
monumental series of Polaroids,
Untitled (1998–99), catalogued the artist's
friends and acquaintances, recording
both front and back views, focusing
on both the faces of his sitters and the
back of their heads. This work refers
to the aestheticized archival posturing
of Harris's own profile portrait, his
1993 Polaroid titled *Face*.

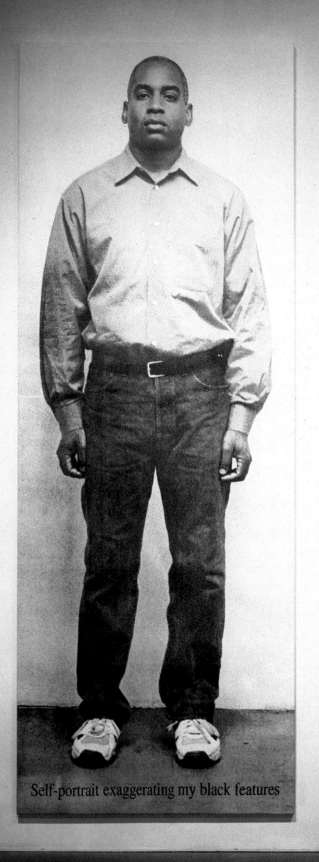

Self-portrait exaggerating my black features

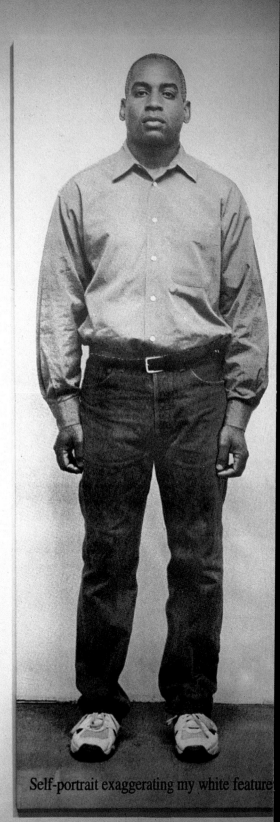

Self-portrait exaggerating my white features

subjects enforce a denial of the action of the gaze and the exchange of the look. The negating gesture of depicting an inaccessible body, pictured in parts, upsets the task of the portrait, which traditionally has been to offer access to personality, or in the case of the archival document, to identify and classify. Simpson's *Gestures/Reenactments* (1985), a monochromatic fragmentary portrait of an anonymous black body, is rendered by cropping the face and fracturing the figure. *Twenty Questions* (1986), a refused portrait, works similarly with minimal but evocative and ambiguous clues that hint at the exploitations of the archive. *Back* (1991) is accompanied by text that reads "eyes in the back of your head" emphasizing projection and desire on the part of the viewer to behold a legible body. Simpson's own discussion of her intervention within the history of portraiture focuses on the artifice of the sitter, a performer enacting a generic role.[10] Kellie Jones comments on this work, "In these pieces from the 1980s, Simpson reacted against the historical image of woman as sexually available, as an object of surveillance. She not so much countered as blocked traditional readings by presenting the renunciatory back, the nonerotic fragment, as a form for contemplation."[11] Simpson's practice refutes the spectacular function of the photograph to capture the body as fetish or curiosity. Moreover, the multipaneled works produce the effect of literally fracturing the photograph, engendering a disorienting and uncanny splintering of the subject. Simpson's strategy of repetition and of ritual representation of the body in only partial form prevents the gaze from fixing on the figure.

Plaques (1986) combines a play on the rock-paper-scissors game with Simpson's mediation on the photographic scientific specimen. Simpson uses serial, detailed images of hands, repeating the formal tropes of the archive.[12] The artist continues the reiteration of the portrait that prevents legibility by repetitiously recording the back of her sitter's head in *Twenty Questions* (1986). Simpson provides futile linguistic clues with impossible recourse. Minimal information is provided—at most a generic white dress. The images are monochromatic, institutional, highly formal, yet vague, prohibiting translation and deciphering of both text and photograph. The triptych *Three Seated Figures* (1989) pictures an interrupted portrait: reductive, repetitive, and incomplete. The frame of the photograph cuts off the kneeling female subject. Disjointed words "her story/prints/signs of entry/marks/each time they looked for proof," gesture directly to the archive as a device of institutional surveillance, particularly the intersection of photography, sexual exploitation, and criminology.

Simpson's photo-triptych *Necklines* (1989) presents segmented closeup views of an unnamed body and focuses on details of the neck

10. Thelma Golden, "Thelma Golden in Conversation with Lorna Simpson," *Lorna Simpson* (New York and London: Phaidon), p. 18.

11. Kellie Jones, "Survey," *Lorna Simpson*, p. 31.

12. Cf., Coco Fusco, "Uncanny Dissonance: The Work of Lorna Simpson," *Lorna Simpson* (Hamilton, NY: Colgate University, 1991); Deborah Willis, "Eyes in the Back of Your Head: The Work of Lorna Simpson," *Lorna Simpson* (San Francisco: Friends of Photography, 1992); bell hooks, "Facing Difference: The Black Female Body," *Art on My Mind* (New York: New Press, 1995).

Glenn Ligon, *Self-Portrait Exaggerating My Black Features/Self-Portrait Exaggerating My White Features*, 1998. Silkscreen on canvas, two panels, each 120 x 40 in. (304.8 x 101.6 cm). Courtesy of D'Amelio Terras Gallery, New York.

thus recalling the history of race murders by hanging, the archive of lynching photographs of the late nineteenth and early twentieth centuries. This association is reiterated in her *Double Negative*, in which rings of braided hair represent nooses. In *I. D.* (1990), a closeup of a woman's back, black hair coifed in the form of a bun, functions as a surrogate subject; it is the replacement of an individual face with a more anonymous but highly erotically charged feature. This visual strategy of object isolation mimics and critiques how cultural identity is rooted in signs, details, and fetishes. Simpson's reenactment and repossession of archival photographic tropes seeks to deflect and deplete the charged signification of their cultural signs. Her text reads "identity and identity," reiterating the function of the photograph to designate and catalogue. The slippage between image and text that occurs in her project is further complicated in this work, because identity is strategically blocked and attention is transferred to the conventions of the archival mode itself.

Simpson's staging of African masks in her critical brand of portraiture extends her inquiry into models of photographic documentation and identification. *Flipside* (1991) displays the interior of a mask. Unable to determine the specific cultural, linguistic, and geographic origin of the mask that is portrayed as a hollow interior, the viewer's reading of surface signs is short-circuited. A culturally specific reading of the mask is restricted in an effort to place pressure on the viewer who can only interpret the inverted mask as a marker of cultural essence, and, in effect, stereotype. The mask, colonially equated with Africa or blackness, references a general, universal trope, or unindividuating sign, and reduces cultures and peoples to base visual signifiers. It is emptied by Simpson, turned inside out and against itself, devoid of meaning. This antiportrait strategy is reiterated in Simpson's *Vantage Point* (1991), for which the accompanying text reads "Inside Out." The mask is critically positioned in this work to be commensurate with an unnamed black subject and yet Simpson's text speaks to the very reversibility of object and subject in the atavistic cultural logic of defining blackness. The repetition of Simpson's conventions of both withholding and framing the process of photographic identification serves to call into question assumptions about both race and the veracity of the medium.

Lorna Simpson's framing of racial fetishization through the medium of photography speaks to Victor Burgin's claim that "the photograph, like the fetish, is the result of a look which has, instantaneously and forever, isolated 'frozen' a fragment of the spatio-temporal continuum... photographic representation accomplishes that separation of knowledge from belief which is characteristic of fetishism."[13] This tendency

13. Burgin, "Photography, Phantasy, Function," p. 180.

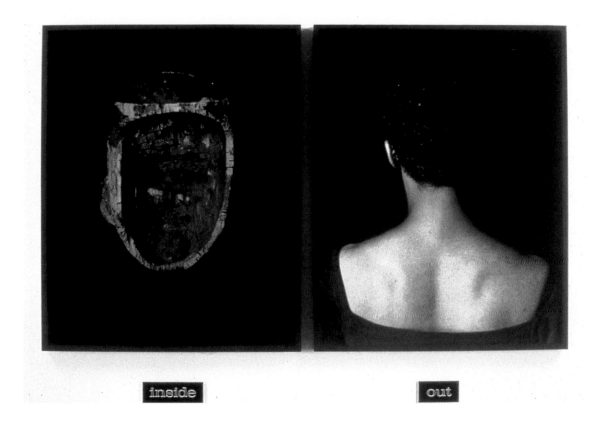

inside   out

is readable in *African Negro Art/Photographs by Walker Evans* of 1935.[14] Engendered from the discourse on primitivism, these images use the photographic conventions of archival portraiture to document a cultural artifact: a mask of the Bamum of Cameroon. This cataloguing impulse is eerily similar to the processing of humans as objects for identification, in that frontal and profile views provide sufficient data. This work reiterates the fetishistic consumption exemplified by Man Ray's photograph *Noire et Blanche* (1926) in which a dark Baule mask is juxtaposed with the preternaturally pale head of a woman that rests on a table top so as to appear disembodied. In *About Face* (1995), Fred Wilson investigates this play between corporeal objectification and anthropomorphization of the object. Wilson's portraits of Mammy and Sambo figurines are introduced into the space of the photographic archive, becoming specimens of stereotyping, meticulously catalogued in the tradition of collecting pictures of the real bodies of the subjects they purport to reference. Wilson uses the anthropological framing device of a neutral white background and positions the popular kitsch figure as a cultural specimen. Furthermore, Wilson's work juxtaposes antique and contemporary dolls. The temporal lapse between the original and the copy is virtually absent, providing a continuum in the

14. This was a large body of photographs by Walker Evans prepared as a record of the Museum of Modern Art exhibition *African Negro Art*, March 18–May 19, 1935.

Lorna Simpson, *Vantage Point*, 1991. Two gelatin silver prints on plastic plaques, overall 50 x 70 in. (120 x 168 cm). Courtesy of Sean Kelly Gallery, New York.

racial logic of visual culture. These signifiers of black stereotypes are reinscribed in the photographic arena, a transposition of the historical format into contemporary terms.

Miguel Calderon's *Evolucion del Hombre (Evolution of Man)* (1995) is a series of six self-portraits of the artist in an Afro wig and baggy pants, with a toy gun. Parodying the Darwinian sequence of modernity and progress, Calderon begins crouched on all fours and gradually becomes upright, mimicking evolutionary development from the posture of a primate to that of an erect Uzi-toting gangster. Calderon plays with stereotypes of racial criminality by means of wardrobe and props, suggesting that through the lens of white cultural convention the most advanced state of development for nonwhites is still one of degeneracy and violence, a residual animalism. These profile portraits reference the ethnographic model of the archive and demonstrate another contemporary approach to the photographic history of stereotype. Likewise, Calderon's series *Historia Artificial (Artificial History)* (1995) uses self-portraiture in a similar guise, to reenter the space of the ethnographic collection. Calderon pictures himself in the Museo de Historia Natural in Mexico City interrogating the vitrines and taxidermy exhibits, literally inquiring into the ways that race and representation coalesce in the fields of anthropology and art.

Maria Magdalena Campos-Pons's Polaroid-portrait diptych *Susurro in Sustenance* (1997) presents the artist in two profile poses. It represents a formal rearticulation of the archival in the vein of Weems and

Fred Wilson, *About Face I*, 1995. Chromogenic prints, each 20 x 16 in. (50.8 x 40.6 cm). Courtesy of the artist and Metro Pictures, New York.

15. Cf.: Lisa D. Freiman, "Constructing Afro-Cuban Female Identity: An Introduction to the Work of Maria Magdalena Campos-Pons" (Ph.D diss., Emory University, Atlanta, 1997), pp. 45–6.
16. Sally Berger, "Maria Magdalena Campos-Pons 1990–2001," *Authentic/Ex-Centric: Conceptualism in Contemporary African Art*, ed. Salah M. Hassan and Olu Oguibe (Venice: Forum for African Arts, la Biennale di Venezia, 2001), p. 131.
17. Campos-Pons discusses her intent to "reconstruct identities, lived or wished for" in Lynn Bell, "A Conversation with Maria Magdalena Campos-Pons," *Third Text* no. 43 (Summer 1998).

Simpson.[15] Campos-Pons's self-portraits of the 1990s investigate Afro-Cuban-American identity by focusing on the iconography of Santeria, syncretic religious and cultural practice of Afro-Cuban origin. Campos-Pons explores the interconnection between the body's role in the field of photography and in the context of Santeria. The artist reveals that in Santeria, as within the domain of photography, "the presence of the body is overwhelming."[16] Her work addresses subjectivity as it is impacted by migration, displacement, expatriation, and transculturation. Performing a multitude of identities for the camera,[17] often in the form of Orisha—Yoruba deities—Campos-Pons's mediation on identity insists on its hybrid and transitory potential. The photograph titled *When I am Not Here/Estoy Alla (from Triptico #1)* (1990) features the artist's bust in a frontal portrait with the text "Identity Could be Tragedy" drawn in mud across her chest. Her eyes shut, Campos-Pons reveals a blank affect to the spectator. *The Nikto Protection* (1996) is an image that also responds to the refusal of the camera's gaze, depicting the artist's fragmentary torso with eyes repeatedly painted onto her nude back. Colonial history and memory are at the heart of her project. These recollections include the role of photographic history in the subjects of such dangerous classes as nonwhites and immigrants. According to Sally Berger, "[Campos-Pons] is simultaneously bared to the world and contained, her actions specific and

Maria Magdalena Campos-Pons, *Susurro in Sustenance*, 1997. Two Polaroid polarcolor prints, 20 x 24 in. (50.8 x 60.9 cm) each. Private collection. Courtesy of the artist.

deliberate. Protective eyes cover her back like a shield, flowers of the bird of paradise family hide and protect her; hair extensions and beads encircle her head and face with the strength of root tendrils; closed eyes and an expressionless face maintain a distance from familiarity."[18] This resistance to possession by the viewer is evident as well in *I Was Told Once* (2000), a multipaneled portrait dividing the artist's body into discreet segments—arm, head, and stomach. Campos-Pons's contribution to contemporary portraiture rests in her interest in a particular body, the diasporal body, as a symbol of dislocation and disarticulation as well as historical memory. Her practice of self-portraiture demonstrates another means of reentering the archive.

Campos-Pons's practice is formally and conceptually linked to that of Dawoud Bey. A street photographer in the seventies, Bey shifted to portraiture in the early to mid-nineties while retaining his interest in documenting American urban culture. Turning to large-format Polaroids, Bey produced broken portraits such as *Oneika 1* (1996), multipaneled pictures of the body severed in a grid of isolated details—head, arm, torso. This dispersal literalizes the way the photograph necessarily cuts up the body, as Burgin insisted, into a frozen fragment, the corporeal fragmentation inherent in the fissured picture plane. Significantly, his formal mutilation splits the subject between the eyes. This stuttered vision of the photographed body also points to the possibility of multiple perspectives of vision. Bey's splintered format presents a self-conscious critique of his medium—the intrinsic capacity of the act of photography to construct and deconstruct. In more recent work such as his portrait *Dowua 1* (2000), a beautifully stark, frontal, closeup, Bey emphasizes the sitter's dynamic engagement with the viewer. Bey explains, "By allowing the subject to return the scrutinizing gaze of the viewer, I seek to decolonize the picture-making process by putting both subject and viewer in equal rooting." Color is manipulated by Bey to animate the canonical portrait format, further emphasizing the sitter as a potent subject.

A similar visual logic is characteristic of Andres Serrano. In his notorious *Klanswoman* (1990), a highly formalized confrontational portrait that is part of a larger series on Ku Klux Klan members, his use of color, lighting, posture, and framing reference formal studio photography but create an enhanced, amplified presence and thus radically individualized images. The artist insisted that his sitters wear masks and regalia, which heightens the ambivalence of these veiled anonymous portraits with regard to notions of identification, masquerade, and mythology. Donald Kuspit reads Serrano's "KKK" series as presenting images of "people rather than…burdensome social objects."[19] Archiving this marginal subculture that is bent on white

18. Sally Berger, *Authentic/Ex-Centric*, p. 132.

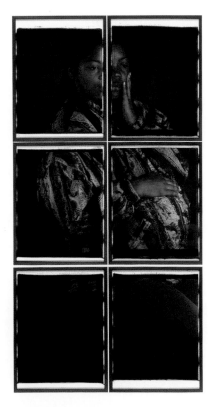

Dawoud Bey, *Oneika 1*, 1996. Polarcolor ER prints; six panels, each 30 x 22 in. (76.2 x 55.9 cm); overall 90 x 46 in. (228.6 x 116.8 cm). Museum of the Art Institue of Chicago, Joseph N. Eisendrath Prize Fund, 1999.

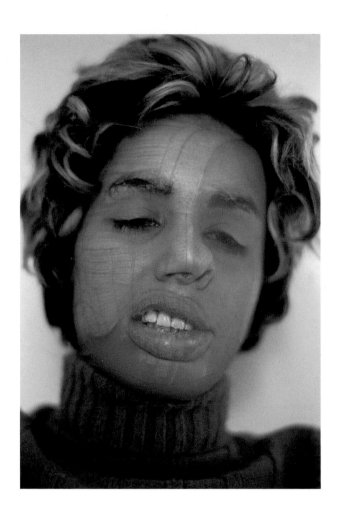

domination problematizes the circuit of exchanges and gazes regarding race, authority, and agency. The self-appointed subjugator is now the photographic subject and open to the revulsion and scorn induced by their marginal identity.

Ana Mendieta's series of self-portraits, "Untitled (Facial Cosmetic Variations)" (1972), are strangely confrontational and disquieting, with a violence that suggests distortions of identity and a gross denaturalization of the subject. Her face is aggressively pressed up against glass or stuffed into sheer stockings, disfiguring the features of lips, eyes, cheeks, and nose. Her skin appears glossed, eerily lustrous in a kind of mutated masquerade. The sheen of her face signals a brutal gesture of self-fetishization. Blond and brown wigs accentuate these corporeal transmutations. Performed within the space of the photograph, Mendieta's theatrics reference the historical fabrications of identity performed for the camera to illustrate deviancy, abnormality, and difference. Following in this tradition, Daniel J. Martinez's *Self-*

19. Donald Kuspit, "Andres Serrano," *Artforum* (March 1991): 124.

Ana Mendieta, *Untitled (Facial Cosmetic Variations)*, 1972/1997. Chromogenic print, 20 x 16 in. (50.8 x 40.6 cm). Courtesy of the Estate of Ana Mendieta and Galerie Lelong, New York.

Portrait #4 (Second attempt to clone mental disorder or How one philos-ophizes with a hammer) (1999) produces a series of grotesque visages, extending the physical violence, mutation, and distortion of Mendieta's self-portraits into the realm of the overtly abject. Collaborating with Hollywood makeup artists Bari Dreiband-Burman and Tom Burman, Martinez creates hyperreal simulations of wounds, scars, stitches, and incisions. Martinez presents the body as battered, severed, raw, and undone, referencing practices of historical documentation of both disfigurement and murder. The kind of grafting and suturing of the skin in Martinez's work mirrors the capacity of the camera to produce images with visual and ideological seams. Mendieta's and Martinez's photographic work can be read as occupied with the intersection of abjection, self-portraiture, and the archive.

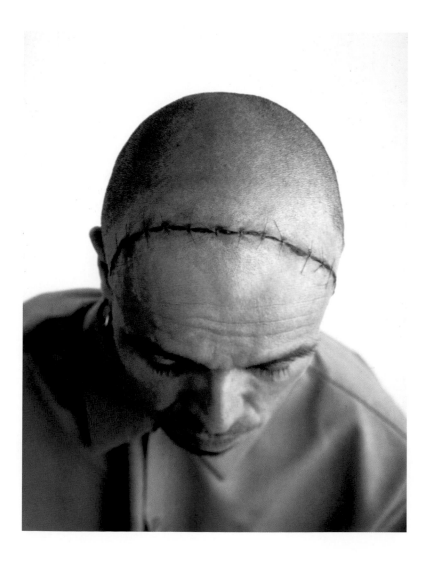

Daniel J. Martinez, *Self-Portrait #4 (Second attempt to clone mental disorder or How one philosophizes with a hammer)*, 1999. Color light jet print, 60 x 48 in. (150 x 120 cm). Courtesy of The Project, New York.

Racial travesty

The legacy of Adrian Piper's persona, *The Mythic Being* (1975), set the groundwork for a host of post-seventies practices focused on various conceptions of masquerade. Assuming a male alter ego—Afro wig, drawn-on mustache, dark glasses—she cruised white middle- and upperclass areas as punk, pimp, criminal, and intruder, staging racist encounters and imitating social constructions of black men. Piper's deft efforts in dramatizing stereotype directly bear on identity as a construct of race, class, and gender. Piper's inclusion of text that actively addresses the viewer emphasizes the spectator as a participant in the staging of race. Her confrontational address "I Embody Everything You Most Hate and Fear" places emphasis on the "you" of the title and points to the subject outside the image field: the act of stereotyping is turned back onto its perpetrators. Piper reveals, "Racism. . .is primarily a visual pathology: It feeds on differences in perceived appearance."[20] Piper's intervention has inspired the work of younger practitioners, including Soon-Mi Yoo. In her *Seeking saf (single asian female)* (1998–99), Yoo mined Boston personal ads listed by white men looking for Single Asian Females. She photographed these men after each encounter (under the category *SWM*), then photographed herself dressed as a geisha (*Self-portrait in Kimono*), performing the fantasies expressed in the advertisements.

Cindy Sherman is represented in *Only Skin Deep* by a selection of photographs that predate her canonical "Untitled (Film Stills)" of 1977–80 which depict stock female cinematic types, a brand of masquerade that has shaped two generations of contemporary photography. The earlier self-portraits present an ironic inhabitation of various typical city dwellers chosen from her survey of a local bus stop. "Untitled (Bus Riders)" (1976) differs from the majority of images represented in *Only Skin Deep* in presentation, in several caricatured images, of a moderate, conventional whiteness. The extreme deidealization of Sherman's bus stop characters is evident in her white caricatures, but most blatant and pungent in the images of Sherman in blackface, which are flagrantly unconvincing performances. In a generic stark white studio setting, she appears in a single standard chair, positioned frontally or in profile. The apparatus of the shutter cable is visible, disclosing the photographic scenario as a space of artifice and pure theater. In blackface, Sherman's legs, neck, face, ears, and lips are painted brown and she wears a black wig. Plain signs point to these willfully counterfeit acts. Sherman takes on the guise of a middle-aged woman with uneven caked-on makeup. Her open-toed shoes expose white skin peeking through the conspicuously messy cosmetic disguise.

20. Adrian Piper, "Goodbye to Easy Listening," *Pretend* (New York: Exit Art, 1990).

In one portrait, Sherman's fingernail is evidently still blackened from the process of tinting her skin. In another the white heel of Sherman's blackened foot, wearing open stacked shoes, is exposed. In the photograph of Sherman as a young black woman she poses in a short miniskirt, which plainly reveals the line of brown makeup that stops at the hem. Contemporary to Sherman's series "Murder Mystery People," which includes early portrayals of the actress, detective, butler, and other cinematic types, "Bus Riders" represents her theatricalization of the epitome of a socioeconomic condition played out in the strange space of cultural distancing. This mode of mimicry is not related to camouflage but to camp. It is purposively inauthentic and outrageous. With no pretense of passing, the camping of race is indicated by the application of thick, messy, unnatural makeup, which focuses the location of race in its ultimate signifier, the surface of skin. Skin color here is blotchy and seamed. The fabrication of race is literalized, externalized, and imbued with the ambivalence intrinsic to the gesture of masquerade.[21] The images are false to an extreme. Identity—more specifically, race—is rehearsed here as travesty. These images can be thought of as performances of otherness or performing through the other. This set of parodic performances may be read as a series of private dramatizations taking on a questionable or confusing gaze. Sherman occupies a collapsed network of positions—inhabiting subject, camera eye, and self-spectator, a brand of masquerade that Kaja Silverman has designated as enacting "identity-at-a-distance."[22] Revealing the constructedness of identity, Sherman photographically plays with a history of social and cultural categorizations.

Lyle Ashton Harris's "Miss America (America's triptych)" (1987–88), a black-and-white photographic series, features the artist masquerading in white face and a blond wig.[23] Readings of Harris's work have focused on his response to the legacy of Mapplethorpe's *Black Book*, as both burden and precursor, serving as a point of departure for re-occupying the discourse of race and representation within the domain of photography. Performing out of the pressures of Mapplethorpe's iconography, Harris complicates both the queer and colonial gaze inherent in Mapplethorpe. However, it is notable in the context of *Only Skin Deep* to examine Harris's burlesque performances as a dialogue with Sherman as well. The level of glamorous artifice in Harris's work is unrivaled. Posed with nude female models swathed in tulle and the American flag, his theatricality is inviolable. Kobena Mercer describes Harris's procedures of unequivocal feigning as "camp[ing] up the categories of identity."[24] Harris is invested in the multiplication of identifications, the plurality and potential shiftings of identity.

21. Homi Bhabha, "The Other Question... Homi K. Bhabha Reconsiders the Stereotype and Colonial Discourse," *Screen* 24, no. 6 (November–December 1983); Homi Bhabha, *The Location of Culture* (London: Routledge, 1994).
22. Kaja Silverman, *The Thresholds of the Visible World* (New York and London: Routledge, 1996).
23. Maurice Berger says of Harris, "He is at once black and white, male and female," in *Ciphers of Identity* (Baltimore: Fine Arts Gallery, University of Maryland, 1993), p. 19.
24. Kobena Mercer, "Dark & Lovely: Notes on Black Gay Image-Making," *Ten. 8* 2, no. 1 (1991): 84.

Cindy Sherman, *Untitled*, 1976/2000. Gelatin silver print, 10 x 8 in. (25.4 x 20.3 cm). Courtesy of the artist and Metro Pictures, New York.

His brand of masquerade specifically calls out the falsity of black stereotypes. Homi Bhabha, in "The Other Question," discusses stereotype in terms of its fixity and maintains, "For it is the force of ambivalence that gives the colonial stereotype its currency; ensures its repeatability in changing historical and discursive conjunctures; informs its strategies of individuation and marginalization; produces that effect of probabilistic truth and predictability which, for the stereotype, must always be in excess."[25] Harris's sardonic mutation of queen culture is most acidic in his "Construct" series (1987–88). He recasts the genre of black male nudes of the Mapplethorpe sort and embodies the act of passing by way of Fanon's conception of the mask.[26] This set of photographs captures Harris undressed and redressed in a coterie of false, rather than fixed, guises. Harris's work embodies Cornel West's "new cultural politics of difference" in its desire "to trash the monolithic and homogenous in the name of diversity, multiplicity, and heterogeneity; to reject the abstract, general, and universal in light of the concrete, specific, and particular; and to historicize, contextualize, and pluralize by highlighting the contingent, provisional, variable, tentative, shifting, and changing."[27]

Mapplethorpe's portraits are marked by techniques of racial fetishization.[28] Devices of cropping and lighting, the sculpturalization of the nude body, and the fetishistic treatment of skin, collapse his subject into pure surface. Harris dramatically reverses these visual terms as the notion of fetish is rendered obscene, absurd, and a sham. He restates the staging of the other for the remaking of the self. Kobena Mercer reads Harris's self-reformulation as "render[ing] black masculinity into a strangely ambiguous version of femininity; that is, a category of identity characterized by its own highly constructed and composite artificiality."[29] Harris's mimetic gestures call into question the legitimacy of the referent: Mapplethrope as source and standard. The ritualized collapse of racial and sexual identification codified in Mapplethorpe's *Black Book* is taken to task in Harris's parodic renditions: the homoerotic gaze is overlaid by a colonialist fantasy that calls into question the intersection of racial and sexual difference in a nondialectical way.[30] Harris locates his own body as the site for a performance of drag queen gone wrong. He exaggerates the female with hyperfeminine wardrobe, and complicates the feminization of Mapplethorpe's black male body through another level of othering and excess. In this way, Harris renders an ambiguous body, reveals the potential for infinite possibilities for the body to take on, and inhabits a series of contradictions to destabilize and dispel singular assumptions of subjectivity.

25. Bhabha, *Location of Culture*, p. 66.
26. Frantz Fanon, *Black Skin White Masks*, trans. Charles Lam Markman (New York: Grove Press, 1967); Alan Read, *The Fact of Blackness, Frantz Fanon and Visual Representation* (Seattle: Bay Press, 1996); "Interior Colonies: Frantz Fanon and the Politics of Identification," *Identification Papers* (New York: Routledge, 1995).
27. Cornel West, "The New Cultural Politics of Difference," in *Out There: Marginalization and Contemporary Cultures* (Cambridge: MIT Press), p. 19.
28. Kobena Mercer, *Imaging the Black Man's Sex Photography/Politics: Two*, ed. Pat Holland, Joe Spence, Simon Watney (London: Comediat Methuen, 1987), p. 66.
29. Kobena Mercer, as cited in Berger, *Ciphers of Identity*, p. 19.
30. Mercer characterizes this operation as "the superimposition of two modes of seeing—sexualizing and stereotyping—[which] inscribes the ambivalence of colonial or racial fantasy, oscillation between erotic idealization and anxiety in defense of the imperial ego." Mercer, *Imaging the Black Man's Sex*, p. 62.

Cindy Sherman, *Untitled*, 1976/2000. Gelatin silver print, 10 x 8 in. (25.4 x 20.3 cm). Courtesy of the artist and Metro Pictures, New York.

Abstracting the portrait, quoting the archive

Jason Salavon's *The Class of 1988* (1998) consists of a collection of blurred portraits. Creating composite pictures from his high school senior class yearbook, Salavon digitally combines several normative images into one elusive multiple portrait. This amalgamation produces a mere specter of subjectivity. His process of obfuscation creates a leveling effect, an effacement of individuality in an effort to provide an average, median appearance. The result is total unrecognizability. This is typical of Salavon's larger project: collecting data from hundreds of images for the development of composite types. From images of porn-stars to those of suburb dwellers, the historical archive model is over-determined; the catalogue is collapsed through superimposition and conglomeration. Regarding his practice, Salavon maintains, "I was thinking about individuals within the whole, and how you define that whole. What are the common characteristics that make this a group, rather than one's individual identity within the group?"[31] These portraits represent the vagaries of the collective. With the assistance of digital technology, photography expands its range of constructions. The photograph is now vulnerable to an infinite number of manipulations and subject to seamless tamperings. Salavon's conceptual reinvention of Galtonian eugenic composite photography illustrates the contemporary technological reconsideration of the archive. Formerly in the service of phrenology, the historical production of archetypal models ends up producing in Salavon's work nonspecific specters, figures beyond identification. Salavon takes his cue from Nancy Burson's *Three Major Races* (1982). Burson's digital rendition of the unity of mankind, rooted in the early twentieth-century discourse of scientific racism,[32] divides and at the same time melds racial categories of white, yellow, and black. The artist morphs physiognomic characteristics of Caucasian, Asian, and African types appropriated from a historical anthropological publication, into a bizarre composite portrait, creating a kind of hybrid clone that reads as a straight, nonmanipulated photograph.

In a similar mode of modifying the conventional portrait, Adal Maldonado creates blurred images of artist Papo Calo and musician Tito Puente, posed in the manner of identity photographs. Titled *Out of Focus Nuyoricans* (1999), it is a mediation of Puerto Rican identity. Likewise, Kori Newkirk's *Channel 11* (1999) turns to the media archive in the production of a highly accentuated pixilated portrait of O. J. Simpson. Newkirk's translation of the most notorious, high-profile mugshot of the twentieth century into the space of painting, à la Chuck Close, inserts the image into the overlapping models of the modernist grid and the digital matrix. In Newkirk's work, devices of abstraction mediate the photographic manufacture of difference. This gesture

31. Jason Salavon as cited in Ann Wiens, "The Message is the Medium," *City Art* (April 2001): 219.
32. Cf., Anne McClintock, *Imperial Leather: Race, Gender and Sexuality in the Colonial Contest* (New York: Routledge, 1995).

Jason Salavon, *Class of 1967, nos. 1–2*, 1998. Gelatin silver prints, two panels, each 25 ¹/₂ x 20 in. (64.8 x 50.8 cm); *Class of 1988, nos. 1–2*, 1998. Gelatin silver prints, two panels, each 25 ¹/₂ x 20 in. (64.8 x 50.8 cm). Courtesy of The Project, New York.

echoes Daniel Tisdale's early nineties practice of appropriation. Tisdale's *Lynching* (1991) and *Rodney King Police Beating* (1991), part of "The Disaster Series," reworks Warhol's silkscreened grid and demonstrates the formation of stereotype through repetition. The serial imagery in Tisdale's work is discussed by Kobena Mercer: "By manipulating the relation between original and copy (both of which are photocopies), the work documents the inexorable power of mass culture to colonize and cannibalize difference—to 'deracialize' identity—all the better to homogenize and hegemonize it under the supremacy of sameness."[33] The image is further abstracted via operations of duplication, negation, and obfuscation. Reiteration of the image serves to neutralize the overmythologized black body.

Artists remain concerned with using the history of the photography of identification, or the archive, to investigate contemporary notions of identity as construction. In particular, the ethnographic archive is a vital source for various current photographic practices. To regard photographs as natural and neutral manifestations of the truth of appearances is a point of departure for recent postmodern photographic practices guided by archival strategies. In the context of South African contemporary photography, Okwui Enwezor suggests:

> [W]hat the archive means goes beyond how to reorganize the fractured memory of a newly emergent sense of the national self. The competing needs to give or strip it of meaning represent the archive both as a legacy of the country's trauma and as its deepest memories. It seems then that it is on this basis that the archive could be said to be both fatal to and a spur of memory. However, such rousing of memory need not always be fatal... the archive could posit new ways to encounter the past without delimiting memory, and thus propose a methodology for the reconstruction of the shattered face of a collective identity. . .the images sealed in the archive call upon the viewer to encounter it without its prior normativity. That is, the experience of the images is diluted and redirected away from its provenance and turns into an object of purely aesthetic discourse and enjoyment once touched by an artistic inclination. Thus the prosthetic of the photographic apparatus contained in the archive rests more on revisioning and reconstruction of the image into other modes of meaning based on the particular inclinations of the artist.[34]

33. Kobena Mercer, *Engendered Species*, p. 75. See Mercer, "Skin Head Sex Thing, Racial Difference and the Homoerotic Imaginary," *How Do I Look? Queer Film and Video* (Seattle: Bay Press, 1991). In this volume, pp. 237–265; Mercer, *Welcome to the Jungle: New Positions in Black Cultural Studies* (New York: Routledge, 1994).

34. Okwui Enwezor, "Remembrance of Things Past: Memory and the Archive," *Democracy's Image: Photography and Visual Art After Apartheid* (Umea, Sweden: BildMuseet) 1998, pp. 26–27.

What the exhibition *Only Skin Deep* reveals is the relevance of the historical archive and its consequence within contemporary practice, particularly for those artists invested in representing the body in photography. Contemporary alliances with the archival are marked by the cooptation of concrete archival material; the reoccupation of the conventions of the archive; the restaging of the subject as performance; and the shifting of photographic authorship in relation to self-portraiture. The contemporary practitioner's alliance with archival material and with the archive as a mechanism of history and memory is timely. British filmmaker Isaac Julien maintains that to reimagine the archive "[is] to imbue it with a certain subjectivity that can be seen in the images but is usually flattened out in the original version… the undoing of the colonial archive"[35]

Perhaps the next question could be: What would postarchival photography look like? It is critical to note that a prevalent strategy in the photographic arena is a total negation of the body in the service of a new brand of portraiture, or antiportraiture, wherein space is a surrogate for the human subject. Identity is abstracted by its absence, indexed by signifiers of landscape in nonfigurative or architectural photography. The obliteration of the figure provides for a new archive of spaces. This shift to visualizing identity as place includes locales of historical memory, such as sites of internment. It is an archiving of the historical landscape. Carrie Mae Weems's *Untitled* from the "Sea Islands" series (1992) features images from Georgia's Sea Islands representing land imbued with West African culture and language. As a limnetic historical zone of the seventeenth century and a place of passage, migration, and settlement, the barrier islands of the Georgia and South Carolina coasts are a geographically isolated and historically overdetermined site. Weems portrays barren unswept graves, documenting territory ridden with cultural memory and unmarred by tourism and urban development. Each marker represents a lost identity and thus is the spirit world of the archive.

35. Coco Fusco, "Visualizing Theory: An Interview with Isaac Julien," *Nka: Journal of Contemporary African Art*, nos. 6/7 (Summer/Fall 1997): 57.

Karin Higa

TOYO MIYATAKE AND "OUR WORLD"

1. All quotes from *Our World* come from a copy owned by Helen Ely Brill, a teacher of "American Life and Institution" at Manzanar High School. It is in the collection of the Japanese American National Museum (95.93.2). A facsimile edition of *Our World* with some additions was edited by Diane Honda and published with funds from the Civil Liberties Public Education Fund in 1998.
2. The official terminology employed by the War Relocation Authority euphemistically referred to the camps as "relocation centers." During the period, they were popularly referred to as "concentration camps." Scholars of American history use this term and I have adopted their usage. See for instance Allan R. Bosworth, *America's Concentration Camps* (New York: W. W. Norton, 1967), and Roger Daniels, *Concentration Camps, U.S.A.: Japanese Americans and World War II* (New York: Holt, Rinehart and Winston, 1971).
3. Executive Order 9066 was issued on February 19, 1942.
4. For a discussion of the "Munson Report," the State Department report concluding that Japanese Americans posed little threat to American security, see Michi Weglyn, *Years of Infamy: The Untold Story of America's Concentration Camps* (New York: William Morrow & Co., 1976). For a discussion of Supreme Court cases and the governmental suppression of information during the period, see Peter Irons, *Justice at War: The Story of Japanese American Internment Cases* (New York: Oxford University Press, 1983).
5. While well-known within the Japanese-American community, Toyo Miyatake's photography in Manzanar was introduced to a larger audience through the exhibition *Two Views of Manzanar: An Exhibition of Photographs by Ansel Adams and Toyo Miyatake*, organized by Graham Howe, Patrick Nagatani, and Scott Rankin for the Frederick S. Wight Art Gallery, UCLA (1978).

The Manzanar High School yearbook of 1944, *Our World*, seems like a typical midcentury high-school annual.[1] But, anticipating questions that might arise through a quick perusal of the yearbook, the student editors ask, "What was Manzanar?" And they answer with only oblique references to the world war and the circumstances that produced this "city" in the desert. In bare facts, Manzanar was an American concentration camp that held over 11,000 Japanese Americans, the overwhelming majority American citizens, from March 1942 to November 1945.[2] Through executive order, President Franklin D. Roosevelt authorized the Department of War to "prescribe military areas" where "any and all persons may be excluded."[3] Despite its own evidence to the contrary, the U.S. State Department orchestrated the largest removal and confinement of citizens in the history of the United States, affecting all persons of Japanese ancestry living in the Western states.[4]

Our World represents one story of incarceration through the voices of teenagers and their faculty advisors. Their perspective is explicitly stated in the first sentence of the foreword, which begins, "The students and faculty have been trying to approximate in all activities the life we knew 'back home.'" And indeed, in what follows, the student editors of *Our World* strive to create, in pictures and words, a world seemingly unmarked by the ravages of war and the abrogation of rights represented by the incarceration. The students also explicitly claim that their goal is for *Our World* to be a "history book of Manzanar, with the school emphasized as the center of the community."

Photographs are a crucial element of any annual and Toyo Miyatake and his studio—Hisao Kimura, Timothy Saito, George Shiba, and Katsumi Igarashi—provided hundreds of images for *Our World*, resulting in a de facto collaboration between Miyatake and the student editors. Toyo Miyatake was known as the "official" photographer of Manzanar.[5] He had smuggled a lens and film holder into Manzanar and found a carpenter friend who used a threaded pipe and scrap wood to construct a wooden camera secretly. In the initial months of incarceration, Miyatake photographed clandestinely with film smuggled into the camp from Los Angeles. The camps were laid out on a grid designed to maximize order and surveillance and to minimize privacy. Each of the thirty-six "blocks" of Manzanar had communal latrines, a mess hall, and fourteen barracks, which, in turn, were divided into compartments housing as many as five families. Hence, it is not surprising that Miyatake's secret activities were easily discovered by the Manzanar administration. But rather than punish Miyatake, Manzanar director Ralph P. Merritt allowed him to set up an officially sanctioned photo studio as part of the comprehensive inmate-run Manzanar

Dorothea Lange, *Just About to Step Into the Bus for the Assembly Center, San Francisco*, 1942. Gelatin silver print, 11 x 14 in. (27.9 x 35.5 cm). Oakland Museum of California, City of Oakland, the Dorothea Lange Collection, gift of Paul S. Taylor.

Cooperative. The "ironing" building of Block 30 became the home of the photo studio. To follow the letter of the law, which prohibited the ownership and use of photographic equipment by Japanese Americans, Merritt required that a European American activate the camera's shutter. The official photographer consisted of a series of people graciously lent by Merritt's office who complied with instructions from Miyatake. After a few weeks, Merritt abandoned this requirement and Miyatake was essentially free to photograph as he wished.

Born in Japan in 1895, Miyatake immigrated with his family to the United States in 1909. At twenty-one, he began his formal study of photography with Harry Shigeta (1887–1964),[6] and he later opened his own photographic studio in the Little Tokyo section of Los Angeles in 1923. Throughout the 1920s and 1930s, Miyatake took portraits, photographs of weddings and funerals, and documented Japanese-American life. At the same time, he and other Japanese photographers—many of whom were key members of the Japanese Camera Pictorialist Club (Miyatake was not an official member)—produced some of the more significant photographs in California.[7] Miyatake participated in international and national photography salons, photographed the 1932

6. For a discussion of Shigeta and his significance, see Christian A. Peterson, "Harry K. Shigeta of Chicago," *History of Photography* 22 no. 2 (Summer 1998): 183–98.
7. See, for instance, Dennis Reed, *Japanese Photographers in America, 1920–1945* (Los Angeles: Japanese American Cultural and Community Center, 1985), and Dennis Reed, "Southern California Pictorialism: Its Modern Aspects," in Michael Wilson and Dennis Reed, *Pictorialism in California: Photographs 1900–1945* (Los Angeles: J. Paul Getty Museum and Huntington Library, 1994).

Ansel Adams, *Roy Takeno at town hall meeting, Manzanar Relocation Center*, 1943. Gelatin silver print, 10 1/4 x 13 1/4 in. (26 x 36.6 cm). Library of Congress, Washington D.C., gift of Ansel Adams, 1965–1968.

Olympics as a correspondent for the *Asahi Shimbun*, and produced a remarkable series of photographs of the choreographer Michio Ito.[8] Miyatake's association with the Shaku-do-Sha, an interdisciplinary group of painters, poets, and photographers based in Little Tokyo and "dedicated to the study and furtherance of all forms of modern art," provided a vehicle for discussion, exhibition, and support for artists in Little Tokyo.[9] These activities included exhibitions of Edward Weston's work during the 1920s. Miyatake's profound and frequent connections with individuals and activities outside of the ethnic enclave of Little Tokyo gave him a special position as both insider and outsider in his photographic practice.

In Manzanar, Miyatake's services were immediately sought out. His studio essentially began where it left off before the war. The high demand necessitated a system of rationing, whereby coupons were distributed to block managers, who then disbursed these to families based on particular events: weddings or the departure of a son for service in the U.S. armed forces ranked high in priority. In addition to photographing family rites, Miyatake roamed the camp and its environs in his trademark black beret making photographic notes on the natural and built surroundings. The incongruity of a fully functioning photographic studio within the confines of a concentration camp attests to

8. See Helen Caldwell, *Michio Ito* (Berkeley and Los Angeles: University of California Press, 1972).
9. Karin Higa, *The View from Within: Japanese American Art from the Internment Camps, 1942–1945* (Los Angeles: Japanese American National Museum, UCLA Frederick S. Wight Art Gallery, and UCLA Asian American Studies Center, 1992), p. 30.

Toyo Miyatake, *Receiving Dolls Donated by the American Friends Society*, ca. 1943. Gelatin silver print, 11 x 14 in. (27.9 x 35.5 cm). Toyo Miyatake Collection.

the strange dichotomies that characterize the incarceration. On the one hand, the government took great pains to exclude and incarcerate Japanese Americans, stripping them of the most basic civil liberties. On the other hand, the infrastructures within the camp itself reproduced mini-cities that simulated freedom.

Our World represented a tremendous organizational and financial feat. Measuring twelve inches high and nine inches wide, its heavy stock cardboard cover and seventy-five pages convey an aura of stability and longevity at odds with the facts of Manzanar and the high school's recent vintage. While funds were allocated for annuals as part of the school's budget, the student editors used their entrepreneurial skills to leverage the initially modest amount of money. Over 1,000 copies of the yearbook were presold to the students and other inmates months before the publication; this group constituted more than 15 percent of the Manzanar population. Despite the strong sense of student control, involvement, and funding, the fact remains that the yearbook bore a direct relationship to the official administration of Manzanar.[10] The first fifty pages of the yearbook are devoted to the activities of the high school: the classes, activities, clubs, and boys and girls sports. By and large, the layout and photographs follow the conventional language of a high school annual: the camp and school administrators are shown at their desks; pages of collaged photographs give the effect of snapshots taken throughout the year; and small head shots of smiling faces depict well-groomed youngsters in regulated rows. (One anomaly: under each student's photograph, after the name, a second line lists his or her "home" high school.) In the "Activities" section, the Baton Club is shown in full costume; the future farmers hold rabbits in their arms; the young journalist reads *Life* magazine; and students in the drama production are photographed performing.

The second section of the annual turns its focus on life beyond the high school. It begins with the section "Democracy," which bears the caption "democracy at work" under photographs of a town hall meeting of block managers (with an American flag prominently displayed on the wall), a group of Nisei soldiers,[11] and the Manzanar police. The following pages cover "Industry," "Agriculture," "Religion," and other aspects of life in Manzanar. It is difficult to reconcile the severe and harrowing experiences of incarceration with a seemingly contradictory picture of utter normality. Inmates experienced anxiety about their future coupled with the daily reminders of their losses of freedom, livelihoods, and possessions, and—though unquantifiable—of their dignity and sense of individual agency. Yet life proceeded in a hyper real enactment of business as usual. In addition to the experiences of births, deaths, weddings, and funerals, there were inmate-run farms;

Ito, Alice
    Theodore Roosevelt
Iwasaki, Isamu
    San Pedro
Kaji, Bruce
    Theodore Roosevelt

Kosaka, Minoru
    Venice
Kunihiro, Luriye
    Van Nuys
Kuniyoshi, Tokiko
    Belmont

Kamimura, Margaret
    Belmont
Katano, Yasunari
    Belmont
Katayama, Shoji
    San Fernando

Kuramoto, Tomoyo
    San Pedro
Kurihara, Goro
    Herbert Hoover
Kuroyama, Noriyuki
    Belmont

Kato, Ayako
    Venice
Kato, Toshiko
    Theodore Roosevelt
Kawaguchi, Saeko
    San Pedro

Kusaba, Torao
    Venice
Kusayanagi, Irene
    Susan M. Dorsey
Kusunoki, Yoshiko
    Thomas Jefferson

Kawamoto, Tom
    Elk Grove
Kikuta, Harry
    Thomas Jefferson
Kimura, Masako
    Whittier

Kuwata, Teruko
    Thomas Jefferson
Lazo, Ralph
    Belmont
Maeda, Arnold
    Santa Monica

Kishi, Jim
    Herbert Hoover
Kitada, Kay
    John Marshall
Kitagawa, David
    University

Maeda, Kunio
    San Pedro
Maruki, Rosie
    Theodore Roosevelt
Maruyama, Shoji
    Santa Monica

Kitaoka, Emiko
    Theodore Roosevelt
Kodama, Umeko
    Theodore Roosevelt
Koga, Mary
    Alameda

Masuda, Setsumi
    San Pedro
Matsumoto, Hideo
    Santa Monica
Matsumura, Tsutomu
    Santa Monica

Toyo Miyatake and others, *Our World, Manzanar, California*, 1943–44 (reprinted 1998). Book. Private Collection.

a cooperative store; a research laboratory; the *Manzanar Free Press* newspaper; a garment factory; an orphanage; a hospital; an internal system of government; Buddhist, Catholic, and other Christian churches; ball games; and an inmate-created garden. Representations of all these activities were part of *Our World*.

Miyatake and his studio took the vast majority of the photographs in *Our World*, though a few images were supplied by Ansel Adams.[12] The incorporation of both Adams's and Miyatake's photographs provides one way to track how the form of the yearbook presents a specific context that changes the meaning of the individual image. High school yearbooks are about conventional stories: the exuberance of youth transformed through education and friendship into adulthood. *Our World* contains the self-conscious "memories" of the experience, already considered in the past tense, as the book simultaneously exists in the present. This conscious fashioning of the experiences of youth takes on greater weight in the context of the concentration camps. The incarceration was predicated on a visual identification as the enemy. Japanese Americans, especially the Nisei, internalized the surveillance of the outside world so that the performance of "American-ness" takes place at all times. Young Nisei were clearly aware that their ancestry marked them as different, a difference that was cast pejoratively. The success of Miyatake's contributions to *Our World* hinges on his canny ability to service his "clients"—the students—at the same time his photographs provide a richness of detail that heightens the irony that their "all-American" experience is taking place in confinement. In *Our World*, Miyatake avoids both direct critique and sentimental juxtapositions of signs of freedom with signs of containment. Instead, the photographs register as naive documentation, seemingly without artful constructions or a documentary edge that reveals hidden truths. In using the conventional language of yearbook illustration, Miyatake succeeds in highlighting what might be missed though in plain sight, producing meaning in addition to creating conventional yearbook illustrations. The excess of information in the photographs duplicates the excessive attempts to be "normal," and in the process, underscores the absurdity of the incarceration itself.

The ability of Miyatake's photographs to serve as more than artifactual documentation is made explicit by comparisons with other photographs of Japanese Americans in the camps. Restrictions against Japanese Americans owning or operating cameras continued throughout incarceration, but by the middle years of the incarceration, snapshots, as well as formal photographs of camp activities, were increasingly common. It is unclear how many of these photographs were produced by Japanese Americans and how many were the work

12. Adams first visited Manzanar in the fall of 1943 at the invitation of director Ralph P. Merritt. The photographs he produced during his visits were exhibited in Manzanar at the inmate-run Visual Education Museum in January 1944. In November 1944, they were shown at the Museum of Modern Art, New York under the title *Born Free and Equal: The Story of Loyal Japanese Americans*, and U.S. Camera published a book under the same title. A photograph of Miyatake and his family in their barracks was included in the publication.

of European American staff or the camp administrations. While these snapshots succeed in capturing moments of individual and collective experience, they do not possess the simple rigor of Miyatake's work. Miyatake employs the standardized language of the snapshot and group picture, but in his emphasis on the telling details, the photographs contain an added layer of information, one that subtly critiques the experience. The photo-essay that opens *Valediction*, the yearbook of the Manzanar High School class of 1945, demonstrates this skill and perhaps most explicitly reveals the ways in which Miyatake's photographs operate. Unlike the large-scale *Our World*, *Valediction* modestly documents the final graduating class of Manzanar. Its construction-paper cover and staple-bound pages lack the weight or ambition of *Our World*. Much had changed in the intervening year. The United States was clearly heading toward victory, and hostility against Japan was lessening. The all-Japanese American 442nd Regimental Combat Team's success and valor in Europe served as incontrovertible proof of Japanese American loyalty, resulting in a less-fervent, less-desperate emphasis on hyper-Americanism than had characterized the earlier

Rea Tajiri, Still from *History and Memory*, 1991. Color and black and white video, 32 minutes. Courtesy of Women Make Movies Inc., New York.

year. With the exclusion orders authorizing incarceration officially lifted, the Manzanar population continually declined, as more inmates relocated to the Midwest and East. War would soon be over. Manzanar would cease to exist.

An elegiac tone tinged with a more nuanced criticality pervades *Valediction*. The first page features a Miyatake photograph of an empty road, curving and receding into dark shadows. The majestic peak of Mount Williamson towers over the solemn road. The following spread features this text:

> *In these years of strain and sorrow one may easily become discouraged and think of the future only as an empty dream. If we are to meet the world with its difficulties and trials, we must not let ourselves be made weak by time and fate.*

Rather like the mariners in "Ulysses" we must

> *Be strong in will to strive, to seek, to find and not to yield.*
>
> *So...to the Future with its joys and its sorrows...not to goals that are found only in the minds of youths but to the achievement of these goals this book is dedicated.*

On the facing page, a photograph depicts in the foreground the wheels of a tractor whose spokes form an iron enclosure; in the background are the barracks and snowcapped mountains. A barbed-wire fence, rough-hewn electrical poles, and the wires strung between them create a diagonal thrust that recedes in space and contrasts with both the massive and rectangular forms of the barracks and the circular bars of the iron wheels. This interlocking web of barriers is captioned with the text, "from 'Our World.'"

Turning the page, the viewer is confronted with the arm of a young person (the model was Miyatake's son Archie) holding a wire clipper— at the moment before cutting—to the taut barbed wire of a fence. A guard tower looms in the background. The caption reads, "through these portals." On the facing page, the caption continues, "to new horizons," with a photograph of a young woman and man stepping forward with suitcases in hand. This attractive, well-dressed couple is shot from a low camera angle to suggest a fresh-faced monumentality. Miyatake is careful to situate the tableau in the physical context of Manzanar—the Manzanar sentry station is clearly visible.

In these pages, photographs similar to ones found in the pages of *Our World* take on new meaning through their clearly articulated and simple layout. The text alludes to the literal product of *Our World* and plays on its multiple meanings while explicitly raising the difficulties forthcoming for the inmates now that they must return to the hostile environment that had previously excluded them. Archie Miyatake recalls that his father created these photographs before it was decided to use them for the yearbook. It is clear that the photographs carefully craft a narrative of future ambiguity, enclosure, and isolation, followed by direct action and a hopeful future. All the while, the motifs and elements depicted in the photographs are the stock images that made up Manzanar. Miyatake uses these components, but through subtle manipulations of composition, camera angle, lighting, and sequencing, he creates another narrative that produces additional meaning. Miyatake's photographic contributions assert the drive to retain an American identity in the face of assaults on personal liberty, property, and political identity in the camps. He captures the relentless optimism and belief in American ideals among the incarcerated. At the same time, his photographs hint at the self-conscious fashioning of young Japanese Americans, who knew that because they looked like the enemy, they were deemed so by their own government. Photography and narrative were used to justify incarceration. In *Our World*, they are used to create an alternative story.

Masumi Hayashi, *Gila River Relocation Camp, Foundations*, 1990. Panoramic photocollage, 28 x 60 in. (71.1 x 152.4 cm).
Japanese American National Museum, Los Angeles, gift of the R. Hayashi Family.

Sally Stein

PASSING LIKENESS

Dorothea Lange's "Migrant Mother" and the Paradox of Iconicity

Dorothea Lange's *Migrant Mother* is arguably the most familiar image from the Great Depression, haunting the nation and, in different ways, both the photographer and the picture's principal subject. Toward the end of her life, Lange was asked to write about her most famous photograph. She began that recollection by noting that some pictures take on a life of their own, overshadowing all the other pictures a photographer may consider to be equally, if not more important. Surely this image fits that description.[1]

Lange made the photograph at a migrant labor camp in Nipomo, California, in early March 1936, as part of her work documenting conditions of rural labor for the New Deal's Farm Security Administration (FSA). Within a few years, the FSA office used this photograph on an in-house poster to proclaim the multiple uses its growing file of government pictures served, for *Migrant Mother* had appeared in major newspapers and magazines, along with photography periodicals and museum exhibitions. In at least one installation photograph from the early 1940s, it already was being represented as worthy of special veneration and, for women, emulation. During and immediately following World War II, it seems to have been retired from active use. But it acquired new legs when its role was reprised for Edward Steichen's book and exhibition *The Family of Man* (1955), Beaumont and Nancy Newhall's book *Masters of Photography* (1958), and then Steichen's final MoMA exhibition and catalogue *The Bitter Years* (1962). As both social documentary and the populist politics of the Great Depression attracted the interest of the postwar generation coming of age in the 1960s, a wide variety of publications made frequent use of *Migrant Mother*. As a government picture in the public domain, it was readily available for minimal cost. Moreover, the picture's extensive prior usage only added to its serviceability as a shorthand emblem of both the depths of misery once wide-spread in this society and its heartfelt recognition by socially engaged New Dealers. Indeed, since the early 1960s, it has been reproduced so often that many call it the most widely reproduced photograph in the entire history of photographic image-making.

Celebrity, we know, attracts critics along with acolytes. It is no surprise, then, that this national icon of maternal fortitude has provoked an unending series of challenges to its documentary authenticity. As much as anyone, the photographer helped lay the groundwork for subsequent skeptics. Two years after Lange made the series that already was gaining exceptional notice, she borrowed the negative from the Washington office in order to make a fine enlargement for a traveling museum exhibition. With art on her mind, she temporarily took leave of her New Deal political senses and decided to have a corner of the

1. Dorothea Lange, "The Assignment I'll Never Forget," *Popular Photography* 46 (February 1960): 42.

Dorothea Lange, *Migrant Mother, Nipomo, California*, 1936. Gelatin silver print, 13 1/2 x 10 1/2 in. (34.3 x 26.7 cm). Oakland Museum of California, City of Oakland, the Dorothea Lange Collection, gift of Paul S. Taylor.

negative retouched. Since the picture had begun gaining special notice, Lange judged the intrusion of a thumb and index finger beside the tent pole to be an extraneous detail, detracting from an otherwise unified composition that was reminiscent of sacred Marian imagery. This embellishment of the picture may have led to her being fired, for one photographic historian has proposed that Lange's FSA boss, Roy Stryker, was so angered by her tampering with a government negative that he named Lange for termination when the FSA faced budget reductions at the end of the 1930s.[2]

Over time Stryker expunged this dispute from memory. In later years, he not only championed Lange's signal contribution to the file but also claimed that of all the thousands of FSA pictures *Migrant Mother* represented the apex of the documentary project.[3] But as the study of photography moved from an infancy of jubilant celebration to a more critical adolescence, others initiated their own investigations. Historian James C. Curtis questioned whether the presumed final picture was absolutely documentary; his reconstruction of the sequence of negatives she exposed in Nipomo demonstrates that Lange worked very selectively to achieve her portrait composition, in the process sacrificing any sense of location and even some family members.[4]

Feminists have brought other concerns to the reexamination of the picture. Cultural historian Wendy Kozol treated *Migrant Mother* as the quintessential example of the FSA traffic in conservative stereotypes. This modern version of the longstanding pictorial genre of mother and child, Kozol argues, chiefly served to reassure the public in the Great Depression that the most fundamental social unit—the nuclear family—was beleaguered but still strong.[5] Subsequent scholarship has extended this critique of the way *Migrant Mother* both drew upon gender conventions and in turn helped keep them in circulation, thereby perpetuating pictorial and social clichés. "Whatever reality its subject first possessed," literary historian Paula Rabinowitz declared, "has been drained away and the image become icon."[6] Some scholars contend more bluntly that study of Depression culture would benefit from shifting attention to less-celebrated pictures, preferably those depicting women engaged in wage work instead of preoccupied with domestic responsibilities.[7]

Despite these critical admonitions, not all have heeded the call to shelve this familiar photograph but instead have explored new avenues for comprehending the picture's persistent power. One lacuna in earlier discussions of *Migrant Mother* was the lack of any detailed information about the woman. Lange spent so little time making the photograph that she did not even record the name of her subject. By the time Lange died in 1965, she had come to think of her model as having only

2. F. Jack Hurley, *Portrait of a Decade: Roy Stryker and the Development of Documentary Photography in the Thirties* (Baton Rouge: Louisiana State University Press, 1972), pp. 142–43.
3. "To me it was 'the' picture of Farm Security," Stryker declared toward the end of his life. Quoted in Nancy Wood's introductory essay, "Portrait of Stryker," in Roy Emerson Stryker and Nancy Wood, *In This Proud Land* (Greenwich, CT.: New York Graphic Society, 1973), p. 19.
4. James Curtis, "'The Contemplation of Things As They Are': Dorothea Lange and *Migrant Mother*," in James Curtis, *Mind's Eye, Mind's Truth: FSA Photography Reconsidered* (Philadelphia: Temple University Press, 1989), pp. 45–67.
5. Wendy Kozol, "Madonnas of the Fields: Photography, Gender, and 1930s Farm Relief," *Genders* 2 (July 1988): 1–23.
6. Paula Rabinowitz, *They Must Be Represented: The Politics of Documentary* (London/New York: Verso, 1994), p. 87. Rabinowitz does not specify whether she means icon in the vernacular sense of shared cultural symbol, or in the more technical, semiotic sense of a sign that works by means of resonant likeness, or in the most traditional religious sense of an image meant for literal veneration, or some combination of these various meanings.
7. See the recent discussions of this image in Laura Hapke, *Daughters of the Great Depression: Women, Work and Fiction in the American 1930s* (Athens: University of Georgia Press, 1995), pp. 29–31; and Michael Denning, *The Cultural Front: The Laboring of American Culture in the Twentieth Century* (London/New York: Verso, 1996), pp. 137–38.

the generic name *Migrant Mother*. But in the 1970s, a younger generation of photographers began to revisit places and people already rendered historic by earlier documentation. In that spirit of rephotography, Nebraska-based photojournalist Bill Ganzel spent years tracking down people and locations photographed by the FSA. With the aid of a story in the *Modesto* (California) *Bee*, Ganzel located Florence Thompson and persuaded her and the same children to pose for him in 1979. The book that resulted from his wide-ranging research was the first major publication to put a name to her face, yet in most other respects, the information supplied was sparse. Apparently wary of further national exposure, the family members offered only general remarks about the hard times they had survived.[8]

Ganzel's photograph offered a bit more information. For this unusual public portrait, Florence Thompson quietly displayed her own sense of style by donning white slacks and a white sleeveless top, adorned only by a Southwest-style squash blossom necklace. In itself, there is nothing conclusive about this detail; one response to the surge of Native American activism in the 1970s was the widespread fashion for silver-and-turquoise jewelry. But for Thompson it was a deliberate, if quiet, statement of identity. During the same period, this long-obscure celebrity made a point of acknowledging her Cherokee heritage in occasional interviews with news media. Thompson also volunteered

8. Bill Ganzel, *Dust Bowl Descent* (Lincoln: University of Nebraska Press, 1984), pp. 10, 30–31.

Bill Ganzel, *Florence Thompson and her daughters Norma Rydlewski (in front), Katherine McIntosh and Ruby Sprague, at Norma's house, Modesto, California*, 1979. Gelatin silver print, 11 x 14 in. (27.9 x 35.5 cm). Courtesy of the artist.

that she always had resented the famed picture by Lange, and would never have allowed its being taken had she understood the way and the extent to which it would be used.[9]

But for more than a decade after her widely reported death in September 1983 and the national circulation of Ganzel's book in 1984, public information about Florence Thompson consisted largely of a proper name. Then, in the early 1990s, Geoffrey Dunn, a freelance journalist and University of California doctoral student, resolved to reconstruct her life story. Extensive interviews with surviving members of the family left him shocked by the gulf between her actual situation and the minimal details Lange had recorded. The varied details of Thompson's life that Dunn pieced together for this first biographical essay were no less stunning than his overriding conclusion of the photograph's betrayal of its immediate subject.[10]

When her path crossed that of Lange's in March 1936, Florence Owens was thirty-two years old. Born Florence Leona Christie in September 1903, she grew up in the Indian Territory of the Cherokee Nation to which both her parents claimed blood rights. Her biological father left her mother before she was born, and her mother soon married a man who did not think of himself as Indian (though his children later came to think that he may have been of part-Choctaw descent). Throughout her youth, Florence believed her mother's second husband to be her biological father. Thus, although she grew up in Indian Territory, she did not identify herself as "pure" Cherokee. In 1921, at the age of seventeen, she married Cleo Owens, a farmer's son from Missouri, and over the next decade they proceeded to have five children.

Oklahoma in the first decades of the twentieth century bore little relation to the locale envisioned in the popular World War II-era musical. The long-running Broadway show simply eradicated the Indian presence and prior claim to the land, while suggesting unlimited opportunities for all newcomers. The historical record is more dramatic. Following the white land rush at the turn of the twentieth century that had been precipitated by the forced allotment system of the federally enacted Dawes Plan, opportunities to homestead turned cutthroat: "Of the thirty million allotted acres more than twenty-seven million passed from Indians to whites by fraudulent deeds, embezzlement, and murder."[11] Florence and Cleo Owens saw no chance of farming on their own, so by the mid-twenties they opted to move west, finding work and temporary housing in the sawmill camps of California's Hill Country. By 1931, they were expecting a sixth child in northern California when Cleo Owens died of tuberculosis.

According to Dunn, Florence supported her family as a waitress and soon became involved with a local businessman. Florence's

9. One such news story circulated by Associated Press appeared in the *Los Angeles Times*, Saturday, II:1 (November 18, 1978), as cited and reproduced in Martha Rosler, *Three Works* (Halifax: Press of the Nova Scotia College of Art and Design, 1981), pp. 67, 75–76.
10. Geoffrey Dunn, "Photographic License," *Santa Clara Metro* 10:47 (January 19–25, 1995): 20–24.
11. Gerald Vizenor, "Manifest Manners," in *American Indian Persistence and Resurgence*, ed. Karl Kroeber (Durham: Duke University Press, 1994), p. 233; Vizenor quotes from the extensive research of lawyer and historian Rennard Strickland's meticulous demographic research in his book *The Indians in Oklahoma* (Norman: University of Oklahoma Press, 1980), particularly chapter 2, "The Dark Winter of Settlement and Statehood," pp. 31–54.

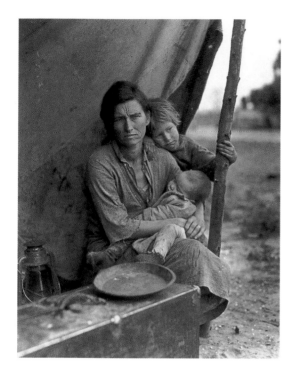

grandson Roger Sprague, who is currently preparing his own biography of the many generations of his grandmother's family, notes that the young widow was fiercely independent but made the mistake of obtaining county aid, which stipulated that any sexual relations with men would result in the removal of her children. When she became pregnant, she immediately left for her home state, determined to avoid any custody dispute.[12] But Oklahoma in the 1930s was devastated by drought and offered even fewer opportunities than it had in the previous decade. Florence quickly set out a second time for California.

After returning to her adopted state, Florence became involved with Jim Hill, an unemployed local man who had turned to migrant work, and with whom she had a child in 1935—the nursing infant in *Migrant Mother*. Hill had temporarily left the camp with one of Florence's sons when Lange happened upon the pea pickers' encampment and made her series of portraits. Though Hill was actually getting a radiator repaired, the photographer soon annotated the closest portrait with

12. I am indebted to Roger Sprague who has allowed me to read his manuscript-in-progress, "Second Trail of Tears." Excerpts from his carefully researched text can be found on his website, *www.migrantgrandson.com*.

Dorothea Lange, From "Migrant Mother" series, 1936. Gelatin silver prints, dimensions vary. Library of Congress.

the detail that the family had been forced to sell the tires from their car. This factual embellishment offended the family's sense of logic as well as accuracy, since mobility was the key to even the poorest migrant's survival. Dunn's article makes no mention of when Florence married Thompson, her last name at the time of her death. But from Roger Sprague's more extensive reconstruction of his family history, I learned that the marriage followed her separation from Hill in the 1940s, and again she outlived her husband.

As Dunn makes clear, Lange was quite careless with the facts. However, this was hardly the first time a scholar has noted the liberties Lange took in her documentary practice (as well as in the facts of her own biography). Accordingly, Dunn's wholesale condemnation of the famous photographer as manipulative, condescending, colonialistic, misleading, and disingenuous made less of an impression on me than the chronicle he had sketched of *Migrant Mother*'s Native American heritage.[13] On this count, I don't think we can condemn Lange for deliberately misrepresenting or burying the information.

From all available evidence, it does not seem that Lange never realized she had cast a Native American for the European American role of New Deal madonna. She never questioned the stranger about her ethnic identity; in fact, making such an inquiry would have risked breaking whatever current of empathy she briefly sought to establish. But if there is anything recognizably "Indian" in this striking face, Lange's misperception is more than a little curious. She prided herself on being able to distill essential truths by looking closely.[14] Moreover, she had spent a fair amount of time studying Native Americans in the southwest. Her first husband, Maynard Dixon, was a plein-air painter who had specialized in idyllic scenes of the pristine West inhabited solely by Native Americans. It was during an early sojourn with Dixon

13. On Lange's radical misquotation in the case of her 1930s portrait of Nettie Featherston ("Woman of the High Plains") long linked to the caption, "If you die, you're dead—that's all," see Maren Stange, *Symbols of Ideal Life* (New York and Cambridge, England: Cambridge University Press, 1989), pp. 119–23; see also my interpretation of the photographer's logic for such counter-factual alteration in "Peculiar Grace: Dorothea Lange and the Testimony of the Body," in *Dorothea Lange: A Visual Life*, ed. Elizabeth Partridge (Washington, D. C.: Smithsonian Institution Press, 1984), pp. 81–84. On Lange's embellishment of her own educational background, see her first biography, Milton Meltzer's *Dorothea Lange: A Photographer's Life* (New York: Farrar, Straus and Giroux, 1978), p. 22.
14. Toward the end of her life she would express this idea in terms of "living the visual life," words that open the 1966 documentary film *The Closer for Me*, produced by Philip Greene and Robert Katz of KQED; transcript of the filmed interviews with the photographer in the Dorothea Lange Collection of the Oakland Museum of California.

Dorothea Lange, From "Migrant Mother" series, 1936. Gelatin silver prints, dimensions vary. Library of Congress.

in the Southwest that Lange began to photograph seriously outside her studio, and those efforts lead to one of her first distinctive portraits. Yet, in the resulting close-cropped print of a Hopi man's face, her framing excluded all conflicting cultural signs like modern, store-bought clothing. In this respect, she continued the quest to find or produce "authentic Indians," a tradition developed by a long line of artists including Dixon and photographers like Edward S. Curtis.[15] That these "authentic" stereotypes were manifestly superficial in spite of being deep-seated, proved especially true in Nipomo, California. The migrant woman who attracted Lange's attention displayed no obvious signs of "Indianness," so Lange proceeded to place her in a distinctly Euro-American scenario of hallowed Christian maternity. In turn, this iconographic context led all, including the photographer, to assume that the model was unarguably white.

Lange's mistaken assumption amplifies the generalizing tendencies in both New Deal culture and subsequent scholarship of the period. Photography and direct observation in that era came close to enjoying the powers of a fetish, magically replete without nominal recourse to factual or reasoned discourse. Though our eyes often deceive us, the objective character of photography encourages viewers to rely on sensory appearance as the incontrovertible bedrock of experienced-based knowledge.

The photograph's history likewise exemplifies the way the New Deal was not only most concerned about "the forgotten man"—in Franklin Roosevelt's words—but equally, if less vocally, about the declining status of whites. The mass media were most inclined to

15. On the deliberately selective practices of staging and framing by Curtis, see Christopher M. Lyman, *The Vanishing Race and Other Illusions: Photographs of Indians by Edward S. Curtis* (Washington, D. C.: Smithsonian Institution Press, 1982).

Dorothea Lange, Left: *Hopi Indian Man* (full frame version), 1926. Gelatin silver print. Private collection.
Right: *Hopi Indian Man*, 1926. Gelatin silver print, 7 1/4 x 7 11/16 in. (18.4 x 19.5 cm). Oakland Museum of California, City of Oakland, the Dorothea Lange Collection, gift of Paul S. Taylor.

focus on the plight of poor whites, and Lange's FSA boss was supremely media-oriented. On one occasion, Stryker rejected Lange's proposal to focus on the situation of blacks and the urban poor, reminding her of the dearth of demand for such pictures.[16] Since there was even less public concern about Native Americans in this period, while traveling for the FSA in the southwest Lange never proposed focusing on the living conditions of Native Americans. But Arthur Rothstein implicitly made such a proposal on one occasion, by sending the FSA a few preliminary studies of Native Americans he had photographed in Montana. Stryker's response was blatant:

> The Indian pictures are fine, but I doubt if we ought to
> get too far involved. There are so many other things to
> be done. You know I just don't get too excited about the
> Indians. I know it is their country and we took it away
> from them—to hell with it![17]

In this unguarded exchange, Stryker may have been expressing a personal and regional bias, for he came from western Colorado where his family had struggled as ranchers. But if his sentiments were at all representative of mainstream opinion in the New Deal, it is reasonable to assume that had Lange recognized her subject as Native American, she might not have bothered to take any photographs. Or if she had discovered from extended conversation that the woman she had photographed was Native American and captioned the picture accordingly, the image's promotion and circulation would have been quite limited. It would have undermined conventional thinking in two ways: it directed attention away from Anglos, and it refused to support the image of Indians as a "vanishing race." Rather, Lange had depicted someone who seems determined to survive and who, as part of that process, had traveled out of the Dust Bowl region and into California—even the most skeletal caption is quick to inform us—thereby challenging the stereotypes of a defeated minority.

Once we recognize that what has been documented inadvertently is the migration not of a poor Anglo-Oklahoman but of an equally poor Native American Oklahoman with children, we may be led to question the basic concept that Lange and her second husband, University of California at Berkeley social scientist Paul S. Taylor, developed to frame their New Deal magnum opus, *An American Exodus*.[18] Together they wove pictures and text to trace the movement of whites and a smaller number of blacks suffering displacement and immiseration as recent (and frequently despised) newcomers to the industrialized agricultural fields of California. It was an ambitious cross-country chronicle, yet after gleaning just a bit about the background of *Migrant Mother*, it is hard to accept the contours of such a black-and-white story. Indeed, to think of exodus and migration with primary emphasis

16. See the exchange of letters between Stryker and Lange, June 18–23, 1937, as well as their correspondence during October 1938; Stryker personal correspondence files, University of Louisville.
17. Stryker to Rothstein in Great Falls, Montana, May 26, 1939; from the Archives of American Art microfilm correspondence of Stryker's personal collection of FSA correspondence.
18. Dorothea Lange and Paul Schuster Taylor, *An American Exodus: A Record of Human Erosion* (New York: Reynal and Hitchcock, 1939).

on the Great Depression fails to comprehend that whites were late-comers to the forced migration across a continent. Okie culture, in particular, was carried to the West not only by whites and blacks, but also by Native Americans who were banished from Georgia and other Eastern states in the early nineteenth century. Those who managed to survive ordeals such as the infamous Trail of Tears were forced to resettle in Oklahoma,[19] and yet the records of so-called Okie migration rarely make reference to Native Americans.[20] Those migrations continue to be relegated to histories devoted exclusively to Native Americans, an example of our intellectual reservation system still in operation. The histories of Oklahoma settlement and resettlement need to be revisited and elaborated to portray the constant flux and mix in populations.

But the continuing gaps in our social histories should not prevent consideration of the symbolic implications in the longstanding assumptions about *Migrant Mother*'s whiteness. How to account for this error? On one hand are the viewers'—including Lange's—deeply ingrained stereotypes. On the other hand, it seems reasonable to assume that the migrant woman made no effort to publicize her identity as a person of color. When she was already living a life of bare-bones subsistence, what was the point of gratuitously announcing her minority status far away from her community of origin (which itself was increasingly dispersed)? The entrenched federal policy of sending Native American children to government boarding schools for training in assimilation provided more incentive to pass.[21]

The concept of passing implies unilateral deception for the sake of upward mobility and the avoidance of stigma. Deliberate misrepresentation is foisted upon another who seeks to police the boundaries of a racialized caste system and guard the gates of exclusivity. While making use of the term, I propose reloading its meanings so that we consider the role of whites, or any privileged group, more actively in the process. Misrecognition of conventional affinities may simply underscore the arbitrary character of such repressive systems of regulation. But misrecognition may also attest to the active desires that are being repressed, at least nominally. Since I find it surprising that it took virtually six decades before anyone began exploring Thompson's ethnic background, I propose that this lack of recognition of difference contains a wish toward generic inclusivity. Such inclusivity may not be motivated by disinterested liberality or the desire to dispense with all social barriers. Rather, for those in the mainstream, there may be other benefits that accrue from imagining oneself more closely connected to the other. At the most banal level, there may be a cosmetic motive (arguably masking an erotic impulse) to reimagine oneself and one's immediate relations with higher cheekbones and a more prominent, "noble" profile. Such a process of physiognomic affiliation may have

19. Strickland, *Indians in Oklahoma*, pp. 1–7; see also Michael Paul Rogin, "Liberal Society and the Indian Question," in Rogin, *Ronald Reagan, the Movie, and Other Episodes in Political Demonology* (Berkeley: University of California Press, 1987), pp. 134–68.
20. For example, Indians and Native Americans do not even appear in the index to the book frequently cited as the definitive social history on Oklahomans in California; James N. Gregory, *American Exodus: The Dust Bowl Migration and Okie Culture in California* (New York: Oxford University Press, 1989).
21. Frederick E. Hoxie, *A Final Promise: The Campaign to Assimilate the Indians 1880–1920* (Lincoln: University of Nebraska Press, 1984).

helped European Americans justify their claims as rightful heirs to the continent. Likewise, the feeling of resemblance might convey the liberating promise of more intimate contact with nature and enhanced physical prowess.[22] What better figure with whom to create such a fantasy set of relations than a woman whose fair-haired child indicates that she has already entered the process of interracial union? Thus, the danger that Mary Douglas reminds us always accompanies thought of purity is conjured into a fantasy of pleasure, revitalization, and legitimation.[23]

Is it not fitting that a society struggling to weather a decade-long capitalist crisis would gravitate toward an image that faintly recalled the strong profiles it had already appropriated to legitimate its business? Gracing coins and government buildings, these figures embodied the natural powers that American capitalism both claimed and coerced so that the New World garden could be worked for profit.[24] That sentiment already found expression in an early Depression report by literary critic and social journalist Edmund Wilson. On a quick visit to the Appalachian region, Wilson was astounded by the visual contrast between the "goggled eyes, thick lips, red, blunt-nosed, salmon-shaped visage" of the County Welfare agent and the "clear oval faces, pale and refined by starvation." These, he ruminates, represent "the pure type of that English race which, assimilated on the frontier to the Indians' hatchet profile and high cheekbones, inbred in Boston and Virginia, still haunts our American imagination as the norm from which our people have departed, the ideal towards which it ought to tend."[25] Wilson's idea allows for a bit of assimilation but mainly stresses the pale refining process in the production of prescriptive norms. By contrast, Lange's image is less concerned with paleness per se, but unwittingly she expresses a similar eugenic sensibility, and in the canonization of this image as mainstream Anglo icon, so too has the entire body politic.

News from the parochial world of photographic studies travels slowly, or perhaps stereotypical thinking proves remarkably tenacious. A recent book on the divisive role of race in twentieth-century America once again reproduces *Migrant Mother*, this time as a negative example of white supremacy. To encourage more critical readings of this familiar picture, the author adds his own interpretive caption:

> *Part of the photograph's appeal lay in the sheer*
> *brilliance of its composition, but part depended, too,*
> *on its choice of a "Nordic" woman. Her suffering*
> *could be thought to represent the nation in ways*
> *the distress of a black, Hispanic, Italian, or Jewish*
> *woman never could.*[26]

22. On the white desire to pass as Indian, at least for brief moments of recreation and resistance, see Philip J. Deloria, *Playing Indian* (New Haven: Yale University Press, 1998).

23. Mary Douglas, *Purity and Danger: An Analysis of the Concepts of Pollution and Taboo* (London: Routledge & Kegan Paul, 1966).

24. While she does not discuss the iconography of the nickel, Barbara Groseclose provides a good basis for such analysis in her genealogy of early official uses of Indian iconography; Groseclose, *Nineteenth-Century American Art* (New York: Oxford University Press, 2000), pp. 62–67. For a trenchant ideological analysis of the contradictory impulses in white paternalism, see Rogin, "Liberal Society and the Indian Question."

25. Edmund Wilson, "Red Cross and Country Agent" (written during Wilson's cross-country travels during 1930–31); reprinted in Wilson, *The American Earthquake* (Garden City, NY: Doubleday, 1958), p. 264.

26. Thanks to Tom Folland for directing me to this passage in Gary Gerstle, *American Crucible, Race and Nation in the Twentieth Century* (Princeton: Princeton University Press, 2001), pp. 180–81.

Even in a text that aims to challenge divisive ideologies, we encounter more evidence of the degree to which race and ethnicity elicits our categorizing impulses and simultaneously mocks them.

One could argue that "reclassifying" *Migrant Mother* as Native American only continues a caste-based tradition of racial labeling. There is something to be said for thinking that the ethnicity of the central subject in this revered picture should not matter, especially because in the past it never seemed to matter. Downplaying the belated revelation of *Migrant Mother*'s Native American identity may serve as proof that our society is moving close to a state of color blindness. Then again, can the eradication of racism ever be achieved if we ignore the racialized ground on which the nation established itself and continually expanded? An alternative goal might be that future generations will come to view *Migrant Mother* beside the highly contrived portrait studies of Edward S. Curtis, for example. Recontextualized thus, both depictions may appear as differing versions of Euro American misrecognitions of Native Americans: either as noble savages magically quite removed from encroaching European society, or conversely as fair-to-passing representative figures of that same civilization, with the Native American lending a fantasy of natural nobility to whites' wishful images of themselves and their supposedly resolute family values. If and when we finally become a society committed to problematizing the historic assumptions of normative whiteness, the notions of passing, and passing likeness, might finally admit thoroughgoing reconsideration of what has been missed with respect to difference and diversity.

Edward S. Curtis, *The Vanishing Race*, 1907. Photogravure, 6 x 8 in. (15 x 20.3 cm). National Anthropological Archives, Smithsonian Insititution, Washington D.C.

V.
PROGRESS /
REGRESS

Osa Johnson and Martin Johnson, *Refrigerator*, ca. 1920. Modern print from original glass negative, 7 x 5 in. (17.8 x 12.7 cm).
George Eastman House, Rochester / New York.

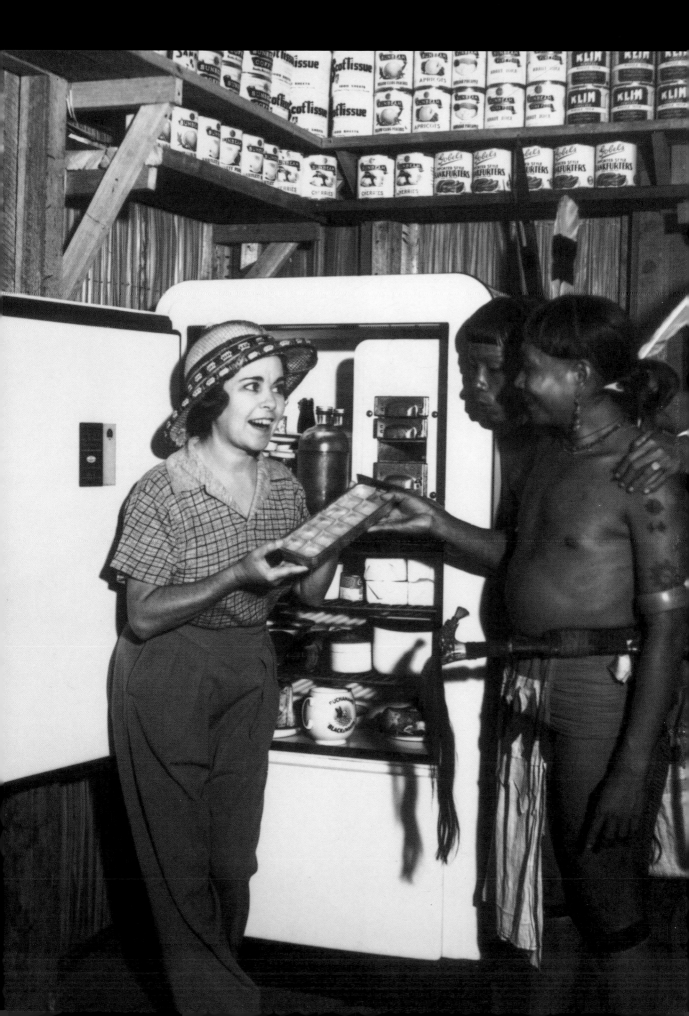

Frances Flaherty, *Moana: A Romance of the Golden Age*, ca. 1925. Gelatin silver print, 11 x 13 in. (27.9 x 33.2 cm).
Claremont School of Theology, The Robert and Frances Flaherty Collection.

Facing page:
Unidentified photographer, *Unidentified group of military, probably sailors, posed at a waterfall with native women*, ca. 1895.
Gelatin silver print, 7 15/16 x 5 15/16 in. (20.0 x 14.2 cm). George Eastman House, Rochester, New York.

Laura Aguilar, *Nature Self-Portrait #12*, 1996. Gelatin silver print, 16 x 20 in. (40.6 x 50.8 cm). Courtesy of the artist and Susanne Vielmetter Los Angeles Projects.

Edward Weston, *Nude on Dunes*, 1939. Gelatin silver print, 7 1/2 x 9 7/16 in. (18.9 x 24.1 cm). Center for Creative Photography, University of Arizona, Tuscon.

Timothy O' Sullivan, *Wagon Darkroom in the Carson Desert, Nevada*, ca. 1868. Albumen print, 7 3/4 x 10 5/8 in. (19.7 x 27 cm).

National Archives, Washington, D.C., Records of the Office of the Chief of Engineers.

Carleton E. Watkins, *Cape Horn Near Celilo, Oregon*, 1867. Albumen print, 25 $^3/_4$ x 29 $^1/_2$ in. (65.5 x 74.9 cm). Stanford University Library, Department of Special Collections.

William S. Prettyman, *Race into the Cherokee Outlet, Ten Seconds After the Gun, Sept. 16, 1893,* 1893. Postcard, 3 ¹/₂ x 5 ¹/₂ in. (9 x 14 cm). Oklahoma Historical Society, Oklahoma City, Archives and Manuscripts Division, Thomas N. Athey Collection.

Herbert J. Spinden, *Green Corn Dance, Santo Domingo Pueblo*, ca. 1920. Cyanotype, 3 $^1/_2$ x 4 $^1/_2$ in. (8.9 x 11.4 cm).
Southwest Museum, Los Angeles.

Unidentified photographer, *Atomic Cloud during Baker Day Blast at Bikini, July 25, 1946*, 1946. Gelatin silver print, 7 $1/2$ x 9 $1/4$ in. (19 x 23.5 cm). National Archives.

Richard Misrach, *Bravo 20 (Crater and Destroyed Convoy)*, 1986. Color photograph, 40 x 50 in. (101.6 x 127 cm). Courtesy of Robert Mann Gallery, New York.

Ignacio Lang, *Interview with a Landscape, Las Acacias*, 2000. Chromogenic print, 24 x 30 in. (60.9 x 76.2 cm). Courtesy of the artist.

O. Winston Link, *Hot Shot East Bound at Lager W. Virginia*, 1956. Gelatin silver print, 16 x 20 in. (40.6 x 50.8 cm). Courtesy of Robert Mann Gallery, New York.

Caroline Vercoe

WHERE TRUTH ENDS AND FANTASY BEGINS

Postcards from the South Pacific

The landing craft roared in over the green and lucid shallows. . . . The door dropped and the sergeant led his men forward in a stumbling rush. . . . They dropped on the sandward side of the logs. Behind them other men carried the tripod of a 50-caliber machine gun…Nothing stirred. Rucinski said: "Jeez! The air boys was right. No Japs!…Where's Dorothy Lamour?" [a native appears on the beach:] "It's a nigger, sergeant. Shall I let him have it?"…The brown figure was coming towards them slowly….His hand swept over his mouth, and he said slowly, pulling out the syllable, "Guten Morgen." "Christ!" said Rucinski. "No Dorothy Lamour and a nigger that speaks German!"
—David Divine, *The King of Fassarai*[1]

Who's to say where truth ends and fantasy begins?
—Esther Williams as Mimi in *Pagan Love Song*, 1950

During World War II, hundreds of thousands of U.S. troops and war workers were stationed around the Pacific. With them came thousands of cameras, and an abundance of photographs were taken for official and private use. No doubt many of the troops would have been well aware that "Paradise" was more fiction than fact, however this did not stop a huge number of photographs being taken that staged and enacted exoticized, Hollywood-style stereotypes. Popular images of the Pacific seen on postcards or in "Paciflicks" such as *Mutiny on the Bounty* (1935), *Bird of Paradise* (1932), and *Waikiki Wedding* (1937), no doubt influenced their perceptions of the Islands.[2] Fueled with this stock of mythologized popular images, many photos effectively blended the real with the imaginary. Today these stereotypes remain firmly entrenched in the collective American popular imagination. The archetypal native, in particular the "hula girl," was a great favorite. She was featured in a vast number of wartime mementos that were staged and photographed by countless GIs and carried back home to adorn walls, wallets, and photo albums. The images have left a legacy of cross-cultural encounters between servicemen and Pacific Islanders that reflected a myriad of truths and fantasies, metanarratives that blended Hollywood legend and invention with firsthand experiences. These pictures of a Pacific paradise contrasted wildly with actual experiences.

1. David Divine (*The King of the Fassarai*, New York: Macmillan, 1950) as quoted in Lamont Lindstrom and Geoff White, *Island Encounters: Black and White Memories of the Pacific War* (Washington, D.C.: Smithsonian Institution Press, 1990), p. 173.
2. Paciflicks are Hollywood movies set in the South Seas. Hollywood's fascination with the Pacific was well established as early as the 1920s, with figures such as Clara Bow and Betty Compson popularizing the hula girl figure in *Hula* (1927) and *The White Flower* (1923). Dorothy Lamour and Jon Hall would go on in the 1930s to be crowned Hollywood's Sarong Girl and Boy.

Unidentified photographer, *Tourists photographing hula show in Waikiki, Honolulu, Hawaii*, ca. 1960. Gelatin silver print, 10 x 8 in. (25.4 x 20.3 cm). Bishop Museum, Honolulu, Hawaii, Laurence Hata Collection.

Since the end of the nineteenth century, America has played an important imperial role in the Pacific. Islands such as the Hawaiian and Eastern Samoan groups held great strategic importance both geographically and commercially. By 1899, the United States had gained dominance over shipping lanes in the Pacific, taking control of Hawaii, Samoa, and the Philippines.[3] In 1898, Hawaii, which formed a natural defense line for the Californian coast, was officially annexed by the United States, and in 1959 became its fiftieth state.[4] The U.S. naval base at Pago Pago, on the island of Tutuila in Eastern Samoa (also known as American Samoa) was important to American interests. Its deep-sea harbor provided a strategic naval base and port for submarines.[5] By 1942, there was one U.S. marine to every six Samoans. Hawaii, in particular, experienced a huge influx of war-related personnel. According to cultural historians David Farber and Beth Bailey, "[H]undreds of thousands of servicemen and war workers spent some significant length of time in Hawaii, and at least a million passed through the islands where the civilian population in 1940 had been only 258,000."[6]

One of the by-products of war was the establishment of a plethora of entertainment and service-related industries that catered to the armed forces. Many women for instance, made a good income from washing soldiers' laundry. Other industries ranged from hot dog and sandwich stands to cinemas, photographic studios, brothels, and hotels. Young men and women were paid in cash for wage-based labor, thus circumventing village and tribal hegemonies. Sexual encounters led to a number of children born with mixed cultural heritage. In *Hawaii Goes to War*, Desoto Brown quotes a Hawaiian local during the war as saying that "some Japanese girls believe it is 'patriotic' to have the babies of our white soldiers."[7] He goes on to say that divorce rates doubled and there was a marked increase in illegitimate births. Wartime occupation in the Pacific also led to the establishment of roads, airports, hospitals, supply bases, and recreation centers, often providing an infrastructure around which urban areas would develop. It also proved to be very important for the development of tourism.

The vast majority of Americans at this time would not have experienced much overseas travel. Traveling abroad prior to the 1940s was very much the domain of the affluent. For instance, before World War II, Hawaii was a tourist playground for the rich and famous. Celebrities would arrive aboard cruise liners and stay at plush five-star hotels. The war, however, put an end to these halcyon days. Luxury Matson cruise liners were stripped and converted for war service. Barbed-wire blanketed Waikiki beach and the famous Hawaiian lei makers set down their flowers and took to weaving camouflage nets to cover civic and

3. See Jean Heffer, *The United States and the Pacific: History or a Frontier*, trans. W. Donald Wilson (Notre Dame, IN.: University of Notre Dame Press, 2002), p. 191.
4. Pre-World War II, many Americans were unaware of its relevance. In a poll taken in 1939, more Americans preferred to defend Canada rather than Hawaii if invaded and a large number did not know where Hawaii was, let alone that the U.S. had annexed it. Desoto Brown, *Hawaii Goes to War: Life in Hawaii from Pearl Harbor to Peace* (Honolulu: Editions Limited, 1989), p. 110.
5. The Japanese attacked Pago Pago, along with Pearl Harbor in 1941, however, it did not sustain major damage or casualties. Samoa was also a staging area for campaigns in the Gilbert (now Kiribati) and Marshall Islands. See Robert W. Franco, "Samoan Representations of World War II and Military Work: The Emergence of International Movement Networks" in *The Pacific Theatre: Island Representations of World War II*, ed. Geoffrey M. White and Lamont Lindstrom (Honolulu: University of Hawaii Press, 1989), pp. 373-394.
6. David Farber and Beth Bailey, "The Fighting Man as Tourist: The Politics of Tourist Culture in Hawaii during World War II" in *Pacific Historical Review* 65, no.4 (Nov. 1996): 7.
7. Desoto Brown, *Hawaii Goes to War*, p. 137.

Edward Steichen, *Advertisement for Matson Cruise Line*, November 1, 1941. *Vogue* magazine, inside back cover, 12 1/2 x 9 1/2 in. (31.7 x 24.1 cm). Courtesy of Vogue, Condé Nast Publications Inc., with permission of Joanna T. Steichen.

Fritz Kraft, *Hula Dancer Erotica (Jojo), Honolulu, Hawaii*, ca. 1940s. Gelatin silver print, 4 $\frac{1}{2}$ x 2 $\frac{1}{2}$ in. (10.8 x 6 cm). Private collection.

strategic buildings. Lands were seized and quickly converted into military camps and housing, while five-star hotels were taken over to serve as leisure centers and provide accommodations for resting troops. By the end of the war, over 200,000 U.S. Navy personnel had stayed at the "R. & R. annex, submarine Base, Pearl Harbor, Rest and Recreation," formally known as the Royal Hawaiian, where they could sleep "in one-time $40 and $50 suites for 25¢ a night."[8] While the war office strove to project Hawaii as a kind of tourist spot for the military, general consensus was that the vast majority of servicemen were mightily disappointed by the lack of women and exotic experiences in paradise.[9] Nightly blackouts, rationing, the vast outnumbering of men to women, and other facts of life imposed by martial law—which lasted for a record-breaking three years—resulted in a strict and often monotonous routine.

When paradise did not measure up, the servicemen often staged their own Hollywood-style scenes in ironic faux reenactments. Photographic studios were set up where GIs could have their picture taken with generic hula girls, who often turned out to be Filipino. In the popular Hawaiian monthly magazine *Paradise of the Pacific*, the popularity of these images did not go unnoticed:

> *Your picture: taken in three minutes with a background drop of Diamond Head on real sand, posed with a happy hula girl, all done up in the best Coney Island style.... Posing with a hula girl is a top attraction on Hotel Street, with a crowd of civilians and service men always present to watch the amusing proceedings. Destination of the picture is unknown, although some are undoubtedly sent to tease the best girl at home, or shock a doting aunt. Others are kept in wallets as mementos of Hawaii.*[10]

These photos belie the incredible gender imbalance in the Islands. Some accounts suggest that men outnumbered women by up to a thousand to one.[11] Dances held at army recreation centers, attended by thousands of men and only thirty or forty women were not uncommon.[12]

> *Lonely men far from home responded to warm Hawaiian alohas and mobbed recreation dances and USOs, where local girls danced with them under strict supervision. At Fort DeRussy the Maluhia ballroom held up to 1,200 people, but occasionally 10,000 men arrived hoping to dance with one of the 100 to 300 local girls who volunteered their time.*[13]

Searching for fun or something to do, thousands of servicemen and war workers crowded the Waikiki area and Honolulu's Red Light District in China Town and Hotel Street, often lining up for hours

8. Ibid., p. 141.

9. See Farber and Bailey, "The Fighting Man as Tourist," pp. 241–261.

10. Bob Dye, ed., "Hotel Street, the Service Man's Domain" in *Hawaii Chronicles III: World War Two in Hawaii, from the pages of Paradise of the Pacific* (Honolulu: University of Hawaii Press, 2000; first published in October 1943), p. 148.

11. This gender imbalance resulted in much tension among servicemen and war workers and no doubt accounted for the thriving trade done in local brothels. It could also account for racist rumors that circulated around Hawaii. Farber and Bailey offer anecdotal evidence of Southern white servicemen spreading rumors prior to the arrival of over 30,000 African American war workers and military that African American men had tails and that if local women fell pregnant to any of them, they would give birth to monkeys. They contend that this most likely resulted in a general fear of African Americans by locals and a refusal by women to socialize with them. See Beth Bailey and David Farber, "The 'Double-V' Campaign in World War II Hawaii: African Americans, Racial Ideology, and Federal Power," in *Journal of Social History* 26, no. 4 (Summer 1993): 817–44.

12. See Beth Bailey and David Farber, *The First Strange Place: Race and Sex in World War II Hawaii* (Baltimore: The Johns Hopkins University Press, 1992).

13. Paul Berry and Edgy Lee, *Waikiki: In the Wake of Dreams* (China: Filmworks Press, 2000), p. 93.

outside brothels, shops, and bars. Packets of black-and-white photographs could be purchased in brown envelopes entitled "Scenic Hawaii" and "Hawaiian Beauties," and featured a mix of generic tropical landscapes as well as images of young women in seminude poses.

> On every corner, photographers crowded the sidewalks with their box cameras, grass huts, and cardboard palm-tree backgrounds: "Two picture with Hula Girl— 75 cents." The rumor was that for $20 you could get an overnight deal with the girl of your choice. Like most rumors, it wasn't true. But the men lined up.[14]

Not surprisingly, prostitution flourished in Honolulu during this time. The demand was such that it became semilegalized. Sex workers paid an annual fee of one dollar to the local police department to be registered and they operated from a number of brothels or "hotels" in the Hotel Street and China Town area in downtown Honolulu. Farber and Bailey claim that, "close to 250,000 men a month paid three dollars for three minutes of the only intimacy most were going to find in Honolulu."[15]

Another common image taken by GIs throughout the Pacific, which also happened to be a favorite of enemy Japanese forces, was the "going native" shot. Indigenous ceremonial dress and adornments would be borrowed or bought from locals and troops would dress "indigene," sometimes adding their own touches for effect. These photos, like the hula girl images, bought into a kind of exoticized myth-making that belied crucial and important interrelationships between the troops and Pacific Islanders. They also worked to fix Islanders into a timeless paradigm, erasing any signs of acculturation or change. Stereotypes of a Hollywood-style other were telescoped into the Pacific, where they were either restaged with Islanders or reenacted by troops. Far from being Edenic natives watching the war unfold before them, however, Islanders often played crucial roles as engineers, carpenters, coast watchers, and service workers. Many donated money and purchased war bonds as a symbol of their allegiance. Thousands fought side-by-side with allied forces and suffered significant casualties. In Papua, New Guinea, Melanesian fighters were nicknamed "fuzzy-wuzzy angels" by Australian forces due to the role they played rescuing and looking after troops. Islanders also worked on beach patrols, often behind enemy lines, risking their own lives for the Allied cause. Often this loyalty did have economic agendas. White tells of Solomon Islanders capturing Japanese troops, marching them to U.S. camps and selling them to the Americans for one packet of cigarettes each.[16]

The war also generated a spate of GI genre Paciflicks, including *South Pacific* (1958) and *Return to Paradise* (1953). They were crucial in

A Haole Hula Girl
PHOTO BY BAKER HONOLULU

14. Bailey and Farber, *The First Strange Place*, p. 96.
15. Ibid., p. 95.
16. Another favorite pose often photographed was of American and Pacific troops lighting cigarettes for each other.

Baker Studio, Ray Jerome Baker, *A Haole Hula Girl (Rose Heather), Hawaii*, ca. 1920. Postcard, 5 1/4 x 3 1/2 in. (14.0 x 8.9 cm). Bishop Museum, Honolulu, Hawaii, General Postcard Collection.

making Polynesia a fantasy space for Westerners. Anne Friedberg has suggested that film allowed a form of virtual travel that blended fantasy and reality. She argues for a mobilized virtual gaze, a viewing dynamic in which people could virtually travel to foreign and exotic places via the cinema screen.[17] Movies substituted for more conventional forms of learning, such as libraries and archives, and their blend of fact and the imaginary provided new points of departure, in relation to viewers' constructions of foreign places.[18] Photographs can function in a similar way. Friedberg alludes to Baudelaire's notion that photography is more an agent of forgetting than remembering history.[19] She sees cinema as functioning in a similar fashion. The myriad of photos taken of servicemen with hula girls and dressed as "natives" also had more to do with forgetting than documenting their wartime experiences, and offered a brief respite from harrowing fighting and the prospect of death. They represent a telescoping of popular culture and Hollywood fancy into the Pacific, staging moments that could have come straight from Paciflick narratives.

The image of the Pacific as phantasm, a kind of exotic and sensual siren for romantic and wayward Westerners, has a long history. World War II, however, brought servicemen and war workers into the Islands on a scale not encountered before and their firsthand experiences did not always translate into the photographs that they took. Many preferred Hollywood's version. Ironically, many Islanders also assimilated the popular American versions of the Pacific into their own cultural practice. For instance, grass skirts were only worn in certain parts of the Pacific. They were, however, in great demand by GI tourists throughout the Islands and were quickly manufactured en mass to become a standard currency in present-day tourism. While popular images taken by servicemen during the war do not have a strong presence in museum collections, they have contributed to an entrenching of exoticized stereotypes that shape U.S. perceptions of Polynesia in the present. Where paradise did not exist, it could be enacted through cultural crossdressing or evoked for a small fee.

17. In the 1920s, the average U.S. movie audience numbered over 25 million per week, and by the 1930s this number had reached up to 110 million.
18. Anne Friedberg, *Window Shopping: Cinema and the Postmodern* (Berkeley: University of California Press, 1993).
19. Ibid., p. 182.

Nate R. Farbman, *Shirley Temple dancing a hula while visiting Honolulu, Hawaii*, 1935. Gelatin silver print, 10 x 8 in. (25.4 x 20.3 cm). Bishop Museum, Honolulu, Hawaii, N. R. Farbman Collection.

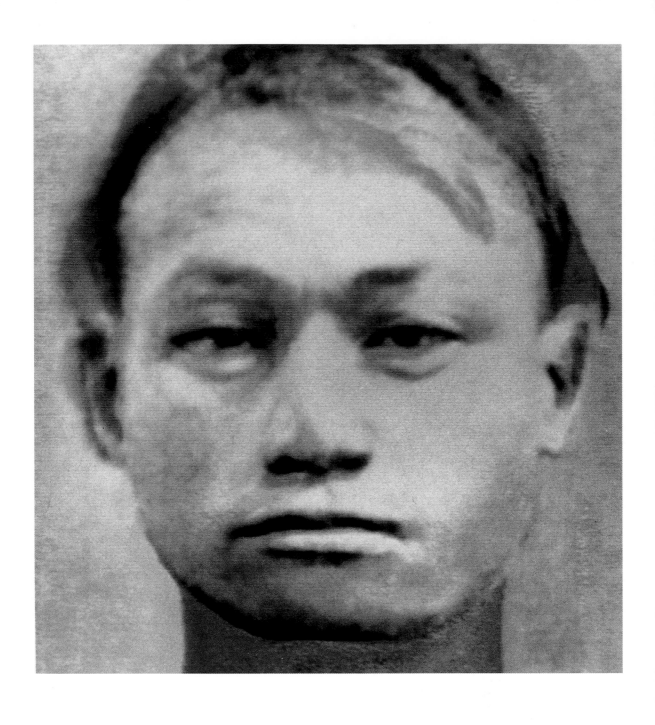

Jennifer González

MORPHOLOGIES

Race as a Visual Technology

Truth effects

As recording device, the medium of photography has always been allied with truth claims: as evidence in courts of law, as the necessary supplement to historical narratives, as the existential proof for the passing of time, or as the unquestioned framework for what might be called the family romance. Historians and theorists have engaged critically with this "truth effect" of photography for over a century, assessing the cultural investment in the indexical quality of the image and the connotations of naturalism that it implies.[1] And nearly every generation of artists has found the interrogation or dismantling of this "truth effect" to be a primary means to engage the medium.

Yet, with every new form of photographic image production, whether analog or digital, a cry goes out in the name of "truth" against subversive forms of manipulation or deception. This cry usually issues from those whose faith in documentary and journalistic image production has not yet been shaken, or from those who hold fast to a belief in the strategic deployment of visual evidence for the sake of larger political and historical concerns. As family snapshots, work-related information exchange, or artistic medium, the easily circulated, digitally produced image no longer has the aura of the new or—perhaps more importantly—the authentic. In this context of mass image production and exchange, questions of verisimilitude seem quaintly out of date. By the mid-nineties a number of anthologies and exhibition catalogues, notably *The Photographic Image in Digital Culture* (1995) and *Photography After Photography: Memory and Representation in the Digital Age* (1996)—offered cogent analyses of the domain of digital photography and its cultural context. Scholars and artists agreed that digital photography is no less and no more susceptible to distortion than its analog counterpart. Similarly, many found that technological or material differences in the new medium do little to change the social effect and cultural function of "realist" images and their "truth effect."[2]

In the era of digital photography and digital art, a photograph is not only anything that *looks like* a photograph but also anything that *acts* like a photograph insofar as it produces a photographic *effect*. Of course, as both historians and practitioners know, the truth effect of photography has real consequences—even when the image lies. Photography, as this exhibition makes clear, played and still plays a central role in the maintenance of a discourse of visibility and the norms it prescribes. This is its rhetorical power and its ideological advantage.[3]

When considering the history of photography and the history of race discourse, it becomes apparent not only that these two histories are intimately interdependent but also that a conceptual parallel exists

1. See, among others, Roland Barthes "Rhetoric of the Image" in *Image/Music/Text* (New York: Hill and Wang, 1977).
2. For other discussions of the photographic image in digital culture, see *Digital Photography: Captured Images, Volatile Memory, New Montage* (San Francisco: SF Camerawork, 1988); *Impossible Presence: Surface and Screen in the Photogenic Era* (Chicago: University of Chicago Press, 2001); *Each Wild Idea: Writing, Photography, History* (2001); Peter Lunenfeld, *Snap to Grid: A User's Guide to Digital Arts, Media, and Cultures* (Cambridge: MIT Press, 2000).
3. Martha Rosler, "Image Simulations, Computer Manipulations: Some Considerations," in *Photography After Photography: Memory and Representation in the Digital Age* (Amsterdam: G+B Arts, 1996).

Nancy Burson, *Three Major Races (an Oriental, a Caucasian, and a Black)*, from the "Mankind" series, 1982. Gelatin silver print, 8 1/2 x 7 1/2 in. (21.5 x 19 cm). Courtesy of the artist and Yossi Milo Gallery, New York.

between the "truth effects" of photography and what might be called the "truth effects" of race. Both kinds of "truth effects" naturalize ideological systems by making them visible and, apparently, self-evident. As with photography, the visual or visible elements of race function to produce truth effects that appear natural. In her essay for this catalogue, Coco Fusco has argued persuasively that there is no visual truth about race. But it is also the case that concepts of race and ethnicity have historically been inseparable from a discourse of display and from the logic of vision. Skin color, hair color, and eye color become marking devices for those who seek to situate the genetic history of humans within the narrow confines of phenotype. Race has always been a profoundly visual rhetoric, evidence of which can be found in the complex vocabularies developed to delineate social hierarchies based on variations in skin color and phenotype over the last few centuries.

In the Americas, for example, sexual reproduction became the site in which the normative condition of hybridity and miscegenation gave rise to a powerfully hierarchical caste system subsequently codified in the arts. In New Spain (Mexico) of the eighteenth century, the tradition of *casta* paintings codified the visual effects of racial mixing by depicting racially distinct parents along with their *mestizo* children. Each painting is inscribed with the ethnic or racial make-up of the mother, the father, and the children, for example, "A Spanish father and an African mother produces a Mulatto child." The categories were elaborate and precise, including variations such as the *criollo*, *mestizo*, *castizo*, *mulato*, *morisco*, *coyote*, *lobo*, *zambo*, and *torna-atras*, among others.[4] Given the passion for scientific categorization during the Enlightenment and the colonial imperative for an artificial means of creating class structure, this elaborate codification is not surprising. Rendered in paint it becomes a striking example of the deep desire to produce a parallel *visual* tabulation of racial hybridity and its physical characteristics. The very concept that a body possesses or reveals a *color* is indebted to the privileging of vision and its attendant systems of representation that measure and quantify the subtle differences of skin hue and tone. Of course, this desire to map the *visible* characteristics of race in a hierarchical taxonomy recurs in photography under the guise of eugenics and now reappears in the automated morphing technologies applied to digital images.

It becomes clear when looking at these and other historical precedents that race has long been an importantly *visual* system of power whose parameters have been the focus of every innovation in visual recording devices. As with photography, the visual "truth effect" of race has also played an important role, socially and culturally, as the necessary supplement to historical narratives, as existential evidence,

4. For an excellent discussion of *castas* paintings, see Maria Concepcion Garcia Saiz, *Las Castas Mexicanas: Un Género Pictórico Americano* (Italy: Olivetti, 1989).

or as the unquestioned framework for the family romance. And as with photography, the visual truth effect of race has very real consequences even if the "facts" about race as a category or discourse reveal it to be primarily an ideological construction.

The concept and lived experience of race are entwined in a discourse of *visibility* that enables subsequent forms of hierarchy or oppression to become naturalized, that enables membership in communities to be established, and that enables categorical distinctions to become reified. In *Against Race*, Paul Gilroy notes, "Cognition of 'race' was never an exclusively linguistic process and involved from its inception a distinctive visual and optical imaginary. The sheer plenitude of racialized images and icons communicates something about the forms of difference these discourses summoned into being."[5] Race, in all its historical complexity, is not an invention of visual culture but, among the ways in which race as a system of power is elaborated as both *evident* and *self-evident*, its visual articulation is one of the most significant.

This essay examines the work of contemporary artists who explore the history and maintenance of the visual discourse of race through digital art practice—particularly but not exclusively digital photography.

Morphology

Despite—and perhaps because of—its historical links to eugenics and the delimiting of racial and criminal types, the composite photograph inherited from the experiments of Francis Galton in the nineteenth century has been the focus of exploration and transformation by contemporary artists working in the tradition of portraiture. Nancy Burson's composite photographs of the 1980s offered a new kind of visual typology by overlaying facial features of cinema stars or politicians to highlight their common traits, or by creating imaginary visual correlates to numerical statistics. Her 1984 image *Mankind* is a composite portrait of three faces weighted according to demographic information about a world population that was "57 percent Oriental, 7 percent Black and 36 percent White." Three "typical" faces are presented as an anonymous computational portrait of a single individual. Its collapsing of normally distinct racial categories was intended as an antiracist gesture, but Burson's effort nevertheless comes across as strangely anachronistic.

In fact, the line between the critique of racial typologies and their reproduction is one that is difficult to draw in Burson's work. Her recent project, the *Human Race Machine* (2002), combines a sophisticated, viewing-booth apparatus with a "patented technology" that will transform the user's photographic image using one of four different

5. Paul Gilroy, *Against Race* (Cambridge, Mass.: Harvard University Press, 2000), p. 35.
6. Vilém Flusser, "Nancy Burson: Chimaeras" in *Photography After Photography*, p. 152. See also, Allan Sekula, "The Body and the Archive" in *The Contest of Meaning: Critical Histories of Photography* (Cambridge, Mass.: MIT Press, 1989).

algorithms: *Age Machine*, *Anomaly Machine*, *Couples Machine*, and *Human Race Machine*. One has the choice of aging one's face, adding disfigurations, combining one's face with another person's, or seeing oneself with the facial characteristics of six different races. Burson claims that the *Human Race Machine* is her "prayer for racial equality" and suggests, "there is only one race, the human one." Presenting the argument that "there is no gene for race" the *Human Race Machine* allows the user to engage in what Lisa Nakamura might call identity tourism. Nakamura writes, "Identity tourism is a type of nonreflective relationship that actually widens the gap between the other and the one who only performs itself *as the other* in the medium of cyberspace."[7] Burson's machine takes a picture of the user and then digitally adjusts bone structure, skin tone, and eye shape in order to achieve a range of racially marked facial features. "The more we recognize ourselves in others," Burson writes, "the more we can connect to the human race." The artist also claims "The *Human Race Machine* allows us to move beyond differences and arrive at sameness."[8] Despite her good intentions, I want to ask, who counts as "us"? Is sameness really where "we" want to arrive? Despite Burson's promise of greater human sameness, the *Human Race Machine* appears to offer satisfaction for a thinly veiled fantasy of *difference*. As form of temporary racial tourism Burson's machine may make the process of cross-racial identification appear plausible, but its artificiality does nothing to change how people live their lives or understand their historical condition.

The technology used by Burson is based in earlier experiments in digital morphing seen first by the mainstream public in Michael Jackson's music video *Black or White* (1991) where he sings:

> *It's a turf war on a global scale/I'd rather hear both sides of the tale/See, it's not about races/Just places/ Faces/Where your blood comes from/Is were your space is/I've seen the bright get duller/I'm not going to spend my life being a color/[...] I said if you're thinkin' of being my baby/It don't matter if you're black or white/I said if you're thinkin' of being my brother/It don't matter if you're black or white [...]*

Throughout the video Jackson's own face morphs in quick, smooth and seamless succession into the faces of men and women of different "races." The uncanny visual transitions are both disturbing and fascinating. One face transforms into the next as if undergoing a physical metamorphosis in which skin and bone are stretched and molded, hair and eyes grow and change. Although each person and racial type appears distinct from the next, the video also suggests that a melding, mixing, or hybridization is taking place in real time—a transformation

7. Lisa Nakamura, *Cybertypes* (New York: Routledge, 2002) p. 57. Emphasis added.
8. http://www.wolfmanproductions.com/racemachine.html

that appears to be entirely the result of the power of the image apparatus. As Peter Lunenfeld suggests, "As we move into the digital, the
aesthetics of form become more and more involved in the aesthetics
of mutable form."9

Morphing quickly became a popular graphical technique in digital
image processing because of the seemingly magical way the computational remix of images provided the truth effect of a real photograph.
Donna Haraway, writing about Morph 2.0 by Gryphon Software designed
for the personal computer, suggests "This technology has proved irre-
sistible in the United States for 1990s mass cultural, racialized kinship
discourse on human unity and diversity."10 The truth effect of photography not only visually demonstrated but also mechanically mimicked
the truth effect of race through an automated process of digital gene-
sis. In the fall of 1993 the canonical image of this renaissance emerged
on the cover of *Time* magazine, for its special issue on "How immigrants
are shaping the world's first multicultural society." "Take a good look
at this woman," reads the text on the cover next to the face of a young
woman, "She was created by a computer from a mix of several races.

9. Lunenfeld, *Snap to Grid*, p. 65.
10. Donna Haraway,
Modest_Witness@Second_Mellinium.
FemaleMan_Meets_OncoMouse™,
(New York: Routledge, 1997), p. 261.

Time, *Special Issue: The New Face of America*, Fall 1993. Photo: Ted Thai; computer morphing: Kin Wah Lam;
design: Walter Bernard and Milton Glaser. Magazine. Private Collection.

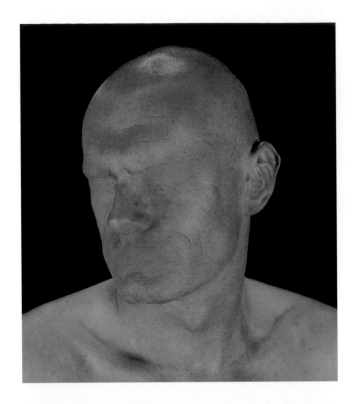

Aziz + Cucher, *Chris*, 1994; *Maria*, 1994. Digitally altered chromogenic prints, each 50 x 40 in. (127 x 101.6 cm).
Courtesy of the artists and Henry Urbach Architecture, New York.

What you see is a remarkable preview of…The New Face of America."
Responding to the image, Haraway writes, "In an odd computerized
updating of the typological categories of the nineteenth and early
twentieth centuries, the programmer who gave birth to SimEve and
her many siblings generated the ideal racial synthesis, whose only
possible existence is in the matrices of cyberspace."[11] Also serving as
an ideological reprise of the *casta* paintings from New Spain nearly
four centuries later, *Time* magazine's new technological hybrid apparently neutralizes the hierarchies of the past with an artificial, clinical
birth in the present, implying that computation is the proper locus
and mode of a new racial mixing. In this Pygmalion fantasy, Haraway
argues, the microchip and the computer program displace the human
being as the origin of life.[12]

Such creationist desires to reformulate the human body abound
in digital photography, some celebratory and others explicitly critical.
Aziz+Cucher's "Dystopia" series of portraits in which human heads are
devoid of any expressive feature or orifice represents a loss of personal
identity that occurs as a result of new forms of digital communication.
The artists write that "With the erasure of the primary facial features—
eyes, nose, mouth, etc.—we intend to suggest an evolutionary change
signifying the loss of individuality in the face of advancing technology
and the progressive disappearance of face to face human interaction."[13]
Looking like unformed creatures in a larval state, the portraits they
construct are disturbingly blank yet remarkably individual. They elicit
the uncanny, eerie sensation of seeing a body caught in the tragic
limbo of genetic error. The unfinished subject, the underdeveloped
social and sensory apparatus, signals the emptiness of the body as
signifier in a world of digitally mediated communication.

Similarly disturbing are the works of Inez van Lamsweerde whose
slick fashion portraits use digital graphics to unsettle expectations of
both gender and age, addressing the sexual politics that makes us read
bodies as desirable or untouchable. Smooth bodies without orifices,
the hands, lips, and eyes of men, women, and children compiled into
single portraits offer a dreamlike condensation of a forbidden unconscious imaginary. "Using the computer to quote plastic surgery,"
writes Collier Schorr, "Van Lamsweerde one-ups the practices of
beautification, suggesting that our preoccupation with perfection
brings us close to science fiction. She also mimics a male desire to
mother by producing a race technologically rather than physically."[14]
Schorr also implies that by working exclusively with "white" bodies,
Van Lamsweerde reveals a white aesthetic that (oppressive or not)
becomes a Western European default for "flesh." She suggests that
"despite their perfect dimensions, her figure's nudity is blank, spongy,

11. Ibid., p. 259.
12. Ibid., p. 261.
13. Aziz+Cucher, *Prospect: Photography
in Contemporary Art* (Frankfurt am Main:
Editions Stemmle, 1996), p. 36.
14. Collier Schorr, "Openings," in
Photography After Photography, p. 214.

their Philip Pearlstein Caucasian flesh humming like a human dooms-day machine."[15]

Paul Pfeiffer's *Leviathan* references whiteness differently. In a digital Chromogenic print, the artist delineates the floor plan of a cathedral in a shimmering outline of pink plastic doll flesh sprouting shiny abundant waves of golden hair. As if rising from a sea or carpet of platinum tresses, this architecturally morphed close-up image of the heads of Mattel dolls looks like a wound or a scar branded on the skin.[16] A leviathan is a Biblical beast, a many-headed serpent that represents a mythical monster eventually slain by the sword of Job. Also the title of Thomas Hobbes's philosophical account of the state's rule over the ills of human nature, *Leviathan* in Pfeiffer's work seems to imply the dynamics of colonial and missionary culture that have ruled over others through ideological and racial domination. Originally exhibited in a solo show called "The Pure Products Go Crazy, " Pfeiffer's *Leviathan* links Christianity to notions of extreme purity, whether moral or racial,

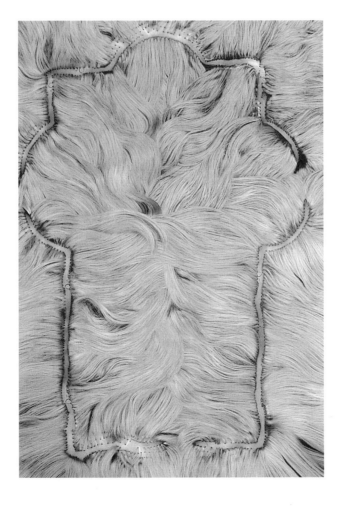

15. Ibid.
16. Franklin Sirmans, "Get a Little Closer," *Artnet.com*, reviews, December 17, 1998.

Paul Pfeiffer, *Leviathan*, 1998. Digital chromogenic print, 36 x 84 in. (91.4 x 213.4 cm). Courtesy of The Project, New York.

which have finally reached a condition of corruption. Much of Pfeiffer's work engages the complex layers of human relations that are at the nexus of mass culture, race, and religious culture in the United States. His use of digital photography produces a shift in the materiality of the visual tropes of race, extending beyond the human body to include the history of architecture and other domains of social spectacle. By equating skin with architecture Pfeiffer asks us to consider the kinds of "pattern language" produced in the historical relations between bodies, religion, and the mapping of space.

Color balance

Technologies of visualization such as photography, film, and video have been mutually constitutive with conceptions of race. It is possible to observe this fact by tracing how technologies of image making have been invented and adapted to the purpose of better elaborating or accommodating racial discourses.[17] Racial hegemony informs the design and use of these technologies, and in turn racial discourse is articulated and defined by them. This feedback loop is rarely acknowledged in studies of the history of photography and other visual media despite the fact that visual recording devices have never been racially neutral. Artist François Bucher's recent digital video work *White Balance* that ties the condition of racial privilege and the production of visual culture in mass media to the politics of global, economic domination, brilliantly illustrates this fact. His title derives from the process by which the digital pixels in the recording device are automatically balanced for the color white. Although the balance is based on the color spectrum, the notion of white balance in Bucher's work refers to white skin color as simultaneously a *cultural* and *technological* default in the United States. It is possible to see how the tradition of photography might be similarly "balanced." Even on a superficial level, the culture of photographic practice is understood to be shaped by the technical capabilities of the medium. New York Institute of Photography's "Tips for Better Photographers" claims, "There is probably no question in portraiture that is more confusing to beginning photographers than how to photograph people with black skin."[18] If black skin creates "confusion" it is because neither the original design of the apparatus, nor common techniques for its use have taken blackness, or other nonwhite skin colors as a standard. [19]

Skin, with all its registers of meaning for the history of race, has also become the focus of questions of color and code in digital art practice. Alba D'Urbano, an Italian artist, used digital imaging techniques available in 1995 to produce a life-sized photographic representation of her own body. Printed on a tailor's pattern, the resulting

17. Stephen Jay Gould, *The Mismeasure of Man* (New York: Norton, 1996); *Colonialist Photography: Imag(in)ing Race and Place* (London: Routledge, 2002), etc.

18. New York Institute of Photography, www.nyip.com/tips/topic_peopleofcolor-0602.php, 2003.

19. Other amateur web sites offer instruction for digitally transforming the "yellow" tones in photographic images of Asians so they will have a rosier glow. Carl Volk's "Color Balancing Skin Tones," (http://www.carlvolk.com/photoshop 18.htm), reveals inherent racial bias when he writes, "In the photo of Christina above that beautiful China doll skin tone color may or may not be entirely *accurate* but the effect is very appealing—it looks (and feels) right." To change a skin color so that it "looks (and feels) right" begs the question of the cultural framework within which one can decide what a "right" skin color might be.

24 People for
Have
Been Mistaken

output was used to create a wearable suit of her own "skin." She writes "The thought of being able to slip out of my own skin for a moment and offer it to another person gave rise to the idea of making a suit out of my own two-dimensional image. This suit would offer others the opportunity, as it were, of walking through the world hidden 'under the skin' of the artist."[20] Somewhat oblivious to the questions of race and passing that lie imbedded in her project, D'Urbano sought to address the idea of the body *as an image* reduced to a passive shell.[21] Digital photography acts in the service of a costume that "defines the contour of the image which forms on the retina of another person."[22] D'Urbano's project grasps the degree to which the subject is always *an image for an other*, and tries to literally slip out of this skin—this image—and imagine it as little more than a costume for exchange.

In a very different kind of project that engages a parallel discourse, artist Keith Townsend Obadike, proposed to sell his "Blackness" on the commercial auction web site *eBay* in August 2001. Although the

20. Alba D'Urbano, "The Project: Hautnah, or Close to the Skin" in *Photography After Photography*, p. 270.
21. Ibid.
22. Ibid., p. 271.

Roger Shimomura, *24 People for Whom I Have Been Mistaken*, 1999. Chromogenic prints and wall text, twenty-four prints, each 5 x 7 in. (12.7 x 17.8 cm). Collection of David E. Schwartz. Courtesy of Greg Kucera Gallery, Seattle.

work makes reference to the history of slavery when black bodies stood on public auction blocks, Obadike is careful not to equate his cultural Blackness (with a capital "B") with a black body, even if this referent is part of its etymology. By not including a photograph, Obadike thwarts the common expectation that objects for sale on *eBay* will be visible on line—further underscoring the difference between the concept of Blackness and skin color. Using the actual *eBay* site, the artist described the object for sale stating that this "heirloom has been in the possession of the seller for twenty-eight years" and that it "may be used for creating black art, ... writing critical essays or scholarship about other blacks, ... dating a black person without fear of public scrutiny," and, among other rights, "securing the right to use the terms 'sista,' 'brotha,' or 'nigga' in reference to black people." Certain warnings also apply, for example the Seller does not recommend that this Blackness be used "during legal proceedings of any sort, ... while making intellectual claims, ... while voting in the United States or Florida," or "by whites looking for a wild weekend."[23] Obadike toys with the idea that Blackness is a commodity that can be bought and sold for the purpose of cultural passing, tapping into a long-standing fantasy in the history of race politics of crossing the "color line." But the artist also writes, "This Blackness may be used to augment the blackness of those already black, especially for purposes of playing 'blacker-than-thou.'" Structured around the perceived desires of others to occupy or "own" Blackness even if they are already black, Obadike's project brings out the hierarchies operative in cultural conceptions of racial identities while revealing the social inequities that always attend Blackness in the United States.

The playful sarcasm of Obadike's work raises the question of how race and color are bought and sold in the digital domain of the Internet. Preema Murthy's *Bindi Girl* is one example of a site that raises the question of how pornography operates as one of the more obvious forms of commodification of bodies that are based on fantasies of racial specificity or difference. Using effectively censored images from an actual porn site, the artist leads the user through a series of links that simultaneously entice and thwart the user's potential desire for the body of a South Asian woman. The love chat turns into a narrative farce of unsuccessful coitus, the souvenirs one can purchase are banal items like knee socks or bindi dots, and the live cam is inoperative. The Bindi Girl says, "At first I thought technology would save me, arm me with my weapons. Then I turned to religion. But both have let me down. They continue to keep me confined to my 'proper' place."[24] The text on the *Bindi Girl* site implies that for the South Asian woman in a Hindu culture, this "proper" place is either as a goddess or whore, the limited

23. For a link to this page see http://obadike.tripod.com/ebay.html.
24. Preema Murthy, http://www.thing.net/~bindigrl/.

range ascribed by a traditionally sexist cultural framework in the context of a booming new high-tech economy. *Bindi Girl* is Murthy's recursive critique of the absurdity of this endless and apparently closed dialectic of positions. By taking up the common graphics and participatory tropes of porn sites, Murthy reiterates the form in order to play out the absurdity of its limits.

In another web site parody, Tana Hargest's digital project *Bitter Nigger Broadcast Network* (2002) offers a humorous and scathingly critical take on the wages of racism in the contemporary United States. Presented in the graphically sophisticated language of high-end web design, the BNBN spoofs both television broadcasting networks and corporate home pages that offer special products and services. Soft and seductive soundtracks and glowing pastel logos lead the user through a series of items to purchase in the BN Pharmaceutical line or the BN Product Division, both "committed to alleviating the bothersome effects of racism." BN Pharmaceutical lists among its products *Melinderm*, a Negro Teflon medicinal lotion, whose "soothing protection" and "gentle yet powerful shielding technology" bonds with the pigmentation of the skin, protecting the wearer from the damaging effects of racist remarks and behavior that subsequently slide right off. *Tominex*, designed for younger clients, helps them to "achieve a level of complacency normally reached after years of deferred dreams and smashed hopes—but without the bitterness." The user is informed by a pleasant voice that by suppressing feelings *Tominex* effectively removes the yearning for fairness or human decency.

If medications don't do the trick, the Product Division recommends the *Holo-Pal* who, like a genie out of a bottle, can be made to materialize when the black user needs a white male friend to provide a legitimizing image during retail shopping, at the bank, purchasing a home, or even developing an art career. The *Holo-Pal* becomes a "passport image" that allows the user to avoid discrimination in encounters with others. Parodying the advertising language that accompanies many new electronic devices, Hargest touts the compatibility of the *Holo-Pal* with other daily planning technologies such as PDAs, suggesting that the new holographic device can be programmed to anticipate the needs of the user. With its self-conscious title, the *Bitter Nigger Broadcast Network* disarms its users with humor while revealing the banality of systematic racism.

A similar critique of racial inequities that uses a parody of technophilia can be found in the work of Los Cybrids. A San Francisco based artists group, Los Cybrids has produced installations, videos, and a number of public art projects, performances, and discussions that address the broader social effects of the new technology revolution.

Responding to the economic boom of Silicon Valley with satirical and ominous predictions, their work poses critical questions concerning the race and class distinctions that underlie the fantasy of a wired world. Making use of public billboard space, their *Digital Mural Project* (2002) served as a public service announcement concerning the role of technology in globalization and in the working lives of Chicanos and Latinos in the Bay Area. Installed outside the Galleria de la Raza in the Mission District of San Francisco, the billboards offered dystopic visions of a future in which the rhetoric of inclusion—"Don't be left behind; last one across the digital divide is a rotten egg"—is shown to be yet another colonizing gesture of capitalism. A different mural announces "El Webopticon: Systema de Vigilancia." The image depicts a young Latino boy looking toward a future populated with computers, robots, and satellites. His innocent features are marred by a sinister bar code printed across his neck, and his face is framed as if part of a police file. Rather than a bridge to a brighter future, the Internet becomes the new panopticon keeping watch over racial minorities. The mural reads, "…you don't have to be connected to be affected…."[25]

Race as a visual technology

In her forthcoming essay "Race as Technology," artist Beth Coleman suggests that race can be understood as a levered mechanism or "a function machine that has already articulated the race-prosthesis algorithm that one inherited from the age of Enlightenment and the age of rational numbers. Race as technology adopts the role of technicity by using race as a tool."[26] Coleman's concept of race *as a technology* is compelling precisely because it allows the discourse to be conceived as a *series of techniques*, rather than a framework

25. See Los Cybrids,
www.cybrids.com/artists.html.
26. Beth Coleman, "Race as Technology,"
an essay in progress. Cited with the
author's permission, 2003.

of ontological conditions. From this perspective, race as a "levered mechanism" can be seen to operate across historical, social, and cultural practices that are geared to carry out operations following a systemic logic.

Some theorists have claimed that digital image production is materially different from traditional photography to the degree that it constitutes a formal avant-garde, a revolution in the concept of the image, a new realism for a new reality.[27] While such pronouncements are no doubt primarily rhetorical, they signal an interest in the idea that the human population is engaged in a major transition—a digital revolution—that is not merely ideological but also phenomenological or even ontological. Our bodies and psyches will become integrated, it is suggested, with systems of information and surveillance, microchips, and nano-technologies. As genetic engineering turns to the computer for its model of analysis and production of experiments, it joins an effort to understand human beings in terms of the atomization that digital technology makes possible. The human body is no longer conceived primarily as a mechanical device with skin, muscles, and bones, but rather as a complex structure of codes that determine micro-processes invisible to the naked eye. Identity and identification become literally more than skin deep when one is defined by genetic code.

Paul Gilroy writes, "Today skin is no longer privileged as the threshold of either identity or particularity. There are good reasons to suppose that the line between inside and out now falls elsewhere. The boundaries of 'race' have moved across the threshold of the skin. They are cellular and molecular, not dermal. If 'race' is to endure, it will be in a new form, estranged from the scales respectively associated with political anatomy and epidermalization."[28] And yet, Gilroy is also quick to point out that despite the fact that science as a discourse has changed the way race is conceived biologically, the brutal simplicity of racial typology still plays itself out in the most basic ways as public forms of violence.[29] For Gilroy it is necessary to find a way to produce an antiracist discourse in *Against Race* that does not simultaneously perpetuate the reification of race as a legitimate human category.

Some of the art projects discussed here are explicitly critical of race categories, while others are engaged in antiracist politics that rely on the ongoing stability of such categories. In both kinds of projects it seems clear, despite Gilroy's suggestion that racial discourses based on the visual logic of color or "epidermalization" are no longer legitimate, that the concept of race and its truth effect are still ensnared in a visual nexus, in a racializing gaze that has been historically produced and is now effectively maintained by popular culture as well as the arts. Even if it is possible to imagine a future in which the

27. See Lev Manovich, *The Language of New Media* (Cambridge, Mass.: MIT Press, 2000).
28. Paul Gilroy, *Against Race* (Cambridge, Mass.: Harvard University Press, 2000), p. 47.
29. Ibid., p. 51.

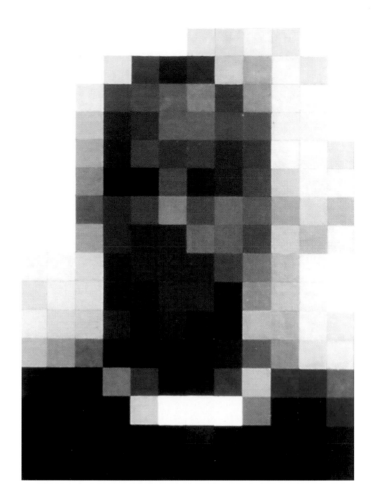

"technology of race" is no longer an oppressive power of domination, it is also likely that visual difference will play itself out as a necessary supplement to other kinds of social dynamics. If, as Gilroy suggests, racial discourse was "summoned into being," at least in part, by the production of a specific image culture, then it is *in image culture* that it must be unraveled and undone. What is required is to recognize that race is, among other things, *a visual technology* consisting of a complex web of intertexual mechanisms tying the present to the past through new and familiar systems of representation. Artists such as those mentioned here explore this intertextuality to better situate the visual frameworks for race in a digital age, or to point to their social and political effects. At the same time, as image-makers, the artists are in the process of producing the *next generation* of visual technologies of race. When looking at these and other contemporary works that engage race as a discourse we should consider to what degree they continue its historical logic or enact its progressive transformation.

Kori Newkirk, *Channel 11*, 1999. Encaustic on wood panel, 65 1/4 x 49 in. (165. 7 x 124.4 cm). Courtesy of The Project, New York.

Checklist of the exhibition

Works are listed in alphabetical order by artist, and chronologically. In the dimensions, height precedes width, followed by depth, when applicable.

Michael Abramson (b. 1944)
March to the United Nations, October 30, 1970, 1970
Gelatin silver print
16 x 20 in. (40.6 x 50.8 cm)
Courtesy of the artist

Adal (b. 1947)
"Out of Focus Nuyoricans"
Ink jet prints; prologue by Pedro Pietri
Four of eighteen prints, each 8 1/2 x 11 in. (21.6 x 27.4 cm)
San Francisco Museum of Modern Art Library Collection

Ansel Adams (1902–1984)
Roy Takeno at town hall meeting, Manzanar Relocation Center, 1943
Gelatin silver print
10 1/4 x 13 1/4 in. (26 x 36.6 cm)
Library of Congress, Washington, D.C., gift of Ansel Adams, 1965–1968

Ansel Adams (1902–1984)
Born Free and Equal, 1944
Book
Japanese American National Museum, Los Angeles

Laura Aguilar (b. 1959)
Nature Self-Portrait #12, 1996
Gelatin silver print
16 x 20 in. (40.6 x 50.8 cm)
Courtesy of the artist and Susanne Vielmetter Los Angeles Projects

Allora y Calzadilla
Jennifer Allora (b. 1974) and
Guillermo Calzadilla (b. 1971)
Landmark (Footprints), 2002
Photo-based installation with text
Four chromogenic prints, each 16 x 20 in. (40.6 x 50.8 cm); overall 32 x 40 in. (81.3 x 101.6 cm)
Courtesy of the artists

Celia Alvarez Muñoz
(b. 1964)
La Honey, Nos. 1–7, 1983
Mixed media (rock maple, gelatin silver print, letterpress text)
Seven boxes, each 12 x 17 x 14 in. (30.5 x 43.2 x 35.5 cm)
Courtesy of the artist

Diane Arbus (1923–1971)
Jewish Giant at Home, 1970
Gelatin silver print
16 x 20 in. (40.6 x 50.8 cm)
Courtesy of the Diane Arbus Estate and the Jewish Museum, New York

Author unknown
The Secret Museum of Anthropology, 1935
Book
Private collection

Bennie Flores Ansell
(b. 1967)
The Collection Box, Morpho Stiletto, 2000
Ink jet transparency film and butterfly collection box
8 x 12 x 3 in. (20.3 x 30.4 x 7.6 cm)
Courtesy of The Frank and Kimberly DeLape Collection, Texas

Eleanor Antin (b. 1935)
Eleanora Antinova in Pocahontas, from the "Recollections of My Life with Diaghilev" series, 1980
Toned gelatin silver print
14 x 11 in. (35.5 x 27.9 cm)
Courtesy of Ronald Feldman Fine Arts, New York

ASCO
Harry Gamboa, Jr. (b. 1951)
No-Movie announcement poster (1977) featuring A la Mode (1975), 1977
Offset lithography
Courtesy of the artist and the Harry Gamboa Collection, Stanford University Library

Decoy Gang War Victim, 1976
Chromogenic print
16 x 20 in. (40.6 x 50.8 cm)
Courtesy of the artist

Aziz + Cucher
Anthony Aziz (b. 1961) and
Sammy Cucher (b. 1958)
Faith, Honor and Beauty, 1992–93
Chromogenic print
86 x 38 in. (218.4 x 96.5 cm) framed
Courtesy of the artists and Henry Urbach Architecture, New York

George Bacon (1918–1993)
Dodie Bacon holding the March 12, 1959 edition of the Honolulu Star-Bulletin, announcing statehood of Hawaii, Honolulu, Hawaii, 1959
Gelatin silver print
8 1/2 x 7 1/4 in. (21.6 x 18.4 cm)
Bishop Museum, Honolulu, Hawaii

Baker Studio
Ray Jerome Baker (1880–1972)
A Haole Hula Girl (Rose Heather), Hawaii, ca. 1920
Postcard
5 1/4 x 3 1/2 in. (14.0 x 8.9 cm)
Bishop Museum, Honolulu, Hawaii, General Postcard Collection

John Baldessari (b. 1931)
California Map Project, 1969
Type R prints and typewritten sheet mounted on board
Eleven prints, each 8 x 10 in. (20.3 x 25.4 cm); text 8 1/2 x 11 in. (21.6 x 27.9 cm)
Private collection

J. P. Ball & Son
James Presley Ball (1825–1905)
William Biggerstaff Portrait seated in a chair with a hand on his face, wearing a flower in his lapel, 1896
Cabinet card
6 1/4 x 4 1/2 in. (15.9 x 11.4 cm)
Courtesy of the Montana Historical Society, Helena

Photograph of the execution of William Biggerstaff, hanged for the murder of "Dick" Johnson, flanked by Rev. Victor Day and Henry Jurgens, sheriff, 1896
Cabinet card
6 1/4 x 4 1/2 in. (15.9 x 11.4 cm)
Courtesy of the Montana Historical Society, Helena

Photograph of William Biggerstaff, former slave, born in Lexington, Kentucky, in 1854, 1896
Cabinet card
6 1/4 x 4 1/2 in. (15.9 x 11.4 cm)
Courtesy of the Montana Historical Society, Helena

George Ballis (b. 1925)
Cesar Chavez, leader of United Farm Workers, confronts Delano policeman during rally and march through city, 1965
Gelatin silver print
10 x 8 in. (25.4 x 20.3 cm)
Courtesy of the artist

Tina Barney (b. 1945)
The Westwater Family, 1999
Chromogenic print
48 x 60 in. (121.9 x 152.4 cm)
Courtesy of Janet Bordon, Inc., New York

Ralph Bartholomew (1907–1985)
Untitled, 1947
Gelatin silver print
10 1/8 x 14 1/8 in. (25.7 x 35.9 cm)
Los Angeles County Museum of Art, gift of the Bartholomew Family, Courtesy of Keith deLellis Gallery

Don Bartletti (b. 1947)
*Border Opinions, San Ysidro,
California. Protestors gather within
sight of the US/Mexico border to
demonstrate their opinions about
immigration*, 1991
Digital chromogenic print
16 x 20 in. (40.6 x 50.8 cm)
Courtesy of the artist and the
Los Angeles Times

Joseph L. Bates
(active 1870–85)
Untitled, ca. 1860
Hand-tinted albumen stereograph
3 3/16 x 6 3/4 in. (8 x 17.1 cm)
Private collection

Romare Bearden (1914–1988)
Untitled, 1964
Gelatin silver print photomontage
35 x 48 in. (88.9 x 121.9 cm)
Private collection

Max Becher (b. 1964) and
Andrea Robbins (b. 1963)
German Indians: Campfire, 1996
Chromogenic print
20 x 24 in. (50.8 x 60.9 cm)
Courtesy of Sonnabend Gallery,
New York

German Indians: Knife Thrower, 1998
Chromogenic print
20 x 16 in. (50.8 x 40.6 cm)
Courtesy of Sonnabend Gallery,
New York

Vanessa Beecroft (b. 1969)
VB48, Palazzo Ducale, 2001
Color video
2 hours and 30 minutes
Private collection
Courtesy of Deitch Projects,
New York

*VB39, US Navy SEALS, Museum of
Contemporary Art, San Diego*, 1999
Digital chromogenic print
Three panels, overall 96 x 120 in.
(243.84 x 304.8 cm)
Private collection
Courtesy of Deitch Projects,
New York

Louis Carlos Bernal (1941–1993)
Rosie Siqueiros, Barrio Anita, 1978
Chromogenic print
9 x 9 in. (22.8 x 22.8 cm)
Center for Creative Photography,
The University of Arizona, Tuscon

*Recamara de Mis Padres/My Parents'
Bedroom*, 1980
Gelatin silver print
8 7/8 x 11 5/8 in. (22.5 x 29.5 cm)
Center for Creative Photography,
The University of Arizona, Tuscon

Dawoud Bey (b. 1953)
Oneika 1, 1996
Polarcolor ER prints
Six panels, each 30 x 22 in.
(76.2 x 55.9 cm); overall 90 x 46 in.
(228.6 x 116.8 cm)
Museum of the Art Institute of
Chicago, Joseph N. Eisendrath
Prize Fund

Blake Brothers
(active ca. 1860)
Portrait of a Man, ca. 1860
Carte-de-visite
4 x 2 7/16 in. (10.1 x 6.2 cm)
International Center of Photography,
Daniel Cowin Collection, 1990

Roland N. Bonaparte
(1858–1924)
*Iga-she (Traveler), 13 years old, in
costume with ornaments beside
wrought iron chair, Omaha Bay, Ca.*,
1883
Albumen prints
15 x 12 in. (38.1 x 30.5 cm)
National Anthropological Archives,
Smithsonian Institution, Washington,
D.C.

Elias A. Bonine (1843–1916)
Yuma, three unidentified women,
ca. 1880
Boudoir card
7 1/4 x 5 1/2 in. (18.4 x 14.0 cm)
Museum of New Mexico, Palace of
the Governors, Santa Fe

Margaret Bourke-White
(1904–1971)
At the Time of the Louisville Flood,
1937
Gelatin silver print
10 x 13 5/16 in. (25.4 x 33.8 cm)
George Eastman House, Rochester,
New York

Mathew B. Brady (1823–1896)
C. Edwards Lester, ed., *The Gallery
of Illustrious Americans*, 1850
Book
George Eastman House, Rochester,
New York

*William Henry Johnson
(Zip the Pinhead)*, ca. 1872
Modern gelatin silver print from
original wet-plate collodion negative
3 9/16 x 2 3/8 in. (9 x 6.1 cm)
National Portrait Gallery, Smithsonian
Institution, Washington, D.C.

Drex Brooks (b. 1952)
*Sweet Medicine: Gnadenhutten
Massacre Site, Ohio*, 1991
Toned gelatin silver print
14 x 21 in. (35.5 x 53.4 cm)
Courtesy of the artist

*Bad Axe Massacre Site, Vernon
County, WI*, 1991
Gelatin silver print
14 x 21 in. (35.5 x 53.4 cm)
Courtesy of the artist

William S. Bryan, ed.
*Our Islands and Their People,
As Seen with Camera and Pencil*, 1899
Book
International Center of Photography

Robert C. Buitron (b. 1953)
Ixta Dates a Nazi Skinhead, from
"The Legend of Ixtaccihuatl y
Popcatepetl" series, 1989
Gelatin silver print
13 3/4 x 17 3/4 in. (34.9 x 45 cm)
Courtesy of the artist

Nancy Burson (b. 1948)
*Three Major Races (an Oriental,
a Caucasian, and a Black)*, from
the "Mankind" series, 1982
Gelatin silver print
8 1/2 x 7 1/2 in. (21.5 x 19 cm)
Courtesy of the artist and Yossi
Milo Gallery, New York

Mankind 2002, from the "Mankind"
series, 2002
Digital iris print
16 x 14 in. (40.6 x 35.5 cm)
Courtesy of the artist and Yossi
Milo Gallery, New York

Will C. Butman
(active 1891–96)
Woman and Two Children, 1890s
Cabinet card
6 9/16 x 4 1/4 in. (16.7 x 10.8 cm)
International Center of Photography,
Daniel Cowin Collection, 1990

Miguel Calderon (b. 1971)
*Evolucion del Hombre
(Evolution of Man)*, 1995
Chromogenic prints
Overall 36 1/2 x 151 in.
(92.7 x 383.5 cm)
Private collection
Courtesy of Andrea Rosen Gallery,
New York

**Maria Magdalena
Campos-Pons** (b. 1959)
Above All Things, 1997
Polarcolor ER prints
Three panels, each 24 x 20 in.
(60.9 x 50.8 cm)
Private collection
Courtesy of Howard Yezerski Gallery,
Boston, Massachusetts

George S. Carney (1868–1941)
*Czech-Slovak Group, American
Pageant, Milwaukee, Wisconsin*, 1919
Gelatin silver print
8 x 33 1/2 in. (20.3 x 85 cm)
Wisconsin Historical Society

Patty Chang (b. 1972)
Contortion, 1999–2000
Digital chromogenic prints
40 x 60 in. each (101.6 x 152.4 cm)
Courtesy of Jack Tilton/
Anna Kustera Gallery, New York

Vivian Cherry (b. 1920)
Untitled, from "The Game of Lynching,
Yorkville, East Harlem" series, 1947
Gelatin silver print
11 x 14 in. (27.9 x 35.5 cm)
International Center of Photography,
purchased by the ICP Acquisitions
Committee, 2003

Untitled, from "The Game of Lynching,
Yorkville, East Harlem" series, 1947
Gelatin silver print
14 3/8 x 11 in. (36.5 x 27.9 cm)
International Center of Photography,
purchased by the ICP Acquisitions
Committee, 2003

Albert Chong (b. 1958)
*Self-Portrait with Garvey's Prison
Docket*, 1995
Gelatin silver print
14 3/8 x 11 in. (36.5 x 27.9 cm)
International Center of Photography,
Museum purchase, 2003

Ed Clark (1912–2000)
Going Home, 1945
Gelatin silver print
10 5/8 x 12 3/8 in. (26.9 x 31.4 cm)
Hallmark Fine Art Collection,
Kansas City, Missouri
Courtesy of Ed Clark/Getty Images

Jennie Ross Cobb (1881–1959)
*Carnival Day at Tahlequah, I.T.
Cherokee Female Seminary Students
Bunt Schrimscher and Pixie Mayes*,
ca. 1900
Modern gelatin silver print from
original negative
Oklahoma Historical Society,
Oklahoma City, Archives and
Manuscripts Division, Jennie Ross
Cobb Collection

Collins Studio
*Geronimo, Apache Chief and
Medicine Man*, 1903
Gelatin silver print on board
7 1/8 x 5 in. (18 x 12.7 cm)
International Center of Photography,
Museum purchase, 2003

Will Connell (1898–1961)
Film still from *Roman Scandals*, 1933
Gelatin silver print
14 x 11 in. (35.5 x 27.9 cm)
UCR/California Museum of
Photography, University of California,
Riverside, Will Connell Collection

Peregrine F. Cooper
(active 1854–70)
As We Found Them, 1864
Carte-de-visite
3 3/8 x 2 1/4 in. (8.6 x 5.8 cm)
George Eastman House, Rochester,
New York

As They Are Now, 1864
Carte-de-visite
3 3/16 x 2 1/8 in. (8.1 x 5.4 cm)
George Eastman House, Rochester,
New York

Edward S. Curtis (1868–1952)
The Vanishing Race, 1907
Photogravure
6 x 8 in. (15 x 20.3 cm)
National Anthropological Archives,
Smithsonian Institution, Washington,
D.C.

Louise Dahl-Wolfe (1895–1989)
Night Bathing, 1939
Gelatin silver print
14 x 10 in. (35.5 x 25.4 cm)
International Center of Photography,
gift of the photographer, 1982

Bruce Davidson (b. 1933)
New York City, 1961–65
Gelatin silver print
14 x 11 in. (35.5 x 27.9 cm)
Courtesy of the artist and
Magnum Photos, Inc.

Voter Registration, 1965
Gelatin silver print
11 x 14 in. (27.9 x 35.5 cm)
Courtesy of the artist and
Magnum Photos, Inc.

F. Holland Day (1864–1933)
Menelek, 1896
Platinum print
9 5/8 x 7 11/16 in. (24.4 x 19.2 cm)
The Metropolitan Museum of Art,
New York, The Alfred Stieglitz
Collection, 1933

Ebony and Ivory, 1897
Platinum print
7 3/16 x 7 7/8 in. (18.2 x 19.9 cm)
The Metropolitan Museum of Art,
New York, The Alfred Stieglitz
Collection, 1933

F. Holland Day (1864–1933) with
Clarence H. White (1871–1925)
F. Holland Day with Model, ca. 1897
Platinum print
9 1/2 x 7 3/8 in. (24.2 x 18.8 cm)
Gilman Paper Company Collection,
New York

Roy DeCarava (b. 1919)
Graduation Dress, 1949
Gelatin silver print
9 1/2 x 13 7/16 in. (24.1 x 34.1 cm)
George Eastman House, Rochester,
New York

Jack Delano (1914–1997)
*In the convict camp in Greene
County, Georgia*, 1941
Gelatin silver print
11 x 14 in. (27.9 x 35.5 cm)
Library of Congress, Washington, D.C.

*Ex-slave mulatta woman in northern
Greene County, Georgia*, 1941
Gelatin silver print
14 x 11 in. (35.5 x 27.9 cm)
Library of Congress, Washington, D.C.

*Guayanilla, Puerto Rico. Family of a
sugar worker living behind the mill.
All these people live in the same
house*, 1942
Gelatin silver print
11 x 14 in. (27.9 x 35.5 cm)
Library of Congress, Washington, D.C.

Thomas Eakins (1844–1916)
*African American Girl Nude Reclining
on a Couch*, ca. 1880
Gelatin silver print
10 1/2 x 12 1/2 in. (26.6 x 31.7 cm)
Museum of the Pennsylvania
Academy of the Fine Arts, Charles
Bregler's Thomas Eakins Collection,
purchased with the partial support
of the Pew Memorial Trust

Adrian J. Ebell (1840–1877)
*White People Escaping from the Riggs
and Williamson Missions Near the
Upper Agency, During the Sioux Revolt
of 1862*, 1862
Albumen print stereograph
3 1/2 x 7 in. (8.9 x 17.8 cm)
National Anthropological Archives,
Smithsonian Institution, Washington,
D.C.

Charles Eisenmann (1850–1909)
*Microcephalics: Maximo and
Bartola—Aztecs of Ancient Mexico*,
ca. 1880
Cabinet card
6 1/2 x 4 1/2 in. (15.9 x 10.8 cm)
Syracuse University Library,
Syracuse, New York, Becker
Collection

Walker Evans (1903–1975)
*Mask; Africa, Cameroon, Bandjoun,
Bamendjo Kingdom, #271*, from
African Negro Art portfolio, 1935
Gelatin silver print
8 7/8 x 7 in. (22.5 x 18.8 cm)
New York University, Institute of
Fine Arts, Visual Resource Collection
Photography

*Mask, profile view; Africa, Cameroon,
Bandjoun, Bamendjo Kingdom, #272*,
from *African Negro Art* portfolio, 1935
Gelatin silver print
8 3/8 x 6 in. (22.5 x 15.2 cm)
New York University, Institute of
Fine Arts, Visual Resource Collection
Photography

Nate R. Farbman (1909–1988)
*Shirley Temple dancing a hula while
visiting Honolulu, Hawaii*, 1935
Gelatin silver print
10 x 8 in. (25.4 x 20.3 cm)
Bishop Museum, Honolulu, Hawaii,
N. R. Farbman Collection

*Members of the Royal Hawaiian Girls
Glee Club performing at the Kodak
Hula Show, Waikiki, Honolulu, Hawaii*,
1937
Gelatin silver print
8 x 10 in. (20.3 x 25.4 cm)
Bishop Museum, Honolulu, Hawaii,
N. R. Farbman Collection

Walter S. Ferguson (1886–1936)
*Geronimo, Apache Warrior, rides in
automobile with three other members
of his tribe*, 1904
Gelatin silver print from
original negative
14 5/16 x 17 7/8 in. (36.4 x 45.4 cm)
National Archives, Washington, D.C.

Frances Flaherty (1883–1972)
*Moana: A Romance of the Golden
Age*, ca. 1925
Gelatin silver print
11 x 13 in. (27.9 x 33.2 cm)
Claremont School of Theology,
The Robert and Frances Flaherty
Collection

Camillus S. Fly (1849–1901)
*Council between Gen. Crook and
Geronimo [Chiricahua Apache], Cañon
de los Embudos, Sonora, Mexico*, 1886
Boudoir card
5 1/2 x 8 1/2 in. (14.0 x 21.6 cm)
Museum of New Mexico, Palace of
the Governors, Santa Fe

Lee Friedlander (b. 1934)
Manuel "Fess" Manetta, 1957
Gelatin silver print
14 x 11 in. (35.5 x 27.9 cm)
Courtesy of Janet Borden, Inc.,
New York

Marlon Fuentes (b. 1954)
Bontoc Eulogy, 1995
Black-and-white film
56:39 minutes
Courtesy of the artist and the
Cinema Guild, Inc., New York

Miguel Gandert (b. 1956)
*Las Camanchas y su Cautivas,
Las Griegos, New Mexico*, 1997
Gelatin silver print
20 x 24 in. (50.8 x 60.9 cm)
Courtesy of the artist

Alexander Gardner (1821–1882)
*U.S. Senator Lewis V. Bogy while
Indian Commissioner at Washington*,
1867–68
Albumen print
12 x 19 in. (30.5 x 48.2 cm)
Harney Collection, Missouri Historical
Society, St. Louis, Missouri

Rico Gatson (b. 1966)
Flaming Hood, 2000
DVD
6:51 minutes
Courtesy of Ronald Feldman
Fine Arts, New York

Gerhard Sisters (active 1910–19)
The Missing Link No. 1 (Photograph of Indigenous Filipino from St. Louis Fair, 1904), 1904
Gelatin silver print
20 1/2 x 11 3/4 in. (52 x 29.8 cm)
Library of Congress, Washington, D.C.

Laura Gilpin (1891–1979)
Hardbelly's Hogan, Arizona, 1932
Gelatin silver print
9 1/2 x 13 1/2 in. (24 x 32.4 cm)
Amon Carter Museum, Fort Worth, Texas, bequest of the artist

Eugene Omar Goldbeck (1892–1986)
Immigration Border Patrol, Laredo, Texas, February 1926, M. M. Hanson, Inspector in Charge, 1926
Gelatin silver print
9 3/4 x 40 3/8 in. (24.7 x 102.5 cm)
Harry Ransom Humanities Research Center, The University of Texas at Austin

Nan Goldin (b. 1953)
At the Bar: Toon, C. and So, Bangkok, 1992
Cibachrome print
30 x 40 in. (76.2 x 101.6 cm)
Courtesy of the artist and Matthew Marks Gallery, New York

Raoul Gradvohl (1898–1976)
Woman with feathered headdress, sitting within light circle, ca. 1940
Gelatin silver print
10 x 8 in. (25.4 x 20.3 cm)
UCR/California Museum of Photography, University of California, Riverside, Raoul Gradvohl Collection

Ed Greevy (b. 1939)
Haunani-Kay, nationalist and leader of the Hawaiian sovereignty movement, speaking before 15,000 people on the 1993 commemoration of the 1893 overthrow of the Hawaiian Kingdom by the American military in support of American businessmen, 1993
Gelatin silver print
20 x 16 in. (50.8 x 40.6 cm)
Courtesy of the artist

John Gutmann (1905–1998)
The Artist Lives Dangerously, 1938
Gelatin silver print
7 5/8 x 10 1/4 in. (19.4 x 26 cm)
Center for Creative Photography, University of Arizona, Tuscon

Ernest Hallen (active 1907–30)
Construction of the Panama Canal, "Looking north from gate, upper east chamber," Jan. 14, 1913, 1913
Gelatin silver print
8 5/8 x 10 1/4 (21.9 x 26 cm)
National Archives, Records of the Panama Canal, Washington, D.C.

Tana Hargest (b. 1969)
Bitter Nigger Broadcast Network (BNBN), 1999–2001
CD Rom
Courtesy of Bitter Nigger, Inc., New York

Alex Harris (b. 1949)
Rodarte, New Mexico, Looking South from Fred Martinez's Chevrolet Impala, 1987
Inkjet print
20 x 24 in. (50.8 x 60.9 cm)
Courtesy of the artist

Lyle Ashton Harris (b. 1965)
Americas Triptych, 1987–88
Gelatin silver print
Three panels, each 30 x 20 in. (76.2 x 50.8 cm)
Private collection

Masumi Hayashi (b. 1945)
Gila River Relocation Camp, Foundations, 1990
Panoramic photocollage
28 x 60 in. (71.1 x 152.4 cm)
Japanese American National Museum, Los Angeles, gift of the R. Hayashi Family

A.R. Henwood (active 1860–65)
General Williams and Servant, ca. 1863
Carte-de-visite
4 1/4 x 3 in. (10.8 x 7.6 cm)
International Center of Photography, Museum purchase, 2003

Lynn Hershman (b. 1941)
Roberta's Body Language Chart, from the "Roberta Breitmore in Therapy Session" series, 1978
Eight gelatin silver prints with text
Overall 60 x 40 in. (152.4 x 101.6 cm)
Courtesy of Gallery Paule Anglim and Robert Koch Gallery, San Fransico

Jack Hillers (1843–1925)
John Chupco, Chief of the Seminole nation, I.T., as he looks today since he has reformed in 1866, now a devoted Christian and farmer, 1875
Albumen print
10 x 8 in. (25.4 x 20.3 cm)
Courtesy of the Archives and Manuscripts Division of the Oklahoma Historical Society, Oklahoma City, C.W. Kirk Collection

Lewis W. Hine (1874–1940)
Composite Photograph of Child Laborers Made from Cotton Mill Children, 1913
Gelatin silver print
6 5/8 x 4 5/8 in. (16.8 x 11.7 cm)
National Gallery of Canada, purchased 1978

Louis Hock (b. 1948)
#1 from the "La Mera Frontera" series, 2000
Digital pigment print
17 x 24 in. (43.2 x 60.9)
Courtesy of the artist

John H. Hogan (1856–1920)
Ishi, Last of the Deer Creek Indians, ca. 1911
Real photo postcard
5 1/2 x 3 1/2 in. (14 x 9 cm)
Pheobe Apperson Hearst Museum of Anthropology and the Regents of the University of California

R.C. Holmes (active ca. 1900–10)
Wilmington, Delaware, 1900
Gelatin siver print on board
4 15/16 x 6 9/16 in. (12.5 x 16.7 cm)
International Center of Photography, Daniel Cowin Collection, 1990

Frank Hudson (1865–?)
The Avengers of Little Myrtle Vance, and the Villian brought to Justice, 1893
Gelatin silver print
6 5/16 x 9 1/4 in. (16.5 x 23.5 cm)
International Center of Photography, Daniel Cowin Collection, 1990

Jack Iwata (1912–1992)
Queen of Manzanar, ca. 1943
Gelatin silver print
9 1/2 x 7 3/4 in. (24.1 x 19.7 cm)
Japanese American National Museum, Los Angeles, gift of Jack and Peggy Iwata

Zig Jackson (b. 1957)
Indian Man on the Bus, from the "Indian in San Francisco" series, 1994
Gelatin silver print
16 x 20 in. (40.6 x 50.8 cm)
Courtesy of the artist

George Wharton James (1858–1923)
Ramona Lubo (Cahuilla) as "The Real Ramona," ca. 1909
Postcard
3 1/2 x 5 1/2 in. (9 x 14 cm)
Courtesy of C. Ondine Chavoya

Simen Johan (b. 1973)
Untitled #100, 2001
Digital chromogenic print
44 x 44 in. (105.6 x 105.6 cm)
Courtesy of Yossi Milo Gallery, New York

Osa Johnson (1894–1953) and **Martin Johnson** (1884–1937)
Refrigerator, ca. 1920
Modern print from original glass negative
7 x 5 in. (17.8 x 12.7 cm)
George Eastman House, Rochester, New York

Rashid Johnson (b. 1977)
Manumission Papers, 2000
Calotype
55 x 44 in. (132 x 105.6 cm)
Smith College Museum of Art Collection, Northampton, Massachusetts

Frances Benjamin Johnston (1864–1952)
Saluting the Flag at the Whittier Primary School, 1899
Gelatin silver print
7 7/16 x 9 1/2 in. (18.8 x 24.1 cm)
Library of Congress, Washington, D.C.

Pirkle Jones (b. 1914)
Window of the Black Panthers Party National Headquarters, 1968
Gelatin silver print
14 3/8 x 11 in. (36.4 x 27.9 cm)
International Center of Photography, purchased by the ICP Acquisitions Committee, 2003

Isaac Julien (b. 1960)
The Long Road to Mazatlan, 2000
Four synchronized DVDs
20 minutes
Courtesy of the Victoria Miro Gallery, London

Myron H. Kimball (active 1850–63)
Emancipated Slaves, 1863
Albumen print
5 1/4 x 7 1/4 in. (13.2 x 18.3 cm)
Gilman Paper Company Collection, New York

Fritz Kraft (active 1940s)
*Hula Dancer Erotica (Jojo), Honolulu,
Hawaii, nos. 1–8 (set #18)*, ca. 1940
Gelatin silver prints
Eight prints, each 4 1/2 x 2 1/2 in.
(10.8 x 6 cm)
Private collection

Barbara Kruger (b. 1945)
Untitled [Your Fictions Become
History], 1983
Gelatin silver print
76 1/4 x 39 1/2 in. (193.7 x 100.3 cm)
Milwaukee Art Museum, gift of
Contemporary Art Society

Heidi Kumao (b. 1964)
Identity Generator, 2003
Digital, interactive web piece
made with Flash MX
http://www.heidikumao.net

Frank Kunishige (1878–1960)
Aida Kawakami, ca. 1927
Gelatin silver print
13 3/4 x 9 1/4 in. (34.9 x 23.6 cm)
University of Washington Libraries,
Manuscripts, Special Collections,
University Archives Division,
Kunishige Collection

Ignacio Lang (b. 1975)
*Interview with a Landscape,
Las Acacias*, 2000
Chromogenic prints
Five prints, each 24 x 30 in.
(60.9 x 76.2 cm)
Courtesy of the artist

Dorothea Lange (1895–1965)
Migrant Mother, Nipomo, California,
1936
Gelatin silver print
13 1/2 x 10 1/2 in. (34.3 x 26.7 cm)
Oakland Museum of California,
City of Oakland, the Dorothea Lange
Collection, gift of Paul S. Taylor

First Braceros, 1942
Gelatin silver print
11 1/4 x 8 1/4 in. (28.5 x 20.6 cm)
Oakland Museum of California,
City of Oakland, Dorothea Lange
Collection, gift of Paul S. Taylor

*Just About to Step Into the Bus for the
Assembly Center, San Francisco*, 1942
Gelatin silver print
11 x 14 in. (27.9 x 35.5 cm)
Oakland Museum of California,
City of Oakland, Dorothea Lange
Collection, gift of Paul S. Taylor

William Larrabee (1841–?)
*Little Chief (Con-way-how-nif,
Cheyenne) Welcoming Two Newcomers
from Dakota Territory*, 1878
Albumen print
9 x 7 1/2 in. (22.8 x 19 cm)
Hampton University Archives,
Hampton, Virginia

Pok-Chi Lau (b. 1950)
*Room for Chinese Bachelor Chef
with Marlboro, Pittsburgh, PA*, 1977
Gelatin silver print
20 x 16 in. (50.8 x 40.6 cm)
Courtesy of the artist

An-My Lê (b. 1960)
Small Wars (Sniper I), 1999–2002
Gelatin silver print
26 x 37 1/2 in. (66 x 95.2 cm)
Courtesy of the artist

Dinh Q. Lê (b. 1968)
Persistence of Memory #10, 2000–01
Chromogenic print and linen tape
45 x 63 in. (114.3 x 160 cm)
Courtesy of P.P.O.W., New York

Nikki S. Lee (b. 1970)
The Ohio Project (7), 1999
Fujiflex print
40 x 30 in. (101.6 x 76.2 cm)
Courtesy of Leslie Tonkonow
Artworks + Projects, New York

Life
How to Tell Japs from the Chinese,
December 22, 1941
Magazine
Private collection

Life
Terence Spencer, photographer
(b. 1918)
Carol Baker with Masai Warriors,
July 17, 1964
Magazine
Private collection

Ken Light (b. 1951)
*Strip Search, Shakedown Room
of Visiting Area*, from the
"Texas Death Row" series, 1994
Gelatin silver print
16 x 20 in. (40.6 x 50.8 cm)
Courtesy of the artist

*Routine traffic check looking
for* indocumentados, *San Ysidro*,
ca. 1985
Gelatin silver print
16 x 20 in. (40.6 x 50.8 cm)
Courtesy of the artist

Glenn Ligon (b. 1960)
*Self-Portrait Exaggerating My Black
Features/Self-Portrait Exaggerating
My White Features*, 1998
Silkscreen on canvas
Two panels, each 120 x 40 in.
(304.8 x 101.6 cm)
Courtesy of D'Amelio Terras Gallery,
New York

Thomas H. Lindsey
(active 1880–1900)
Stripes But No Stars, ca. 1892
Boudoir card
5 x 8 in. (12.7 x 20.3 cm)
Wm. B. Becker Collection/American
Museum of Photography

O. Winston Link (1915–2001)
*Hot Shot East Bound at Lager,
W. Virginia*, 1956
Gelatin silver print
16 x 20 in. (40.6 x 50.8 cm)
Courtesy of Robert Mann Gallery,
New York

John L. Lovell (1825–1903)
Composite of Class of '87, Harvard,
1887
Gelatin silver print
3 1/8 in. (7.9 cm) diameter
The Hallmark Photographic
Collection, Kansas City, Missouri

Composite Class of Harvard Annex,
1887
Gelatin silver print
3 1/8 in. (7.9 cm) diameter
The Hallmark Photographic
Collection, Kansas City, Missouri

Charles F. Lummis (1859–1928)
Procession of the Penitents, 1888
Gelatin silver print
5 1/2 x 8 1/2 in. (14.0 x 21.6 cm)
Southwest Museum, Los Angeles

George Platt Lynes (1907–1955)
*Untitled (Francisco Moncion
with Medallion)*, 1948
Gelatin silver print.
10 x 8 in. (25.4 x 20.3 cm)
Courtesy of Robert Miller Gallery,
New York

Untitled, ca. 1952
Gelatin silver print
8 x 10 in. (20.3 x 25.4 cm)
Courtesy of Kinsey Institute for
Research in Sex, Gender, and
Reproduction, Bloomington, Indiana

Danny Lyon (b. 1942)
*Atlanta, Georgia. Segregated
water fountains*, 1962
Gelatin silver print
14 x 11 in. (35.5 x 27.9 cm)
Courtesy of the artist and
Magnum Photos, Inc.

Parker Yia-Som MacKenzie
(1897–1999)
*Lucy Sumpty, Kiowa, at Phoenix
Indian School*, 1916
Oklahoma Historical Society,
Oklahoma City, Archives and
Manuscripts Division, Parker
MacKenzie Collection

Robert Mapplethorpe
(1946–1989)
Isaiah, 1981
Gelatin silver print
20 x 16 in. (50.8 x 40.6 cm)
The Robert Mapplethorpe
Foundation, Inc., New York

Thomas, 1986
Gelatin silver print
24 x 20 in. (60.9 x 50.8 cm)
The Robert Mapplethorpe
Foundation, Inc., New York

Lee Marmon (b. 1925)
*White Man's Moccasins
(Jeff Sousea)*, 1954
Gelatin silver print
20 x 16 in. (50.8 x 40.6 cm)
Courtesy of the artist

Daniel J. Martinez (b. 1957)
*Self-Portrait #4 (Second attempt to
clone mental disorder or How one
philosophizes with a hammer).
After Mary Shelley, 1816*, 1999
Color light jet print
60 x 48 in. (150 x 120 cm)
Courtesy of The Project, New York

Victor Masayesva, Jr.
(b. 1951)
Cold Moon, 1996
Digital chromogenic print
20 x 24 in. (50.8 x 60.9 cm)
Courtesy of the artist

Frank Matsura (1881–1913)
*A Cowboy Named Barrett and Paul
"Long Paul" Timentwa, a Colvile
Rancher*, ca. 1905
Modern print from original
glass plate negative
11 x 8 in. (27.9 x 20.3 cm)
Okanogan County Historical
Society and Museum

James E. McClees (1821–1887)
These children were turned out of the St. Lawrence Hotel, Chestnut St., Philadelphia, on account of color, 1863
Carte-de-visite
4 x 2 in. (10.1 x 5 cm)
International Center of Photography, Daniel Cowin Collection, 1990

McCrary & Branson
F. B. McCrary and
Lloyd Branson (1853–1925)
Alligator Bait, ca. 1897
Gelatin silver print
8 3/8 x 23 in. (21.2 x 58.4 cm)
International Center of Photography, Daniel Cowin Collection, 1990

Larry McNeil (b. 1955)
The Raven Series, 1999
Digital chromogenic prints
Courtesy of the artist

McPherson & Oliver, attr.
William D. McPherson
(1833–1867)
The Scourged Back, 1863
Carte-de-visite
3 15/16 x 2 3/8 in. (10 x 6 cm)
International Center of Photography, Museum purchase, 2003

Hector Mendez Caratini
(b. 1949)
Acting as human shields, peaceful civil disobedients were able to shut down the U.S. Navy's bombing range in Vieques, P.R., for a whole year, 1999
Gelatin silver print
20 x 24 in. (50.8 x 60.9 cm)
Courtesy of the artist

Ana Mendieta (1948–1985)
Untitled (Facial Cosmetic Variations), 1972/1997
Chromogenic prints
Three prints, each 20 x 16 in. (50.8 x 40.6 cm)
Courtesy of the Estate of Ana Mendieta and Galerie Lelong, New York

Pedro Meyer (b. 1935)
In Search of Liberty, N.Y., 1986
Gelatin silver print
16 x 20 in. (40.6 x 50.8 cm)
Courtesy of the artist

Mexican Migrant Workers, Highway in California, 1986/90
Ink jet print
44 x 31 in. (105.6 x 78.6 cm)
Courtesy of the artist

Andrew Miller (d. 1899)
Was a Yuma Chief in Days of Prosperity, ca. 1888
Albumen print
6 1/2 x 4 1/4 x in. (16.5 x 10.8 cm)
Museum of New Mexico, Palace of the Governors, Santa Fe

Richard Misrach (b. 1949)
Bravo 20 (Crater and Destroyed Convoy), 1986
Color photograph
40 x 50 in. (101.6 x 127 cm)
Courtesy of Robert Mann Gallery, New York

Toyo Miyatake (1895–1979)
Receiving Dolls Donated by the American Friends Society, ca. 1943
Gelatin silver print
11 x 14 in. (27.9 x 35.5 cm)
Toyo Miyatake Collection

Toyo Miyatake (1895–1979)
and others
Our World, Manzanar, California, 1943–44 (reprinted 1998)
Book
Private collection

Tracy Moffat (b. 1960)
and **Gary Hillberg**
Lip, 1999
Color video
10 minutes
Courtesy of Women Make Movies, Inc., New York

Mole & Thomas
Arthur S. Mole (1889–1983) and
John D. Thomas
The Human Liberty Bell, 1918
Gelatin silver print
14 3/8 x 11 in. (36.5 x 27.9 cm)
International Center of Photography, Museum purchase, 2002

Delilah Montoya (b. 1955)
La Guadalupana, 1998
Kodacolor photo mural
with mixed mediums
120 x 60 in. (304.8 x 152.4 cm)
Museum of New Mexico, Palace of the Governors, Santa Fe, museum purchase with funds donated by J. Michael O'Shaughnessy, 1999

Charles Moore (b. 1931)
Martin Luther King, Jr. Arrested on a Loitering Charge, Montgomery, September 3, 1958, 1958
Gelatin silver print
14 x 11 in. (35.5 x 27.9 cm)
Courtesy of the artist and Black Star

Birmingham Riots. Demonstrators attacked by water cannons, Birmingham, Alabama, 1963
Gelatin silver print
16 x 19 7/8 in. (38.4 x 47.2 cm)
International Center of Photography, gift of the Professional Division, Eastman Kodak Company

Ku Klux Klan rally, near Salisbury, North Carolina, 1965
Gelatin silver print
14 x 11 in. (35.5 x 27.9 cm)
International Center of Photography, gift of the artist, 1991

Clarence G. Morledge
(1871–1948)
In My Fighting Clothes [Portrait of Nat Love, Buffalo Soldier], from Nat Love, Life and Adventures of Nat Love . . . , 1907
Gelatin silver print mounted in book
7 x 5 in. (17.8 x 12.7 cm)
Denver Public Library, Western History and Geneaology Collection

Vik Muniz (b. 1961)
Frederick Douglass, from "Pictures of Ink" series, 2000
Cibachrome print
60 x 48 in. (144 x 115.2 cm)
International Center of Photography, purchased by the ICP Acquisitions Committee, 2003

Nickolas Muray (1892–1965)
Paul Robeson, ca. 1925
Gelatin silver print
9 1/4 x 7 in. (23.4 x 18 cm)
George Eastman House, Rochester, New York

Prema Murthy (b. 1969)
e.rase, 2003
Interactive net.art with Javascript, Flash, and Hypertext
http://www.premamurthy.net/ works/erase

Wangechi Mutu
Pin Up Series, 2001
Mixed mediums
13 x 10 in. (31.2 x 24 cm)
Courtesy of the artist

Study, from "The Historical Romance" series, 2002
Mixed mediums
12 x 9 in. (30.4 x 22.8 cm)
Collection of Eileen Harris Norton, Santa Monica

Eadweard J. Muybridge
(1830–1904)
The "Heathen Chinee" with Pick and Rocker, ca. 1868
Albumen print stereograph
3 1/2 x 7 in. (8.9 x 17.8 cm)
California Historical Society

Patrick Nagatani (b. 1951) and
Andree Tracey (b. 1948)
Radioactive Reds, 1986
Polacolor ER print
24 x 20 in. (60.9 x 50.8 cm)
Center for Creative Photography, University of Arizona

Bruce Nauman (b. 1941)
Self-Portrait as a Fountain, 1966–67/1970
Chromogenic print
20 1/16 x 23 15/16 in. (50.9 x 60.8 cm)
Whitney Museum of American Art, New York

Kori Newkirk (b. 1970)
Channel 11, 1999
Encaustic on wood panel
65 1/4 x 49 in. (165. 7 x 124.4 cm)
Courtesy of The Project, New York

Barbara Norfleet (b. 1926)
Private Home, New Providence Is., Lyford Cay Club, 1982
Gelatin silver print
11 x 14 3/8 in. (27.9 x 36.5 cm)
International Center of Photography, purchased by the ICP Acquisitions Committee, 2003

Don Normark (b. 1928)
Gilbert Madrid and Johnny Johnson visiting over the Johnson Gate, from the "Chavez Ravine, 1949" series, 1949/1997
Gelatin silver print
14 3/8 x 11 in. (36.5 x 27.9 cm)
International Center of Photography, purchased by the ICP Acquisitions Committee, 2003

Lladro Madrid, home from WWII, from the "Chavez Ravine, 1949" series, 1949/1997
Gelatin silver print
14 3/8 x 11 in. (36.5 x 27.9 cm)
International Center of Photography, purchased by the ICP Acquisitions Committee, 2003

Timothy O' Sullivan (1840–1882)
Wagon Darkroom in the Carson Desert, Nevada, ca. 1868
Albumen print
7 3/4 x 10 5/8 in. (19.7 x 27 cm)
National Archives, Washington, D.C., Records of the Office of the Chief of Engineers

Catherine Opie (b. 1961)
Self-Portrait, 1993
Chromogenic print
40 x 30 in. (101.6 x 76.2 cm)
Los Angeles County Museum of Art, the Audrey and Sydney Irmas Collection, Courtesy of Regen Projects, Los Angeles

Rubén Ortiz-Torres (b. 1964)
El Rey Feo, San Antonio, Texas, 1999
Chromogenic print
20 x 24 in. (50.8 x 60.9 cm)
Courtesy of Jan Kesner Gallery, Los Angeles.

Keith + Mendi Obadike
(b. 1973) and (b. 1973)
My hands/wishful thinking, 2000
World Wide Web, HTML, Animated GIFs, REALAUDIO
http://obadike.tripod.com/
Adiallo2.html

Paul Outerbridge (1896–1958)
Asian Nude with Ornament, ca. 1936
Carbro print
16 x 12 in. (40.6 x 30.5 cm)
Private collection

Gordon Parks (b. 1912)
American Gothic, 1942
Gelatin silver print
20 x 16 in. (50.8 x 40.6 cm)
Courtesy of the artist

Dr. Kenneth B. Clark conducting the "Doll Test" with male child, 1947
Modern gelatin silver print from original negative
11 x 14 in. (27.9 x 35.5 cm)
Library of Congress, Washington, D.C.

Emerging Man, Harlem, 1952
Gelatin silver print
16 1/8 x 19 7/8 in. (40.9 x 50.4 cm)
International Center of Photography, purchased by the ICP Acquisitions Committee, 2003

L.A. Courtroom, Malcolm X displaying picture of Muslim Ronald Stokes, killed by police a year earlier, 1963
Gelatin silver print
11 x 14 3/8 in. (27.9 x 36.4 cm)
International Center of Photography, purchased by the ICP Acquisitions Committee, 2003

Charles Paxton
(ca. 1841–1880)
Learning is Wealth, Wilson, Charley, Rebecca and Rosa, Slaves from New Orleans, 1864
Carte-de-visite
4 x 2 7/16 in. (10.1 x 16.2 cm)
International Center of Photography, Daniel Cowin Collection, 1990

Roz Payne (b. 1940)
Yellow Peril Supports Black Power, 1968
Gelatin silver print
14 3/8 x 11 in. (36.4 x 27.9 cm)
International Center of Photography, purchased by the ICP Acquisitions Committee, 2003

Paul Pfeiffer (b. 1966)
Leviathan, 1998
Digital chromogenic print
36 x 84 in. (91.4 x 213.4 cm)
Courtesy of The Project, New York

Adrian Piper (b. 1948)
It Doesn't Matter #1
("It doesn't matter who you are"), 1975
Crayon oil drawing on gelatin silver print
24 x 18 in. (60.9 x 45.7 cm)
Spencer Museum of Art, University of Kansas, Museum purchase, Helen Foresmen Spencer Art Acquisition Fund

It Doesn't Matter #2
("If what you want to do to me"), 1975
Crayon oil drawing on gelatin silver print
24 x 18 in. (60.9 x 45.7 cm)
Spencer Museum of Art, University of Kansas, Museum purchase, Helen Foresmen Spencer Art Acquisition Fund

It Doesn't Matter #3
("Is what I want you to do to me"), 1975
Crayon oil drawing on gelatin silver print
24 x 18 in. (60.9 x 45.7 cm)
Spencer Museum of Art, University of Kansas, Museum purchase, Helen Foresmen Spencer Art Acquisition Fund

Prentice H. Polk (1898–1984)
The Boss, 1932
Gelatin silver print
14 x 11 in. (35.5 x 27.9 cm)
International Center of Photography, gift of P. H. Polk and Southlight

Horace Poolaw (1906–1984)
Trecil Poolaw Unap, Mountain View, Oklahoma, 1929
Gelatin silver print
11 7/8 x 8 1/2 in. (30.1 x 21.6 cm)
Courtesy of Charles Junkerman

Cletus Poolaw's Honor Dance, Carnegie, Oklahoma, ca. 1952
Gelatin silver print
9 15/16 x 12 15/16 in. (25.2 x 32.8 cm)
Courtesy of Charles Junkerman

William Pope.L (b. 1955)
Susan Smith Goes to Haiti, 2001
Digital chromogenic print
67 1/2 x 37 in. (171.4 x 93.9 cm)
Courtesy of The Project, New York

William S. Prettyman
(1858–1932)
Race into the Cherokee Outlet, Ten Seconds After the Gun, Sept. 16, 1893, 1893
Postcard
3 1/2 x 5 1/2 in. (9 x 14 cm)
Oklahoma Historical Society, Oklahoma City, Archives and Manuscripts Division, Thomas N. Athey Collection

Richard Prince (b. 1949)
Untitled (Cowboy), 1991–92
Chromogenic print
48 x 72 in. (122 x 182.9 cm)
San Francisco Museum of Modern Art

James W. Queen (1815–1990)
The Darkey's Vanity, ca. 1860
Hand-tinted albumen print stereograph
3 1/2 x 7 in. (8.9 x 17.8 cm)
Wm. B. Becker Collection/
American Museum of Photography

Man Ray (1890–1976)
Noire et Blanche, 1926
Gelatin silver print
6 3/4 x 8 3/4 in. (16.2 x 21 cm)
Private collection

Jacob A. Riis (1899–1914)
The First Patriotic Election in the Beach Street Industrial School, ca. 1890
Gelatin silver print
7 3/4 x 9 5/8 in. (19.7 x 24.4 cm)
International Center of Photography, purchased by the David Schwartz Foundation, 1982

Alex Rivera (b. 1973)
Why Cybraceros?, 1997
Video
5 minutes
Courtesy of the artist

Robertson Studio
Alice Mary Robertson
(1854–1931)
Principal Chief Pleasant Ponter, 1904
Modern print from original glass plate negative
7 x 5 in. (17.8 x 12.7 cm)
Oklahoma Historical Society, Oklahoma City, Archives and Manuscripts Division, Alice Robertson Glass Plate Collection

Chief Pleasant Porter, of the Creek Nation, 1890
Modern print from original glass plate negative
7 x 5 in. (17.8 x 12.7 cm)
Oklahoma Historical Society, Oklahoma City, Archives and Manuscripts Division, Alice Robertson Glass Plate Collection

Martha Rosler
Vital Statistics of a Citizen, Simply Obtained, 1977
Video
40 minutes
Courtesy of the artist and Video Data Bank, Chicago

Charles E. Rotkin (b. 1916)
PRRA Promotional Photos: Women in grooming class to train as maids, 1948
Gelatin silver print
8 x 10 in. (20.3 x 25.4 cm)
Archivo General de Puerto Rico

Jason Salavon (b. 1970)
Class of 1967, nos. 1–2, 1998
Gelatin silver prints
Two panels, each 25 1/2 x 20 in. (64.8 x 50.8 cm)
Courtesy of The Project, New York

Class of 1988, nos. 1–2, 1998
Gelatin silver prints
Two panels, each 25 1/2 x 20 in. (64.8 x 50.8 cm)
Courtesy of The Project, New York

Andres Serrano (b. 1950)
Klanswoman (Grand Kaliff II), 1990
Cibachrome print
60 x 49 1/2 in. (152.4 x 125.7 cm)
Courtesy of Paula Cooper Gallery, New York

Ben Shahn (1898–1969)
A Medicine Show, Huntingdon,
Tennessee, 1935
Gelatin silver print
6 1/2 x 9 3/4 in. (15.6 x 23.4 cm)
International Center of Photography,
anonymous gift

Cindy Sherman (b. 1954)
Untitled, 1976/2000
Gelatin silver print
10 x 8 in. (25.4 x 20.3 cm)
Courtesy of the artist and
Metro Pictures, New York

Untitled, 1976/2000
Gelatin silver print
10 x 8 in. (25.4 x 20.3 cm)
Courtesy of the artist and
Metro Pictures, New York

Untitled, 1976/2000
Gelatin silver print
10 x 8 in. (25.4 x 20.3 cm)
Courtesy of the artist and
Metro Pictures, New York

Untitled, 1976/2000
Gelatin silver print
10 x 8 in. (25.4 x 20.3 cm)
Courtesy of the artist and
Metro Pictures, New York

Untitled, 1976/2000
Gelatin silver print
10 x 8 in. (25.4 x 20.3 cm)
Courtesy of the artist and
Metro Pictures, New York

Untitled Film Still #50, 1979
Gelatin silver print
8 x 10 in. (20.3 x 25.4 cm)
Courtesy of the artist and
Metro Pictures, New York

Roger Shimomura (b. 1939)
24 People for Whom I Have Been
Mistaken, 1999
Chromogenic prints and wall text
Twenty-four prints, each 5 x 7 in.
(12.7 x 17.8 cm)
Collection of David E. Schwartz
Courtesy of Greg Kucera Gallery,
Seattle

J. Shimon & J. Lindemann
John Shimon (b. 1961) and
Julie Lindemann (b. 1957)
R.J. as Glade Boy in an abandoned
K-mart parking lot, Manitowoc,
Wisconsin, 1996
Gelatin silver contact print
10 x 8 in. (25.4 x 20.3 cm)
Courtesy of the artists

Bharat Sikka (b. 1974)
Anurag, 2002
Chromogenic print
32 1/2 x 42 1/2 in. (82.5 x 108 cm)
Courtesy of Riva Gallery, New York

Coreen Simpson (b. 1942)
Masqued Nude, 1999
Gelatin silver print
20 x 24 in. (50.8 x 60.9 cm)
Courtesy of the artist

Lorna Simpson (b. 1960)
Vantage Point, 1991
Two gelatin silver prints
on plastic plaques
Overall 50 x 70 in. (120 x 168 cm)
Courtesy of Sean Kelly Gallery,
New York

Benjamin L. Singley (b. 1864)
The Philippines, Porto Rico and
Cuba—Uncle Sam's Burden
(with apologies to Mr. Kipling), 1899
Albumen print stereograph
3 1/2 x 7 in. (8.9 x 17.8 cm)
Private collection

Aaron Siskind (1903–1991)
Harlem, ca. 1936
Gelatin silver print
10 3/8 x 7 1/2 in. (26.3 x 19 cm)
International Center of Photography,
gift of Roger P. Smith, 1984
Courtesy of Robert Mann Gallery,
New York

Will Soule (1836–1908)
Wichita Woman (Squaw 2), ca. 1867
Albumen print
7 x 5 in. (17.8 x 12.7 cm)
National Anthropological Archives,
Smithsonian Institution, Washington,
D.C.

Southworth & Hawes
Albert Sands Southworth
(1811–94) and **Josiah Johnson**
Hawes (1808–1908)
The Branded Hand of Captain
Jonathan Walker, Boston, Mass., 1845
Sixth-plate daguerreotype
2 3/4 x 3 1/4 in. (7 x 8.3 cm)
Massachusetts Historical Society

Bently Spang (b. 1960)
Modern Warrior Series: War Shirt #1,
1998
Mixed mediums
36 x 56 x 10 in. (91.4 x 142.2 x 25.4 cm)
Collection of Sandra Spang

Herbert J. Spinden (1879–1973)
Green Corn Dance, Santo Domingo
Pueblo, ca. 1920
Cyanotype
3 1/2 in x 4 1/2 in. (8.9 x 11.4 cm)
Southwest Museum, Los Angeles

Edward Steichen (1879–1973)
Advertisement for Matson Cruise Line,
November 1, 1941
Vogue magazine, inside back cover
12 1/2 x 9 1/2 x in. (31.7 x 24.1 cm)
Courtesy of Vogue, Condé Nast
Publications Inc., with permission
of Joanna T. Steichen

Portrait of Hawaiian Model
Kaaloalaikini "Toots" Notley, 1937
Chromogenic print
8 x 9 3/4 in. (20.4 x 25.1 cm)
George Eastman House, Rochester,
New York, bequest of Edward
Steichen by direction of Joanna
T. Steichen, with permission of
Joanna T. Steichen

Rea Tajiri (b. 1963)
History and Memory, 1991
Color and black and white video
32 minutes
Courtesy of Women Make Movies,
Inc., New York

Charlene Teters (b. 1952)
Mound to the Heroes, 1999
Mixed medium installation
Dimensions variable
Courtesy of the artist

Tamiko Thiel (b. 1957) and
Zara Houshmand (b. 1953)
Beyond Manzanar website, 1998–2003
Documentation of the Beyond
Manzanar 3D virtual
reality installation
http://mission.base.com/manzanar/
index.html

Richard Throssel (1882–1933)
Unidentified Crow Couple Sitting
in Tipi, ca. 1905
Modern gelatin silver print from
the original glass plate negative
8 x 10 in. (20.3 x 25.4 cm)
American Heritage Center,
University of Wyoming, Richard
Throssel Collection

Time
(Unidentified photographer)
O.J. Simpson portrait, June 27, 1984
Magazine cover
Private collection, New York

Time
Special Issue: *The New Face*
of America, Fall 1993
Photo: Ted Thai; computer morphing:
Kin Wah Lam; Design: Walter Bernard
and Milton Glaser
Magazine cover
Private collection

Daniel Tisdale (b. 1958)
Rodney King Police Beating,
from "The Disaster Series," 1991
Screenprint on canvas
24 x 33 in. (60.9 x 83.8 cm)
Courtesy of the artist

George Trager (1861–1948)
Big Foot Lying Dead in the Snow at
Wounded Knee, South Dakota,
1891/ca. 1920
Real photo postcard
3 x 4 7/8 in. (7.6 x 12.3 cm)
International Center of Photography,
purchased by the ICP Acqusitions
Committee, 2001

Tseng Kwong Chi (1950–1990)
Reagan Inauguration, Mudd Club, 1981
Fifty-four Polaroids on poster collage
47 x 33 in. (119.3 x 83.8 cm)
Estate of Tseng Kwong Chi/Muna
Tseng Dance Projects, Inc., New York

Statue of Liberty, New York,
from the expeditionary series
"East Meets West," 1979
Gelatin silver print
36 x 36 in. (91.4 x 91.4 cm)
Estate of Tseng Kwong Chi/Muna
Tseng Dance Projects, Inc., New York

Hulleah Tsinhnahjinnie
(b. 1954)
This is Not a Commercial,
This is My Homeland, 1998
Digital chromogenic print
16 x 20 in. (40.6 x 50.8 cm)
Courtesy of the artist

Doris Ulmann (1884–1934)
Untitled, ca. 1933
Photogravure
11 1/4 x 8 in. (28.4 x 20.3 cm)
International Center of Photography,
gift of William Clift

Underwood & Underwood
Bert E. Underwood (1862–1943)
and **Elmer Underwood**
(1860–1947)
"Three Cheers for 'Old Glory'!"—
The first flag raising in Pinar del
Rio, Cuba, 1899
Stereograph
3 1/2 x 7 in. (8.9 x 17.8 cm)
Research Library, The Getty
Research Institute, Los Angeles

Primitive Cuba—Oxen Power and
Solid Wheel Cart, Pinar del Rio, 1899
Stereograph
3 1/2 x 7 in. (8.9 x 17.8 cm)
Research Library, The Getty
Research Institute, Los Angeles

Spanish American War Philippine
Islands "Civilized Warfare—Restoring
men we had to shoot—Reserve
Hospital," Manila, Philippine Islands,
1899
Stereograph
3 1/2 x 7 in. (8.9 x 17.8 cm)
Museum of New Mexico, Palace of
the Governors, Santa Fe

Border Guard inspecting suspicious
Mexican, ca. 1916
Gelatin silver print
9 3/16 x 7 1/8 in. (23.3 x 18 cm)
Courtesy of National Archives,
Washington, D.C.

Unidentified photographer
Ethnographic portrait—Indian woman,
ca. 1845
Quarter-plate daguerreotype
4 1/4 x 3 1/4 in. (10.8 x 8.3 cm)
George Eastman House, Rochester,
New York

Unidentified photographer
Abolitionist Button, ca. 1849
Daguerreotype
5/8 in. (1.5 cm) diameter
Gilman Paper Company Collection,
New York

Unidentified photographer
Portrait of An African American
Woman Holding A White Child,
ca. 1855
Hand-colored ruby ambrotype
4 7/8 x 3 5/8 in. (12.3 x 9.1 cm)
Library of Congress, Washington, D.C.

Unidentified photographer
Stirrup Branch Plantation. Bishopville,
S.C., on the 75th birthday of Capt.
James Rembert, June 8, 1857 (Front
view of house shows Capt. Rembert
and family), 1857
Tintype
2 1/4 x 5 1/2 in. (5.8 x 8.9 cm)
Library of Congress, Washington, D.C.

Stirrup Branch Plantation. Bishopville,
S.C., on the 75th birthday of Capt.
James Rembert, June 8, 1857 (Rear
view of house shows slave families),
1857
Tintype
2 1/4 x 5 1/2 in. (5.8 x 8.9 cm)
Library of Congress, Washington, D.C.

Unidentified photographer
Civil War Soldiers with a
"Contraband," ca. 1863
Carte-de-visite
4 x 2 1/2 in. (11.6 x 6.3 cm)
Wm. B. Becker Collection/American
Museum of Photography

Unidentified photographer
Sojourner Truth: I Sell the Shadow
to Support the Substance, 1864
Carte-de-visite
4 x 2 3/8 in. (20.3 x 6 cm)
International Center of Photography,
Museum purchase, 2003

Unidentified photographer
John Chupco, Seminole, I.T., as he
looked in 1865 when a drunkard, 1865
Oklahoma Historical Society,
Oklahoma City, Archives and
Manuscripts Division, C.W. Kirk
Collection

Unidentified photographer
Ku Klux Klansman, 1869
Tintype
3 1/4 x 1 7/8 in. (8.1 x 4.9 cm)
Gilman Paper Company Collection,
New York

Unidentified photographer
Woman and Baby, ca. 1890
Gelatin silver print
9 5/16 x 7 3/16 in. (23.7 x 18.3 cm)
International Center of Photography,
Daniel Cowin Collection, 1990

Unidentified photographer
Hawaiian woman posed in photo
studio, ca. 1890
Postcard
5 1/2 x 3 1/4 in. (14 x 9 cm)
Bishop Museum, Honolulu, Hawaii

Unidentified photographer
Portrait of Young Kru Woman from
Village Near Monrovia with Body
Paint and in Costume, 1893
Postcard
6 x 4 in. (15.2 x 10.2 cm)
National Anthropological Archives,
Smithsonian Institution, Washington,
D.C.

Unidentified photographer
Unidentified group of military, probably
sailors, posed at a waterfall with
native women, ca. 1895
Gelatin silver print
7 15/16 x 5 15/16 in. (20.0 x 14.2 cm)
George Eastman House, Rochester,
New York

Unidentified photographer
Philippines, soldiers interrogating
two Filipinos, P.I., ca. 1899
Stereograph
4 1/8 x 7 1/8 in. (10.5 x 18.0 cm)
UCR/California Museum of
Photography, University of California,
Riverside, Keystone-Mast Collection

Unidentified photographer
Dead insurgents in a rice field near
Imus, P.I., 1899
Stereograph
4 1/8 x 7 1/8 in. (10.5 x 18.0 cm)
UCR/California Museum of
Photography, University of California,
Riverside, Keystone-Mast Collection

Unidentified photographer
"Fun in black," ca. 1900
Albumen print stereograph
4 1/8 x 7 1/8 in. (10.5 x 18.0 cm)
UCR/California Museum of
Photography, University of California,
Riverside, Keystone-Mast Collection

Unidentified photographer
Lynching, ca. 1900
Gelatin silver print on board
5 3/4 x 4 in. (14.6 x 10.2 cm)
International Center of Photography,
Daniel Cowin Collection, 1990

Unidentified photographer
Geronimo whom General Miles named
the Human Tiger, ca. 1903
Hand-colored gelatin silver print
5 x 8 in. (12 x 20.3 cm)
Library of Congress, Washington, D.C.

Unidentified photographer
Geronimo and Apaches at St. Louis
Fair, 1904
Gelatin silver print
7 9/16 x 10 in. (19.3 x 25.4 cm)
Library of Congress, Washington, D.C.

Unidentified photographer
Portrait of Ishi, ca. 1911
Modern print from original glass
plate negative
5 x 7 in. (12.7 x 17.8 cm)
Pheobe Apperson Hearst Museum
of Anthropology and the Regents
of the University of California

Unidentified photographer
Ishi posing in furs with a San
Francisco Call *reporter*, ca. 1911
Gelatin silver print
4 11/16 x 6 11/16 in. (11.9 x 17.0 cm)
Pheobe Apperson Hearst Museum
of Anthropology and the Regents of
the University of California

Unidentified photographer
Typical Revolutionist, ca. 1911–14
Real photo postcard
5 1/2 x 3 1/2 in. (14 x 9 cm)
Research Library, The Getty
Research Institute, Los Angeles

Unidentified photographer
Assassination of Pancho Villa, 1923
Real photo postcard
3 1/2 x 5 1/2 in. (9 x 14 cm)
Research Library, The Getty
Research Institute, Los Angeles

Unidentified photographer
Student, Sylvenia Scott, at the Sherman
Institute in Riverside, ca. 1926
Gelatin silver print
7 1/2 x 4 3/4 in. (19 x 12 cm)
Sherman Indian Museum,
Riverside, California

Student, Sylvenia Scott, at the Sherman
Institute in Riverside, ca. 1926
Gelatin silver print
7 1/2 x 4 1/2 in. (19 x 11.4 cm)
Sherman Indian Museum,
Riverside, California

Unidentified photographer
This Negro was burned by a mob at
Sherman, Texas, on May 9, 1930, 1930
Gelatin silver print
6 5/16 x 4 7/8 in. (16. x 11.2 cm)
International Center of Photography,
Daniel Cowin Collection, 1990

Unidentified photographer
Outside Tule Lake Internment Camp,
Tule Lake, Calif., 1942
Gelatin silver print
6 x 4 in. (15.2 x 10.1 cm)
International Center of Photography,
Museum purchase, 2001

Unidentified photographer
"Hello Gorgeous! Kimona See me Sometime," ca. 1943
Gelatin silver print
8 3/16 x 10 (20.8 x 25.4 cm)
American Image Collection,
National Archives, Washington, D.C.

Unidentified photographer
Beautiful Baby Contest, NAACP Baltimore, MD (Baby Contest Winners), 1946
Gelatin silver print
8 x 10 in. (20.3 x x 25.4 cm)
Library of Congress, Washington, D.C.

Unidentified photographer
Atomic Cloud during Baker Day Blast at Bikini, July 25, 1946, 1946
Gelatin silver print
7 1/2 x 9 1/4 in. (19 x 23.5 cm)
National Archives, Washington, D.C.

Unidentified photographer
Tourists photographing hula show in Waikiki, Honolulu, Hawaii, ca. 1960
Gelatin silver print
10 x 8 in. (25.4 x 20.3 cm)
Bishop Museum, Honolulu, Hawaii,
Laurence Hata Collection

John Vachon (1914–1975)
Billboard, 1948
Modern print from original negative
8 x 10 in. (20.3 x 25.4 cm)
International Center of Photography,
Museum purchase, 2003

Carl Van Vechten (1880–1964)
Pearl Bailey, 1946
Gelatin silver print
9 1/2 x 7 1/8 in. (24.1 x 18 cm)
Yale University, Beinecke Rare Book and Manuscript Library, American Literature Collection

James VanDerZee (1886–1983)
Beau of the Ball, 1926
Gelatin silver print
10 x 8 in. (25.4 x 20.3 cm)
Collection of Donna Mussenden VanDerZee

Sergio Vega (b. 1959)
Within (Dante's Inferno) nos. 1–9, 1995–96
Chromogenic prints with text
Nine prints, each 30 x 24 in.
(76.2 x 60.9 cm)
Courtesy of the artist

Walery Studio (1860–1955)
Josephine Baker, 1926
Gelatin silver print
10 x 8 in. (25.4 x 20.3 cm)
Private collection

Andy Warhol (1928–1987)
Cowboys and Indians: Geronimo, 1986
Screenprint on Lenox Museum Board
36 x 36 in. (86.4 x 86.4 cm)
The Andy Warhol Museum, Pittsburgh

Carleton E. Watkins (1829–1916)
Cape Horn Near Celilo, Oregon, 1867
Albumen print
25 3/4 x 29 1/2 in. (65.5 x 74.9 cm)
Stanford University Library,
Department of Special Collections

Carrie Mae Weems (b. 1953)
From Here I Saw What Happened And I Cried, 1995/96
Chromogenic prints with sandblasted text on glass
Four prints, each 14 3/8 x 11 in.
(36.4 x 27.9 cm)
International Center of Photography,
purchased with funds from the ICP Acquisitions Committee, 2000

Frank Wendt
Little Levey Sisters, ca. 1880
Cabinet card
6 1/2 x 4 1/2 in. (16.5 x 11.4 cm)
Syracuse University Library,
Syracuse, New York, Becker Collection

Little Levey Sisters, ca. 1880
Cabinet card
6 1/2 x 4 1/2 in. (16.5 x 11.4 cm)
Syracuse University Library,
Syracuse, New York, Becker Collection

Edward Weston (1868–1958)
Nude on Dunes, 1939
Gelatin silver print
7 1/2 x 9 7/16 in. (18.9 x 24.1 cm)
Center for Creative Photography,
University of Arizona, Tucson

Tehuana Costume [worn by Rose Roland, wife of Covarrubias], ca. 1920
Gelatin silver contact print
9 5/8 in x 6 in. (24.9 x 15.2 cm)
Courtesy of Throckmorton Fine Art,
New York; Center for Creative Photography, University of Arizona, Tucson

Joel Emmons Whitney
(1822–1986)
Portrait of Sha-kpe (Little Six) in Costume, ca. 1865
Carte-de-visite
2 x 3 in. (5.1 x 7.6 cm)
National Anthropological Archives,
Smithsonian Institution, Washington, D.C.

Pat Ward Williams (b. 1948)
Accused/Blowtorch/Padlock, 1986
Mixed mediums
59 1/2 x 107 x 4 1/2 in.
(151.1 x 271.8 x 11.4 cm)
Whitney Museum of Art, New York,
purchased with funds from
The Audrey and Sydney Irmas Charitable Foundation

Fred Wilson (b. 1954)
About Face I, 1995
Chromogenic prints
Two prints, each 20 x 16 in.
(50.8 x 40.6 cm)
Courtesy of the artist and
Metro Pictures, New York

Albert J. Winn (b. 1947)
Jewish Summer Camp, Southern California, 1997
Gelatin silver print
14 x 11 in. (35.5 x 27.9 cm)
Courtesy of the artist

Edie Winograde (b. 1964)
The Flaying, from "The Legend of the Rawhide" series, 1999/2003
Chromogenic print
30 x 35 in. (76.2 x 88.9 cm)
Courtesy of the artist

Boys Putting on Iron Ore, from "The Legend of the Rawhide" series, 1999/2003
Chromogenic print
10 x 8 in. (25.4 x 20.3 cm)
Courtesy of the artist

Indians on Horseback, from "The Legend of the Rawhide" series, 1999/2003
Chromogenic print
8 x 10 in. (20.3 x 25.4 cm)
Courtesy of the artist

Death of a Maiden, from "The Legend of the Rawhide" series, 1999/2003
Chromogenic print
13 x 19 in. (33 x 48.3 cm)
Courtesy of the artist

Pull the Wagons in a Circle, from "The Legend of the Rawhide" series, 1999/2003
Chromogenic print
13 x 19 in. (33 x 48.3 cm)
Courtesy of the artist

Garry Winogrand (1928–1984)
Central Park Zoo, New York City, 1967
Gelatin silver print
8 1/2 x 13 1/2 in. (21.6 x 32.5 cm)
Courtesy of The Fraenkel Gallery,
San Francisco; Center for Creative Photography, University of Arizona

Ernest C. Withers (b. 1922)
Bilbo Brown, Brown Skin Follies, Memphis, 1949–50
Gelatin silver print
20 x 16 in. (50.8 x 40.6 cm)
Courtesy of Panopticon Gallery,
Waltham, Massachusetts

Special Issue: Mississippi, 1955
Jet magazine
International Center of Photography,
Museum Purchase Fund, 2002

Soon Mi Yoo (b. 1962)
Seeking saf (single asian female), 2003
Mixed medium installation, wall paper, and gelatin silver prints
Dimensions variable
Courtesy of the artist

403

Selected bibliography

Abramson, Michael, and the Young Lords Party. *Palante: The Young Lords*. New York: McGraw-Hill, 1971.

Adams, Ansel. *Born Free and Equal, photographs of the loyal Japanese-Americans at Manzanar Relocation Center, Inyo County, California*. New York: U.S. Camera, 1944.

Aguilar, Dugan. *Wa'tu Ah'lo: Dugan Aguilar, Northern California Indigenous Photography*. Davis: University of California at Davis, 1996.

Albright, Peggy. *Crow Indian Photographer: The Work of Richard Throssel*. Albuquerque: University of New Mexico Press, 1997.

Alland, Alexander. *Jacob A. Riis: Photographer and Citizen*. New York: Aperture, 1974.

Allen, James, et al. *Without Sanctuary: Lynching Photography in America*. Santa Fe: Twin Palms Publishers, 2000.

Alloula, Malek. *The Colonial Harem*. Translated by Myrna Godzich and Wlad Godzich. Minneapolis: University of Minnesota Press, 1986.

Appadurai, Arjun. *Modernity at Large: Cultural Dimensions of Globalization*. Minneapolis: University of Minnesota Press, 1996.

_____. "The Colonial Backdrop." *Afterimage* 24, no. 5 (March–April 1997).

Ahern, Wilbert H. "'The Returned Indians': Hampton Institute and its Indian Alumni, 1879–1893." *Journal of Ethnic Studies* 10, no. 4 (1983): 101–24.

Alison, Jane, ed. *Native Nations: Journeys in American Photography*. London: Barbican Art Gallery, 1998.

Back, Les, and John Solomos, eds. *Theories of Race and Racism*. London and New York: Routledge, 2000.

Banta, Melissa, and Curtis M. Hinsley. *From Site to Sight: Anthropology, Photography, and the Power of Imagery*. Cambridge, Mass.: Peabody Museum, 1986.

Barringer, Tim, and Tom Flynn, eds. *Colonialism and the Object: Empire, Material Culture and the Museum*. New York: Routledge, 1998.

Barron, Stephanie, Sheri Bernstein, and Ilene Susan Fort, eds. *Reading California: Art, Image and Identity, 1900–2000*. Los Angeles: University of California Press, 2000.

Barthes, Roland. *Camera Lucida: Reflections on Photography*, translated by Richard Howard. New York: Hill and Wang, 1981.

_____. *Image, Music, Text*. Translated by Stephen Heath. New York: Hill and Wang, 1977.

_____. *Mythologies*. Translated by Annette Lavers. New York: Hill and Wang, 1977.

Batchen, Geoffrey. *Each Wild Idea: Writing, Photography, History*. Cambridge, Mass.: MIT Press, 2001.

Bate, David. *Renegotiations: Class, Modernity, and Photography*. Norwich, Eng.: Norwich Gallery, 1993.

_____. "Photography and the Colonial Vision." *Afterimage* 20 (summer 1992): 11–13.

Belous, Russell, and Robert Weinstein. *Will Soule: Indian Photographer at Fort Sill, Oklahoma, 1869–74*. Los Angeles: Ward Ritchie Press, 1969.

Berger, Maurice. *Fred Wilson: Objects and Installations, 1979–2000*. Baltimore: Center for Art and Visual Culture, University of Maryland, 2001.

_____. "Picturing Whiteness: Nikki S. Lee's Yuppie Project." *Art Journal* 60, no. 4 (winter 2001): 55–57.

_____. *Adrian Piper: A Retrospective*. Baltimore: University of Maryland Fine Arts Gallery, 1999.

Berkhofer, Robert, Jr. *The White Man's Indian: Images of the American Indian from Columbus to the Present*. New York: Vintage Books, 1979.

Bhabha, Homi K. *The Location of Culture*. London: Routledge, 1994.

_____, ed. *Nation and Narration*. New York: Routledge, 1990.

Blackman, Margaret. "'Copying People': Northwest Coast Native Response to Early Photography." *BC Studies*, no. 52 (winter 1981–82): 86–112.

_____. "Posing the American Indian." *Natural History* 89, no.10 (October 1980): 68–75.

Blanton, Casey, ed. *Picturing Paradise: Colonial Photography of Samoa, 1875 to 1925*. Miami: Southeast Museum of Photography, 1995.

Bloom, Lisa, ed. *With Other Eyes: Looking at Race and Gender in Visual Culture*. Minneapolis: University of Minnesota Press, 1999.

Blount, Marcellus, and George P. Cunningham. *Representing Black Men*. New York: Routledge, 1996.

Bolton, Richard, ed. *The Contest of Meaning: Critical Histories of Photography*. Cambridge, Mass.: MIT Press, 1989.

Bourdieu, Pierre. *Photography: A Middle-Brow Art*. Stanford: Stanford University Press, 1990.

Braddock, Alan C. "Eakins, Race, and Ethnographic Ambivalence." *Winterthur Portfolio* 33, nos. 2–3 (1998): 135–61.

Breitbart, Eric. *A World on Display: Photographs from the St. Louis World's Fair, 1904*. Albuquerque: University of New Mexico Press, 1997.

Brown, Julie. *Contesting Images: Photography and the World's Columbian Exposition*. Tuscon: University of Arizona Press, 1994.

Bryan, William S., ed. *Our Islands and Their Peoples, As Seen with Camera and Pencil*. New York: Thompson Publishing Co., 1899.

Butler, Judith. "Endangered/Endangering: Schematic Racism and White Paranoia." In *Reading Rodney King, Reading Urban Uprising*. Edited by Robert Gooding-Williams. New York: Routledge, 1993.

Burgin, Victor, ed. *Thinking Photography*. London: MacMillan, 1982.

Bush, Alfred L., and Lee Clark Mitchell. *The Photograph and the American Indian*. Princeton: Princeton University Press, 1994.

Cahan, Susan, and Zoya Kocur, eds. *Contemporary Art and Multicultural Education*. New York: Routledge, 1996.

Caratini, Héctor Méndez. *Haciendas: Cafetaleras de Puerto Rico*. San Juan: n.p., 1990.

Carby, Hazel. *Race Men.* Cambridge, Mass.: Harvard University Press, 1998.

Chalfen, Richard. *Turning Leaves: The Photograph Collections of Two Japanese American Families.* Albuquerque: University of New Mexico Press, 1991.

_____. "Japanese American Family Photography." *Visual Sociology* 3, no. 2 (fall 1987): 12–17.

Chandra, Mohini. "Pacific Album: Vernacular Photography of the Fiji Indian Diaspora." *History of Photography* 24, no. 2 (summer 2000): 236–42.

Chavoya, Ondine C. "Collaborative Public Art and Multi-Media Installation: David Avalos, Louis Hock, and Elizabeth Sisco's 'Welcome to America's Finest Tourist Plantation' (1988)." In *The Ethnic Eye: Latino Media Arts.* Edited by Chou Noriega and Ana López. Minneapolis: University of Minnesota Press, 1996.

_____. "Orphans of Modernism: the Performance Art of ASCO." In *Corpus Delecti: Performance Art of the Americas.* Edited by Coco Fusco. New York: Routledge, 2000.

Clifford, James. *The Predicament of Culture: Twentieth-Century Ethnography, Literature and Art.* Cambridge, Mass.: Harvard University Press, 1988.

_____. *Routes: Travel and Translation in the Late Twentieth Century.* Cambridge, Mass.: Harvard University Press, 1997.

Cole, Carolyn Kozo, and Kathy Kobiyashi. *Shades of L.A.: Pictures from Ethnic Family Albums.* New York: New Press, 1996.

Collins, Kathleen. "The Scourged Back." *History of Photography* 9, no. 1 (January 1985): 43–45.

_____. "Portraits of Slave Children." *History of Photography* 9, no. 3 (July–Sept. 1985): 187–207.

Coombes, Annie E. *Reinventing Africa: Museums, Material Culture and Popular Imagination.* New Haven: Yale University Press, 1994.

Corrin, Lisa, ed. *Mining the Museum: An Installation by Fred Wilson.* New York: New Press, 1994.

Crimp, Douglas. *On the Museum's Ruins.* Cambridge, Mass.: MIT Press, 1988.

_____. "The Museum's Old/The Library's New Subject." *Parachute*, no. 22 (spring 1981).

Curtis, James C. "Race, Realism, and the Documentation of the Rural Home During America's Great Depression." In *The American Home: Material Culture, Domestic Space, and Family Life.* Hanover, N.H.: University Press of New England, 1998.

Daniel, Pete, and Raymond Smock. *A Talent for Detail: The Photographs of Miss Frances Benjamin Johnston.* New York: Harmony Books, 1974.

Davidov, Judith Fryer. "The Color of My Skin, The Shape of My Eyes: Photographs of the Japanese-American Internment by Dorothea Lange, Ansel Adams, and Toyo Miyatake." *Yale Journal of Criticism* 9, no. 2 (fall 1996): 223–44.

Dent, Gina, ed. *Black Popular Culture: A Project by Michele Wallace.* Seattle: Bay Press, 1992.

Dewey, Rob, ed. *Dawoud Bey: Portraits, 1975–1995.* New York: Distributed Art Publishers, 1995.

Dippie, Brian. *The Vanishing American: White Attitudes and U.S. Indian Policy.* 1982; reprint, Lawrence: University of Kansas Press, 1991.

Doll, Don S.J. *Vision Quest: Men, Women and Sacred Sites of the Sioux Nation.* New York: Crown Publishers, 1994.

_____., and Jim Alinder, eds. *Crying for a Vision: A Rosebud Sioux Trilogy, 1886–1976.* Kansas City: Mid-America Arts Alliance, 1976.

Dominguez, Virginia. "Exporting U.S. Concepts of Race: Are There Limits to the U.S. Model?" *Social Research* 65, no. 2 (summer 1998): 369–99.

Donovan, Susan. *Texas Death Row: Photographs by Ken Light.* Jackson: University Press of Mississippi, 1997.

Doy, Gen. *Black Visual Culture: Modernity and Postmodernity.* New York: I.B. Tauris and Co., 2000.

DuBois, W.E.B. "The American Negro in Paris." *American Monthly Review of Reviews* 22, no. 5 (November 1900): 575–77.

Ducille, Ann. "Black Barbie and the Deep Play of Difference." In *The Feminism and Visual Culture Reader.* Edited by Amelia Jones. London: Routledge, 2003.

Durham, Michael. *Powerful Days: The Civil Rights Photography of Charles Moore (Modern and Contemporary).* Birmingham: University of Alabama Press, 2002.

Dyer, Richard. *White.* London: Routledge, 1997.

_____. "White," *Screen* 29, no. 4 (autumn 1988): 44–65.

Edwards, Elizabeth. *Raw Histories: Photographs, Anthropology, and Museums.* Oxford: Berg, 2001.

_____. "Postcards: Greetings from Another World." In *The Tourist Image: Myths and Myth Making in Tourism.* Edited by Tom Selwyn. London: John Wiley and Sons, 1996.

_____, ed. *Anthropology and Photography, 1860–1920.* New Haven: Yale University Press, 1992.

Edwards, Susan. "Ben Shahn and the American Racial Divide." In *Intersections: Lithography, Photography, and the Traditions of Printmaking.* Albuquerque: University of New Mexico Press, 1998.

Faris, James. *Navajo and Photography: A Critical History of the Representation of an American People.* Albuquerque: University of New Mexico Press, 1996.

Farr, William. *The Reservation Blackfeet, 1882–1945, A Photographic History of Cultural Survival.* Seattle: University of Washington Press, 1984.

Firstenberg, Lauri, and Marc H.C. Bessire. *Beyond Decorum: The Photography of Iké Udé.* Cambridge, Mass.: MIT Press, 2000.

Fleming, Paula Richardson, and Judith Luskey. *The North American Indians in Early Photographs.* New York: Dorset Press, 1988.

Foster, Hal. "The Artist as Ethnographer." In *The Return of the Real: The Avant-Garde at the End of the Century.* Cambridge, Mass.: MIT Press, 1996.

Fox, Claire F. *The Fence and the River: Culture and Politics at the U.S.-Mexico Border.* Minneapolis: University of Minnesota Press, 1999.

Fox, Paul. "The Imperial Schema: Ethnography, Photography and Collecting." *Photofile* 7, no. 4 (1989): 10.

Foucault, Michel. *The Order of Things: An Archeology of the Human Sciences.* New York: Random House, 1970.

Frankenberg, Ruth, ed. *Displacing Whiteness: Essays in Social and Cultural Criticism.* Durham: Duke University Press, 1997.

Furedi, Frank. *The Silent War: Imperialism and the Changing Perception of Race.* London: Pluto Press, 1998.

Fusco, Coco. *Bodies That Are Not Ours.* London: Routledge, 2002.

_____. "Uncanny Dissonance: The Work of Lorna Simpson." In *English Is Broken Here.* New York: New Press, 1995.

_____. "Fantasies of Oppositionality." *Screen* 29, no. 4 (Autumn 1988): 80–93.

_____, ed. *Corpus Delecti: Performance Art of the Americas.* New York: Routledge, 2000.

Gamboa, Harry, Jr. *Urban Exile: Collected Writings of Harry Gamboa Jr.* Edited by Chon Noriega. Minneapolis: University of Minnesota Press, 1998.

Gandert, Miguel. *Nuevo México Profundo: Rituals of an Indo-Hispano Homeland.* Santa Fe: Museum of New Mexico Press, 2000.

Gates, Henry Louis, Jr. "The Face and Voice of Blackness." In *Facing History: the Black Image In American Art, 1710–1940.* Edited by Guy C. McElroy. San Francisco: Bedford Arts Publishers, 1990.

_____, ed. *"Race," Writing, and Difference.* Chicago: University of Chicago Press, 1986.

Geary, Christraud M., and Virginia-Lee Webb, eds. *Delivering Views: Distant Cultures in Early Postcards.* Washington, D.C.: Smithsonian Institution Press, 1998.

Gelburd, Gail, and Thelma Golden. *Romare Bearden in Black and White: Photomontage Projections 1964.* New York: Whitney Museum of American Art, 1997.

Gilroy, Paul. *Against Race: Imagining Political Culture Beyond the Color Line.* Cambridge, Mass.: Harvard University Press, 2000.

_____ *The Black Atlantic: Modernity and Double Consciousness.* Cambridge, Mass.: Harvard University Press, 1993.

_____. *"There Ain't No Black in the Union Jack":* *The Cultural Politics of Race and Nation.* Chicago: University of Chicago Press, 1991.

Glenn, James R. "'The Curious Gallery': The Indian Photographs of the McClees Studio in Washington, 1857–1858." *History of Photography* 5 (1981): 249–62.

Golden, Thelma. *Black Male: Representations of Masculinity in Contemporary American Art.* New York: Whitney Museum of American Art, 1994.

_____, et al. *Freestyle.* New York: Studio Museum in Harlem, 2001.

Goldin, Nan. *I'll Be Your Mirror.* New York: Whitney Museum of Art, 1996.

González, Jennifer A. "The Appended Subject: Race and Identity as Digital Assemblage." In *Race in Cyberspace.* Edited by Lisa Nakamura et al. London: Routledge, 2000.

Gordon, Avery F., and Christopher Newfield, eds. *Mapping Multiculturalism.* Minneapolis: University of Minnesota Press, 1996.

Gould, Stephen Jay. *The Mismeasure of Man.* New York: W.W. Norton, 1981.

Graybill, Florence Curtis, and Victor Boesen. *Edward Sheriff Curtis: Visions of a Vanishing Race.* Albuquerque: University of New Mexico Press, 1976.

Green, David. " Veins of Resemblance: Photography and Eugenics." *Oxford Art Journal* 7, no.2 (1985): 3–16

_____. "Classified Subjects: Photography and Anthropology: The Technology of Power." *Ten.8,* no. 14 (1984): 30–37.

Green, Rayna. "Gertrude Käsebier's 'Indian' Photographs: More Than Meets the Eye." *History of Photography* 24, no. 1 (spring 2000): 59–60.

Guimond, James. *American Photography and the American Dream.* Chapel Hill: University of North Carolina Press, 1979.

Hall, Michael. "Race, Ritual, and Responsibility: Performativity and the Southern Lynching." In *Performing the Body/Performing the Text.* Edited by Amelia Jones and Andrew Stephenson. London: Routledge, 1999.

Hall, Stuart. *Different.* London: Phaidon Press, 2001.

_____. "New Ethnicities." In *Race, Culture and Difference.* Edited by James Donald and Ali Rattansi. London: Sage, 1992.

_____. "Reconstruction Work." *Ten.8,* no. 16 (1984): 2–9.

_____, ed. *Representations: Cultural Representations and Signifying Practices.* London: Sage, 1997.

Hallam, Elizabeth, and Brian V. Street, eds. *Cultural Encounters: Representing 'Otherness.'* New York: Routledge, 2000.

Hammond, Joyce D. "Photographic Tourism and the Kodak Hula Show." *Visual Anthropology Review* 14 (2001): 1–32.

Harlan, Theresa. "Adjusting the Focus for an Indigenous Presence." In *OverExposed: Essays on Contemporary Photography.* Edited by Carol Squiers. New York: New Press, 1999.

Higa, Karin. *Bruce and Norman Yonemoto: Memory, Matter, and Modern Romance.* Los Angeles: Japanese American National Museum, 1999.

_____. "Some thoughts on National and Cultural Identity: Art by Contemporary Japanese and Japanese American Artists." *Art Journal* 55, no. 3 (fall 1996): 6–13.

Hight, Eleanor M., and Gary D. Sampson, eds. *Colonialist Photography: Imag(in)ing Race and Place.* New York: Routledge, 2002.

Hill, Mike, ed. *Whiteness: A Critical Reader.* New York: New York University Press, 1997.

hooks, bell. "Carrie Mae Weems: Diasporic Landscapes of Longing." In *Inside the Visible: An Elliptical Traverse of Twentieth Century Art In, Of, and From the Feminine.* Edited by Catherine de Zegher. Cambridge, Mass.: MIT Press, 1994.

_____. *Black Looks: Race and Representation.* Boston: South End Press, 1992.

Hulick, Diana Emery. "James VanDerZee's *Harlem Book of the Dead*: A Study in Cultural Relationships." *History of Photography* 17, no. 3 (fall 1993): 277–83.

Hutchinson, H.M., J.W. Gregory, and R. Lydekker. *The Living Races of Mankind, A Popular Illustrated Account of Customs, Habits, Pursuits, Feasts and Ceremonies of the Races of Mankind Throughout the World.* London: Hutchinson, 1901.

Isaak, Jo Ann, ed. *Looking Forward, Looking Black.* New York: Museum Press, 1999.

Isles, Chrissie, and Russell Roberts, eds. *In Visible Light: Photography and Clarification in Art, Science and the Everyday.* Oxford: Museum of Modern Art, 1997.

Jacobson, Matthew Frye. *Whiteness of a Different Color.* Cambridge, Mass.: Harvard University Press, 1998.

Jenkins, David. "The Visual Documentation of the American Indian: Photography and Popular Culture in the Late Nineteenth Century." *Museum Anthropology* 17, no. 1 (February 1993).

Jezierski, John Vincent. *Enterprising Images: The Goodridge Brothers, African American Photographers, 1847–1922.* Detroit: Wayne State University Press, 2000.

Johnston, Frances Benjamin. *The Hampton Album.* Edited by Lincoln Kirstein. New York: Museum of Modern Art, 1966.

Johnston, Patricia Condon. "The Indian Photographs of Roland Reed." *American West* 15, no.2 (March/April 1978): 44–57.

Johnson, Thomas L., and Phillip C. Dunn, eds. *A True Likeness: The Black South of Richard Samuel Roberts, 1920–1936.* Chapel Hill: Algonquin Books of Chapel Hill, 1986.

Jones, Kellie. "In Their Own Image: Black Women Artists Who Combine Text With Photography." *Artforum* 29 (Nov. 1990): 132–38.

Kaplan, Amy, and Donald E. Pease, eds. *Cultures of United States Imperialism.* Durham: Duke University Press, 1993.

Kasher, Steven. *The Civil Rights Movement: A Photographic History.* New York: Abbeville Press, 1996.

Karp, Ivan, and Stephen Lavine, eds. *Exhibiting Cultures: The Poetics and Politics of Museum Display.* Washington, D.C.: Smithsonian Institution Press, 1991.

Kelley, Robin D.G. *Race Rebels: Culture, Politics, and the Black Working Class.* New York: Free Press, 1994.

Kester, Grant. "Riots and Rent Strikes: Documentary During the Great Society." *Exposure* 27, no. 2 (1997): 21–37.

_____, ed. *Art, Activism, and Oppositionality: Essays from Afterimage.* Durham: Duke University Press, 1998.

Kirshenblatt-Gimblett, Barbara. *Image Before My Eyes.* New York: Schocken, 1995.

Kolko, Beth E., Lisa Nakamura, and Gilbert B. Rodman, eds. *Race in Cyberspace.* New York: Routledge, 2000.

Krauss, Rosalind. "Photography's Discursive Spaces." In *The Originality of the Avant-Garde and Other Modernist Myths.* Cambridge, Mass.: MIT Press, 1985.

Lamunière, Michelle C. "Roll, Jordan, Roll and the Gullah Photographs of Doris Ulmann." *History of Photography* 21, no. 4 (winter 1997): 294–302.

Langford, Martha. *Suspended Conversations: The Afterlife of Memory in Photographic Albums.* Montreal: McGill-Queens University Press, 2001.

Levinthal, David. *Blackface.* Santa Fe: Arena Editions, 1999.

Ligon, Glenn. *Glenn Ligon: Un/becoming.* Philadelphia: Institute of Contemporary Art, 1997.

Lin, Jan. *Reconstructing Chinatown.* Minneapolis: University of Minnesota Press, 1998.

Linker, Kate. *Love For Sale: The Words and Pictures of Barbara Kruger.* New York: Harry N. Abrams, 1990.

Lippard, Lucy, ed. *Partial Recall.* New York: New Press, 1992.

Lokko, Lesley Naa Norle, ed. *White Papers, Black Marks: Architecture, Race, Culture.* Minneapolis: University of Minnesota Press, 2000.

Lord, Catherine, ed. *The Theater of Refusal: Black Art and Mainstream Criticism.* Irvine: Fine Arts Gallery, University of California, Irvine. 1993.

Lott, Eric. *Love and Theft: Blackface Minstrelsy and the American Working Class.* New York: Oxford University Press, 1993.

_____. "White Like Me: Racial Cross-Dressing and the Construction of American Whiteness." In *The Cultures of United States Imperialism.* Edited by Amy Kaplan and Donald E. Pease. Durham: Duke University Press, 1993.

Lutz, Catherine, and Jane Collins. *Reading National Geographic.* Chicago: University of Chicago Press, 1993.

Lyon, Danny. *Memories of the Southern Civil Rights Movement.* Chapel Hill: University of North Carolina Press, 1992.

Maitland, Gordon. "Two Sides of the Camera: Nineteenth-Century Photography and Indigenous People of the Pacific." *Photofile* 6, no. 3 (1988): 47–58.

Malmsheimer, Lonna M. "'Imitation White Men': Images of Transformation at the Carlisle Indian School." *Studies in Visual Communication* 2, no. 4 (fall 1985): 54–75.

Mamiya, Christin. "Greetings from Paradise: The Representation of Hawaiian Culture in Postcards." *Journal of Communication Inquiry* 16 (summer 1992): 86–101.

Mapplethorpe, Robert. *Black Book*. New York: St. Martin's Press, 1986.

Martinez, Natasha Bonilla, ed. *La Frontera/ The Border: Art About the Mexico/United States Border Experience*. San Diego: Centro Cultural de la Raza, 1993.

Masayevsa, Victor, and Eric Younger, eds. *Hopi Photographers/Hopi Images*. Tucson: University of Arizona Press, 1983.

Mayer, Robert A. *Blacks in America: A Photographic Record*. Rochester: International Museum of Photography at George Eastman House, 1986.

McAdory, Jeff, ed. *I am a Man: Photographs of the 1968 Memphis Sanitation Strike and Dr. Martin Luther King Jr.* Memphis: Memphis Publishing Company, 1993.

McAuley, Skeet. *Sign Language: Contemporary Southwest Native America*. New York: Aperture, 1989.

McMaster, Gerald, ed. *Reservation X: The Power of Place in Aboriginal Contemporary Art*. Seattle: University of Washington Press, 1998.

Mellinger, Wayne Martin. "Toward a Critical Analysis of Tourism Representations." *Annals of Tourism Research* 21, no. 4 (1994): 756–79.

Mercer, Kobena. *Welcome to the Jungle: New Positions in Black Cultural Studies*. New York: Routledge, 1994.

———, and Chris Darke. *Isaac Julien*. London: Ellipsis, 2001.

Meyer, Pedro. *Truths and Fictions: A Journey from Documentary to Digital Photography*. New York: Aperture, 1995.

Michaels, Barbara L. "New Light on F. Holland Day's Photographs of African Americans." *History of Photography* 18, no. 4 (winter 1994): 334–47.

Millstein, Barbara Head, and Sarah M. Lowe. *Consuelo Kanaga: An American Photographer*. Brooklyn: Brooklyn Museum, 1992.

Mitchell, Timothy. "Orientalism and the Exhibitionary Order." In *Colonialism and Culture*. Edited by Nicholas Dirks. Ann Arbor: University of Michigan Press, 1992.

Mirzoeff, Nicholas, ed. *Diaspora and Visual Culture: Representing Africans and Jews*. New York: Routledge, 2000.

———. *Visual Culture Reader*. New York: Routledge, 1998.

Motz, Marilyn. "Visual Autobiography: Photograph Albums of Turn-of-the-Century Midwestern Women." *American Quarterly* 41, no. 1 (March 1989): 63–92.

Moy, James S. *Marginal Sights: Staging the Chinese in America*. Iowa City: University of Iowa Press, 1993.

Murray, Carolyn B., and J. Owens Smith. "White Privilege: The Rhetoric and the Facts." *Multiculturalism from the Margins, Non-Dominant Voices on Difference and Diversity*. Edited by Dean A. Harris. Westport: Bergin and Garvey, 1995.

Nakamura, Lisa. *Cybertypes: Race, Ethnicity and Identity on the Internet*. London: Routledge, 2002.

Nathanson, Nicholas. *The Black Image in the New Deal: The Politics of FSA Photographs*. Knoxville: University of Tennessee Press, 1992.

Newhall, Beaumont. *The History of Photography: From 1839 to the Present*. 1939; reprint, New York: Museum of Modern Art, 1982.

Nordstrom, Alison Devine. *Voyages (Per)Formed: Photography and Travel in the Gilded Age*. Miami: Southeast Museum of Photography, 2001.

———. "Paradise Recycled: Photographs of Samoa in Changing Contexts." *Exposure*, no. 28 (winter 1991–92): 6–13.

Norfleet, Barbara. *The Champion Pig: Great Moments in Everyday Life*. New York: Viking, 1980.

Normark, Don. *Chavez Ravine, 1949: A Los Angeles Story*. San Francisco: Chronicle Books, 1999.

Nott, Josiah Clark. *Types of mankind: or, Ethnological researches, based upon the ancient monuments, paintings, sculptures, and crania of races, and upon their natural, geographical, philological and biblical history*. Philadelphia: Lippincott, Grambo and Co., 1854.

Omi, Michael, and Howard Winant. *Racial Formation in the United States: From the 1960s to the 1980s*. New York: Routledge, 1986.

Packard, Gary, and Maggy Packard. *Southwest 1880 with Ben Wittick, Pioneer Photographer of Indian and Frontier Life*. Santa Fe: Packard Publications, 1970.

Panzer, Mary. *Mathew Brady and the Image of History*. Washington, D.C.: Smithsonian Institution Press, 1997.

Patterson, Vivian. *Carrie Mae Weems: The Hampton Project*. New York: Aperture, 2000.

Phillips, Sandra. *Crossing the Frontier: Photographs of the Developing West, 1849 to the Present*. San Francisco: San Francisco Museum of Modern Art, 1996.

Pinney, Christopher, and Nicolas Peterson, eds. *Photography's Other Histories*. Durham: Duke University Press, 2003.

Poolaw, Linda. *War Bonnets, Tin Lizzies, and Patent Leather Pumps: Kiowa Culture in Transition, 1925–1955: The Photographs of Horace Poolaw*. Stanford: Stanford University Press, 1990.

Post, Robert, and Michael Rogin, eds. *Race and Representation: Affirmative Action*. New York: Zone Books, 1998.

Przyblyski, Jeannine M. "American Visions at the Paris Exposition 1900: Another Look at Francis Benjamin Johnston's Hampton Photographs." *Art Journal* 57, no. 3 (fall 1998): 60–68.

Prochaska, David. "Postscript: Exhibiting Hawai'i." In *Post-Colonial America*. Edited by C. Richard King. Urbana: University of Illinois Press, 2000.

Rafael, Vincente L. *White Love and Other Events in Filipino History*. Durham: Duke University Press, 2000.

Rahder, Bobbi. "Gendered Stylistic Differences Between Photographers of Native Americans at the Turn of the Century." *Journal of the West* 35, no. 1 (January 1996): 86–95.

Read, Michael, ed. *Ancestral Dialogues: The Photographs of Albert Chong*. San Francisco: Friends of Photography, 1994.

Roe, Jo Ann. *Frank Matsura, Frontier Photographer*. Seattle: Madrone Publishers, 1981.

Roediger, David R. *The Wages of Whiteness: Race and the Making of the American Working Class*. New York: Verso, 1991.

Rogin, Michael. "Democracy and Burnt Cork: The End of Blackface, The Beginning of Civil Rights." *Representations*, no. 46 (spring 1994): 1–34.

———. "Making America Home: Racial Masquerade and Ethnic Assimilation in the Transition to Talking Pictures." *Journal of American History* 79, no.3 (December 1992): 1050–77.

Rony, Fatimah Tobing. *The Third Eye: Race, Cinema, and Ethnographic Spectacle*. Durham: Duke University Press, 1996.

Root, Deborah. *Cannibal Culture: Art, Appropriation and the Commodification of Difference*. Boulder, Col.: Westview Press, 1995.

Rosler, Martha. *3 Works*. Halifax: Nova Scotia College of Art and Design, 1982.

Ruby, Jay. *Secure the Shadow: Death and Photography in America*. Cambridge, Mass.: MIT Press, 1995.

Rydell, Robert W. *All the World's a Fair: Visions of Empire at American International Expositions, 1876–1916*. Chicago: University of Chicago Press, 1984.

Sancho, Victoria A-T. "Respect and Representation: Dawoud Bey's Portraits of Individual Indentity." *Third Text*, no. 44 (fall 1998): 55–68.

Scherer, Joanna Cohan. "You Can't Believe Your Eyes: Inaccuracies in Photographs of North American Indians." *Exposure* (winter 1978): 6–19.

———. *Indians: The Great Photographs that Reveal North American Indian Life, 1874–1929*. New York: Crown, 1973.

Sekula, Allan. *Photography Against the Grain*. Halifax: Nova Scotia College of Art and Design, 1986.

———. "The Body and the Archive." *October*, no. 39 (winter 1986): 3–6.

Seshadri-Crooks, Kalpana. "The Comedy of Domination: Psychoanalysis and the Conceit of Whiteness." In *The Psychoanalysis of Race*. Edited by Christopher Lane. New York: Columbia University Press, 1998.

Slemmons, Rod. *Shadowy Evidence: The Photography of Edward C. Curtis and His Contemporaries*. Seattle: Seattle Art Museum. 1989.

Smalls, James. "Public Face, Private Thoughts: Fetish, Interracialism, and the Homoerotic in Some Photographs by Carl Van Vechten." *Genders*, no. 25 (1997): 144–93.

Smith, Shawn Michelle. "Photographing the 'American Negro': Nation, Race, and Photography at the Paris Exposition of 1900." In *With Other Eyes: Looking at Race and Gender in Visual Culture*. Edited by Lisa Bloom. Minneapolis: University of Minnesota Press, 1999.

Stange, Maren. "'Illusion Complete Within Itself': Roy DeCarava's Photography." *Yale Joutrnal of Criticism* 9, n0. 1 (Spring 1996): 63–92.

———. *Symbols of Ideal Life: Social Documentary Photography in America, 1890–1950.* Cambridge: Cambridge University Press, 1989.

Stein, Sally. "On Location: The Placement (and Replacement) of California in 1930s Photography." In *Reading Calfornia: Art, Image and Identity, 1900–2000.* Edited by Stephanie Barron et al. Los Angeles: Los Angeles County Museum of Art, 2000.

Stocking, George W., Jr., ed. *Colonial Situations: Essays on the Contextualization of Ethnographic Knowledge.* Madison: University of Wisconsin Press, 1991.

Stoler, Ann Laura. *Race and the Education of Desire.* Durham: Duke University Press, 1995.

Suderburg, Erika. "Written on the West: How the Land Gained Site." In *Space, Site Intervention: Situating Installation Art.* Edited by Erika Suderburg. Minneapolis: University of Minnesota Press, 2000.

Taft, Robert. *Photography and the American Scene: A Social History, 1839–1889.* 1938; reprint, New York: Dover Publications, 1964.

Tchen, John Kuo Wei. *New York Before Chinatown: Orientalism and the Shaping of American Culture, 1776–1882.* Baltimore: Johns Hopkins University Press, 2001.

———. *Genthe's Photographs of San Francisco's Old Chinatown.* New York: Dover Publications, 1984.

Thomas, Nicholas. *Entangled Objects: Exchange, Material Culture and Colonialism in the Pacific.* Cambridge, Mass.: Harvard University Press, 1991.

———, and Diane Losche. *Double Vision: Art Histories and Colonial Histories in the Pacific.* Cambridge: Cambridge University Press, 1999.

Tomkins, Jane. *To The Promised Land: Photographs by Ken Light.* New York: Aperture, 1988.

Trachtenberg, Alan. "Wanamaker's Indians." *Yale Review* 86, no. 2 (1998): 1–24.

———. *Reading American Photographs: Images as History, Mathew Brady to Walker Evans.* New York: Hill and Wang, 1989.

———. "Walker Evans's America: A Documentary Invention." In *Observations: Essays on Documentary Photography.* Edited by David Featherstone. Carmel, Calif.: Friends of Photography, 1984.

Trenton, Patricia, and Patrick Houlihan. *Native Americans: Five Centuries of Changing Images.* New York: Harry N. Abrams, 1989.

Tsinhshjinnie, Hulleah. *Photographic Memoirs of an Aboriginal Savant: Hulleah Tsinhshjinnie.* Davis: University of California, Davis, 1994.

Vergara, Benito M., *Displaying Filipinos: Photography and Colonialism in Early Twentieth Century Philippines.* Manila: University of the Philippines Press, 1995.

Verdelle, A.J. "Beyond Shack Photography: The Humanist Imagery of Roy DeCarava." In *Tracing Cultures: Art History, Criticism, Critical Fiction.* Edited by Miwon Kwon. New York: Whitney Museum of American Art, 1994.

Viera, Ricardo, et al., eds. *Outside Cuba: Contemporary Cuban Visual Artists (Fuero de Cuba: artistas Cubanos).* Miami: University of Miami, 1989.

Viola, Herman. *North American Indian Photographs from the National Archives of the Smithsonian.* Chicago: University of Chicago Press, 1975.

Vizenor, Gerald. *Fugitive Poses: Native American Indian Scenes of Absence and Presence.* Lincoln: University of Nebraska Press, 1998.

Wagner, Anne M. "Warhol Paints America, or Race in America." *Representations,* no. 55 (1996): 98–119.

Wallace, Maurice O. *Constructing the Black Masculine: Identity and Ideality in African American Men's Literature and Culture, 1775–1995.* Durham: Duke University Press, 2002.

Wallace, Michele. "Passing, Lynching, and Jim Crow: A Genealogy of Race and Gender in U.S. Visual Culture, 1895–1929." Ph.D. diss., New York University, 1999.

———. *Invisibility Blues.* New York: Verso, 1990.

Wallis, Brian, and Jeffrey Kastner. *Land and Environmental Art.* London: Phaidon Press, 1998.

———, Marianne Weems, and Philip Yenawine, eds. *Art Matters: How the Culture Wars Changed America.* New York: New York University Press, 1999.

Watriss, Wendy, and Lois Parkinson Zamora, eds. *Image and Memory: Photography from Latin America, 1866–1994.* Austin: University of Texas Press, 1998.

Webb, Virginia-Lee. *Perfect Documents: Walker Evans and African Art, 1935.* New York: Metropolitan Museum of Art, Harry N. Abrams, 2000.

———. "Manipulated Images: European Photographs of Pacific Peoples." In *Prehistories of the Future: The Primitivist Project and the Culture of Modernism.* Edited by Elazar Barkin and Ronald Bush. Stanford: Stanford University Press, 1995.

Webb, William, and Robert Weinstein. *Dwellers at the Source—Southwestern Indian Photos of A.C. Vroman, 1895–1904.* Albuquerque: University of New Mexico Press, 1978.

West, Cornel. "The New Cultural Politics of Difference." In *Out There: Marginalization and Contemporary Culture.* Edited by Russell Ferguson, Martha Gever, Trinh T. Minh-ha, and Cornel West. Cambridge, Mass.: MIT Press, 1990.

Wiegman, Robyn. "Whiteness Studies and the Paradox of Particularity." *Boundary 2* 26, no. 3 (fall 1999): 115–50.

Wexler, Laura. *Tender Violence: Domestic Visions in an Age of U.S. Imperialism.* Chapel Hill: University of North Carolina Press, 2000.

———. "Seeing Sentiment: Photography, Race, and the Innocent Eye." In *Familial Gaze.* Edited by Marianne Hirsch. Hanover, N.H.: University Press of New England, 1999.

———. "Black and White and Color: American Photographs at the Turn of the Century." *Prospect,* no. 13 (winter 1988): 341–90.

Williams, Carol Jane. "Framing the West: Race, Gender, and the Photographic 'Frontier' on the Northwest Coast, 1858–1912." Ph.D. diss., Rutgers State University, 1999.

Willis, Deborah. *Reflections in Black: A History of Black Photographers.* New York: W.W. Norton, 2000.

———. *VanDerZee: Photographer 1886–1983.* New York: Harry N. Abrams, 1993.

———, ed. *Picturing Us: African American Identity in Photographs.* New York: New Press, 1994.

———, and Carla Williams. *The Black Female Body: A Photographic History.* Philadelphia: Temple University Press, 2002.

Wilson, Judith. "What Are We Doing Here? Cultural Difference in Photographic Theory and Practice." *San Francisco Camerawork Quarterly* 17 (fall 1990): 27–30.

Wride, Tim. B. *Retail Fictions: The Commercial Photography of Ralph Bartholomew Jr.* Los Angeles: Los Angeles County Museum of Art, 1998.

Wright, Barton, Marnie Gaede, and Marc Gaede. *The Hopi Photographs, Kate Cory, 1905–1912.* Albuquerque: University of New Mexico Press, 1988.

Wyatt, Victoria. "Interpreting the Balance of Power: A Case Study of Photographer and Subject in Images of Native Americans." *Exposure,* no. 28 (winter 1991–92): 21–31.

Contributors

C. Ondine Chavoya is assistant professor of art at Williams College where he teaches courses on contemporary art and Chicana/o visual culture with an emphasis on performance, conceptual art, and film/video. Chavoya's research interests revolve around the social production and use of space, and the ways artists have represented and intervened in the urban landscape.

Richard Dyer teaches film studies at the University of Warwick in Coventry, England. His many publications include *Stars* (1982), *Now You See It: Studies on Lesbian and Gay Film* (1990), and *The Culture of Queers* (1999). Richard Dyer's research has focused on notions of entertainment and representation with particular emphasis on the relationship between them. His approach emphasizes the aesthetic and historical specificity of cultural texts.

Lauri Firstenberg is curator for Artists Space in New York City. She was associate curator for Okwui Enwezor's exhibition *The Short Century: Independence and Liberation Movements in Africa,* which was presented at the Museum Villa Stuck, Munich; Haus der Kulturen der Welt, Berlin; Museum of Contemporary Art, Chicago; and the Museum of Modern Art/PS1, New York. She is also an art critic, independent curator, and Harvard University Ph.D. candidate in the history of art and architecture.

Coco Fusco is a New York-based interdisciplinary artist and director of graduate study for the visual arts division at Columbia University's School of the Arts. She is the author of *English Is Broken Here: Notes on Cultural Fusion in the Americas* (1995) and *The Bodies That Were Not Ours and Other Writings* (2002). Fusco has curated exhibitions and public programs for London's Institute of Contemporary Art, The Brooklyn Museum of Art, The Oberhausen Festival of Short Films, and other venues.

Jennifer González is assistant professor in the history of art and visual culture department at the University of California, Santa Cruz. Her essays on art, technology, and the body have appeared in periodicals such as *Frieze, World Art, Art Journal, Bomb,* and *Inscriptions,* and in anthologies such as *The Cyborg Handbook* (1996), and *Race in Cyberspace* (2002).

Karin Higa is curatorial and exhibitions director at the Japanese American National Museum in Los Angeles. She recently co-curated an exhibition of Japanese-American art from 1896 to 1945 for the Tokyo Metropolitan Teien Museum of Art; the exhibition traveled to Hiroshima and Oita, Japan. Higa was also curator of the traveling exhibition *The View from Within: Japanese American Art from the Internment Camps 1942–1945.* Her publications include *Living in Color: The Art of Hideo Date* (2002).

Kobena Mercer is a critic whose varied work on the politics of representation in African diasporic visual arts has inaugurated an important line of inquiry into post-identitarian cultural politics. His publications include *Welcome to the Jungle: New Positions in Black Cultural Studies* (1994), and *Keith Piper: Relocating the Remains* (1997).

Nicholas Mirzoeff is professor of art and comparative literature at Stony Brook University. He is the author of *Silent Poetry: Deafness, Sign and Visual Culture in Modern France* (1995); *Bodyscape: Art, Modernity and the Ideal Figure* (1995); and *An Introduction to Visual Culture* (1999). Mirzoeff also edited *The Visual Culture Reader* (1998), and *Diaspora and Visual Culture: Representing Africans and Jews* (1999).

Javier Morillo-Alicea is completing a Ph.D. in anthropology and history at the University of Michigan, Ann Arbor. His dissertation, "The Paper Trails of Empire: Spanish Bureaucratic Knowledges, 1863–1900," analyzes the imperial bureaucracy that administered Spain's late-nineteenth-century colonies of Cuba, Puerto Rico, the Philippines, and Guam.

Leigh Raiford is a postdoctoral fellow at Duke University's John Hope Franklin Humanities Institute.

Aleta M. Ringlero is an independent curator and writer. She was director of Native American Public Programs for the Smithsonian Institution National Museum of Natural History from 1989 to 1993.

Allan Sekula is a photographer, writer, and critic, who teaches at the California Institute of the Arts. His published books include *Photography Against the Grain* (1984); *Fish Story* (1995); *Geography Lesson: Canadian Notes* (1997); *Dead Letter Office* (1997); *Dismal Science, Calais vu par: Deep Six/Passer au bleu* (1998); *Performance under Working Conditions* (2001); and *TITANIC's Wake* (2001). His work has been shown in solo exhibitions in Austria, Belgium, England, France, Germany, the Netherlands, Portugal, Sweden, Australia, Canada, and the United States.

Sally Stein is an associate professor in the department of art history at the University of California in Irvine. She has coauthored and cocurated *Official Images: New Deal Photography* (1988), and *Montage and Modern Life* (1992). Her monographic essays include an early critical essay on FSA photographer Marion Post Wolcott, and the introductory essay to the published memoir of photographer and filmmaker Jack Delano. Stein also curated a retrospective of Delano's photography and graphic art.

Caroline Vercoe is a lecturer in art history at Auckland University, New Zealand, and teaches courses in Pacific art and postcolonial theory. Vercoe's writings have been included in *Body Politics and the Fictional Double* (2000), *The Bodies That Were Not Ours* (2002), and *Pacific Art Niu Sila* (2002).

Brian Wallis is director of exhibitions and chief curator at the International Center of Photography. He was formerly a curator at the New Museum of Contemporary Art in New York, and senior editor at *Art in America.* His books include *Art After Modernism: Rethinking Representation* (1984); *Blasted Allegories: Writings by Contemporary Artists* (1986); *Rock My Religion: Writings and Art Projects by Dan Graham, 1965–1990* (1993); *Land Art* (1998); and *Art Matters: How the Culture Wars Changed America* (1999).

Deborah Willis is a MacArthur Fellow (2000) and professor of photography and imaging, New York University, Tisch School of the Arts. Her recent publications include *Reflections in Black: A History of Black Photographers 1840 to the Present* (2000), and *The Black Female Body: A Photographic History* (2002) with Carla Williams.

Howard Winant is professor of sociology at the University of California, Santa Barbara. He is the author of *The World is a Ghetto: Race and Democracy Since World War II* (2001).

Lenders to the exhibition

We would like to thank the following individuals and institutions for their generous assistance in securing loans for this exhibition: Michael Abramson at Flatiron News; Jennifer Allora & Guillermo Calzadilla; Gallery Paule Anglim; Bennie Flores Ansell; The DeLape Family Collection; Josè Flores and Juan Carlos Romàn at the Archivo General de Puerto Rico; ARS; SCALA/Art Resource; Aziz + Cucher; Don and Diana Bartletti; Wm. B. Becker at the American Museum of Photography; Katrina Bernal and Lisa Bernal Brethour; Desoto Brown and Deanne DuPont at the Bishop Museum; Ben Chapnick, Joyce Rodriguez, and Barbara Gottlieb at Black Star Publishing; Janet Borden at Janet Borden, Inc.; Drex Brooks; Robert C. Buitron; Nancy Burson; Steven A. Baker and Maren Jones at the California Historical Society; Steve Thomas at the California Museum of Photography; Jack Coogan at the Robert and Frances Flaherty Collection, Claremont School of Theology; Douglas Nickel, Betsi Meissner, and Diane Nilsen at the Center for Creative Photography; C. Ondine Chavoya; Vivian Cherry; Albert Chong; Condé Nast Publications; The Cinema Guild; Richard Clarke; Steven P. Henry at the Paula Cooper Gallery; CRG Gallery; Gregory Miller; Christopher D'Amelio and Lucien Terras at the D'Amelio Terras Gallery; Bruce Davidson Photography; Lalla Essaydi; Suzanne Geiss at Deitch Projects; Keith deLellis Gallery; James X. Kroll at the Denver Public Library; Karen Kelly at the Dia Center for the Arts; Ronald Feldman, Jenny Aborn, and Frayda Feldman at Ronald Feldman Fine Arts; Frish Brandt at The Fraenkel Gallery; Marlon Fuentes; Harry Gamboa Jr.; Anthony Bannon, Miguel Gandert; Rick Hock, Therese Mulligan, Becky Simmons, Joseph Struble, Rachel Stuhlmann, Stacey Vandenburg, Janice Madhu, and Barbara Puorro Galasso at the George Eastman House; Weston Naef and Brett Abbott at the J. Paul Getty Museum; Irene Lotseich-Phillips and Wim de Witt at the Getty Research Institute; Pierre Apraxine and Maria Umali at the Gilman Paper Company Collection; Rosalie Benitez and Carter Mull at the Barbara Gladstone Gallery; Lissa McLure at the Marion Goodman Gallery; Ed Greevy; Keith Davis, Pat Fundom, and Melissa Roundtree at the Hallmark Fine Art Collection, Hallmark Cards; Mary Lou Hultgren at the Hampton University Museum Archives; Alex Harris; Zsolt Kadar and Jean Pagan at the G. Ray Hawkins Gallery; Roger Hollander; Leslie Freund, Therese Babineau, and Joan Knudson at the Phoebe Apperson Hearst Museum of Anthropology, University of California; Lynn Hershman; Louis Hock; Rhona Hoffman Gallery; Diane Honda; Garry Henkel at Image Conscious; Zig Jackson; Karin Higa, Theresa Manalo, and Cris Paschild at the Japanese American National Museum; Joan Rosenbaum, Norman Kleeblatt, Mason Klein, and Barbara Treitel at the Jewish Museum; Pirkle Jones; Charles Junkerman; Amy Goltzer, Cecile Panzieri, and Debra Vilen at the Sean Kelly Gallery; Jan Kesner at the Jan Kesner Gallery; Catherine A. Johnson at the Kinsey Institute for Research in Sex, Gender, and Reproduction; Robert Koch Gallery; Greg Kucera Gallery; Susan Maruska at the Jack Tilton/Anna Kustera Gallery; Ignacio Lang; Pok-Chi Lau; An-My Lê; Mary Sabbatino and Lanka Tattersall at Galerie Lelong, New York; Margaret Brown and Carol Johnson at the Library of Congress; Ken Light; Estate of O. Winston Link; Robert Sobieszek and Nancy Thomas at the Los Angeles County Museum of Art; The Los Angeles Times; Estate of George Platt Lynes; David Strettell at Magnum; Debra Bosniak at Robert Mann Gallery; Marisa Cardinale, Michael Stout, and Gillian Cuthill for the Robert Mapplethorpe Foundation; Victoria Cuthbert and Jill Sussman at Matthew Marks Gallery; Lee Marmon; Victor Masayevsa; Anne E. Bently at the Massachusetts Historical Society; Larry McNeil; Hector Mendez-Caratini; Estate of Ana Mendieta; Janelle Reiring at Metro Pictures; Maria Morris Hambourg, Malcolm Daniel, Jeff Rosenheim,

Lisa Hoefstetler, Eileen Sullivan, and Virginia Lee-Webb at the Metropolitan Museum of Art; Royce Howes at the Robert Miller Gallery; Yossi Milo at the Yossi Milo Gallery; Brian Ferriso at the Milwaukee Art Museum; Nina Overli and Glenn Scott-Wright at the Victoria Miro Gallery; Richard Misrach; Ellen Thomason at the Missouri Historical Society; Archie Miyatake; Mon Muellerschoen at MM Artmanagement; Lory Morrow at the Montana Historical Society; Kim Sajet at the Museum of the Pennsylvania Academy of the Fine Arts; Celia Alvarez Muñoz; Melissa Altman and Karen Hanus at the Museum of Contemporary Art, Los Angeles; Marsha Bol, Joan Tafoya, and Steve Yates at the Museum of New Mexico; David Travis, James Rondeau, and Lisa D'Acquisto at the Museum of the Art Institute of Chicago; Pedro Meyer; Wangechi Mutu; Patrick Nagatani; Paula Richardson Fleming, John Homiak, Shannon Perish, and Jeanie Sklar at the National Anthropological Archives; Edward McCarter and Jim Zeender at the National Archives; Raven Amir, Sonja Dumais, Martha King, Lori Pauli, Pierre Théberge, Ann Thomas, Jacqueline Warren at the National Gallery of Canada; John McMahon, Ann Shumard, and Kristen Smith at the National Portrait Gallery; Jennie Rodda and Jason Varone at the New York University, Institute of Fine Arts; Don Normark; Eileen Harris Norton; Kris Kuramitsu at the Norton Family Office; Deborah Cooper, Drew Johnson, and Bill McMorris at the Oakland Museum of California; David Lindeblat at the Okanogan County Historical Society and Museum; Chester R. Cowen at the Oklahoma Historical Society; José Olmo; Antony Decaneas at the Panopticon Gallery; Gordon Parks; Roz Payne; P.P.O.W; Regen Projects; Heather D'Angelo and Anjali Suneja at the Riva Gallery; Alex Rivera; Third World Newsreel; Sarah Cohen at the Andrea Rosen Gallery; Alvin D. Hall; Martha Rosler; Video Data Bank; Neal Benezra, Sandra Phillips, Ellen Shershow, and Maria Naula at the San Francisco Museum of Modern Art; David E. Schwartz; Lorene Sisquoc at the Sherman Indian Museum; Aaron Siskind Foundation; SITE Santa Fe; Roger Shimomura; J. Shimon & J. Lindemann; Coreen Simpson; Suzannah Fabing, Aprille Gallant, and Louise LaPlante at the Smith College Museum of Art; Ileana Sonnabend, Laura Bloom, and Antonio Homen at the Sonnabend Gallery; Kim Walters at the Southwest Museum; Sandra Spang; Kate Meyer and John Pultz at the Spencer Museum of Art, University of Kansas; Roberto G. Trujillo at the Stanford University Library; Carol Davis at the Syracuse University Library; Matt Herron at Take Stock Photos; Charlene Teters and Don Messec; Giovanni Garcia-Fenech at The Project; Time-Life Pictures; Daniel Tisdale; Julie Baranes and Leslie Tonkonow at Leslie Tonkonow Artworks + Projects; Andree Tracey; Muna Tseng; Hulleah J. Tsinhnahjinnie; Kathleen Howe and Bonnie Varado at the University of New Mexico Art Museum; Roy Flukinger at the University of Texas at Austin, Harry Ransom Humanities Research Center; Nicolette Bromberg and Carla Rickerson at the University of Washington Libraries; Leslie Shores at the University of Wyoming, American Heritage Center; Henry Urbach Architecture; Donna Mussenden VanDerZee; Bruce Kellner for the Estate of Carl Van Vechten; Sergio Vega; Susanne Vielmetter at Susanne Vielmetter Los Angeles Projects; Tom Sokolowski, Julie Chill, and Jesse Kowalskik at The Andy Warhol Museum; The Andy Warhol Foundation for the Visual Arts; Cara Weston at the Weston Gallery; Sylvia Wolf, Jennifer Belt, and Barbi Spieler at the Whitney Museum of American Art; Albert J. Winn; Edie Winograde; Andy Kraushaar at the Wisconsin Historical Society; Women Make Movies, Inc.; Nancy Kuhl, John Monahan, and Patricia C. Willis at the Beinecke Rare Book and Manuscript Library, Yale University; Timothy Welsh at the Howard Yezerski Gallery; and Soon Mi Yoo.

Trustees of the International Center of Photography

Credits

Photography

©1979 Amon Carter Museum: 28; ©Aaron Siskind Foundation: 300; ©The Andy Warhol Foundation for the Visual Arts, Inc./ARS New York: 209; ©George Ballis/Take Stock: 284; ©1999 Vanessa Beecroft, Photo Todd Eberle: 64; ©Lisa Bernal Brethour and Katrina Bernal: 160, 309; ©Black Star Press: 56; Photo by Ben Blackwell: 289 ©Miguel Calderon, Photo by Peter Muscato: 65; ©1989 Center for Creative Photography, Arizona Board of Regents: 2, 294, 361; ©Patty Chang and David Kelly: 76; ©Flatiron News, New York: 290; ©Hallmark Cards, Inc., Kansas City, Missouri: 103; ©1990 Charles Junkerman: 150, 210; ©Nikki S. Lee: 50; ©Copyright The Robert Mapplethorpe Foundation, Courtesy A+C Anthology: 236, 240, 242; ©1954 Lee Marmon: 214; ©Charles Moore/Black Star: 277, 278; ©O. Winston Link Estate: 369; ©1999 The Metropolitan Museum of Art: 67, 88, 206, 241, 248; ©The Museum of Modern Art/ARS: 219; ©National Gallery of Canada: 105; ©Carl Mydans, Time Life Pictures/Getty Images: 56; ©Patrick Nagatani and Andree Tracey: 57; Paul Outerbridge, Jr. ©G. Ray Hawkins Gallery, Los Angeles: 213; ©George Platt Lynes Estate: 255; ©ARS, NY, Digital image ©The Museum of Modern Art/Licensed by SCALA/Art Resource, NY: 260; ©Estate of Ben Shahn/Licensed by VAGA, New York: 218; ©The Heirs of W. Eugene Smith: 96; Photo by Benlly Spang. 226; ©Time Life Pictures/Getty Images: 285; ©Courtesy Estate of Tseng Kwong Chi/Muna Tseng Dance Projects, Inc. New York: 56; back cover; ©Ernest C. Withers: 121, 307; ©Donna Mussenden VanDerZee: 212; ©1984 Estate of Garry Winogrand: 15; ©UC Regents: 17, 66, 81, 156

Reprinted texts

Howard Winant, "The Theoretical Status of the Concept of Race" was published in Les Back and John Solomos, eds., *Theories of Race and Racism*. London and New York: Routledge, 2000.

Allan Sekula, "The Traffic in Photographs" appeared in Allan Sekula, *Photography Against the Grain: Essays and Photo Works 1973–1983*. Halifax: The Press of the Nova Scotia College of Art and Design, 1984.

Javier Morillo-Alicea, "Looking for Empire in the U.S. Colonial Archives" first appeared in *Historia y Sociedad*. Puerto Rico: University of Peurto Rico, 1998.

C. Ondine Chavoya, "Orphans of Modernism: The Performance Art of ASCO" first appeared in Coco Fusco, ed. *Corpus Delecti: Performance Art of the Americas*. London and New York: Routledge, 2000.

Kobena Mercer, "Skin Head Sex Thing: Racial Difference and the Homoerotic Imaginary" first appeared in Bad Object-Choices, ed. *How Do I Look? Queer Film and Video*. Seattle: Bay Press, 1991.

Richard Dyer, "The Matter of Whiteness" was excerpted in Les Back and John Solomos, eds., *Theories of Race and Racism*. London and New York: Routledge, 2000.

Karen Higa, "Toyo Miyatake and Our World" evolved from "Manazanar Inside and Out: Photo Documentation of the Japanese Wartime Incarceration" by Karen Higa and Tim B. Wride which appeared in Stephanie Barron, Sheri Bernstein, and Ilene Susan Fort, eds., *Reading California: Art, Image, and Identity, 1999–2000*. Los Angeles and Berkeley: Los Angeles County Museum of Art and University of California Press, 2000.

Index

Page numbers in *italics* refer to illustrations.